# THE
# BIG WHITE LIE

### THE DEEP COVER OPERATION THAT EXPOSED
### THE CIA SABOTAGE OF THE DRUG WAR

*Other Books by Michael Levine*

Deep Cover
Fight Back

# THE
# BIG WHITE LIE

## THE DEEP COVER OPERATION THAT EXPOSED
## THE CIA SABOTAGE OF THE DRUG WAR

*An Undercover Odyssey*

## Michael Levine

with

## Laura Kavanau-Levine

THUNDER'S MOUTH PRESS

First trade paperback edition, 1994

Published by
Thunder's Mouth Press
632 Broadway, 7th Floor
New York, NY 10012

LIBRARY OF CONGRESS CATALOGING IN PUBLICATION DATA
Levine, Michael
    The big white lie: the deep cover operation that exposed the CIA sabotage of the
    drug war / Michael Levine with Laura Kavanau-Levine.
        p.   cm.
    Includes bibliographical references and index.
    ISBN 1-56025-084-4 : 13.95
        1. Cocaine habit—United States.   2. Crack (Drug)—United States.   3. United
States. Central Intelligence Agency.   I. Kavanau-Levine, Laura.   II. Title
HV5810.L48      1993
363.4'5'P0973—dc20                                                    93-5814
                                                                        CIP

Printed in the United States of America

Distributed by
Publishers Group West
4065 Hollis Street
Emeryville, CA 94608
(800) 788-3123

In memory of my son, New York City Police Sergeant Keith Richard Levine, killed on December 28, 1991 while trying to stop an armed robbery by a crack addict with a record of two murder convictions.

While the CIA and other covert agencies betrayed us, and while our leaders looked the other way, they left it to law enforcement to clean up the mess they made of America. And we continue to pay with our blood and the blood of our children.

To all law enforcement officers who have died trying to take drugs off the street.

For Laura, whose insight, wisdom, talent, and vision are on every page of this book, and on the strength of whose love it was written.

To those many outraged, frustrated readers of my first book, *Deep Cover*, who wrote to me, this is the story I promised would follow, the one the politicians will not be able to ignore.

# CONTENTS

## PART THREE: SONIA'S SECRET

# Author's Note

The story you are about to read is true. Certain names have been changed and descriptions altered to avoid jeopardizing current law enforcement agents and informants, to avoid violating secrecy laws, and to protect the identities of people protected under the Witness Protection Program.

I have also changed the names of some criminals with whom I dealt with in my undercover role. For reasons unknown—despite having violated numerous state and federal laws from drug smuggling to homicide—they were never prosecuted, and in some cases never even fully identified. Our government's failure to take action against these drug dealers and murderers makes me vulnerable to civil action if I use their true names. However, if elected officials find the events described herein as scandalous as you will, I will furnish them with the true identities of these criminals.

I have reconstructed the incidents, events, and conversations I was party to with the aid of transcripts of taped conversations, personal diaries, copies of reports, court transcripts, and interviews of other participants. Those incidents, events, and conversations I was not party to were reconstructed from statements made by participants, statements made to me by criminals I associated with while working undercover, interviews of informants, historical research, and government reports.

A good portion of the evidence gathered in Operation Hun, including videotapes and tape-recorded conversations, were mysteriously destroyed by the Drug Enforcement Administration. Thus some of the recorded conversations recounted in these pages had to be recon-

1

structed from court transcripts, personal diary notes, and other documents.

The Prologue is a fictionalized dramatization of a meeting and transaction that actually occurred and is based on my personal knowledge of all the parties, informants' statements, and statements made to me by drug dealers during my deep cover assignment in Operation Hun.

The "suits" are the drug war bureaucrats—the armchair generals who direct the drug war from behind desks and in front of television cameras, and whom for the most part are more concerned with their own careers and images than the lives of the men and women they command.

# Introduction

Senator John Kerry, after hearing evidence of our own government's massive involvement in drug trafficking during his Iran-Contra Senate hearings, including testimony indicating that at least two presidents might have been criminally implicated, said that "our system of justice had been perverted; that [our covert agencies] had converted themselves into channels for the flow of drugs into the United States." He noted with astonishment that while American taxpayers were taxed (more than a $100 billion) to stop drugs, their own government was complicit in flooding their country with them. In a great show of outrage, he proclaimed that the American people had been betrayed.

Senator Kerry's rhetoric notwithstanding, not a single U.S. official was ever officially charged with violating our drug laws. Evidence that should have put many high government officeholders behind bars for crimes with minimum sentences of 10–20 years—not the community service given those convicted of lying to Congress—was heard by Kerry's committee in secret session and will never be revealed to the American people.

This secrecy was allegedly for reasons of national security. After you read this book, you will know that this reason could not be true; more damage was done to our national security by those responsible for this falsehood and the flood of drugs that has followed than any foreign enemy.

On his resignation, Kerry's chief investigator, Jack Blum, said, "I am sick to death of the truths that cannot be spoken." As a 25-year veteran undercover agent for the Drug Enforcement Administration working deep-cover drug cases from Bangkok to Buenos Aires, I was witness to the most scandalous of these truths. Now, in this book, these truths will be told for the first time.

In these pages I will lead you through the deep cover odyssey that I lived for six years. You will hear the words I heard, witness what I and others did, and learn the real reasons behind our cocaine and crack epidemic—the ones your elected representatives hid from you behind closed doors and a misuse of the secrecy laws that must have had our founding fathers clog dancing in their graves.

I will give you a fly-on-the-wall look at how the CIA perverts the American justice system by protecting drug dealers and murderers from prosecution; at how even federal judges and prosecutors alleged to have violated narcotic laws were protected from investigation; at how a beautiful South American woman known as "the Queen of Cocaine," responsible for shipping more cocaine into the United States than any one person I had ever known of—was able to seduce the CIA into destroying her competitors, protecting her from prosecution as she sold drugs to Americans, and paying her a small fortune in taxpayer dollars for her "services"; at how the only ruling government of Bolivia—a nation that produces the raw material for as much as 90 percent of the cocaine entering the United States—that ever wanted to help DEA defeat their drug barons was paid for its faith in our sincerity with torture and death at the hands of CIA-sponsored paramilitary terrorists under the command of fugitive Nazi war criminal (also protected by the CIA) Klaus Barbie. And finally, you will realize, as I did, the ultimate betrayal of America—how, without the CIA's protection of and support for Nazi war criminals and drug dealers, *La Corporacion,* South America's "General Motors of cocaine" and the resultant crack/cocaine epidemic might never have occurred.

A white lie is a well-meaning or diplomatic untruth. The CIA would have us believe that their protection of drug dealers for the past two decades—from the heroin-producing tribes of Southeast Asia during the Vietnam War to the cocaine-dealing Nicaraguan Contras—was well-meaning and in the interests of national security; and that their lies to the American people were harmless.

The truth is that the only thing white about their lies is the thousands of tons of cocaine powder that has almost buried us because of their actions. These lies are anything but little; to date, they have killed more Americans than the Vietnam and Korean wars combined—including my son, a New York City police officer killed by a gang of

4

crack addicts, and my brother, who committed suicide after 19 years of heroin addiction. These lies have caused the worst deterioration in American life and family values in our history, cost us trillions of dollars in taxes, drug-related crime, injury, and other costs to society, and two generations of brain-damaged crack babies whom sociologists tell us are destined to become conscienceless sociopaths. And none of those responsible for these lies has gone to jail . . . yet.

Without further ado, enter the inner sanctum of the biggest, whitest, deadliest lie of them all—the war on drugs.

# Prologue

Cali, Colombia, November 11, 1980, 2 A.M. The 10-piece salsa band rocked and swayed, their sweating bodies moving with the driving rhythms they were creating. The four-man brass section reared back as their horns shrieked while the rhythm section launched a precision, head-bobbing attack with drums, gourds, hollowed sticks, and cowbells. The dance floor was packed with gyrating multihued bodies dressed in expensive imported silks, satins, and jewelry. The scents of exotic perfumes merged with the stench of the jungle, which seeped in despite the best efforts of a huge air conditioner. The lead singer, a black Panamanian, danced forward and sang, *"Me abriste tu corazon, mamita. Colombia te canto."*

Outside the amplified music blasted far into the jungle night, and the lights of the mansion and the security lights posted around the perimeter fence could be seen for miles. A khaki-clad guard moved between rows of glistening luxury cars, an Uzi slung over his shoulder. Doing a little dance step, the guard joined in the chorus, singing, *"Colombia te canto, mamita linda, Colombia te canto."* The singers stopped and the brass section wailed again.

The guard paused—*"Dios mio, no aguanto mas."* Resting his gun on the hood of a black Porsche, he extracted a tiny bottle of white powder from his shirt pocket and held it up to the light. There was nothing else in this world so bright, so white, so inviting.

*"Que cosa mas linda,"* he breathed, as if to a lover.

The bottle had a straw that he inserted deep into his right nostril; pinching off the left nostril, he inhaled deeply. As his brain sizzled in chemical fire, he laughed and snapped up the gun as if it were a woman and danced grotesquely to the music.

Another security man in dark glasses, his Uzi held at port arms, watched expressionless from a few feet away.

Two other guards stood at the entrance to the compound, where the circle of light ended and the incessant chittering of the jungle drowned out the music. As they watched several sets of distant headlights moving toward them, their hands shifted to their gun handles and their fingers rested lightly on the triggers.

One guard, a thickset Colombian wanted on drug-trafficking charges in the United States, moved behind a small aluminum gatehouse and disappeared in the shadows. The other, also Colombian and wanted on multiple homicide charges in Miami, was a small thin man who would never be recognized from his photos on the wanted posters. His face had been disfigured by a bomb blast, leaving him with only a fraction of his upper lip and a permanent toothy smile. He moved to the center of the road and continued to watch the approaching lights bounce over the pitted jungle track.

Inside the mansion the band swung into another hot salsa number and the party rocked into higher gear. Some of the most recognizable faces in North and South America—businesspeople and politicians, sports figures and celebrities—rubbed elbows nervously with the elite of the Colombian Mafia. The guests were either packed onto the dance floor in the main room or grouped off in corners and smaller rooms helping themselves to mounds of cocaine offered in silver bowls by uniformed servants. Some shoveled powder up their nostrils with tiny silver spoons, offered as party favors, that had miniature devil's-head handles which grinned evilly at the guests. The faces seemed to be caricatures of the party's host, Octavio "Papo" Mejia.

Papo, flanked not so discreetly by bodyguards, moved among his guests. He was dressed in nothing but the best, from his handmade Italian shoes and custom Italian white silk suit to his diamond-studded Rolex watch, he was the picture of what a Hollywood producer might have cast as an evil drug baron; only there was nothing Hollywood about him. Mejia was very real and more deadly than any screenwriter would dare invent.

In Miami, Papo was said to have shot a man for failing to say hello to his father, at whose knee he learned the inseparable businesses of death and cocaine. His father, at the age of 42, was machine-gunned to death in a Miami shopping mall in broad daylight. His killers, three members of a rival cocaine gang headed by the infamous "Godmother," Griselda Blanco, had blasted his body beyond recognition with a brutal glee that had so impressed the scores of people who saw the event that not one eyewitness came forward. It was the beginning of the Cocaine Cowboy Wars that raged from Miami to Medellin during the early 1980s.

As the apocryphal story goes, Young Papo was to have been killed next but his enemies did not move fast enough. The wily killer with jungle instincts began a savage killing spree that left blood running in the Miami streets and a flotilla of corpses in the South Florida waterways. During those years, Drug Enforcement Administration agents and cops called the Colombian drug-dealing community "the Dixie Cup people" because they were so quickly murdered and replaced. And in that bizarre subworld sustained by the river of powder flowing from the Amazon basin directly into the heart of Miami, populated by some of the coldest killers in the history of crime, none was more feared than Papo.

Papo's aura emanated from his body like a forcefield. People spoke of feeling a cold chill when he was near. Yet it was this aura that seemed to attract the glitterati to him. To the rich and powerful, bored and overburdened with time and money, rubbing elbows with Papo Mejia was living on the edge—a high they couldn't resist.

As Mejia moved through the crowd, people parted before him as if by magic. Having the most frivolous of conversations with the bulldog-faced Colombian could have unforeseen and deadly consequences. Guests, their eyes averted, slithered aside as if on roller skates. This night there was extra reason to stay out of his way.

Papo was furious.

Papo checked his watch. Who did this Bolivian whore Atala think she was? Espinosa said she would arrive at midnight. If she didn't come, he'd have her gutted on the main street of Panama City, or wherever he found her, in broad daylight. He'd send Eduardo Pineda to do it. No, he would do it himself; then he would feed her entrails to the stray dogs.

The party was in her honor, and everyone had come to see this fabled beauty who sold cocaine for the Bolivian government. He had even invited his biggest American customer, *El Aleman* (the German), who had flown in from Miami. Opening up a line with this woman would be a signal to the drug world that Octavio Mejia had scaled the highest mountain of achievement—direct access to the storehouse of the world's richest lode of coca paste and cocaine: the Bolivian government's warehouses. He would be an equal to those other *hijos de putas*—Pacho Cuervas, the Ochoa family, even Pablo Escobar.

If she didn't show—no matter who's protection she was under—he would make her an example that those spineless *Bolivianos* would never forget. And that fucking Mario Espinosa . . . It was his idea in the first place to offer her jewelry and the Mercedes.

"Nobody alive knows what's going on in her head," Espinosa had said. "She's *chiflada*, you can never figure what she'll do next. But for Sonia Atala, if it sounds like kicks, she'll come. We offer her jewelry and a nice, slick Mercedes along with the money. Have a wild party. Invite a lot of freaky people."

If that *maricon* was wrong there would be a special death for him. The thought of it pacified him for the moment.

Sonia Atala settled back into the soft leather seat of the Mercedes limousine next to Nati and lit a cigarette. She nodded her head lightly with the rhythm of a conga drum solo coming from the stereo. Sonia smiled to herself. She loved the hot, racy salsa music that was so different from the bucolic, peaceful Bolivian *musica folklorica*. Maybe tonight, after the business, if the atmosphere was right and the people *simpatica*, she would have an opportunity to dance. What was life worth without *un poquito de salsa*?

The car made a sharp turn on the jungle track and was suddenly illuminated by a spotlight. A short distance ahead she could see an open gate and a man with a submachine gun slung under his arm standing in their path.

"*Ai, Dios mio,*" Nati gasped, "look at his face." Her long nails dug into Sonia's arm.

"Don't be frightened, *mi amor,*" Sonia laughed. "He looks like he's smiling, doesn't he?" She pulled Nati to her, enjoying the feel of her quivering body, the pleasurable bite of her nails. She loved to have Nati with her wherever she went. To see the world through Nati's eyes was to experience it with an innocence she was no longer capable of feeling.

"I don't know why you are doing this," said Nati, her eyes fixed on the nightmare face that seemed to float toward her in the glare of the headlights. "You have the biggest customers in the world begging you to come. Why do you need this?"

Sonia brushed Nati's dark hair away from her pretty face. "It's just

9

business, *querida mia,*" she said. "His money is as good as any man's."

She couldn't tell Nati the real reason they were there. Nati would be paralyzed with terror, unable to control herself. Papo was no fool; he would understand this and recognize Sonia's intentions immediately. Dealing with a mad-dog killer made no sense, unless you had a plan.

The great American demand for cocaine was exploding as it never had before. And working for Lucho—Luis Arce-Gomez, Bolivia's Minister of Interior—had put Sonia in an immensely powerful position. She was an underground celebrity, one of the highest-ranking members of *La Mafia Cruzeña*—the Santa Cruz Mafia—which supplied 80 percent of the world's cocaine. She was invited into the homes of ambassadors, movie stars, diplomats, and military leaders and treated with a deference reserved for heads of state and royalty.

"We will flood America's borders with cocaine," Lucho had bragged to Sonia shortly after he had taken power. And in the six months since the Bolivian revolution Sonia had almost single-handedly made that boast come true. She had shown the fools now running her country how to turn the tons of seized powder they had stored in government vaults into gold, and had introduced them to her best Colombian and American customers. And now that she had the pipelines to the great gringo gold mine filled with white powder northbound and gold coming south, the *hijos de putas* were repaying her by cutting her out of the deal. And the idea that they thought they could get away with it because she was a woman filled her with a seething rage.

She would make them pay—all of them. She had built them up, and she would now bring them down. There was no man she couldn't bring to his knees—Lucho in particular. And when he fell, the others would follow.

The driver lowered his window, and the jungle heat flooded the car. The bodyguard tensed in his seat, eyes fixed on the guard's mutilated face and the weapon leveled in his direction. As the music from the house reached her, Sonia felt a surge of adrenaline. Nati's nails dug deeper, but it was an exquisite pain. She was on a roller coaster that had just peaked and stood ready for the plunge.

The guard ducked his head to peer inside. He quickly dismissed pale, gawking Nati, and his eyes shifted to Sonia. She returned his gaze directly and smiled. He studied her for a long moment, nodded in satisfaction, and then waved the caravan through. For a moment he watched their taillights moving over the road toward the big house, and then he turned and nodded at the other.

The thickset Colombian reached inside for a field phone. He cranked it and said, *"Acaba de llegar, ella."*

Papo heard the news of Sonia's arrival and did not smile. He looked at his watch again. She was exactly two hours and nine minutes late. If she did not come through, he would make it the most expensive 129 minutes of her life.

# PART ONE

# THE COCAINE COUP

The first sign of corruption in a society . . . is that the end justifies the means.

—Georges Beranos, "Why Freedom?" (1955)

# 1

# A Kidnaping and a Premonition

"**Y**ou speak Spanish, right Levine?" said Assistant Special Agent in Charge (ASAC) Jim Hunt. It was 10 A.M. on May 26, 1976 in the DEA New York City Field Division office. The powerfully built ex-Marine spotted me across his smoke-filled office the moment I stuck my head in. The room, crowded with dour-faced suits, was suddenly silent. All eyes were on me.

"Yes," I said, taken aback by the electricity in the air and the sight of so many unfamiliar faces—usually a sign that a joint operation with other enforcement agencies was underway.

My heart was still racing from my tire-screeching drive down the West Side Highway. "Urgent," the base radio operator had said. "Report to Mr. Hunt's office ASAP." This meant that, wherever I was, I had to get my butt into headquarters within minutes; Jim Hunt was not a man you wanted pissed off at you.

Hunt looked at his watch. "It's ten hundred hours. I want you out at the JFK office by eleven. Report to Bob Nickeloff. Call your family. Tell 'em you won't be home tonight, and that's all you know. You got that?" Jim Hunt was not one for a lot of conversation when shit was happening—and shit was definitely happening.

"Yes sir," I said.

Minutes later I was racing along the Grand Central Parkway toward John F. Kennedy Airport in my undercover (UC) Eldorado, my siren screaming and a redball emergency light whirring over my head. I was feeling good. My face was flushed and I could practically hear my heart pounding. This was why I had become a DEA agent. I was conscious of the blurred faces in other cars trying to get a look at me as I raced by, and I tried not to smile. I really thought I was hot stuff.

An hour later I was traveling southbound on a chartered Boeing 707 with 17 other DEA undercover agents—14 men and 3 women. We didn't have the slightest idea where we were going or what we were going to do when we got there, but everyone was kind of giddy. The adrenalin rush was almost too hard to handle, and some of the guys were pacing the aisles of the big empty plane, their eyes wild.

We were frontline soldiers in one of America's longest and dirtiest wars. "The war on drugs," our leaders had told us time and time again, "is the number one priority of our nation. The very future of America is at stake." It was a war that had to be won "at all costs." We were the protectors of the youth of America—kids like my little son and daughter, Keith and Niki, and my brother David, who was already a heroin addict. Our government had chosen the 17 of us for a top-secret mission in that war. We felt privileged and honored, and were ready to do anything we were told, without question.

About six hours into the trip Bob Nickeloff, Associate Special Agent in Charge of DEA's New York office, came out of the cockpit and told us that we were on our way to Argentina to pick up three of the most wanted fugitives in the drug world: Miguel Russo, Yolanda Sarmiento, and Françoise Chiappe. The three were part of the French Connection case; they had sent tons of heroin into our country and were under indictment in New York. They had found refuge in Argentina, a country with which the United States had no extradition treaty for drug violators. But DEA had convinced the Argentines to give them to us.

"Argentina is going to expel them from their country," explained Nickeloff, a scholarly looking man with a salt-and-pepper brushcut, "and we'll just happen to be there to 'accept' them into ours." We all laughed like we were being let in on a dirty trick on some guy everyone hated. "This is the first time an operation like this has ever been attempted. It's expensive and risky." He paused to let this sink in, his eyes roving our faces with a faint look of amusement. For the first time I noticed how different he was from all of us. As usual, he was dressed in conservative suit and tie, while we were a bunch of ragtag street narcs looking more like a planeload of muggers than the James Bond-type spies we were all suddenly feeling like. Nickeloff seemed to realize this and appeared to be enjoying the moment. "It's important," he continued, "that you follow your orders to the letter."

Nickeloff tried to explain that we were treading a fine legal line, but I hardly listened to a word. I thought of my brother David, a heroin addict by the time he was 15, and his nightmare life. Then my mind drifted to a fall day in Plattsburgh, New York when I was 19 and in the Air Force. After an argument over a $3 debt, a man shoved a .45 pistol into my stomach and pulled the trigger. The gun misfired.

The MPs arrested the guy, seized his gun, and later test-fired it. That gun never misfired again. The MPs showed me the bullet where the firing pin had struck the rear precisely where it was supposed to. The tiny explosive cap was dented. It should have fired. No one could figure out why it hadn't.

For months after that incident I lay awake nights thinking about what it all meant. I came out of the experience with a sense of destiny about things; that if there was a logical purpose for all life, then the same could be said for each individual life and perhaps for each individual event. I came to believe that each of us has, if not a destiny, at least a certain role to play in life.

At that moment, 30,000 feet in the air and halfway to Argentina, I had no doubts about my role. This was what I had been spared for—to be the valiant drug warrior defending my nation against the "white death." I was proud of this, and I was proud of what my country was doing. During that plane ride I was a fulfilled man.

We landed at Eseiza Airport, Buenos Aires, just before dawn. I looked out the window as our plane taxied to a stop on the tarmac about a quarter mile from the terminal, and suddenly experienced an odd feeling of familiarity. I'm supposed to be here, I thought. I knew it with a certainty that startled me. Minutes later I stepped onto the tarmac and took a deep breath of the chill air. The lights of the terminal shone dully through a thick mist. Bobby Joura, an agent and friend from my New York street group, was alongside me. "You know Bobby," I said, "I have this feeling I'll be coming back here to live."

"Sure you will," he said and gave me a strange look.

I felt embarrassed and shut up. I was acting like a giddy kid. Besides, for a DEA agent to even think of getting a transfer to Buenos

Aires—at the time one of the juiciest plums on the DEA tree—he had to have one hell of a "rabbi," and I had none.

The sky had begun to turn a soupy gray when the airfield sprang to life. A procession of about a dozen military jeeps and trucks filled with armed soldiers in full battle dress and a half dozen unmarked Ford Falcons suddenly appeared and raced toward us. Emergency lights flashed from the vehicles' grills, dashboards, and roofs. Another dozen vehicles, with all kinds of lights flashing crazily, seemed to appear from nowhere. For a moment it looked as if we were under attack.

"They're here," said Nickeloff casually.

The cars and trucks screeched to a halt around the plane. Soldiers clutching rifles and submachine guns leapt from trucks, and a group of about 20 soldiers and a half-dozen mustachioed men in European-cut suits and trenchcoats surrounded a truck with a canvas cover. I watched them, fascinated. They were the Argentine Secret Police—stone killers, as I had been told.

Within moments soldiers flanked by secret police were half-leading, half-dragging three figures toward us. As they drew closer, I saw that the hands and feet of each prisoner were heavily shackled and their heads were covered by filthy canvas bags of the type used to feed horses.

"We don't take custody of them till they're on the plane," ordered Nickeloff.

We all scrambled back onboard. I stood in the doorway along with the gawking civilian flight crew as the Argentines prodded and shoved the three toward the stairway. The first prisoner up the metal gangway was a huge, bearlike man whose wrists were so thick that leg irons had been used to manacle them. This was Chiappe, the notorious Corsican gangster and drug smuggler, and he was being turned over to me on Hunt's orders. I felt so proud I could hardly breathe.

Chiappe's incredible size seemed to fill the doorway of the aircraft. Even though I was 6'1" and weighed about 220 pounds, I felt dwarfed beside him.

"The fucking Hulk," whispered someone.

"Shut up!" snapped someone else. We had been given orders that there was to be "no talking whatsoever" until the plane was off the ground.

"Where?" whispered one of the secret policemen, a slim man with predatory eyes. I motioned for them to follow me down the aisle toward the rear of the plane where I had been assigned to sit with Chiappe. The Argentines, their eyes on the huge man as if expecting him to explode at any moment, led him slowly down the aisle by his chains like a circus gorilla. I noticed that the soldier just behind Chiappe held his submachine gun pointed at Chiappe's back. His eyes never blinked, and his finger was tensed on the trigger. He made me more nervous than the prisoner did.

It was about 20 minutes before Chiappe was wedged into his seat, his leg irons were off, and I had squeezed in beside him. The huge man's clothes were grimy and bloodstained, and he reeked of body odor and excrement. It was not going to be a pleasant ride home, but I didn't care. If I had to, I would have made the trip standing on my head.

I had to replace the Argentine leg irons around Chiappe's wrists with handcuffs, which didn't fit. The secret policeman watched me struggling with the them, and suddenly reached over and squeezed the metal hasps shut, cutting off Chiappe's circulation. The huge man grunted in pain, and the Argentine winked at me. The canvas bag was to stay on his head until we were off the ground.

The other two prisoners had been seated without incident and the flight crew was preparing for a quick takeoff. The Argentine cop grinned and shook my hand; there was something unnerving about his smile. "Good luck," he said. "Now there are three less of these bastards."

"Thanks," I said gripping the man's hand and feeling a revulsion that I tried to ignore.

Chiappe suddenly began to twist in his seat. Muffled noises came from beneath the bag. The Argentine started to reach for something inside his coat. I leaned close to Chiappe and raised a corner of the bag. "My money," he said in Spanish, spraying blood. A glob of it and something else stuck to my fingertip. I shook it off. "My jacket pocket," he said. "I had money there."

I felt both jacket pockets and then his pants pockets. There was nothing.

"*Usted habla español?*" asked the Argentine, nervously eyeing me. "*Sí,*" I replied.

"He had nothing," the Argentine said in Spanish, uncomfortable but still smiling. "Let him go fuck himself, anyway."

I didn't know if Chiappe could hear with the bag over his head so I leaned close and said, "He said you didn't have any money." I heard a short laugh beneath the bag, then he lay his head back on the seat. I looked up and the Argentine cop was on his way down the aisle. He turned once and waved at me.

Twenty minutes after takeoff, I was ordered to remove the bag from Chiappe's head, read him his constitutional rights, and explain what was happening. I reached around his head to remove the canvas bag. The bottom of it was damp and crusted with blood. As I struggled to raise it gingerly over his head, blood trickled down my hands. What I found underneath was a mess.

It was hard to tell whether Chiappe's head was simply enormous or if it was swollen and misshaped from the beating. He looked to be in his late forties. His thick, graying hair was matted with blood, and there were scabs and patches of fresh blood in half a dozen places. He seemed to be smiling, only it was no smile—all his front teeth had been battered out, leaving only jagged and broken stumps.

"What happened?" I asked.

"Three days ago," he said, dipping his head to keep from spraying me with blood, "I was enjoying a barbecue with my family when suddenly soldiers and police were crashing into my house from every direction. I demanded to know what was going on. They knocked me to the ground and held me. A soldier smashed out my teeth with his rifle butt. 'That's what's going on,' he said. 'Anything else you want to know?'" Chiappe coughed; his face twisted into a horror smile. "So I didn't ask any more questions.

"It didn't matter, though. They blindfolded me, brought me someplace, chained me spread-eagled to the floor and kept beating me. And now they brought me here." He suddenly held up his manacled hands. "Can you take these off?" The steel had cut deeply into his wrists. He nodded his head toward the window. "I'm not going anywhere." I took the cuffs off.

By the time we were halfway back to New York I learned that the other two prisoners had been treated similarly. Later we shifted babysitting duties and I was assigned to sit with Yolanda Sarmiento, a middle-aged Chilean drug dealer and the only one of the three who had ever been in the United States. She told me that the Argentine police had killed her only son. "I don't care what happens to me now," she sobbed, laying her head on my shoulder. "I have nothing to live for."

I felt her sorrow enter me for a moment and put my arm around her. She looked so sweet and helpless; she reminded me of my grand-mother. She had been indicted for murdering a drug dealing competitor on the Upper West Side of Manhattan, and was alleged to have hacked the body to pieces in a bathtub by herself because her husband didn't have the stomach for it. I tried to picture her doing it, but couldn't.

Later, when I was given a break to eat and get some sleep, I thought about everything that had happened. I was troubled that a part of me was feeling sympathy for these people, and had to remind myself about what drugs had done to my brother. Whatever a drug dealer gets he deserves, I thought, and fell into a deep sleep.

I had a lot to learn.

Ten months later, on February 27, 1977, my brother David ended his 19-year battle against heroin addiction by shooting himself in the head with a .38. His note said, "To my family and friends, I'm sorry. I just can't stand the drugs anymore."

I blamed my brother's death on the drug dealers; I couldn't shovel them into jails fast enough. I threw myself into undercover work with a vengeance, working seven days a week, often around the clock. Sometimes I would make three or four undercover drug buys a day. My life's activities were narrowed to making undercover buys, arresting drug dealers, and testifying in court. I even slept in the DEA gym. I never stopped.

In August 1978, when I first learned that I was being transferred to Buenos Aires, I was shocked and then ecstatic. Like a World War II Kamikaze ready to die for his emperor, my dream was to be sent into battle where the real action was—where my undercover talent and ability with Spanish could best be utilized—where the biggest drug dealers in the world seemed to operate with impunity—South America. And now that dream was coming true. There had to be something to all my notions of destiny; this was too much for chance.

And so it was that in December 1978 I moved to Buenos Aires, Argentina—the land of the tango, Nazi war criminals, and government-sponsored death. I was a confirmed believer in the righteousness and purity of America's war on drugs, and was one of its most dedicated warriors. I felt it was truly my destiny to make a difference.

Could I have been so innocent? I was. But in Argentina, I would learn that the drug war I'd been married to for the past 13 years was a faithless whore who'd been cheating on me from day one.

# 2

# Argentina

## 1

*T**he Star Spangled Banner* erupted over loudspeakers, and a three-man Marine color guard snapped to attention like the crack of a rifle bolt. Old Glory fluttered in the breeze as it was raised up the sparkling white pole on the front lawn of the American embassy in Buenos Aires as the eyes of 150 invited guests raised with it. It was Friday, July 4, 1980. I had been a federal agent for more than 15 years and could not have been more proud of my job and of being an American. But I was just 48 hours away from my first glimpse of how deeply involved my own government was in drug trafficking; 48 hours from the first time I would hear the name of Sonia Atala.

As DEA's Country Attache to Argentina and Uruguay, I spent that morning at the embassy greeting and having my picture taken with foreign dignitaries, Argentine military officers, and celebrities attending the Independence Day ceremonies. I took advantage of the opportunity to talk drug enforcement policy with the head of Argentina's 27,000-man border patrol, the *Gendarmeria Nacional*.

Later that afternoon, Argentine secret police and one of my informants came to my office at the embassy to plan an undercover operation. A Bolivian cocaine trafficker named Hugo Hurtado-Candia was coming to Buenos Aires on Sunday to meet me in my role as Latino representative of the American Mafia—one of the several roles I'd been playing for the past 18 months. I would con the Bolivian into delivering cocaine to me in Buenos Aires and the Argentines would arrest him. Another routine victory in the drug war.

Forty-eight hours later I was Luis Garcia, a Cuban American with diamonds on my fingers, a fake Rolex on my wrist, and three thick gold chains around my neck, sitting in a smoke-filled suite (monitored by the Argentine police) at the Buenos Aires Sheraton facing a founding member of *La Mafia Cruzeña*—the Cocaine Mafia of Bolivia.

"You know Luis, I think we're going to do a lot of business together," said Hugo Hurtado. The barrel-chested Bolivian took another sip of Chivas Regal and flashed a smile that showed a lot of gold. "I really like you."

"And what about me?" said Alfredo (name changed), the informer who had arranged the meeting. "You don't like me?" He gave me a quick sly wink. I ignored him.

Alfredo was crazy even for an informant. He was a blond, blue-eyed Argentine of German ancestry, and a fearless pilot who would fly his Piper Cub anywhere. I used to call him "The Bolivian Ferret," and I'd send him into Bolivia hunting drug dealers the way I imagined a hunter might send a trained ferret into a burrow to chase small animals out into the open. He'd sucker some Bolivian doper into coming to Buenos Aires to meet his "New York friend" every time. Sometimes I was a Puerto Rican, sometimes a Cuban, usually a half-breed Sicilian; but I was always a representative of the American Mafia looking for drugs. The doper would deliver cocaine to me in Buenos Aires and the Argentine cops would bust him. I made sure Alfredo was well paid, but the way his maniacal eyes gleamed before each of his trips told me that he was a danger junkie who'd have done the work for nothing.

"I think you're a fucking Nazi," I used to tell him. "I'll bet half your family is hiding out from Simon Wiesenthal. If you ever give me any trouble I'm going to be sneaking around your house with my friends from the Mossad, taking pictures." When I said this to him—and I said it often—he'd give me a strange look and a thin-lipped smile, but he'd never laugh.

"Of course I like you, Alfredo," laughed Hurtado. "What are you worried about?"

"I just didn't want you two to forget I'm part of this thing," said

Alfredo. "I arranged this meeting." It was a nice touch of realism—men who set up drug deals always worry about their money. And a Bolivian drug dealer would detect anything that fell short of real.

Alfredo was slick. He worked on a drug dealer as if he were seducing him—calling him constantly to see if there were any special favors he could do, sending presents to his family (paid for by the U.S. government), making himself liked and trusted. He had Hurtado so convinced that the Bolivian showed up carrying a hefty sample of pure cocaine, and it was hardly any work at all for me to reach an agreement for the delivery of 200 kilos to Buenos Aires.

Hurtado was easy to like. He was a typical farmer who had turned cocaine dealer because of the weak Bolivian economy and the exploding U.S. cocaine demand. He had a wide mestizo face, a pencil mustache, and a ready smile, and he loved to drink scotch, tell jokes, and talk, in any order. In fact, he loved to talk so much that he began to talk his way out of leaving Argentina alive.

"You know, Luis, I'd like to get this transaction done before the changes in my government," he said, "because things could get complicated . . . I could get involved."

"What do you mean, 'changes?'" I asked. A drug dealer involved with changes in his government was always an interesting notion.

He considered his words for a long moment, glancing at the half-bottle of Chivas remaining. Finally, he said, "Did you hear about that big cocaine case in Miami? The one with Roberto Suarez and this one they call *El Judio Triqueño?*"

Hear about the case—I had created it. He was talking about the case that had dominated my life for the past six months. *I* was *El Judio Triqueño*—The Dark Jew.

"Yes, I heard something about it." I could see Alfredo grinning at me out of the corner of my eye. I felt my face flame; I couldn't look at him.

"You know 50 kilos of that load was mine," bragged Hurtado. (He had just said enough to be indicted in the United States.) "Not only that, they used my ranch to load the plane. I have a good landing strip there."

"That's too bad," I said, hoping the hidden microphones had picked up his voice clearly. "You see, that's why I came to Argentina. The gringos are strong in places like Miami, Colombia, and Bolivia. They . . . the DEA . . . doesn't even know Argentina exists."

Hurtado laughed ironically and poured himself a half tumbler of scotch. "That's where you are wrong, my friend. That case began right here in Argentina. *El Judio Triqueño,* the guy that set Suarez up, lives here; he was an agent or possibly an informer for *la DEA.* (He pronounced this *la day-ah.*) They say his name was *Mitch-ay-el.*"

My blood pressure surged. Alfredo's face lit up, and he was grinning like an idiot. I couldn't believe that Hurtado didn't notice.

"This Jew really fooled them," continued Hurtado, shaking his head in wonder, "the Suarez people."

"And you, too," I said, looking directly into his eyes.

"No, I never met him . . . I just invested."

"This *Mitch-ay-el* must really be something," said Alfredo, winking at me again. "What did he look like?"

At first I wanted to smack him, but I realized that what he was doing was perfect—even if he was enjoying himself a little too much.

"I never saw him," said Hurtado. "They say he's big and dark . . . like a negro."

"Those fucking Jews," said Alfredo.

"It's causing a lot of trouble in my country," said Hurtado, looking at me.

"How so?" I said, conscious of my skin, now dark brown from the Argentine sun; a gift of nature that has always helped me to change identity; a gift that at the moment I wished I didn't have.

"Bolivia is a poor country. Coca feeds the people. We can't have bastards in our own government who betray us . . . who collaborate with the gringos . . . who spy on us for *la DEA.*" He raised his glass in a silent toast and downed the remains. Then he said, "The Suarez people are planning a *golpe* [revolution]. It will be soon."

For a long moment the room was quiet. I thought I heard a stirring behind a wall. The adjoining rooms were filled with Argentine secret police who were recording the conversation. I was grateful for the recording, but afraid of the police.

"You see," continued Hurtado, pouring more scotch into his tumbler, "*la DEA* could never have gotten away with what they did without help from within our own government."

As he spoke I flashed back to my first meeting with Roberto Suarez's righthand man, Marcelo Ibañez, in a Buenos Aires *confiteria* six months earlier. He had been trying to convince me to bring $9 million to Bolivia to make a buy of 1,000 pounds of cocaine. "In Bolivia," Ibañez had said, "you will be as safe as in your own home."

"Then why do you want to do the transaction before the change?" I asked Hurtado.

Hurtado shrugged. "In my country you can start a change in government, but you can't predict how it will turn out."

"I don't understand. I thought the change would be a good thing for you."

"It's being done out of anger. Everything, as far as I am concerned, is protected enough. Right now I pay $100,000 a year to the head of the narcotics police and $100,000 to the Minister. Once it's in the hands of the military . . . " He shrugged again. "That's why I'd like to finish this deal before the change."

Hurtado rambled on for a while about "the change" with Alfredo questioning him. I watched, trying to decide if Hurtado was one of the grandiose bullshitters that the drug world was so full of—men who come at you with mind-boggling stories of mountains of drugs and money. Who the hell could believe drug dealers were powerful enough to take over a whole country?

There was a sudden loud knock. Alfredo opened the door, and a waiter entered with a fresh bottle of Chivas. We had never ordered it, but Hurtado didn't seem to regard it as out of the ordinary.

The waiter took a long look at Hurtado as I signed the bill. Both Alfredo and I knew he was no waiter. This was supposed to be a straight undercover meet with no police action. The Argentine cops had agreed to let Hurtado return to Bolivia; he would be arrested when he returned to Buenos Aires with the 200 kilos. Something had changed.

The waiter took a last look at Hurtado, memorizing every detail of his face, and left. The tipsy Bolivian noticed nothing, and once he started talking again it was hard to stop him. If he was trying to impress us, he was succeeding beyond his wildest expectations.

According to Hurtado all his country's major coca producers had joined an organization under the control of Roberto Suarez. Many top members of the government were already on the organization's payroll, and Hurtado himself was the "bagman" in charge of collecting from the coca dealers and paying the officials.[1] He described the confiscation of 854 pounds of cocaine in the Suarez case as a group loss. "I invested 50 kilos. Others also invested."

"If Suarez is so big and powerful, why were so many people involved? I thought it was all his stuff."

[1] This was the beginning of *La Corporacion*, the organization that would dominate cocaine production in South America for the next decade, supplying from 50 to 90 percent of the world's cocaine. The organization was the target of Operation Trifecta, the subject case in my book *Deep Cover*.

"No, no, no, Luis," he said, tapping his forehead. "Why should one person risk everything? If there's a problem . . . a loss . . . we all lose." Hurtado gulped down the rest of his drink. Alfredo rolled his eyes at me.

The room was suddenly quiet. I wanted to keep Hurtado talking, but what he had already said had opened up so many possibilities that I just couldn't think fast enough.

Alfredo broke the silence. "How's Sonia?" he asked with a sly grin.

"She's very well," said Hurtado, taken aback.

"Who's Sonia?" I asked. When I had debriefed Alfredo earlier, he'd never mentioned her.

"My niece," said Hurtado.

"*Jesu Cristo,* is she beautiful," said Alfredo knocking back the rest of his drink. "She's in the business, right *Che*?"

"Yes," said Hurtado.

"Now I know you're bullshitting," I said, laughing, relieved by the diversion.

"She's married," said Hurtado solemnly.

"Come on, *Che* . . . with those eyes how married can she be?"

Hurtado suddenly looked very uncomfortable. He sipped his drink. "With the new government, Sonia's going to be in a very strong position."

"How so?" I asked, noting fear in his voice. He had spoken openly about Suarez taking over the Bolivian government, but about Sonia he was guarded.

"She's already very strong . . . and very popular with the military."

"Did she have anything invested in that Miami thing?" I asked.

"I wouldn't be surprised. She's very . . . secretive." We were silent for an uncomfortable moment.

"What about the 200 kilos I'm ordering," I said. "Does that come from a whole corporation, or am I dealing with just you?"

"What difference does it make?" said Hurtado. For a moment I was afraid I had probed too hard. "You deal with me. I'm responsible to the others."

"Does Sonia have part of this?" asked Alfredo.

"Sonia?" said Hurtado, as if he'd never heard the name before. "No. In this one, no. She does a lot on her own."

I had rarely heard of a female dealer of any consequence in the male-dominated South American drug scene, and never one who worked on her own.

Taking another gulp of Chivas, Hurtado said, "Sonia is strong. She has her own lab, she sells base and crystallized [forms of cocaine] . . . She has her own lines [customers] in Venezuela, Colombia, and Brazil for base . . . The crystallized she sells direct to North America."

"*Jesu Cristo,*" said Alfredo, rolling his eyes.

"Well, Sonia . . . my niece . . . does her own thing."

There was a long silence.

"I never dealt with Bolivians before," I said, hoping that changing the subject would get him talking again. "I'm used to just dealing with one person."

"Understand, just a week ago I lost a plane with 158 kilos in Venezuela . . . a mistake . . . It was North Americans . . . I told them before the plane took off that it was the wrong equipment. But at least there were other investors with me."

Bingo! I had just received a teletype from DEA in Caracas, Venezuela, describing a plane with 158 kilos of cocaine from Bolivia that had crashed. The pilots had been interrogated by Venezuelan police and would only say that the drugs were destined to "Michael" in Miami. It was Suarez rubbing my name in DEA's face, I thought.

On the plane, the Venezuelan cops had found photographs of a clandestine landing field that had very unusual topography. It could be Hurtado's. If the DEA UC pilots could identify it as the strip they'd used in the Suarez case, we had the beginnings of a huge conspiracy case. Anyone who'd had anything whatsoever to do with the downed plane in Venezuela or the Suarez seizure—whether investing money or dope or pumping gas into the plane, or whether he was the president of Bolivia, a barefooted *campesino,* or a beautiful Bolivian drug dealer—could be indicted and sent to jail in the United States, if we could identify them. I had to keep Hurtado talking.

"The plane took off from that same strip?" I asked.

"Yes," he said, sipping his drink and eyeing me speculatively. "Well, it's not exactly mine. It's on *Perserverancia,* Sonia's ranch." Hurtado suddenly shifted uncomfortably in his seat.

I had to back off. I was pushing too hard, becoming more cop than undercover, and Hurtado was sensing it. When he sobered up I was afraid he might remember how much he had talked and go bad on me, and this was one undercover deal that I did not want to fail. Hurtado had said some things that had incredible implications about the drug world. The Bolivian coca producers were about to take over their country. And I thought I was the only American who knew about it.

# 2

I stood at my window anxiously watching the hotel entrance six floors below me. Hurtado had left the room minutes before—taking the unopened second bottle of Chivas with him—after we agreed on a shipment of 200 kilos of cocaine to Buenos Aires for $27,000 a kilo. I was to contact him through Alfredo in a week as to where and when the payment of $5.4 million would be made. The Argentine secret police had promised they would let Hurtado return to Bolivia, but I had a feeling they were about to renege.

"Why didn't you tell me about Sonia?" I asked Alfredo.

"The story sounded so fantastic that I wanted you to hear it directly from him first. He's her son-of-a-bitching uncle and he's afraid of her! Couldn't you tell?"

Thoughts of Sonia vanished as I saw Hurtado step out from beneath the hotel marquis and into a cab. As his cab drove off, three nondescript cars appeared as if from nowhere and followed him out of the parking area. Another car raced up to the front of the hotel and the room service waiter, now in a dark trenchcoat, quickly slipped inside. The car raced off after the others. The Argentine cops obviously had plans for Hurtado that they hadn't discussed with me.

"You know where he's staying?" I said to Alfredo.

"The Plaza."

"Get over there. Stay with him. I don't care what excuse you use. You want to make sure about your profit, you want to screw me out of money, anything. I don't want anything happening to him."

In 1980, death was very much a way of life in Argentina. The military government believed itself to be in a life-and-death struggle against communism. It was called *la guerra sucia*—"the dirty war." If you were an idealistic Argentine with sympathies that could in any way be construed as leftist, you kept your mouth shut or got your butt out of Argentina. Otherwise, you stood a good chance of hearing a knock on your door at any time and greeting cold-eyed men in civilian clothes carrying official government identification cards. They would take you to a secret subbasement of a military or government building, where they would methodically savage your body and brain with the latest "advances" in torture methods, designed to inflict the maximum pain a human can tolerate without losing consciousness or dying, until you named all the other "leftists" you knew. You would then be "disappeared" from the face of the earth, and these men would pay a visit to everyone you had named. From 1976 to 1982, it was estimated that some 25,000 Argentines had been turned into *desaparecidos*—"disappeared ones." Scores of them are now being found in mass graves and floating in the Rio de la Plata and Parana rivers.

I had heard stories from other agents assigned overseas that the torture methods used by the Argentines and other South American police agencies were taught by our own CIA. However, when I was stationed in Argentina, I found those stories hard to believe. Unfortunately, the events in Bolivia that Hurtado had alluded to and published revelations of other ex-deep cover agents have since given convincing evidence of the truth of these stories.[2]

With mass murder a quasi-official tool of government, many of the Argentine military and law enforcement officials that the American embassy's intelligence and law enforcement sections had to work with were involved with mass murder. Week after week I attended top-level Country Team meetings with Ambassador Raul Castro and the other embassy section chiefs during which the number of *desaparecidos* from the previous week would be announced. Ambassador Castro was grieved by what was going on, and we always discussed how we could pressure the Argentine government into changing its ways. The CIA representatives, who were present at every meeting, would sit in stony silence, never offering a single suggestion. The U.S. government was not resolved to end the mass murders, so the prevailing feeling at the embassy was one of helplessness and hopelessness.

Thus, I found myself wrestling with my conscience. The mission assigned to me—stopping drug trafficking whenever and wherever I found it—along with my personal safety depended on the cooperation I got from the different branches of the Argentine military, police, and intelligence agencies. Some of the Argentine officers and agents upon whom I depended might have been the cold-blooded murderers of men, women, and children. In most instances I could only guess how involved each man was; in some cases there was little doubt.

A rapid, light knocking on my hotel room door brought me up short. I opened the door and the room quickly filled with Argentine secret policemen from a Special Intelligence unit. Their leader, a tall,

---

[2] See A. J. Langguth, *Hidden Terrors: The Truth About U.S. Police Operations in South America* (New York: Pantheon Books, 1978).

dark, mustachioed man with slicked-back tango-dancer's hair, entered with a sly smile on his face.

Mario's (name changed) eyes gave him away—they told you what he was. If you studied his pupils you saw that they were as dead and lusterless as tiny brown tombstones; the eyes of someone who kills often and without conscience, like a professional hitman or a serial killer. A CIA agent I knew once called them "executioner's eyes."

To Mario, murder had become an addiction, a need, even an aphrodisiac. Once, at a U.S. embassy function, I heard him, half-drunk, telling some other Argentine cops, "Nothing turns me on more than killing. Right after I kill I must fuck . . . I'm desperate to fuck." Although he had pretended not to see me enter the room, he seemed to want to scandalize me. "You know why Argentina doesn't have a drug problem, Señor Levine," he used to delight in telling me, pronouncing my name *lay-vee-nay*, "because we send our drug dealers to a better place. In fact, if you've got the stomach, you ought to come with us and watch—it might do you some good." Then he would laugh, but his stone killer eyes told me he wasn't joking.

I could never permit myself to show even a hint of the hatred I felt for Mario and others like him, nor could I allow myself to forget how easily I could become a *desaparecido.* I was simply determined to keep anyone I worked on alive.

"What's happening, Mario?" I demanded. "Something is going on. We had a deal."

"What do you mean, *Che*?" he said, flushing. He knew exactly what I meant.

"Where's the Bolivian right now?" I said, trying to speak evenly.

He shrugged. "Back at his hotel, I suppose."

"Alive or dead?"

The smile vanished. "Can we go someplace?" He pointed at one of the walls, indicating that the room was bugged.

"My house?"

He grinned. *"Fenomino!"*

I wanted to scream at the son of a bitch, or punch his heartless lights out. I knew that Hurtado might already be dead, and he was just playing with me. The Argentine cops had pulled stunts like that before.

I smiled. "You know where it is."

One hour later, Mario arrived at my home in La Lucila, a suburb north of Buenos Aires, with two of his men. They'd been to the house before. The established routine with Argentine cops was that they would help me with a case, then everyone would go to my house, where I would pay them a "reward." The reward was the most important part, for when all was said and done, these guys were working for money, and DEA paid well.

The usually talkative cops were silent as they sat in the overstuffed armchairs that came with the rented house. They watched Mario, their *jefe*, for their cue.

Mario helped himself to a bottle of Johnny Walker, took a swig, and then slumped on an easy chair with the bottle at his feet. His casual actions reminded me that for a DEA agent assigned overseas there was no such thing as "home." Wherever you lived was to be used to "entertain" or do anything else necessary to get your job done.

The living room extended out from the ground floor of the ancient, two-story, concrete-and-fieldstone house into a beautiful subtropical garden, and the glass wall gave those inside the feeling of being in the middle of a lush forest. The setting sun painted the scene with a breathtaking golden hue. I had never seen the room look more beautiful and peaceful. It seemed so incongruous to talk of death and to have what had been my life's devotion for 15 years begin to come apart.

Mercedes, my maid, served drinks and a huge platter of hand-rolled *empanadas*. The room was quiet for a long time. Watching me, Mario chewed an *empanada* and sipped his scotch. He was still playing with me, waiting for me to come to him. Everything with him was some kind of a head game, but this time I wasn't playing. "The Bolivian's not going to make it, is he?"

Mario shrugged. "It may be out of my hands."

I felt a sinking sensation. "Is he gone already?"

"No, no, no. Tsk, tsk, tsk." He waved his index finger. "My men have him under surveillance." Sly grin. "I think Alfredo is with him, no, *Che*?"

"Then what's going on?"

"You heard what he said about the coup . . . the change?"

"Yes. So what does that have to do with anything?"

Mario laughed and shook his head in wonder. "You North Americans amaze me. Don't you speak to your own people?"

"What do you mean?"

"To your friends on the third floor."

I knew the son of a bitch was on the CIA's payroll as well as the DEA's. The CIA's mission was to destroy communism, and Mario's guys were killing off a couple of thousand "communists" a year. That was why the CIA was always silent during those Country Team meetings when we discussed the Argentines' policy of mass murder—the most prolific of the murderers were on their payroll.

"We're just like you guys and Toxicomania," I said, naming the Argentine Federal Police narcotics unit. "Sometimes we talk, sometimes we don't." The rivalry between Mario's elite unit and the federal unit was just like the rivalries between American spy and law enforcement agencies, each vying for turf and glory. It was something I exploited, playing one agency off against the other.

Mario took another swig of scotch and leaned forward, his forearms resting on his knees. "*Che*, what this Bolivian is saying can be very embarrassing to your country and mine."

"What are you saying?"

"Levine, are you really that innocent? Do you think you are the first to know about what's happening in Bolivia?" He cast a sidelong glance at his men; he enjoyed demonstrating his superiority over American diplomats.

"So you're saying that what Hurtado was telling me was real?"

"Could it be that you're the only one in your embassy who doesn't know?" said Mario, smiling thinly. His minions studied my reaction. "Do you think Bolivia's government—or any government in South America—can be changed without your government and mine being aware of it?"

"Okay, so everybody knows," I said. "What's that got to do with Hurtado not making it?"

"Because the same people he's naming as drug dealers are the people we are helping to rid Bolivia of leftists."

"I don't understand. Who is *we*?"

"Us. The Argentines . . . working with your CIA. Levine, don't you see how embarrassing this Hurtado can be to both our countries?"

I was stunned. How could I have missed it? Dozens of inexplicable events of the past six months flickered through my mind. Mario had just explained them all.

Six months earlier, I had telephoned DEA headquarters in Washington, D.C. to inform them that a man by the name of Roberto Suarez was uniting all the major Bolivian cocaine producers into one umbrella organization. Suarez himself had offered me the opportunity to be the organization's main customer if I agreed to purchase 1,000 kilos per month—a staggering amount considering that the largest drug seizure up to that point was 200 kilos of cocaine by a Border Patrol agent in South Florida. I requested authorization to set up a sting operation.

Headquarters refused permission. "He's not in the computer," I was told. "No one knows who he is."

I suppose I should have suspected that something was amiss. How could a man who six months later would be acknowledged by *60 Minutes* as the "biggest drug dealer alive," a man delivering tons of drugs to the United States, not be in the DEA computer system, which had not only the names of every nickel-and-dime drug dealer from Bogota to Bangkok, but also the names of everyone they telephoned—even wrong numbers. Someone had to be protecting Suarez. However, I couldn't conceive of anyone in my government protecting a drug dealer for any reason.

For weeks I kept meeting with informants, working undercover, and gathering information about Suarez and his organization without DEA support. I kept bombarding headquarters with phone calls and cables trying to get authorization and money to spend on the case. Finally, one man in headquarters, Ralph Saucedo, stuck his neck out. On February 13, 1980, I received a cable from headquarters that said, in essence, that Suarez was unknown and that headquarters had refused me permission to spend any money on the investigation; however, the cable concluded with these surprising words: "Please resubmit if additional intelligence can be found to support importance of Suarez. Case appears sound and achievable and should be pursued."

Later, I would meet more men like Saucedo whom, out of a sense of conscience and duty, tried to carry out the mission for which they had taken an oath to the American people despite of powerful political pressures. Unfortunately, in the upper ranks of DEA, these people have always been few and far between.

I "pursued" the hell out of the Suarez organization. After two months of undercover work, I managed to work out with Suarez himself an experimental first delivery of 500 kilos. When I sent recorded conversations and photos of undercover meetings to DEA headquarters, the suits were embarrassed into allowing me to set up a sting in Miami.

"A lot of people in headquarters want this thing to fail," Saucedo told me just before I left for Miami and the final undercover phase.

Either he didn't know why or wouldn't tell me why, but since there is a lot of competition in narcotics enforcement, I figured that it all had to do with internal jealousies. I didn't give a damn about who got the credit—I just wanted to make the case. I forgot Saucedo's words and dove in undercover.

On May 24, 1980, the sting ended with our UC plane making a miraculous takeoff from a ranch (Sonia Atala's) in the middle of the Bolivian jungle. Within hours I arranged for the payment of $9 million to Suarez's U.S. representatives, Alfredo "Cutuchi" Gutierrez and Jose Roberto Gasser, two major drug traffickers.

While counting out the $9 million in the bank vault, I offered Gutierrez help in getting the money out of the country. "Don't worry," he said, "my man [Gasser] has many legitimate interests in the U.S. and carries this much [drug] money out every week." So much for money laundering. Both men were arrested as they left the bank.

The world was rocked by the news. It was the biggest drug case in history. The suits fought each other for space in front of the television cameras, where—with the piles of cocaine and $9 million in cash behind them—they told America of their heroics. Suddenly every DEA suit was an expert on Suarez. Mike Wallace reported on *60 Minutes* that the DEA told him that Suarez had been arrested in Bolivia in 1976 for drugs, and that in 1979 Brazil had named him that country's "chief source of [cocaine]." Yet three months earlier they were telling me, their top enforcement officer in Argentina and Uruguay, that Suarez wasn't in the DEA computer.

An article by Jonathan Kandell entitled "The Great Bolivian Cocaine Scam," which appeared in the August 1982 *Penthouse,* was typical of what America was told:

> There had been weeks of patient negotiations with Suarez lieutenants in Buenos Aires, Miami, and Santa Cruz, Bolivia. A dozen DEA agents, men and women, had carefully rehearsed their roles as racketeers, underworld financiers, bodyguards, prostitutes, and cocaine chemists. A posh Fort Lauderdale beach house and limousines had been placed at the disposal of the Bolivian mobsters. Entertainment tours of Las Vegas and Broadway were booked. And $9 million had been borrowed from the Federal Reserve Bank in Miami as projected payment to Suarez for the first delivery of cocaine.

It was all lies.[3]

Saucedo's warning about DEA wanting the case to fail turned out to be an understatement. The undercover plane assigned to pick up the cocaine was so woefully inadequate that the Bolivians were betting on whether it would get off the ground. Headquarters also refused to change the plane's serial numbers, even though the plane had been used just months before to ferry corrupt Bolivian drug police from one location to another. The undercover team, which was supposed to pose as a close-knit Mafia family, was assembled only hours before Suarez's representatives were to arrive. The elaborate rehearsals were in reality a single three-hour meeting. The luxury mansion was an empty, two-bedroom tract home that we filled with cheap rental furniture paid for with most of our $2,500 total budget—minuscule for such an elaborate sting—and the limousines were Budget rental cars.

In spite of all these obstacles, a miracle was accomplished thanks to the heroic efforts of a small team of undercover agents whose rallying cry became, "Do it in spite of DEA."

After the initial media coverage died down, Jose Roberto Gasser, the son of Edwin Gasser, one of the richest and most powerful industrialists in Bolivia and a staunch anti-communist, was quietly released from jail and the U.S. Attorney's office, Southern Judicial District of Miami dropped all charges against him. Gasser immediately returned to Bolivia, where he ran a full-page ad in Bolivia's largest newspapers with a photo of his unconditional release signed by the U.S. Attorney. Overnight our war on drugs became a joke among South American drug traffickers.

The Assistant U.S. Attorney who authorized Gasser's release was Michael "Pat" Sullivan, who would later prosecute Manuel Noriega. He was quoted as saying there wasn't enough evidence against Gasser. The American public was not apprised of this, and the DEA suits refused to be interviewed about the details of the case.

I had blamed the wreckage of the case on jealous suits and bungling prosecutors. It was not until I heard Mario's words that I began to put the pieces together.

"You must understand the predicament I am in," said Mario. "I have a superior who I report to. Everything the Bolivian said was recorded."

[3]Another good example of the fiction DEA put out about the Suarez case can be found in Brian Freemantle, *The Fix* (New York: Tom Doherty Associates, 1986).

"Mario, I'm a DEA agent, not a CIA agent," I said, getting to my feet and trying to stop a flood of frightening thoughts. "You heard what Hurtado said about drug trafficking; a lot of very heavy things—I don't care about the political shit. That man is invaluable to DEA and the war on drugs—alive. Through him we can bring down people who threaten all our kids—American and Argentine. If he's dead he's worth nothing to us, and he'll be worth nothing to you. He's promised to return anyway—you heard him—with 200 kilos. That will be the biggest case in Argentina's history, and it will be worth one hell of a lot to DEA. And if there's anyone in Argentina who could see that he gets out of here alive, it's you."

I was now standing over Mario. His usually flat black eyes glowed with an excitement I'd never seen there before. I wasn't even sure if what I had said made sense, but I figured I had hit the man's three strongest psychological buttons—his ego, his love for money, and the warped sense of patriotic duty that seems to motivate some Argentines. Whatever the case, I had struck a responsive nerve in Mario and his men.

Mario nodded his head thoughtfully. "I'll see what I can do."

Before the policemen left, Mario cornered me. "Listen *Che*," he said, drilling me with his stone-killer eyes, "this conversation never happened."

"You know me better than that," I said.

"I just wanted to be sure. There's something else I think you'll find interesting. It will soon be no secret anyway. You know the one you arrested in Miami; the one they released?"

"Gasser?"

"Yes," said Mario, forming the devil smile that usually preceded one of his mental probes. "Do you know who he is?"

"All I know is he's a drug trafficker."

"Would it surprise you to know that he and his father are two of the big fishes behind this *golpe*?"

"No, Mario, after today I don't think anything would surprise me."

"Well did you ever consider why your own people let him out of jail?"

"Go ahead Mario, tell me."

His eyes bored into mine. "I don't know, Levine, but I think if I were in your shoes I would want to know why."

# 3

# A Peanut Butter Sandwich

## 1

At 6 A.M. the morning after I had met with Hurtado, I aimed my big four-door Chevrolet south on Avenida Libertador toward my office at the embassy. It had been almost 14 hours since I'd sent Alfredo to babysit Hurtado, and there was still no word from him. I had not been able to sleep, so I figured I might as well miss the 80-mile-per-hour game of bumper cars that is the Buenos Aires rush hour; during which any oversized American car with diplomatic plates becomes a target for every overworked, underpaid, oversexed Argentine who can fit behind a steering wheel.

By midmorning my assistant, Max Pooley, and our secretary, Linda Alcalumbre, had arrived, and I still hadn't heard from Alfredo. I didn't want to call his home in case he'd been out all night. Alfredo had a very nervous wife, and his life-style was going to drive her into an asylum; I didn't want to help. I telephoned DEA headquarters to report what I knew so far.

"I wouldn't put that in a cable if I were you," said Gordon Groot (name changed), one of the suits I reported to in the Latin American section. I'd just given him a brief rundown on what Hurtado had said.

"Believe me," I said, "I'm not going to. I'll call it a 'change in government.' But that's what he said, though. He called it . . . "

"Well you know there's elections going on there, maybe he was referring to that."

"I don't think so. He said a *golpe*. That translates to 'coup' or 'revolution.'"

I started to tell him what Mario had said about the CIA supporting the drug dealers, but decided against it. I was talking on an embassy telephone that I was sure was being monitored, and I wasn't sure I trusted Groot. He was one of those long-time overseas agents who, I had a feeling, had either transferred into DEA from CIA and possibly still worked for them, or wished he did.

"Can you run Hurtado's name in the computer for me?" I asked.

"Sure."

I gave him a full description of Hurtado along with everything I knew about him, including three telephone numbers in Bolivia that he'd given me. "And I got a woman's first name, but no last. See if you got anything on her, too."

"Go ahead."

"Sonia LNU [last name unknown]. A Bolivian female. Age unknown. She's Hurtado's niece. May own a big ranch with a landing strip. It's the same place the coke was picked up in the Suarez operation."

"Uh-huh."

"If he told me the truth there's gotta be something on her . . . or someone named Sonia."

"Um-hmm."

"She might be tied into the military."

"Okay, I'll get back to you."


An hour later Groot called. "Negative NAADIS check."

"Both names?" I said.

"Nothing."

I flashed back to the first time I mentioned Suarez's name to a headquarters suit. He wasn't in the computer either.

I telephoned DEA's La Paz, Bolivia office and spoke to a sharp street agent named Craig Chretien. He had heard of both Sonia and Hurtado, but nothing about a revolution.

"You know they've got elections going on, maybe that's what he was talking about."

"I don't think so," I said. "Is there any reason SRF [CIA] would be interested in this thing?"

"Are you kidding? That's their thing! And there's a leftist coalition leading."

"No shit."

"Yeah, but it's complicated. Elections here, well they're somethin' else. But the other thing . . . I haven't heard anything like it. But it's tough here—we're kind of limited."

"I know what you mean," I said. It was also tough talking on a telephone knowing that every spy in the Western Hemisphere was probably listening in. "And this Sonia," I said. "Big?"

"From what I hear, real big. I think her husband is political or something. But like I said, we've been limited here lately."


After I hung up I prepared teletypes to DEA headquarters and DEA Caracas, Venezuela detailing what Hurtado had said during our meeting, referring to the coup as the "change in government." I was sure the CIA was reading all cables in and out of the embassy, and I was no longer so sure about the coup. It was possible that Hurtado was just bullshitting me, and Mario couldn't resist playing mind games. He and his goons probably had a hell of a laugh last night.

In the cable I requested that DEA Caracas forward the photos of the landing strip found on the plane that had been downed with Hurtado's 158 kilos to Dave Kunz, Dave Gorman, and Rich Vandiver—the three UC pilots who'd flown the Suarez mission—to see if the strip was the same one they'd used during that operation; the one Hurtado said belonged to Sonia.

I also suggested a couple of game plans to bust Hurtado, including having him meet me in Miami to get paid. Hurtado had mentioned that he sometimes traveled to Miami and might accept payment there. Arresting him in Miami seemed too good to be true, but we had managed to do it in the Suarez case. The thought reminded me of the release of Jose Gasser and Mario's last words to me the night before—"if I were in your shoes I'd want to know why."

✿　✿　✿

I had been notified of Gasser's release after he was already back in Bolivia. My first thought was why had they waited until the guy was back in Bolivia before telling me? I was the case agent, the one responsible for the case's direction. I should have been the first to know. And then came the news of the ad Gasser took out in the Bolivian newspapers, followed by information that he was still traveling in and out of the United States carrying drug money. I took it all very personally.

I had telephoned Assistant U.S. Attorney Scott Miller in Miami, the man charged with prosecuting the Suarez case. It was the first time we spoke.

"We had more evidence against this guy than I've had against half the street dealers I've convicted," I said.

"It wasn't my decision," said Miller. "Pat Sullivan, my boss, said there's not enough evidence to convict him."[1]

"I disagree," I said. "But even if there wasn't enough to convict, there was sure as hell more than enough to indict and lock his ass up. This guy is no ordinary drug dealer; he's the biggest fish DEA's ever caught."

"It was out of my hands," said Miller. "There was nothing I could do."

"Scott, we're a laughingstock down here. The biggest case in history . . . Our informants are asking us 'How can that happen?' Everyone knows the guy is huge, and he just walks free? No grand jury, no trial?" (With Gasser's release we had lost about 90 percent of our effectiveness in the Southern Cone. The traffickers appeared all-powerful. Informers were afraid to work with us, particularly in Bolivia, from where every day the amount of cocaine crossing American borders multiplied geometrically.)

"If you want to, take it up with Pat Sullivan. He's the boss," Miller said, sounding annoyed.

✿　✿　✿

[1] In an earlier case in Florida, I had put an unemployed guitar player named John Clements away for 30 years for merely being present during a drug deal. He didn't take part in the deal, and didn't even say a word. The evidence against him was so flimsy that the judge had at first thrown the case out. But the Assistant U.S. Attorney, believing that all drug dealers should at least be tried by a jury, got Clements indicted and convicted of conspiracy. All we had to prove was that Clements knew about the conspiracy and had in some way taken part in it. We had at least that against Gasser, and he was one of the biggest drug violators in our history. Apparently, Gasser had friends who had unusual influence on our justice system. For full details of the Clements case, see Donald Goddard, *Undercover* (New York: Times Books, 1988.)

Maybe, I thought, there was a way I could reopen the Gasser case. I decided to go through the file again. Among the reports concerning his arrest I found one indicating that his codefendant Gutierrez had stated that Gasser "knew he was picking up drug money." The report also indicated that Gutierrez had been anxious to make a statement. Perhaps Sullivan had missed this; it was only one little paragraph in a long report. I prayed that that was the case.

I telephoned Miami DEA and spoke to Richie Fiano, Miami case agent on the Suarez operation. He searched the file for a follow-up statement by Gutierrez, but couldn't find a thing. A man trafficking in tons of cocaine willing to make a statement to DEA, and no one took it? How could that be?

I drafted another cable listing all the evidence against Gasser—emphasizing the paragraph I thought Sullivan might have missed—requesting that his indictment be "reconsidered" so he could be arrested during one of his megabuck excursions through Miami. Both Hurtado and Gasser traveled to the United States, and I was certain we had more than enough to indict and arrest both of them. If I could convince DEA headquarters and the U.S. Attorney's office to present the case before a grand jury for a sealed (secret) indictment, we could send them directly to jail as soon as they entered the United States. We still had Gutierrez, and if two of the three cooperated, we could damn near indict the whole Bolivian government. Our drug war would regain some of the effectiveness it had lost.

I sent out the cables and mailed the cocaine sample Hurtado had given me via diplomatic pouch to the DEA laboratory in Miami, and then began calling DEA headquarters and Miami, trying to get support in convincing the U.S. Attorney's office to start a special grand jury investigation into the whole Bolivian cocaine network with an emphasis on a Gasser-Hurtado indictment.

Late in the afternoon, Linda buzzed me; Alfredo had just passed through the Marine guard checkpoint. I watched the long carpeted hallway, and Alfredo appeared, walking fast as usual, a man on a mission. His face glowed and he was grinning from ear to ear. The Marine guard hustled to keep up with him.

"He is somethin', ain't he?" said Linda. The tall, friendly Oklahoma woman had been working in the office for five years.

"He sure is," I said. I signaled the guard, who let Alfredo come the rest of the way on his own.

"There's only one Alfredo," laughed Linda, "thank God."

"*Che,*" said Alfredo excitedly when we were alone in my office, "I just left him at the airport. It's going perfect. That *hijo de puta* can drink, can't he?" He sat down on a long imitation leather couch, fidgeting. His head nodded slightly, a leg moving, then a hand, then the leg again. He always looked like he was going someplace, even when he was sitting still.

"You see Mario or his people?" I asked.

"Sure."

"No trouble? Hurtado notice anything?"

"Not a thing. He loves me." Big grin. "He talks. I keep filling his glass. He keeps talking. He finished the whole second bottle." He mimed pouring and drinking as he spoke.

"Yeah, and you didn't help him, right?"

"Well . . . maybe just a little," said Alfredo, wagging his head from side to side. "But he puts it away fast. He gave me all the details, the protection payments, the names, the amounts. I wrote it down." He fished scraps of paper out of his pockets that were covered with scribblings of what Hurtado had told him of his work as bagman for the Bolivian cocaine traffickers. Hurtado claimed that he was in charge of the payments.

If true, this information was political dynamite. It would help those in the present Bolivian government who had collaborated with us in the Suarez sting and who seemed sincere in their antidrug efforts to clean house.

"He told me more about the Suarez case," said Alfredo. "He said he's good friends with the guy you met . . . Ibañez." Marcelo Ibañez was ex-Minister of Agriculture and Suarez's righthand man. I had spent three days with him in Buenos Aires working out the deal that eventually became the sting.

"Sure," said Alfredo. "He said Ibañez told him that the Dark Jew had fronted him a million bucks. He said, 'Now even DEA fronts money. You don't know who you're dealing with.' He's scared shitless about DEA."

"You sure he doesn't suspect I'm the Dark Jew?"

"No," said Alfredo. "The guy thinks you're a Cuban." He laughed.

"Cuban. Where'd that come from?"

He shrugged in mock innocence. "Don't ask me. I heard him say it on the phone—'a big, black Cuban with gold chains around his neck.'" Alfredo slapped his thigh and laughed.

I laughed. It was impossible to watch Alfredo without laughing. "You fucking Nazi. Did you tell him I was a black Cuban?"

Alfredo doubled over, wheezing and pounding his leg. "What's the difference, *Che*? Hurtado's so sold on you that he made phone calls to Bolivia to start his people putting oversized fuel tanks in his Piper Cub . . . to make the delivery."

"Here in Argentina?"

"Of course, where else?"

"And what about the coup, did he say anything?"

Alfredo shrugged. "The only thing he said was that if it doesn't happen, Roberto Suarez is going to be in bad shape. A lot of people are gunning for him. People in the government are after him."

I studied Alfredo. He met my gaze easily. He was such a whacky, likable son of a bitch that it was easy to forget he was an informant. And that's something a narcotics agent must never do.

"You think this guy Hurtado is the real thing?" I asked. "He talks so fucking much; what's the chances he's just a lying *chanta* [con man]? Like that landing field. One minute it's his then he says it's really his niece's—Sonia's."

"It is Sonia's," declared Alfredo. "This guy's no *chanta*."

"How come you're so sure?"

"He always said it was hers, *Che*. When I was [in Bolivia] with him I saw it. We landed on it and took off."

"Damn! Describe it for me. No wait." I ran out to Linda's desk and borrowed crayons and coloring paper that she kept for the times she had to bring her little girl Mariela to work with her. "Draw it for me."

Alfredo began to draw the landing field. "There's a river," he said as he drew a curved blue line. "As you land you have to cross over it. And on the right—you see it on the right as you're landing—there's a little building, more like a shack." He picked up a black crayon and drew a little house.

"Fantastic," I said, watching him add little trees and flowers to the drawing. The topography was distinctive enough to be easily identified. If the pilots who flew the Suarez mission said it was the same place, we had enough evidence for a conspiracy case.

"Did he say anything else about this mysterious Sonia?"

Alfredo looked offended. "*Che*. He's not the only place I heard about Sonia. And he's no *chanta*."

"Well she's not in the fucking computer, and neither is he."

"What?"

"Never mind," I said. "Believe me, it's not important. Is there any-thing else I should know?"

Alfredo thought for a long moment. "No . . . Yeah, one thing. He spoke about a deal he's working on with some Colombians. And Sonia's got a load—I think he said 200 kilos—going to Venezuela. But he didn't say any more. And I didn't think I should keep pushing him."

"*Gutsadankum!*"

"What's that?"

"That's something you wouldn't know. Yiddish. It means 'Thank God.'"

After Alfredo left, I prepared another cable updating the earlier one, adding his description of Sonia's landing field. I didn't call it Sonia's, because I was suddenly paranoid about the whole operation. I'd been in Argentina about 19 months and had met some of the greatest *chantas* in the world. Alfredo wouldn't be above conning me out of my underwear, and he hung out with Mario and his crew, whose greatest pleasure would have been making the American diplomat look like the biggest boob in the world. Adding them together with a Bolivian drug dealer who liked to bullshit could result in a very embarrassing situation.

Drug traffickers planning to take over Bolivia with CIA support? A mystery woman with her own drug organization and a landing field used for the biggest drug case in history? Nothing in the computer on anybody?

And I'm a black Cuban.

But I had spent three hours with Hurtado, and enough of what he said checked out. The cocaine sample he'd given me was real enough. DEA Bolivia knew Hurtado and Sonia were big, and then there were Mario's words about finding out why Gasser had been released. But I just couldn't believe my government was involved—at least not yet.

## 2

I spent the next week bombarding DEA and the Department of Justice with telegrams and phone calls, trying to get DEA headquar-ters to concentrate some of its resources on the Bolivian cocaine scene and the Miami U.S. Attorney's office to indict Gasser and Hurtado. Alfredo tried to stay in telephone contact with Hurtado. I was afraid it was just a matter of time before he figured out that I was the Dark

Jew and Alfredo was my stool pigeon. Then we'd never get Hurtado out of Bolivia, a country with no extradition treaty with the United States.

By Wednesday, July 16, none of my cables to headquarters had been answered and no one was returning my phone calls. To make matters worse, Alfredo was unable to reach Hurtado at any of his three phone numbers.

Something was up. Craig Chretien had called the day before with a hint of what the problem might be. "I'm hearing rumors of a move by the military here," he had said. "I'm not sure how good it is, but something's brewing. A lot of the big guys are suddenly hard to find."

And the photos of what I now believed was Sonia's landing field had vanished.

Part of my communications barrage had been directed at headquarters Latin American section and the Caracas and Miami offices, trying to determine how vital evidence that could link Hurtado and his niece to more than 1,200 pounds of cocaine seized in Miami and Venezuela—allegedly sent via diplomatic pouch—could disappear without a trace. Venezuela said they sent the photos to Miami, Miami said they never received them, and one of the headquarters suits said, "Why don't you just forget about the damned things. They're just gone!"

By late afternoon Wednesday I sat staring out my office window considering my options. The notion that there were dealers whom I could easily indict and arrest right next door in Bolivia getting ready to take over their country and not a single high-ranking DEA bureaucrat or Justice Department attorney seemed interested enough to make a move to stop them just wouldn't sink in.

Looking back, I have a hard time believing I was so naive, but I believed to the very depths of my soul in what I was doing. I believed that my brother's suicide was the fault of people like Suarez, Gasser, Hurtado, and Atala. All I wanted to do was put these people in cages and maybe dissuade a few others from going into the business. That was the mission I was sent to South America to carry out. Why were the people who sent me trying to stop me?

# 3

Later, Tanya, the frog-faced informant who had introduced me into the Suarez organization, rushed into my office in a panic. Dressed completely in black with a large hat and veil hiding her face, she looked like an overweight, frightened Ninja. Without a word she ducked, moved in a crouch to the window, and closed the blinds. I didn't know whether to laugh or get worried.

"What's wrong with you?"

When she removed her hat and veil, I saw mascara stains around her bulbous eyes, making them look more frog-like than ever. "He is offering money for us," she said, her thick features trembling. Since the Suarez case, she had been in hiding in Buenos Aires but in daily telephone contact with her family in Bolivia.

"What are you talking about?"

"Suarez has offered $150,000 for each of us, dead. He calls you the Dark Jew."

"I know," I said, and she looked at me, puzzled. "Does anyone in Bolivia know where you are?"

I had already started making arrangements for Tanya to get into the Witness Protection Program and moved to the United States under a new identity. The process normally took forever, and Tanya's case was probably one of the most complicated the program would ever see. She had served eight years in a U.S. prison for drug dealing and had been deported, so she was persona non grata in the United States. DEA was trying to get her readmitted and supplied with American identification, with American taxpayers footing the bill for hiding and protecting her. And all for a case that the American government was doing all it could to destroy.

"Only my family," she whispered in a choked voice. Her body shook and her thick lips quivered.

"Can you be sure they won't tell anyone where you are?"

"Yes, absolutely sure. Or I would be dead already."

"*We* would be dead already. Who told you about the money?"

"People who know. The money's been offered to a lot of people. Some of them know my family."

"Do they know where you are?"

"They only know I am in Argentina."

"Wonderful." Tanya was a typical stool, willing to sell her loyalty for money but too terrified to face even the possibility of consequences.

"I have to call my family." She began pacing nervously. "People came to their house yesterday, and last night. My son is there."

"Why the hell is your son there?" We had moved her teenage son

Ricardo to Buenos Aires with her. In Bolivia he was a natural hostage.

"He's a child," she blubbered, laying her head on my shoulder. "He misses his friends . . . the family . . ."

Linda peeked in the doorway and I told her to put a call into Tanya's family in Bolivia. While we were waiting for the call to go through, I calmed Tanya down by calling local police contacts and arranging for extra security at her home. Ironically, she was probably a lot safer in Argentina, a police state where people without identification could not loiter or walk the streets without being arrested, than in the United States, where drug gangs and contract hit men roam the cities, killing at will.

When the call was ready, I sat Tanya on the couch beside me. She took the receiver in a trembling hand. *"Hola."* For an instant, she sat bolt upright and the color in her face drained away. "No! No! No!" she screamed, and she held the phone away from her as if it were attacking her. I grabbed it.

"This is Tanya's friend, Miguel."

"They're all around the house!" said a frightened woman's voice. "They have guns! They are banging on the doors!"

"Who are they?"

"I don't know." She was crying, and I could hear banging, shouts, and screams in the background. "Don't open it!" she yelled at someone. "Get away from the door!"

"What are they dressed like? Soldiers? Police?"

"Gringos, in cowboy hats and dark glasses."

"Gringos?" Suddenly I was listening to a dial tone.

It took the embassy operator about 90 minutes to put the call through again, during which time Tanya was sprawled on the couch in shock. I got La Paz DEA on the phone and learned that coup rumors were increasing, but that there was not much they could do about Tanya's problem. "We're not sure if we have a problem ourselves," an agent told me.

Finally the call was put through. Tanya sat up and grabbed the phone from my hand. *"Hola!"* She listened for a moment, then breathed a sigh of relief. She was talking with her son.

"The gringos have left," he told her. He described what happened and Tanya repeated it to me:

Men in black, wearing cowboy hats and dark glasses, and carrying machine guns—"definitely not Bolivians"—surrounded the house.

They banged on the door, saying they were looking for Tanya. They claimed they were the FBI.

I took the phone from Tanya. "Ricky, what kind of accents did they have?"

"*Norte Americano,*" he said, "but I think they might be faking it. I heard another speaking Spanish with an Argentine accent. I'm sure they work for Suarez." What Ricardo had described was a brush with *los Novios de la Muerte*—the Fiances of Death—a group of men who were hours away from making history.

"Do they know who you are?"

"I don't think so."

"Do you have enough money to get out of there and back to Buenos Aires as soon as you hang up?" He was silent. "If you don't have enough I can arrange it for DEA to get you money, but I'd rather not take a chance that anyone will see."

"I have a ticket," he said.

"Good. I want you out of there as fast as you can."

A vastly relieved Tanya hung up the phone. Ricardo would be leaving within the hour and would be on an afternoon flight to Buenos Aires. "I almost forgot to tell you," she said. "Ibañez is in hiding. Suarez wants to kill him too. He's blaming the whole thing on him." Ibañez, the man who had recommended that Suarez do business with *El Judio Trigueño*, was also Hurtado's close friend. Perhaps Ibañez being in hiding explained why Hurtado had not yet realized who I was. "I'm going to try to reach him," said Tanya, "and convince him to turn himself into the DEA."

"Good idea," I said. "As long as you don't tell him where you are."

I walked Tanya "incognito" with everyone staring at her to the front gate, where squads of Argentine cops and plain-clothes embassy security guards scrutinized everything that moved. I called a taxi for her. Before she got in I gave her a reassuring hug, and then remembered something I had intended to ask her.

"Did you know someone in Bolivia named Sonia?"

"Sonia?" she said, suddenly alert as a cobra. "Her husband races cars?"

I had learned to be extremely cautious about mixing my cases together. I had made that mistake once and almost paid for it with my life. If Sonia's ranch was used in the Suarez case, Tanya should have known her. And if she did, she had to have reasons for not telling me about her.

"I don't know," I said. "All I know is her name and that she's supposed to sell a lot of dope."

"That sounds like her," said Tanya, cautious. "She's very dangerous. How did you hear about her?"

"I don't even know if we're talking about the same person," I said. "Someone just mentioned the name to me. But why didn't you ever mention her before?"

Tanya looked at me for a long moment. "I gave you Roberto Suarez, and look what happened."

Alfredo arrived moments after Tanya departed. "This is your day," said Linda, as he rushed by her into my office, grinning like a clown and waving a cassette.

"I finally got the *hijo de puta*," he said. He had recorded a conversation with Hurtado. Hurtado agreed to deliver the drugs to Argentina—but first he wanted Alfredo to come to Bolivia as soon as possible.

"We've got to finish this thing," said Hurtado on the recording, "before the changes in government." I listened for some hint of suspicion, that it was some kind of trap, but his tone was calm and friendly.

"*Jefe*, I'm ready to go anytime you say," said Alfredo saluting, his madman's eyes blazing.

"You're not afraid you'll get your ass shot off in a revolution?"

"I'll believe it when I see it happen."

"When can you leave?"

His face lit up. "The next flight to Santa Cruz is on Sunday."

I gave Alfredo enough cash to pay for his airline tickets and a couple of days in Bolivia and watched him go bustling down the hall and out of sight. My assistant Max Pooley, a veteran of DEA and Customs on the Texas border, was at Linda's desk watching.

"That's one crazy son of a bitch," said Max.

"He does like living on the edge," I said.

Max laughed. "Nah, he's just nuts."

## 4

On the following morning, I sent off another cable with Alfredo's travel itinerary, once again requesting that DEA push the U.S. Attorney's office to indict Hurtado as soon as possible. Hurtado was liable to find out who I was at any moment, and if Alfredo happened to be with him then, that would be the end of the crazy blue-eyed ferret. A suit in the Latin American section said, "I can't force Miami to do their job," and then hung up on me when I yelled, "Well what the fuck am I supposed to do from here?"

I sat in my office for a very long time trying to focus my thoughts. Linda buzzed me—there was a call from headquarters.

"How are you doing, Mike?" said a calm voice.

"Fine," I said.

"That's not what I hear."

I recognized the voice of the Rabbi. It was hard to believe that two years had passed since our first strange meeting.

Late in September 1978, as a prelude to my transfer to Buenos Aires, I was called into DEA headquarters to meet some of the middle and upper management to whom I would be reporting. It was to be a tense day for me among the dour-faced leaders of the war on drugs, with whom I was somewhat less than popular even before they'd met me.

My promotion and transfer to Buenos Aires had not been a gift. Between 1973 and 1978 I led the New York office in arrests, undercover buys, and drug seizures, and had never lost a case in court, yet I was never even considered for promotion. To inflame my impetuous and egotistical young heart even further, the agents being promoted had little or no enforcement accomplishments and no street expertise; in some cases, they were even considered office jokes. What they did have were good political connections. I was not the only DEA street agent hurt and deceived by this policy; it was agencywide.

The idiosyncrasy in my situation was the rumor that my "main problem" was that I was Jewish. I documented the rumors and was about to take DEA to court. When it became apparent that I would win, the suits decided to offer me a transfer and promotion to a place they thought I was least likely to accept—Buenos Aires.

The Rabbi was one of many who introduced himself to me that day. He was one suit who had the respect of a lot of street agents. "Why don't you stop by my office before you leave," he murmured in a tone that seemed to add, "for your own good."

I poked my head into his office at the end of the day. He was alone in shirtsleeves, staring out the window. He smiled and invited me to take a seat, and for the next few minutes we chatted generally about the job and the working conditions in Argentina. Suddenly he said,

"The fact that you are a Jew worry you at all, about going to Argentina?"

The question took me by surprise. It was the kind of thing I might have expected from another Jew, but not from the Rabbi, who was as un-Jewish as they come.

"No," I said, "should it?"

"I know some people who thought it might."

"Well I hope they were disappointed," I said.

His smile said they had been, and that he had enjoyed it. "You know you're the first man that I can remember who's gotten into the Latin American section without a rabbi." He was thoughtful for a long moment, eyeing me. "I just wanted you to know something," he said finally. "I've been very much aware of your career, Mike. I think we're lucky to have you." He suddenly smiled broadly, stood, and offered me his hand.

I was so surprised by this that for a second I didn't move. I didn't trust flattery; most undercovers don't. But his handshake was firm; his smile was open and sincere. I felt myself flush. Whenever I suspected that flattery might be sincere, I was embarrassed.

The Rabbi put his arm on my shoulder and walked me to the door. "Mike, you're going to find that it's another world down there—it's not the streets of New York or Miami. If ever you need any help, a little friendly advice, I want you to call me."

I had the feeling that there was something else he wanted to tell me, but for some reason had changed his mind. We had no further contact. And now, the sudden phone call after two years had me nervous.

"What do you hear?" I said, trying to make my voice sound light and friendly.

"That you're pushing the envelope pretty hard."

"Is that bad or good?"

"That, I'm afraid depends on what you're referring to—your health or your career. If you're losing sleep, it's bad for your health; if you're upsetting your superiors, I'd say it's bad for your career. You tell me!"

"If you're trying to make me nervous, you're doing a hell of a job," I said, attempting a laugh that sounded more like a cough.

"Mike, I once told you that it's another world down there; and to call me if you wanted some advice. I decided I wouldn't wait for your call. I happen to believe DEA needs men like you, but you've got to learn to pick and choose your wars. You're a great agent, Mike, but your timing and your sense of proportion is way off, and that can be very dangerous."

"I don't follow you," I said.

He was quiet for along moment. "Years ago I was a cop . . . a uniformed patrolman. Did you know that?"

"No, I didn't," I said, really surprised.

"There's a lot you don't know," he said. "In some ways you remind me of me when I was a rookie."

"I'm not that young."

"It's more your attitude. When I started out I wanted to arrest the world, go on every radio run, check out every suspicious character, investigate every crime. I thought I could really make a difference. I remember I was once assigned to ride with an oldtimer just a few months from retirement. We were doing a four-to-midnight in a really bad neighborhood. We had just parked the wagon to take a coffee break when all hell broke loose.

"A lot of people came running around the corner. We heard shots, then an explosion. The oldtimer starts our wagon rolling slowly toward the corner; so slowly that I wanted to scream, 'Turn on the siren and move, you idiot!' But I kept my mouth shut. When we reached the corner I could see that a full-scale riot had broken out; hundreds of people were looting stores, turning over cars, setting them on fire—it was bedlam.

"So what does the oldtimer do? He backs up to the middle of the block and parks. 'Call it in,' he tells me. I was furious, I could hardly contain myself, but I kept my mouth shut and did as he ordered. It took four minutes for assistance to arrive while we just sat there and did nothing.

"At that moment I despised that old son of a bitch. But when I thought about it later—after life taught me a few hard lessons—I realized that that old beat-pounder might have saved my life. That four-minute wait might have been the most valuable of my life."

"What are you saying?" I asked, still so possessed by my one-man drug war that I couldn't even consider what his words meant.

"I'm saying that your timing is off and you've got no backup. If you turn the next corner, you're on your own; you've got to lose."

"I'm only doing what's right; isn't that what they sent me here for?"

"Look Mike, our country has many diverse interests and you're one man in one little corner of the world. There are a lot of people a lot smarter than you and I involved in this business who might know a few things we don't. So just because an action might seem right doesn't mean it is; and even if it's the right thing to do, sometimes it's not the healthiest."

"What do you suggest I do?"

"Relax," he said. "Take it easy. The Suarez case was a great accomplishment; bigger than anyone expected. Finish all your reports, make your recommendations; then let someone else carry the ball. You made the agency look good; now take a little vacation."

"I'm having a hard time with that."

He was silent for a long moment. "Mike, don't ever forget a peanut butter sandwich."

"You're kidding."

"No, I'm not. I'm telling you this because I like you."

I hung up feeling chilled to the bone. They were words that would follow me to the end of my career; words that, at that moment, I was still unwilling to believe.

The Rabbi was talking about what happened to Sante Bario. Bario was one of the best and most committed undercover agents in DEA; he had done some of the agency's highest-level deep cover work. He was also a friend of mine. A year earlier he had been arrested for smuggling heroin from his post of duty in Mexico. While in jail in a Texas border town awaiting a removal hearing, he took a bite of a peanut butter sandwich and went into convulsions, and then a deep coma. He died a month later. His wife was told by the prison warden that strychnine had been found in his blood. The official autopsy report listed the cause of death as asphyxiation—he choked on a peanut butter sandwich.

Many of Bario's fellow agents were aware that he was involved in cases that overlapped CIA interests. The rumor was that he "knew too much" about the CIA smuggling drugs into the United States to support its own interests and that he was killed by either members of DEA's Internal Security (who were in reality CIA) or by the CIA itself. I had always been one of those who had placed little credence in the rumor. Who could really believe that a branch of the U.S. government would assassinate its own people for any reason?

That night driving home, I decided to try to follow the Rabbi's advice. I was exhausted, and my nerves were frazzled. My bosses and the U.S. Attorney's office were ducking my phone calls. Suarez had offered a reward for my death. It had to be nature's way of telling me to slow down.

# 4

# The Cocaine Coup

Just after dawn on July 17, 1980, a bent old man pedaled a bicycle slowly through the center of the rustic town of Trinidad, Bolivia. The long, dusty road was silent except for the creaking of the bicycle's wheels and the harsh breathing of the old man as he fought a slight upgrade with a jaw full of *hoja de coca*—coca leaf.

The quiet was suddenly broken by the sound of cars approaching at high speed from behind the old man. A car horn sounded. Then another. Someone leaned on a horn and held it; the continuous blast echoed across the distant hills, shattering the pastoral calm for miles.

A pickup roared past the old man, spraying him with gravel and dust. A pebble opened a tiny cut on his cheek. A half dozen men in featureless combat fatigues with black ski masks covering their faces watched him from the back of the truck. The sound of laughter and a shouted message in a language he did not understand floated back to the old man.

Another pickup loaded with men in masks roared by, this time a little closer. The old man felt something brush him lightly, and he fought to keep his balance. More laughter and shouts in a foreign tongue, but this time the old man recognized the language. He had worked for a German *patron* for many years. This time, all the men were aiming guns at him. There was a succession of clicks and laughter, then one of the guns suddenly barked smoke and flame. There was a rapid series of explosions. Dust and gravel kicked up around the old man.

He stopped pedaling and watched the pickup move off in the distance.

A flatbed truck on which rode more masked men bristling with armament roared by, giving the old man a wide berth. In the distance he could hear gunfire erupting. The men on the truck watched him solemnly as they drew away. One of them, moving as if in slow motion, slid into a prone position. He had a rifle with a telescopic sight that for an instant flashed a reflection of morning sunlight. Pulling his ski mask up over his head, he brought the rifle up to his cheek.

The old man started pedaling again. He could barely distinguish the man with the rifle. The last thing he saw was a minute puff of smoke from the back of the truck, and then a .22 slug slammed through his head, exploding it like a melon. A cheer went up from the back of the truck.

The Cocaine Coup had begun.

Explosions and gunfire began to echo through the surrounding hills. More men in combat fatigues and ski masks roared into Trinidad, firing at everything that moved. They broke into stores and homes, looting and shooting. The masked thugs were not Bolivians; they spoke Spanish with German, French, and Italian accents. Some, like Mario and his men, had Argentine accents. Their uniforms bore neither national identification nor any markings, although many of them wore Nazi swastika armbands and insignias. The foreigners were soon joined in the frenzy by mutinying Bolivian soldiers calling for a Bolivian army colonel named Luis Arce-Gomez to lead a national revolution.

The news of this bizarre uprising spread quickly across Bolivia. Word reached the heads of the democratically elected government of President Lidia Gueiler, the administration that had collaborated with DEA to accomplish the Suarez operation. A state of emergency was declared and a crisis meeting called at the La Paz headquarters of Bolivia's national labor union—the COB building.

Marcelo Quiroga, an outspoken deputy of the newly elected but not yet seated socialist coalition and a strong antidrug advocate, called for a national strike. The measure was adopted. The call went out and the entire nation of Bolivia was instantly on strike.

Meanwhile, on the outskirts of La Paz more men in ski masks and fatigues commandeered ambulances at the Bolivian Social Security Institute and raced off toward the center of town firing indiscriminately at men, women, children, and even stray dogs and cats.

The blood began to flow in torrents.

The mad dogs killing anything in their gunsights were *los Novios de la Muerte,* a group of more than 600 paramilitary, swastika-wearing, Nazi-worshiping mercenaries recruited by Klaus Altmann, a/k/a Klaus Barbie, a fugitive Nazi war criminal and long-time CIA asset.

Barbie had first recruited the Fiances of Death for Roberto Suarez's exclusive use in protecting his drug empire. But from this day on they would be under the command of Colonel Arce-Gomez, called "Lucho," the leader of the coup, a pot-bellied gangster in the medal-laden uniform, ornate military cap, and dark glasses of Hollywood's classic Latin American dictator. Arce-Gomez, Suarez's cousin, turned the bloodthirsty neo-Nazis loose on his own people for the worst torture and killing spree in Bolivia's history.

The men in the ambulances knew exactly where they were going. The operation had been planned by Barbie himself along with international terrorist Stefano Della Chiaie, under the authority of Arce-Gomez. They reached the COB building and charged up the stairs. Racing through the ancient marble hallways, they fired at anyone in their path.[1]

In the room where the meeting was taking place, pandemonium broke loose. Noel Vasquez, an official of the Bolivian central labor union, was an eyewitness:

> We all hit the floor. . . . Moments later they burst in—
> hooded civilians with automatic weapons . . . they were very
> ferocious.
>
> They ordered us outside. They took the leaders out first.
> And as we were going downstairs one of them ordered
> Marcelo [Quiroga] to stay behind. He refused, but they

---

[1] I would later learn that the actual planning of the military action for the coup was done during a meeting between the Argentine and Bolivian military in June, and that a tape recording of that meeting was turned over to the CIA.

pushed the others out in front and fired a burst of automatic fire at him. I lifted Marcelo's head and he was still alive, but bleeding heavily. Later we heard he was dead.

Unfortunately for the heroic Quiroga—who had spearheaded attempts to indict Bolivia's former military dictator, Hugo Banzer, on drug and corruption charges—he did not die instantly. Wounded by a bullet in his head, he was dragged off to police headquarters to be the object of a game played by some of the torture experts imported from Argentina's dreaded Mechanic School of the Navy—where many of Argentina's 25,000 *desaparecidos* were used as guinea pigs in refining the skills of keeping a person alive while inflicting maximum pain. These experts applied their "science" to Quiroga as a lesson to the Bolivians, who were a little backward in such matters. They kept Quiroga alive and suffering for hours. His castrated, tortured body was found days later in a place called "The Valley of the Moon" in southern La Paz.

The other survivors of the COB raid were taken to the headquarters of the Bolivian joint chiefs of staff, where they were beaten and tortured. The women were given "special" treatment, being gang-raped in addition to the torture and beatings.

"We spent days in a cement cell, without food, living in our own excrement," said Vasquez. "We were tortured by hooded paramilitaries with Italian or Argentine accents."

By the evening of July 17, it was clear that the primary goal of the revolution was the protection and control of Bolivia's cocaine industry. All major drug traffickers in prison were released, after which they joined the neo-Nazis in their rampage. Government buildings were invaded and trafficker files were either carried off or burned. Government employees were tortured and shot, the women tied and repeatedly raped by the paramilitaries and the freed traffickers. The revolutionaries next turned to crushing the national strike.

A paramilitary group launched a heavy attack on the Catholic radio station, Radio Fides, and silenced it. Over the next 24 hours, 20 trade union leaders were executed or tortured to death. The leader of the Bolivian peasant's union, Simon Reyes, was so brutally tortured he would never walk again. The national strike was crumbling. Only the miner's union resisted, but with most of its leaders killed or captured, they too would collapse after two weeks.

By July 18 the Bolivian borders were closed and the country was declared a military zone. In La Paz, General Garcia Mesa and Colonel Arce-Gomez were officially sworn in as President and Minister of Interior, respectively. Argentina quickly recognized the new government. Although some resistance continued, the revolution was almost an unqualified success.

A diplomat described the streets of La Paz: "Overnight it became the weirdest place imaginable, with creeps with carbines running around and everybody normal off the streets. It was as though the Mafia had taken over in downtown Washington."

The revolutionaries made heavy use of the Argentine technique of using innocent-looking vehicles to "disappear" people. "For a while," said a Bolivian student, "every time you saw an ambulance, you ran like hell."[1] The main enemies of the revolution were union leaders, student leaders, journalists, progressive clergy, political activists, and just ordinary Bolivians who happened to be in someone's gunsight. Thousands were herded into sports stadiums in a style reminiscent of the 1973 Chilean coup, from where special groups were selected for torture and execution.

By mid-August all resistance was ended. As Minister of Interior, Arce-Gomez had a virtual monopoly of power within Bolivia's security apparatus and total control over the country's cocaine industry. Barbie, whom Arce-Gomez had once called "my teacher," and who was also known as "The Butcher of Lyon" for the atrocities he'd committed against the French people during his reign as Gestapo chief in that city, was made an honorary colonel in the Bolivian army and given command function in the state security apparatus. His expertise was in counter-intelligence and the drug trade.

Under Arce-Gomez's protection, all Bolivian cocaine trafficking was put under the control of a small group of drug barons—those who had financed the coup. Three key members of this group were Suarez, Gutierrez (still sitting in jail in Miami awaiting trial), and Jose Gasser. A percentage of the drug proceeds was paid to Arce-Gomez, and each of the drug barons was given a squad of neo-Nazis for protection and to suppress competition.

Ostensibly to show the United States that the new government was tough on drug dealers, but actually to eliminate competition and streamline and improve cocaine production, Arce-Gomez drew up a

---

[1]Magnus Linklater, Isabel Hilton, and Neal Ascerson, *The Nazi Legacy* (New York: Holt, Rinehart and Winston, 1984).

list of 140 small and midlevel drug dealers who were to be suppressed (killed or jailed). This campaign, put in the hands of the Fiances of Death, resulted in massive drug seizures. Cocaine valued in the billions of dollars on the U.S. market was stored in Bolivian national bank vaults. In pursuit of their suppression duties, Barbie's goons were furnished a private torture house across the street from Los Tajibos hotel in Santa Cruz. The house belonged to a 30-year-old drug trafficker—Hugo Hurtado's niece, Sonia Atala.

Sonia, married to Walter "Pachi" Atala, race car driver and one-time Undersecretary of Labor for Hugo Banzer, was also given her own squad of neo-Nazis to command, with good reason. Of all the drug barons in Bolivia, Sonia's connections in Colombia and the United States—where most Bolivians had feared to go—were the best. Arce-Gomez quickly recognized her value to the government and put her in charge of selling the government's cocaine, then piling up in bank vaults and beginning to rot.

The Cocaine Coup had turned Sonia Atala into the chief international sales representative of the country then producing 80 percent of the world's cocaine—beyond any doubt the biggest drug dealer in the world.

# 5

# Loss of Illusions

## 1

The reports about the Cocaine Coup coming into DEA were mind-blowing, particularly for the five street agents stationed in Bolivia. Although the DEA suits supposedly had no idea who Roberto Suarez was until he was close to taking over his country, Suarez had a copy of each of their personnel files, including intimate personal histories, photos, and medical histories of their families. These records are customarily furnished to the interior ministry of a host country when a DEA agent is transferred overseas; and in Bolivia the Minister of Interior was now Luis Arce-Gomez, Suarez's cousin.

For me the coup was a very personal blow, since I had with a small team of undercover agents worked so hard in the preceding months to penetrate Suarez's organization and arrest its top people. They just shook us off and took over their government so that such a sting could never happen again. And I just couldn't shake Mario's words that they had done it with the help of the CIA.

Intelligence we were receiving indicated that one of the instigators and heavy contributors to the bloody coup was Erwin Gasser, father of

61

Jose Roberto Gasser. Would Gasser, one of the wealthiest and most powerful men in Bolivia, have supported the coup if his son had remained in U.S. custody? And why was Jose Gasser—now known to be one of those controlling Bolivian cocaine production—released in the first place? Could he have been released without the help of the CIA? The Rabbi had advised me to back off, but I found that was not possible. There were too many unanswered questions whose answers, I was afraid, might invalidate everything my life had stood for during the past 15 years.

During the week after the revolution I walked around in a daze, unable to decide my next move. Alfredo was still incommunicado in Bolivia with Hurtado. I tried to tell myself that Alfredo was a paid professional who knew the risks.

In the meantime, despite the coup, despite the torturing and killing of antidrug Bolivian officials who had collaborated with DEA to complete the Suarez operation, I couldn't get the suits interested in indicting Gasser or Hurtado or in pushing the Miami U.S. Attorney's office to start a grand jury investigation into the Bolivian cocaine scene. I couldn't even persuade them to try to find the missing photos of what I now felt certain was Sonia Atala's airstrip—or at least determine how they disappeared. There was something going on that I was not being told about—something hidden and ugly, and I didn't have the slightest idea what to do about it.

It was during this time that I realized I was under attack. Everything I believed in was being torn apart before my eyes by an enemy that hid behind a Kafkaesque wall of overlapping bureaucratic curtains, and I was doing nothing to defend myself. I resolved to push for all I was worth for a Hurtado-Gasser indictment. With any luck an indictment of Sonia Atala would follow. And then, who knew, maybe Arce-Gomez, Klaus Barbie, and the whole damned Bolivian government.

On Saturday morning July 26, there was a loud pounding on my front door. It was Alfredo just back from Bolivia.

"You wouldn't believe it," said Alfredo pacing my living room, head bobbing, his eyes ringed and bloodshot from lack of sleep. "We were in [Hurtado's] Piper Cub . . . an Aztec. Two air force officers were at the controls—he lent it to the military for the coup; he lent them a couple of planes. And we're sitting in the rear talking about the deal.

"Below us there's shooting, bombs going off. They are mowing down these *campesinos* . . . women, kids. I mean it was ugly . . . I mean son-of-a-bitching ugly." Alfredo collapsed in an easy chair and rested his head on his hands. I was seeing a side of him I had never seen before. I poured him a half-tumbler of scotch and he gulped it down. He took a deep breath. "Perfect," he said.

Alfredo, like the pro he was, had made notes of everything he'd seen, from the serial number of Hurtado's plane to complete descriptions of the two Bolivian colonels at the controls. (I later had an Argentine police expert make composite sketches of the two men; one was identified as Colonel Ariel Coca, one of the leaders of the coup.) They had flown over the mining town of Oruro, which was still holding out against the government.

"What about the drug deal?" I asked.

"He said he's not doing anything until they're finished with the coup. But at the same time he told me he's going to Colombia next week, to Cali, to collect for 100 kilos, either for himself or Sonia—he said both. Then he mentioned deliveries he just made in Panama, Brazil, and Puerto Rico."

"Why won't he deal with me? You think he's finally suspicious?"

"I don't think so," said Alfredo uncertainly. "I mean he took me with him on the plane. We talked about the deal in front of the two colonels. If he knew who you were I wouldn't be here." His maniacal eyes suddenly lit up. "Send me back next week. I'll stay there with him until he's ready."

"Not so fast," I said. "I want to see if I can get an arrest warrant for him before you go back. That way, if he won't do the drug deal, you can invite him to meet me in Miami or Puerto Rico. You think he'll come if you tell him I'm going to front him some of the money?"

"Are you joking? He'll be on the next plane out."

I wasn't even sure if I wanted to send Alfredo back. We'd already pushed his luck too far. But if I could get the arrest warrant for Hurtado, I could make the offer myself over the phone. Maybe he'd bring Sonia with him if I made it attractive enough.

I sent Alfredo home to his wife and kids and headed into my office, where I began another barrage of cables and phone calls to headquarters that continued over the next few days. I gave up hope of DEA ever finding the missing photos of Sonia's landing strip and sent the map Alfredo had drawn directly to the undercover pilots at their office in Texas.

❖    ❖    ❖

On Wednesday, July 30, Tanya was back in my office, this time shrouded in an off-white hat and veil. She had upsetting news.

"Cutuchi is getting out of jail," she said breathlessly. "My people called. The word is all over Santa Cruz . . . all the traffickers are saying a deal has been made in America and he's going to walk out of Miami."

I called the embattled DEA office in Bolivia and spoke to Craig Chretien. "We've been hearing the same thing," he said. "If it happens, we might as well just close down this office."

I fired off another cable to DEA headquarters, urging that a secret indictment naming Gasser be expedited so that he might be arrested while he was still traveling back and forth to the United States with drug money, and while Gutierrez was still in jail. I made it very clear that Gutierrez was not going to remain in jail for very long unless they acted quickly.

I was afraid to put what Tanya had said in a cable. The CIA read everything that left the embassy. If they were behind Gasser's release, why wouldn't they do the same for Gutierrez?

On August 1, pilot Dave Kunz called me to say that he and the other pilots had identified Alfredo's drawing of Sonia's landing field as the same location they'd landed to receive the Suarez cocaine. Then, after weeks of pressuring headquarters to convince the Miami U.S. Attorney's office to indict Gasser and Hurtado, I got a phone call from an exasperated suit. "We're authorizing you to travel to Miami. You present it to Pat Sullivan yourself."

Supercharged, I telephoned the Bolivia DEA office to see if they had anything that might help me convince Sullivan to indict Gasser.

"Forget it, you might as well not even go," said an agent with too many years on the street. "Did you see the fucking cable we sent him before he released Gasser?"

"What cable?"

"About the murder."

"Murder? How the hell did I miss that?"

"Check your chron file. If you don't have it I'll send you a copy."

"What's it say?"

"Around 1972 Gasser killed this army major named Rojas. Who knows if it was political or dope or both—but we do know he was officially charged."

"What was the disposition?"

"We couldn't get it. His family's so politically hung we couldn't find any disposition. An informant inside the [Bolivian] government said they paid a bribe and had him absolved."

"Jesus," I said. "Sullivan had this before he released him?"

"Fuck yeah, and that ain't the half of it. Suarez's people went to Selum, the old Minister of Interior, and tried to get him to sign a paper saying Gasser and Gutierrez had no arrest record. They were gonna present it to the judge in Miami to try and get 'em out on bail. The feisty son of a bitch told 'em to fuck off. Can you imagine the kind of balls that took?"

"He's the guy that helped us in the first place, right?"

"That's him . . . Jorge Selum. He was ready to go balls to the wall for us in this. He said that if the Bolivian police would take a stand against Gasser and Suarez he would fucking support them."

"And Sullivan had all this info?"

"All of it."

I asked him if there was anything new on Hurtado or his niece Sonia.

"We're limited as hell since the coup, but from what I hear the broad is heavy now . . . very heavy. If anything, Hurtado's gotta be workin' for her."

The cable about Gasser wasn't in our files, so I called back Bolivia DEA and had them re-send it. I would have it with me when I met with Sullivan.

## 2

It was a sweltering morning in Miami when I arrived for my meeting with Sullivan, chief of the criminal division of the U.S. Attorney's office, Southern District of Florida. I had not slept in almost 48 hours; the events of the past four months kept materializing in my mind like frightening shadow spirits, jabbing me awake with whispered threats and vanishing before I could grasp their meaning.

Before leaving Buenos Aires I tried to find out what I could about the suits I was about to meet. A couple of agents said that Scott Miller was no more than a publicity hound who forgot a case existed as soon as he got his name in the paper. One agent said he never had a problem with Miller. About Sullivan, however, those whom I called were unanimous. He had heavy political connections and as one street agent put it, "He's no one to fuck with, Levine."

At 10 A.M. I found myself seated in a government office across a desk from Sullivan, a clean-cut, quiet man in his early thirties with a thin-lipped smile and humorless eyes. The Miami heat was already starting to overpower the air conditioning, but Sullivan, in tie and shirtsleeves, looked cool and bored.

Seated beside me was Miller, the man officially charged with prosecuting the Suarez case. We'd never met in person although I had spoken with him several times on the phone, until he stopped returning my calls. Our conversations had usually ended with him telling me "the decision is out of my hands" or "that's up to my boss, Pat Sullivan." Miller was short, bearded, balding, and dressed like a preppie yachtsman in a gold-buttoned, double-breasted blue blazer and penny loafers—with the penny inserted.

In a ten-minute monologue I reeled off the facts to Sullivan. I had spent the entire weekend rehearsing it. I went through the whole mind-boggling series of events—the Suarez bust in Miami; the Hurtado undercover meeting; the Cocaine Coup; the DEA pilots' identification of Sonia's landing field and everything else I'd heard about her; Alfredo's flight with Hurtado over the massacre in Oruro, Bolivia; the rumor that Gutierrez was going to be released from jail in Miami.

As I spoke Sullivan watched me, expressionless. Once or twice he checked his watch. I finished my monologue with an urgent recommendation that Gasser and Hurtado be indicted as soon as possible.

"Hurtado's suspicious," I said. "I don't think he'll do a drug deal, but I'm sure I can con him into meeting me here and we can bust him. Gasser is still flying in and out of the U.S.; we can take him off when he comes through customs."

Sullivan looked at me for a long moment; then he said, "Is that all?"

"Isn't that enough?" I said, looking at Miller for support. Miller was looking at his penny loafers.

"Not for me it isn't," said Sullivan. "I just don't think you have enough." He glanced at his watch and stretched; the meeting was over.

I fought to control my temper. "Right now, Mr. Sullivan, drug dealers all over South America are laughing at us. We can still turn this thing around. With Hurtado talking and maybe Gasser, who knows how far we can go? These dopers are running Bolivia now; we could indict about half of 'em."

Sullivan stared at me, while Miller studied a spot on the wall. "In my opinion," said Sullivan slowly, "you just don't have enough."

"With all due respect, Mr. Sullivan," I said, "I totally disagree with you. I've been an agent for 15 years and seen people indicted for a lot less."

"Not in my district you haven't."

I handed him a copy of the cable from DEA Bolivia telling of the accusation of homicide against Gasser and his attempts at coercing the Minister of Interior. "I just wanted to make sure you saw this." He glanced at it without a word and laid it down in front of him.

"I even have a tape recorded conversation with Suarez himself describing Gasser and Gutierrez as his most trusted people. Hell, it was Gasser who telephoned Suarez after the arrest to warn him— Gutierrez was ready to cooperate."

"That's not admissible evidence," said Sullivan.

"For an indictment?" I shot back. "We're talking about one of the biggest drug dealers alive. I've seen ounce dealers indicted for a hell of a lot less. And this guy's liable to help us bring down a whole drug-dealing government."

Sullivan gave me a cold look and said, "I never indict a case I'm not sure I am going to win."

"Mr. Sullivan," I said, "by releasing a drug dealer of Gasser's importance without giving a grand jury the opportunity to hear the evidence against him is short-changing the American people."

I could not believe I had said those words. Sullivan was too powerful a man for me to have said what I did.

Sullivan smiled a thin smile and said, "I'm sorry you feel that way."

I had turned the corner in the Rabbi's cop parable. I was now alone.

## 3

I stepped out into the Miami sunlight. The meeting had lasted less than 20 minutes. Why had DEA sent me 6,000 miles for this? Before I left Argentina I had made arrangements to fly to DEA headquarters, Venezuela, Bolivia, Colombia, and Puerto Rico for what I had hoped would be a full-scale investigation into the Bolivian drug scene. But what was the sense if I couldn't get the support of the U.S. Attorney? Why had the DEA suits approved my arrangements in the first place?

It was a setup. The Bolivians were untouchable and everyone except me had known it. I had been sent on a wild goose chase to keep me occupied.

❖   ❖   ❖

I called headquarters and announced I was canceling my travel plans and that I was going to take some annual leave. The leave was approved without a question. None of the suits even bothered to ask what had happened.

I rented a car and wandered around Miami for a couple of days. I had a feeling that I was in imminent danger, yet I could not identify the source. When I drove north to my mother's home in Delray Beach, I saw a blue, late model Chevrolet behind me. The car stayed in my rearview mirror, keeping the same distance no matter how fast or slow I drove. I veered off sharply at my mother's exit, and it continued past.

"You look terrible," my mother greeted me. She is a beautiful woman who looks 20 years younger than her age. She speaks with a British accent—not because she was born there. She immigrated to the United States from Derechna, Poland in her early teens, and learned English by watching Leslie Howard movies.

I dropped my bag and gave her a hug. For a moment, I was in a warm, safe place, and it felt good. "I'm just tired ma."

"You're not eating sushi are you?" She pulled away and looked me up and down. "You look skinny. You're losing too much weight. You laugh at me, but three people in this development died from eating sushi."

"Ma, half the people here are over 80 years old."

"They died from eating sushi—parasites."

"Why wasn't it in the newspapers?"

"The papers wouldn't print it; they're in cahoots with the Japanese restaurants."

"Ma, you should be the agent, not me."

"Very funny, Michael. When will you listen to your mother?"

She was so terrified about my job that she couldn't talk about it, and her fears came out in other ways, like sushi. Spending the evening with her and my step-father—feeling their warmth and love, eating a huge Jewish-mother dinner, looking at the pictures of my children, my brother, my relatives and ancestors from Poland, some of whom survived the Holocaust and lived in Israel, dancing with mom to some Xavier Cugat rhumbas, enjoying the feel of the furniture I grew up with—put a long-missing smile on my face.

As I drove out of my mother's development, there was still enough sunshine to see the blue Chevrolet behind me. It followed me all the way to my hotel in Miami.

That night I flew to New York.

I spent most of the the next eight or nine days in New York living like a fugitive. I was afraid to talk on telephones and kept checking for tails, but saw nothing.

On August 15 I stopped in at DEA headquarters and spoke to a couple of suits about some administrative matters that I had fallen behind in. None of them mentioned the Suarez case, and for the first time since the case began, neither did I.

I left headquarters and headed home to Argentina. I was weary of battling the bureaucracy. I was just one man in one little corner of the world. I could use a real vacation, I thought. Maybe I would spend the rest of my tour in South America traveling and working out in the gym.

A week later, Mario the killer cop and his boss visited my office. He asked me about the progress of the Hurtado case. It was his way of letting me know that his boss expected a reward for letting the talkative Bolivian leave Argentina alive. I told them they'd be the first to know if the case went down, shook his boss's hand, and walked them to the elevator. The boss gave me a cocky little smile as the elevator door closed.

It rose to the third floor and the CIA office.

I returned to my office in a rage. News of the atrocities in Bolivia had been filtering back through informants all week. I could not shake the idea that my own government was behind it. I had to know. Why would the CIA support those drug dealers whom we were told were the number one threat to our national security?

I toyed with calling a man known in the cloak-and-dagger world of Argentina as "the Doctor." In the Southern Cone there was probably no better source of information about the overlapping worlds of espionage and international crime. But dealing with him—even talking to him—came with a certain amount of discomfort and risk.

I had met the Doctor soon after I was transferred to Buenos Aires. He had come to the embassy with two of his assistants, former Argentine military intelligence operatives, who always accompanied him. They had appeared in my office doorway, smiling politely, waiting for Linda to make the introductions—three impeccably dressed, well-spoken, mustachioed men in custom three-piece suits. The Doctor had passed through embassy security without anyone notifying me—he had those kinds of connections everywhere.

The Doctor—tall and powerfully built with unwavering brown eyes that never stopped probing—was one of the most impressive men I had ever met. He was also one of the most frightening. His visit was not totally unexpected. Weeks earlier one of the suits had told me he'd be paying me a visit.

"He used to head up an SAU unit for us," the suit had said during a phone call from headquarters.

"What's that?"

"It's a Special Action Unit. We used to use him down in the Southern Cone . . . any country . . . Bolivia, Uruguay, Brazil—whatever you need—just call the Doctor. We're thinking of going back to that concept. It's one of the things I want you to look into."

"But what exactly do they do?"

"Anything and everything. You've got a fugitive in Bolivia and you want to get him to Argentina to be extradited? Call the Doctor. Forty-eight hours later, he's delivered to the back door of the embassy in the trunk of a car. You want a phone tapped in Chile? Call the Doctor and it's done. His intelligence files are better than the [CIA's]—anything and everything. He can do it all. He's expensive as hell, but he's worth it."

"How expensive?"

He was quiet for a moment. "You work that out with him. He's got the top talent in Argentina—everything from safecrackers and electronic experts to hit men—and that's expensive. But it's in your budget. I just want you to look into it. Come to terms with him . . . work out a contract . . . I'm sure it'll be approved."

My first meeting with the Doctor was strange and disquieting. We drank coffee and talked for about an hour. His assistants barely said a word. They sipped coffee and studied me, smiling politely every time I looked in their direction. The Doctor used small talk beautifully to take a complete inventory of me with an efficiency that I couldn't help but admire. He slipped in questions about my background, my family, my education, the weapons I preferred, my martial arts training almost subliminally. He was never pushy, just politely insistent, and always friendly.

The Doctor finally got to the purpose of his visit. He mentioned a few jobs his team had done for DEA—tapping phones in Paraguay, locating a fugitive in Uruguay, nothing heavy—all the time gauging my reaction. In his dark, piercing eyes was the question, "How far can I go with this gringo?" Being as cordial as I could be, I told him that headquarters might be interested in returning to the SAU concept and that it was something I was looking into. That seemed to satisfy him, and the visit was over.

I never did make full use of his SAU unit. For the right price they would do anything—the kind of weapon you couldn't use without hurting yourself. I checked the office records. Just a few years back the Doctor had been getting very big money for his services, which I was certain were also for sale to other agencies and embassies. I found it hard to trust people who offered those kinds of services for money; they took no oaths and their only allegiance was to the highest bidder. While they worked for you, they devoured all the information they could about you—information with a high market value.

Nevertheless, I stayed friendly with him; now and then coffee and a little chat in my office; from time to time using his services on a limited basis for intelligence that I needed badly—such as information about which agents, cops, spies, and politicians could be trusted and how far, and which ones were dangerous and why—and could get from no other source. He came through with detailed, accurate information. His intelligence-gathering capabilities extended far beyond Argentina. I was certain, for instance, that through his DEA contacts he had access to DEA files and U.S. sources—perhaps better access than I had. As risky as dealing with the Doctor was, he was a necessary evil. You never knew when he might be the last option left—the difference between success and failure, life and death.

I found his number on the Rolodex and dialed.

"*Hable!*" said a male voice. I told the man who I was and asked for the Doctor by name.

"*Un momento.*" The phone clicked.

I could hear a faint ticking at the other end, and wondered what exotic electronic gadget I had dialed into. Sophisticated electronics was one of the Doctor's specialties and his personal passion. I was certain there was some machine at the other end giving a digital readout of my phone number while a recorder taped me and fed my voice waves into a computer to be analyzed for stress. If there was a machine that could read minds over the telephone, the Doctor either had it or was developing it.

"*Hola, don Miguel,*" said the deep baritone voice, always affable. "To what do I owe the pleasure?" Right to business.

"Well, the reason I'm calling . . . are you up to date on the events in Bolivia?"

"The coup, of course. Very interesting."

"Yes, very. What I needed . . . well, there are some events . . . related to it, that are bothering me . . . perhaps you can help me."

"Of course."

"You know about the Roberto Suarez case we just did?"

"Sure."

"How much do you know about it?"

Silence. "I know the investigation."

"You know the name Jose Gasser then?"

"The Bolivian."

"Yes."

"I don't mean to interrupt you," said the Doctor, "but is this something we should be talking about on the telephone?"

"Probably not," I said, a little taken aback. We had previously discussed other sensitive topics on the telephone.

The Doctor invited me to his office, which surprised me. I had never been there before. My hands shook as I wrote down the directions, and I put on my ankle holster with a heavy 9mm automatic when I left.

An hour later a cab deposited me in the middle of a street lined with dismal-looking apartment buildings of European architecture. It might just as well have been a rundown neighborhood in Frankfurt, Paris, or London in the 1920s. The address was a featureless, six-story, concrete bunker of an apartment building. The block was deserted. I double-checked the address. This was the place.

The hallway was pitch dark as I entered, but then a light came on, illuminating an elevator door that looked like an upright coffin with a small, wire-glass window. The hallway went black as I entered the tiny elevator, and the only light was a dim overhead bulb. The elevator groaned loudly as it slowly rose to the third floor. I pulled open the gate and pushed against the door, but it didn't budge. Suddenly a key turned in the lock and the door swung open.

One of the Doctor's assistants, the Colonel, greeted me politely, locked the elevator door, and then led me through a maze of hallways and locked doors to the Doctor's office. When I entered the small, sparsely furnished office, the Doctor was seated behind a large wooden desk. He stood to greet me.

"Welcome, welcome, welcome, don Miguel," he said, as cordial as if we were old friends, his dark eyes skewering me. "Have a seat, please, make yourself comfortable. Would you like some coffee? Of course you would. Colonel, would you bring us both some coffee."

When the Colonel left, I glanced around the room. It was bare except for rows of bar-locked file safes and a couple of metal chairs. I wondered why alarm bells announcing my 9mm weren't going off.

The Doctor's seat was directly in front of the only window in the room, which was heavily barred and wired. "So . . . what can I do for you?" he said.

"About the Suarez case . . . you know that Jose Gasser was released immediately after his arrest in Miami?" I said, being extremely careful. The Doctor had a relationship with the CIA, the closeness and nature of which I could only guess at.

"Yes, I am aware."

"Now, according to my sources, he and Roberto Suarez are up to their necks in the coup—they financed it." I noticed a file about two inches thick on the desk between his outstretched fingers. "What I don't understand . . . maybe you can help me . . . is why Gasser was released from our jail."

The Doctor looked at me for a long moment. "What makes you think I can help you?"

"I don't know anyone who knows more of what is going on down here than you."

The Doctor smiled. The Colonel appeared with a tray of strong Argentine coffee in delicate little cups, and we were silent as he served us. After he left the Doctor said, "It was an American court that released him."

I shrugged, waiting for him to speak; to tell me if he knew something, rumors, anything. But the Doctor never volunteered information. He wanted to find out what was on my mind first.

"Why do you think they released him?" he asked.

"The U.S. Attorney supposedly didn't feel that he had enough evidence against him."

"But you don't believe that."

"No, I don't."

"What do you suspect?"

"The CIA."

The room was quiet as I waited for men in black-hooded Ninja outfits to come charging through the doors to get me. The Doctor smiled, sat back in his seat, and brought his fingertips together in front of his nose. "It's interesting that you say that."

"Why, do you know something?"

"No, no, no," he replied quickly. "But it is a logical assumption."

"What do you mean?" I was on the edge of my seat.

"Are you familiar with the history of these Bolivians . . . the traffickers?"

"Some," I said. Actually, I was woefully ignorant. They were just dopers to me. I did my undercover, locked them up, and tried to forget about them, as I had done with thousands of dopers before them.

He opened the file before him. "Please excuse me," he said.

I watched him leaf through the file, feeling a little queasy. Had I made a mistake coming here? I was sure I was being videotaped or at least tape-recorded, and I knew the Doctor reported to at least one of the DEA suits and possibly to the CIA.

"Nothing new," he said, closing the file. "You have heard of General Echevarria, a Bolivian army general?"

"No. Should I have?"

"It was his special Ranger division that worked closely with your CIA to track down Che Guevara in 1967."

"I was working the streets of New York then," I said.

The Doctor smiled politely. "General Echevarria in those years was protecting Suarez. It is nothing definite, but it is something to consider. Now the Gasser family is a more interesting story. You know of course that they are immensely wealthy?"

"Who in that business is not?" I said.

The Doctor smiled politely again. "They have been a behind-the-scenes power in Bolivia for many years. Have you heard of the World Anti-Communist League?"

I felt like a dunce. "No."

"This is an organization strongly supported by the CIA. The elder Gasser—the father of Jose, I think Erwin is his name—is a key member of this organization. Señor Gasser is also the man who financed the 1971 coup putting General Banzer in power . . . this coup, by the way, was also strongly backed by the CIA. This was the beginning of cocaine's rise to prominence in the Bolivian economy."

"Yes," I said, trying not to look too stunned.

"So with the Gassers supporting this last coup, I would say your . . . assumption . . . may have a certain amount of validity."

"That the CIA is behind it?" I said, my heart beating faster.

"Well, of course Argentina backed the coup to the hilt, supported it, took part in it; we were the first to recognize the new government; we are granting them emergency loans. We wouldn't have done anything without at least some words of encouragement from your government. As a matter of fact, we have information that a group of 10 of your private banks headed by Bank of America postponed Bolivia's loan repayments, giving the new government a chance to consolidate its power base and its new cocaine economy."

I felt like crying.

The Doctor continued. "And, of course, many of the same players from the Banzer coup are involved in this one, including Herr Barbie and General Banzer himself."

"Barbie?"

"Oh yes. You know who he is?"

I nodded.

"Well, in 1971 he used the name Klaus Altmann. He worked for General Banzer as a security advisor—in fact, he reorganized the secret police. I believe he now has similar duties for Arce-Gomez."

I could think of nothing to say. "What this Bolivian is saying can be very embarrassing to your country and mine," were Mario's words. He had been ready to kill Hurtado. The Doctor waited for me to speak.

"Why?" I finally said.

"Why?" The Doctor looked puzzled.

"Why . . . why would the CIA back this?"

"Aside from the obvious and most probable—that the newly elected government was leftist—I think I have an interesting theory about an added incentive." He was smiling a Cheshire smile. "Your presidential elections are at the end of this year, true?"

"Yes."

"Well you know President Carter isn't very popular with your associates."

"I don't get it." What I really meant was that I didn't want to believe it. Most of the CIA agents I knew were passionate in their anti-Carter sentiments. Carter and his CIA director, Admiral Stansfield Turner, had reduced the agency's manpower dramatically. I was not a great admirer of Carter, either. I thought his drug policies were idiotic and bad for our country. A statement by his drug policy adviser, Dr. Peter Bourne, that cocaine was "the most benign" of the illicit drugs and the birth of the term "recreational drug use" had gone a long way, I thought, toward giving Americans license to indulge, and were key factors contributing to the massive surge in demand for cocaine and the disastrous effects on our nation that soon followed. But to help drug dealers take over Bolivia to defeat President Carter seemed bizarre.

"Sure," said the Doctor. "How popular is he going to look with your people if he loses a whole country to drug dealers?"

"I don't buy it," I said.

The Doctor chuckled. "It's an interesting theory though, isn't it?"

Was the Doctor's theory believable? Eleven years later, news of the "October Surprise" came out—the allegation that the CIA and the Reagan election committee conspired to delay the release of American hostages in Iran to ensure Carter's defeat in the 1980 elections. This was going on at exactly the time that the neo-Nazis in Bolivia were on their rampage of torture, rape, and murder. In addition, as I have learned, Gasser, Suarez, and three other traffickers met with Arce-Gomez and members of the Argentine and Bolivian military on June 17, 1980 to plan the coup, and a tape-recording of that meeting was given to the CIA by one of the Argentines present.[1]

If the Cocaine Coup were part of a worldwide plot by the CIA to throw the election to Reagan, Carter could not have played into their hands any better. His administration canceled $200 million in aid payments to Bolivia and on August 21 ordered DEA to close its offices there. A State Department spokesman called Bolivia the "first government in history to be taken over by drug traffickers." Arce-Gomez, the new Bolivian Minister of Interior—dubbed "Minister of Cocaine" by DEA—hinting that Carter was favoring communism by opposing his junta, announced, "At this time, having suspended aid [Carter] will be the sole author of the increase of cocaine consumption in the United States." Arce-Gomez promised to "flood" the United States with cocaine, and then made good his promise. It was truly the beginning of the cocaine explosion of the 1980s.

Events seemed beyond my control, but I was unable to let go. I found myself back at the typewriter drafting cable after cable, trying to get the interest of the street agents stationed in headquarters, Miami, and South America to make the case in spite of the suits. I had lost any illusions I'd ever had about winning a drug war; my own government had knocked them out of me. But the people who had taken over Bolivia epitomized a kind of evil that transcended drugs.

I was back at war again.

---

[1] This meeting and its participants soon became well known throughout the covert world, and eventually made it into the regular media. See Jonathan Kandell's article "The Great Bolivian Cocaine Scam" in the August 1982 *Penthouse* for one mention of the meeting.

# 6

# Loss of Hope

1

Tanya, in black and her face covered in a veil, swept into my office looking like a Bedouin mourning tent. The blinds went down. The veil came off. She was whimpering and wheezing. Another crisis.

"They want me back," she said, her chest heaving with excitement.

"Who wants you back, where?"

"The minister, Lucho. He wants me to help with the new government . . . to help them find the traffickers." She was hyperventilating, gasping for breath.

"You? To help them find the what?"

"The traffickers."

"What are you talking about? How did this happen?"

"I met with Esther [Aranda], Lucho's daughter-in-law, and she told me to call Alberto Alvarez . . . his nephew. I called him, and . . . "

"Tanya, are you out of your head? I'm trying to keep you alive and you're jumping head first into a pizza oven." Tanya was in front of me, her barrel chest heaving, her hand pressed to her heart, her frog eyes bulging and tearing. "You met with Lucho's daughter-in-law?"

She nodded, about to cry. "She told me they want to talk to me; they want my help."

"Where did you meet with her?"

"Here . . . in Buenos Aires."

"She knows where you live?" Now I was the one gasping for breath. It was late August; her son was safe in Argentina; I was still fighting with the State Department, Immigration, Justice, and DEA to get her into the Witness Protection Program, but Tanya just couldn't seem to stay away from the people who wanted to kill her.

"No, I met her. I called her. And we met, but she doesn't know where I live."

"Doesn't know where you live—Jesus! Why the hell didn't you tell me?"

Tanya's eyeballs darted up and down and her thick lips trembled—she was getting ready to lie.

"I tried to call you but you weren't here."

"When?"

"On Sunday."

"You know I'm not here on Sunday. Why didn't you call me at home?"

"I didn't have your phone number with me."

I could not speak. For a moment my 15 years of dealing with informants—trying to straighten out their intrigue-knotted, lying lives and their never-ending family and financial problems; trying to keep them alive in spite of themselves—overwhelmed me. I wanted to choke her. Instead, I sat her down beside me on the couch.

"Tanya, just tell me what happened."

"I met with Esther. She's so sweet, she would never do anything to hurt me. She said that Alberto wanted to speak to me. She wanted my telephone number. I wouldn't give it to her, so she gave me his. So I called him."

"You called him without telling me?" Alvarez was second-in-command to the Minister of Cocaine, one of the chiefs of the new Bolivian government

"I called him because he wanted me to help." She was on her feet, angry. I made her sit. She continued, her voice between a whine and a wail, "He said since I know the top *traficantes,* they wanted me to come there to help the government get them. They wanted me to collaborate with them. He said he would even come to Argentina to meet with me."

"And what did you say?"

"I said, if he would prove himself by delivering to the DEA some of the names he already knows, then I would come to Bolivia."

"And you don't think he knows you're an informant?"

"But he said he's in agreement, Miguel. He said he would have to consult with General Mesa and Arce-Gomez and then he would come to Buenos Aires. What could be wrong with that?"

"You don't think he wants to kill you?"

"Why would he want to kill me?" she whined. "If they wanted to kill me he wouldn't call."

"All that shows is how desperate they are to find you, Tanya. We just cost Suarez $9 million in cocaine. Arce-Gomez is his cousin."

"But they don't know I'm working for you. They think you fooled me too, and that . . . "

"How the hell can you say that?"

"He told me no one really believes I could be an informer; he said they want me to come back to make peace."

Now her voice had a little-girl-lost quality, and for a moment I felt sorry for her. She wanted so badly to undo what could never be undone. She would never be able to return home.

"And you believe it?" I said, as softly as I could. Informers were reporting that Suarez spent most of his waking hours fantasizing about our deaths, and she wanted to go back to Bolivia to make peace.

"I don't know."

"Did he ask for your phone number?"

"Yes."

"Did you give it to him?"

Long pause. "No."

"Thank God, Tanya."

Tanya stared at me for a long moment with tears in her eyes. She suddenly laughed. *"Mi Negro Judio de Mierda,"* she said. It was her pet name for me. I gave her a hug and kissed her on the head.

"Does anyone in your family have your phone number here?" Informers had reported that more than 200 of Argentina's secret police, including some of the world's foremost experts in torture (like Mario's men), were still in Bolivia busily teaching the Bolivians the finer points of the "art." Besides, if loose lips were hereditary, Tanya's family had probably already told everything they knew.

"No, I call them."

"Whatever you do, Tanya, never, never, never give anyone your phone number. If someone needs to contact you, you give them my number at the embassy. With any luck at all you will be a U.S. citizen by Christmas." God bless America.

"What if Alvarez agrees?"

"You tell him, fine. You'll meet him right here in my office. He can turn over his drug dealers and you can collaborate; but right here, on this couch."

Alvarez never called back, although four days later on September 2 he was in Buenos Aires to attend the Fourth Congress of the Latin American Anti-Communist League, along with Stefano Della Chiaie (neo-Nazi lieutenant of Barbie's wanted in Europe for various homicides and bombings) and top Argentine government officials. The organization was a branch of the CIA-supported World Anti-Communist League.

"I almost forgot to tell you," said Tanya, "I am still hearing that Cutuchi is going to get out of jail very soon."

"DEA knows all about it," I said.

After Tanya left, I sent the information to headquarters in a NIACT IMMEDIATE cable. Then I made some more calls trying to expedite Tanya's paperwork and get herself and her son up to the United States and out of harm's way.

On Monday morning, September 1, Mario showed up at my house with Alfredo in tow. There was fire in Mario's usually dead eyes, and Alfredo was unusually subdued. The two slumped down in chairs without a word. I asked Mercedes to serve coffee, and Mario had a shot of Chivas with his.

"What's up?" I said.

"I wanted to discuss our Bolivian friend," said Mario, eyeing me closely, "so I picked Alfredo up."

I understood immediately. It was going on two months since Mario had allowed Hurtado to leave Buenos Aires alive, and he wanted his payoff. He knew that unless a drug case was made there'd be no money.

In recent weeks developments in the Hurtado case had me jittery. Informants in Puerto Rico, Venezuela, Colombia, Brazil, and California had reported Hurtado involved in shipments of hundreds of kilos of cocaine, yet Alfredo couldn't get him to deliver a gram to Argentina. The same informants were saying that Hurtado was working for Sonia, yet her name never appeared on any of the cables and she still was not listed in the DEA computer. It seemed that whenever the CIA had an "interest" in a doper, the doper never appeared in the DEA computer.

I shrugged. "I don't know what to do, Mario," I said. "The man is stalling us."

"No he isn't, *Che*," said Mario, holding up an audiocassette. "We got him on the phone this morning."

"Great!" I said. "Let's hear it."

Alfredo was bobbing his head and blushing. He knew he'd done wrong working a DEA case with Mario without notifying me. I wasn't sure whether he'd done it to manipulate me into sending him back to Bolivia or because he was an Argentine living in a police state, where Mario was one of the deadliest cops of all.

The tape was just like all the other recent conversations Alfredo had had with Hurtado. Near the end of it Hurtado said, "Look Alfredo, I can't do anything with you right now. There are some problems." He wouldn't say what the problems were.

"It doesn't sound too encouraging to me," I said.

"I say we send Alfredo there to find out what those problems are," said Mario, his cold eyes watching me. I always had the creepy feeling that he was picturing what I'd look like dead.

"What if that problem is that he knows who I am and Alfredo doesn't come back?"

Mario laughed, an ugly bark. "You afraid to go, Alfredo?" he challenged.

"Afraid?" said Alfredo grinning. "What the hell is there to be afraid of?"

"Well, Levine," said Mario in his taunting way, "what do you say, you want this big fish or don't you?"

I looked at Alfredo. He was suddenly himself again—head bobbing, grinning, his eyes blazing. "You're nuts, you know that don't you?"

"Sure," said Alfredo.

Two days later Alfredo left for Bolivia.

In the meantime an informer in San Diego, California began dealing with Hurtado. I sent a copy of the Hurtado case file to California in hopes that—if their deal didn't work out—they would combine their evidence with mine and at least indict him. Nothing came of it and Hurtado was not indicted, but there was an enigmatic woman involved in the deal whom the San Diego informant felt might have been calling all the shots in Bolivia.

No one knew her name.

## 2

"Are you the Mike Levine that did the Roberto Suarez case?" said a man speaking through overseas static. A tight, harried quality in his voice set my heart hammering. I had been halfway out the door of my house on the way to the embassy when the phone rang.

"Yes, I am."

"I'm a deputy U.S. Marshal; I'm calling from Miami. It's kind of an emergency, so I got your number from the Marine guard at the embassy."

"That's fine, what's up?"

"I just wanted to tell you that, as I'm talking to you right now, Alfredo Gutierrez is being released on $1 million bail."

"You've got to be fucking kidding!" I yelled. It was happening exactly as our informants had said it would. "What about DEA in Miami, you call them? Are they—"

"I called everyone I knew over there. I can't get anyone to come over here to follow this guy. You know he's gonna leave the country. So I figured I better get hold of you."

"I can't thank you enough. I'm gonna get on the phone right now with my people."

"Well, good luck to ya buddy," he said with an ironic laugh.

I sprinted for my car and made the half-hour drive to the embassy in about 15 minutes. The embassy guards saw me racing toward the compound and had the heavy iron gate open before I reached it. I bounced up the driveway past a gawking Marine security guard, parked, and sprang out of the car, leaving the keys in it and the car door open.

"Emergency calls!" I shouted at Linda as I barged past her into my office, peeling off my jacket and shirt. It was the beginning of the Argentine summer and I was thoroughly soaked with perspiration. "Get Frank White and Richie Fiano in Miami and Ralph Saucedo in Washington."

"Who first?" said Linda.

"Anyone! Just get me anyone. And also get me Scott Miller at the Miami courthouse."

"What's the matter?" called Linda, running for the phone.

"Gutierrez is getting out. He's making bail."

Richie Fiano, who had worked the streets of New York with me as ATF and DEA agent was the first on the phone. Richie had been on the plane that took off from Sonia Atala's airstrip with Suarez's 854 pounds of cocaine. He was also case agent on the Suarez case in Miami.

"How the fuck did this happen?" I gasped to Richie.

"Judge Hastings lowered the bail and he made it," said Richie.

Judge Alcee Hastings, a federal judge in Miami, had lowered Gutierrez's bail from $3 million to $1 million, exactly as our informants had predicted. (Hastings would later be impeached and fired by Congress for unrelated charges.)

"And nobody's down there at least following the guy?"

"They're sending me out to do a half-million quaalude case, Mike."

"Richie, this is the biggest drug dealer ever arrested. The biggest case! These fucking people just took over their government. What is it, do they really want him to escape?"

There was a long silence. "I only work here Mike." I could hear the exasperation in his voice. He just wanted me out of his hair, and I couldn't blame him. He was in no position to buck the suits, and I had no right to expect him to.

By the time I spoke to White and Saucedo, Gutierrez was already on a plane. There was nothing to do and nothing to talk about. The last defendant in the Suarez case was free and on his way back to Bolivia to help rule the country.

The last person I talked to was Miller, Pat Sullivan's buddy. "How are you doing?" Miller said cheerfully.

"Not real good. I just heard about Gutierrez."

"Oh, yeah," he said, as though it had slipped his mind. "I opposed the bail reduction, but the judge just didn't see it my way," he said matter-of-factly, and then he droned on for a while about the hearing. I hardly listened. In my mind's eye I saw Gutierrez in the back of a limousine using back roads to avoid surveillance—only there was no surveillance to worry about. Then, as if I were right there, I saw the cars pull into a hidden airstrip in the wilds of South Florida. Gutierrez—big, dark, and dangerous-looking in his guayabera shirt— looking as he did four months ago when I was handing over the $9 million dollars, left the limo. He paused to look around, and laughed in disbelief at how easy it had been. Then he boarded a sleek Learjet that swept down the runway and disappeared heading due south.

After hanging up on Miller I closed my office door and laid down on the couch. Suddenly it struck me that Gutierrez was on his way back to Bolivia, and he and Hurtado were business associates.

Alfredo was with Hurtado.

# 3

Within days, I received word from DEA headquarters that Gutierrez was safely back in Bolivia and that informants were reporting that he had added $50,000 dollars to the price Suarez had already put on the heads of Tanya and myself, making the total offered for our deaths $200,000 each. Thank you Judge Hastings! Thank you DEA suits! Thank you Miami U.S. Attorney's office! Thank you, thank you, thank you!

Alfredo's luck had held out once again. He had spent four days with Hurtado, narrowly missing the arrival of Gutierrez. He was back in my office all psyched up. This time Max Pooley sat in on the meeting.

"*Che,* you can't imagine what's going on up there," said Alfredo, eyes wide. "It's like all Bolivia's a cocaine supermarket. There's people from everywhere up there doing deals. Hurtado told me that they're getting rid of all the small dealers and putting everything in the hands of a couple of big fish, so that the government can control the whole thing."

"You sense any suspicion at all?" I asked.

Alfredo clucked his tongue, shook his head, and waggled his finger back and forth—the most emphatic *no* an Argentine can give you. "He's doing deals right in front of me. He told me about deals with Colombians and Cubans from Miami. Here's one you can check on. He said a pilot, a Colombian, was coming in and couldn't find the jungle landing strip. The guy was running low on fuel, so what does he do? He lands right in the middle of the main airport in Santa Cruz and gets himself busted. Hurtado had to get him out of jail to do the deal."

"What about Sonia, did he mention her?"

"Not a word."

"Doesn't that seem odd?" I said. "He talked about her before. Why the sudden change?"

(Later, I would learn that the pilot was a Cuban American and that it was actually Sonia's transaction, her landing field he had missed, and she who had gotten the pilot out of jail. Also, Sonia was one of the "big fish" now controlling Bolivian cocaine trafficking.)

"Who knows?" said Alfredo, shrugging. "I mean he's talking to me; he's doing business right in front of me."

"But he's not doing any with you."

"But he wants to do it, *Che!* He said that you should come there."

"I should come to Bolivia? They're offering $200,000 for the head of the Dark Jew, and he wants me to come there?"

"He said he's got the chief of police and the Minister of Interior protecting him. You won't have a thing to worry about, *Che.*"

"You have to be fucking kidding."

"No," said Alfredo. "He said he'll meet you on the Bolivia-Argentina border. He'll have the Minister of Interior there and the head of the narcotics police, just to assure you of your security.

"He said Arce-Gomez would be there? And you believe him?"

"Yes," said Alfredo, watching me intently. He had the ultimate in maniac missions in his sights and he wanted me to accompany him.

The room was quiet as I contemplated the risks of going into Bolivia. My biggest danger was that the two men I'd dealt with face-to-face during the Suarez operation were running around loose up there, and I had good reason to believe they were close associates of Hurtado. But it was a terrific opportunity to show America what a monster we had created in Bolivia.

"Okay, I'll do it," I heard myself say. Was I losing my mind?

*"Fenomino!"* said Alfredo, executing a sitting jump like his team had just scored. Max looked at me quizzically. I just shrugged.


# 4

Once again fate stepped in to send me a message—a deadly one.

With Max and Alfredo still in my office, I received a call from Scott Miller telling me that Tanya and I would be needed in Miami to testify against a Bolivian drug dealer named Pedro Castillo, whom Tanya had introduced me to over a year before. I had conned Castillo into delivering 10 kilos to me in Miami, where he was arrested.

I told Max to send a cable to headquarters detailing everything Alfredo had said and asking permission for me go to Bolivia undercover with phony Argentine identification. I had to get Tanya ready to travel to Miami with me. It would be her first time testifying in open court against a top-level drug dealer whom she had betrayed. I dialed her number.

"I'm frightened," said Tanya, her voice a low whine.

"Don't worry. We'll have an army protecting us."

When I hung up I cabled DEA headquarters and Miami with the time and date of our arrival, requesting that agents be assigned to protect us. The whole agency knew about the $200,000 price on our heads. Informants in Brazil and Colombia had reported the contracts and the news had been sent to all DEA offices.

On Thursday, September 18 at 6 A.M., our flight bounced down at Miami International. Minutes later Tanya and I were moving with the flow of passengers through the long airport corridors. Tanya's high-heel shoes were so tight that her ankles were swollen like balloons, and she had kept me awake all night babbling away a mile a minute, wheezing and whining about her fears.

She was afraid of everything. She was sure the price tags on our heads would attract hundreds of South American hitmen. But I was no longer listening. I was watching the hallway ahead, expecting to see a half-dozen armed undercover agents, probably in dark glasses and Miami Vice shirts.

No one was there.

"They're probably waiting for us in the baggage area," I told Tanya. I was worried, and I had to leave Tanya. I could go through the line for American citizens, but she had to go through the "All Others" line. "I'll meet you on the other side of that door."

I showed an Immigration inspector my badge and hustled through the door and down a long hall to the baggage claim area. At first I didn't see anyone. Then the forlorn-looking Fiano in shorts and sneakers stepped out from behind a pole.

"Where's our protection?" I asked.

"I'm it," said the red-faced Richie.

"You mean they aren't going to give us any protection?"

"I'm not even supposed to be here, Mike," Richie said softly. "I took annual leave so I could come in my own car."

"It's a fucking shame, Richie. Drug dealers take better care of their own," I said, feeling as if my heart was breaking.

Richie and I talked about old times while we waited for Tanya to clear Immigration. After about half an hour I got worried about Tanya, and at that moment there was a muffled POP, POP, POP from somewhere outside the terminal, like a car backfiring.

Richie looked at me. We both knew it could be gunfire.

"Lemme go see about Tanya."

I walked quickly back to Immigration. All the passengers were gone and there was one lone inspector at his desk. I described Tanya and asked him if he'd seen her.

"Oh, her." He pointed to a plain door. "They got her in there."

I rushed over to the door and banged on it. When a uniformed Immigration officer opened it, I saw Tanya sitting there raccoon-faced from running mascara. Her name was on a list of "undesirables," and she had been arrested. Immigration was about to put her on the next plane back to Buenos Aires.

"Tanya's a witness in a federal drug trial," I said.

"She's a convicted felon who's been deported," said the Immigration suit.

The impasse lasted two hours. Phone calls to Washington, Buenos Aires, and the Miami U.S. Attorney's office finally straightened the problem out, and we were on our way. Richie was still waiting for us, but he looked pale. As we gathered our bags and started toward the door of the terminal, Richie said, "You know those sounds we heard before? Somebody got hit coming out of the terminal."

I dropped my bag. "You gotta be kidding."

"What is it? What's happening?" Tanya, who understood no English, was staring at me, just waiting for a reason to panic.

"Nothing," I said, picking up my bag.

"I think the guy might have been on your flight," Richie explained. "Two guys came up on a motorcycle—South American style—and did him right there. The witnesses say the shooter got off and gave him the *coup de grace* right in the head. Then gone."

"What is he saying?" asked Tanya.

"He said that he got us hotel reservations at a hotel by a race track."

Tanya smiled for the first time. "Oh, that's nice."

## 5

By mid-October it seemed that all investigations into Bolivian cocaine trafficking had died; the traffickers were in firm control of the government. Coca base and cocaine became Bolivia's chief exports and the source of most of its national income. In the meantime, the U.S. demand for cocaine began to explode as it never had before. In a mass migration reminiscent of the California gold rush, tens of thousands of Bolivians moved from the cities to coca-leaf growing areas to cash in on this Bolivian "gold." Minister of Interior Arce-Gomez had promised to inundate the United States with cocaine, and with the help of people within my own government, he was succeeding beyond his wildest dreams.

Events in Bolivia were far from secret in the intelligence community. Within DEA, cables and reports buzzed back and forth with the results of investigations and informant debriefings. The names of all the people running the Bolivian government's "Cocaine Corporation" seemed to be well known: Arce-Gomez, Suarez, Gutierrez, Gasser, Hurtado, and so on. One name remained conspicuous by its absence—Sonia Atala.

In Miami, Tanya and I spent a week testifying at the Castillo trial without any government protection—slipping in and out the back door of the courthouse, driving a rented car over back roads and side streets, hiding out like fugitives—feeling depressed and betrayed. I had called headquarters to complain, and a suit told me to cool my heels; that he would call Miami DEA and straighten it out. He never called back, and we never got our protection.

Tanya ended the trip in a lot better shape than me. I was instructed to pick up her reward money for the Suarez case in Washington on my way back to Argentina. When I handed her the U.S. government check for $175,000, she took two deep breaths and transformed herself into Zsa Zsa Gabor. Why was she wasting time with me when she could be out buying things?

As for my proposal to cross into Bolivia undercover to do the 200-kilo deal with Hurtado and Arce-Gomez, the suits did not even bother to answer my cable. Perhaps the delay was the final straw for Hurtado, for he was no longer returning Alfredo's calls. And the truth was, it no longer mattered to me. I had had it. I had lost all hope for this drug war and my part in it.

# 7

# Torture

## 1

"Look chief, if you ain't doin' nothin' with it, whyntchu let me run with it a little?"

Max Pooley was sitting across from me, his ten-gallon hat tipped back on his head, his alligator boots resting on the end of my desk. It was the second week in October and Alfredo the ferret wanted to return to Bolivia. I was sure I'd be authorizing his death if I let him go, so I'd been stalling him.

"What do you want to do with it, Max?"

"Let Alfredo tell Hurtado,'Okay you don't wanna deal with the black Cuban, I gotcha another buyer—a Texas cattle rancher.'"

If there was a prototypical Texas cowboy, Max Pooley was it. He was tall, angular, and bald, with piercing blue eyes and a slow-talking, easy-going, impossible-to-ruffle manner that was at once beguiling and deceiving. Beneath the calm was the tenacity of a pit bull.

"Who you gonna work it with?" I asked.

"Mario and the boys."

"Mario's been talking to you?"

"Yup." That explained why Mario had suddenly stopped calling me.

I no longer had the energy to push the Hurtado case, or any other case. But just turning it over to Max could have deadly consequences.

"Let me sleep on it, Max."

On October 17, I flew to Albuquerque, New Mexico to receive the Octavio Gonzalez award from the International Narcotic Enforcement Officers Association for the Suarez case. The award was named for a DEA agent who'd been gunned down in his office in Bogota, Colombia by a drug-dealing informant. As I made my acceptance speech, I thought of the events of the past year. I had the feeling I was somehow defiling Gonzalez's memory by laying down.

That night, I was sitting in my room staring at the plaque given to me for a case whose existence screamed that the war on drugs was a fraud, seeing my name engraved just below that of a man who had died because he believed in that fraud. Plaguing me was the question of whether I could be party to other agents risking their lives in that same fraud. I had a terrible foreboding about Max taking over the Hurtado case. I knew that if I stalled I could destroy the case suit-style. But I just couldn't cross that line.

I picked up the phone and called Max in Argentina. When he came on the line, I told him that the case was his to run with.

## 2

At exactly noon on November 6, Alfredo was staring at the phone in his hotel room in downtown Santa Cruz, Bolivia. Sweat beaded his brow—and it wasn't the heat. A car with two men in it had followed his taxi right to the front of the hotel, and just moments ago, downstairs in the lobby, two men in dark glasses and guayabera shirts alerted like hunting dogs as he entered. One even stood beside him watching him fill out his registration card.

Alfredo dialed Hurtado's phone number. *"Hable!"* answered Hurtado.

"I'm here."

"Good," said Hurtado. "Stay there. I'll be right over." He hung up without asking for the room number.

Alfredo put the phone down slowly. He didn't like the tightness he'd heard in Hurtado's voice. His survival instinct, a little snarling creature deep inside that had kept him alive through a hundred situations no normal man would ever put himself into, was telling him to run for his life. But where would he go? And what in *el nombre del Diablo* could be going on?

Maybe Levine had been right about them suspecting he was from *la DEA*. The moment he had told Hurtado the black Cuban was no longer in the picture, the Bolivian had relaxed and the deal had gone forward smoothly. He was going to deliver 200 kilos across the border to Max; it would be the biggest drug case in Argentina's history, and it would mean a huge reward payment in American dollars for his work. Alfredo and Max had gone out to dinner to celebrate. That *hijo de puta* Levine was going to go nuts when he got back from the United States to find that he and Max had been successful without him.

But a few days later Hurtado had called to say that he was having a problem with Arce-Gomez, and that the transaction had to be postponed. And then a few days after that he called again to say that the problem had been resolved and that Alfredo should come to Santa Cruz as soon as possible to finalize the deal.

Alfredo had been happy that Levine was in the United States. The sudden changes would have upset him, and he might not have authorized the trip. Hurtado's behavior had seemed normal to Alfredo then; the sudden reversals and phony excuses were the usual machinations of all *traficantes*—especially those *boludos Bolivianos*.

But now Alfredo was not so sure. He thought of calling Max, but what could Max do? The DEA no longer had an office in Bolivia. Calling Mario would be better.

Mario had given Alfredo an undercover phone number to call if he needed to communicate. He could let Mario know, in code, that there might be trouble; that if he didn't call in 24 hours to come looking for him. But what if I'm panicking for nothing? They'll laugh at me; especially Mario.

At 12:30 there was a light rapping at the door. Alfredo opened the door and Hurtado entered, his eyes scouring the room cautiously. This was not the relaxed, gregarious Hurtado of the Buenos Aires Sheraton meeting.

"I don't have too much time," said Hurtado, "I have to be going out of town. I'll have 10 kilos ready for you in a few days."

"Ten!" Alfredo forgot his fears. The difference in reward money between a 200-kilo seizure and a 10-kilo seizure would be tremendous, and Alfredo had already started spending the money. "I thought we were getting 200 kilos. This is hardly worth my time."

"I'm sorry," Hurtado said softly, "but I never met your new customer. And the truth be known, you and I have never done business before." Hurtado smiled a strange smile. "I thought it would be better for both of us to proceed cautiously. Next time you can have as much as you like."

After Hurtado left, an incensed Alfredo—his previous worries forgotten—telephoned another drug-dealing relative of Hurtado's named Milton Mendez to try to salvage the 200-kilo deal. If Hurtado was too afraid to do it, maybe Mendez would. There was no way these *maricon* Bolivian *hijos de putas* were going to screw him out of his reward money.

At 4 P.M. Mendez, a swarthy, barrel-chested Bolivian, entered Alfredo's room. They had been introduced by Hurtado during Alfredo's last trip to Bolivia. As well as being a world-class cocaine dealer, Mendez also happened to be the head of the Bolivian Immigration Service at the Santa Cruz airport. But the usually friendly Mendez was tense and apprehensive. The survival beast was shrieking at the top of its lungs, but Alfredo wasn't listening.

"I can deliver 200 kilos with no problem," said Mendez, "but how do I know you can pay for it?"

Alfredo was prepared for this; he pulled out a letter on Bank America of Buenos Aires stationery verifying that a bank account Max had opened (fictitious) had a balance of $5 million. Mendez examined it carefully. He seemed impressed. "I will speak to my people," he said, getting to his feet. "I'll call you later."

At 9:30 P.M., three dark men in guayaberas entered Alfredo's room without a word. Two brushed past him; one—a tall, mustachioed man wearing reflector sunglasses—blocked the door. One of the men began rifling through Alfredo's suitcase; the other began searching bureau drawers.

"Who are you? What's going on?" asked Alfredo.

"Police," snapped Sunglasses. "Just keep your mouth shut!"

When they were finished, Sunglasses said, "You're coming with us."

"Where are we going?"

Sunglasses stepped close to Alfredo. "Keep your scummy mouth shut," he hissed.

The three men hustled Alfredo out of the hotel and into a waiting police van. He was forced to lie face down on the floor of the van. The men piled in after him, and one stepped on his back.

The drive over rutted, bumpy streets took about 15 minutes. The van screeched to a halt. The doors were flung open, and Alfredo was roughly brought to his feet. Outside the van he was surrounded by men, some in police uniforms, and led into a thick-walled house. He got a quick glimpse of a hotel across the street—Los Tajibos. As he was led through the house and into a room that looked like a barracks, he heard a voice somewhere speaking German. From somewhere else in the house there was a sudden terrifying wail followed by a moan— a man in excruciating pain. Then a door slammed and all was silent again.

Alfredo was ordered to sit on a straight-backed chair in the middle of the room. The three men stood over him silently. All he could hear was the loud ticking of a clock. It seemed to go on forever. Finally, the door opened and in walked a man in a Bolivian police officer's uniform, wearing tinted glasses and an ornate military cap with a brightly polished bill. He bore the rank of captain.

"Who are you, and what are you doing in Bolivia?" said *El Jefe.* He was slowly smacking his palm with a riding crop.

Alfredo had spent half his adult life preparing himself for a moment like this. Without hesitation, he said, "I am an Argentine businessman. I'm just here trying to purchase some wood for an American company I work for."

Alfredo never saw the blow coming. The right side of his head exploded with pain and the world went black. The next thing he knew he was on the floor looking up at *El Jefe,* the vision in his right eye blurred.

"I have no patience with liars," said *El Jefe.*

Alfredo felt where his right temple and eye were beginning to swell. His hand came away sticky with blood. "Why did you do that?" he asked, struggling to his feet.

The next blow caught Alfredo full in the groin and lifted him off the ground. It had been delivered from behind, driving upward between his legs. Alfredo landed hard, vomiting and gasping for air. Pain raged through his body from his testicles to his eyeballs. He opened his eyes just in time to see a well-aimed foot about to hit him in the face. There was no pain, only a blinding flash followed by cool blackness.

When Alfredo next opened his eyes, he was spread-eagled on his back on a table, nude. He could hear something that sounded like fat sizzling in a skillet. He turned his head, and with his good eye saw that he was in a kitchen. The room was crowded with men—some in police uniforms, some in plainclothes, and some in combat fatigues. At a stove Sunglasses was holding a frying pan over a high flame. In it was oil.

Now Sunglasses was leaning over Alfredo, smiling. He filled an eye-dropper with the boiling oil and held it just over Alfredo's penis.

"Who is Mitch-ay-el?" said Sunglasses very softly.

"I don't know."

"Are you working for DEA in Buenos Aires?"

"I'm just trying to buy some wood here. I'm just trying to make a living!"

Sunglasses said, "You're lying!" and dropped a heavy glob of sizzling oil onto the head of Alfredo's penis. A cry from deep in Alfredo's bowels ripped the air and echoed off the heavy walls of the room.

Outside the house not a sound could be heard. In the past five months the heavy walls of the house had muffled the agonized shrieks of hundreds of victims, making the house the favorite torture chamber of the Fiances of Death. Lately the Bolivian narcotics police had begun using it more frequently. They would eventually take it over completely once they became a little more proficient in their methods.

The house belonged to neither the neo-Nazis nor the Bolivian police. Its owner was Sonia Atala.

# 3

"His old lady's been callin' every day," said Max, pacing my office. "I don't know what to tell her." This was the most troubled I'd ever seen Max.

"I got a feeling he's all right, Max," I said, trying to reassure myself.

"Lord, I hope that crazy son of a bitch's luck holds out," said Max. "I think we oughtta do somethin'."

"If DEA makes an inquiry about him, that'll be his death warrant." If he wasn't dead already.

"Well we gotta do something."

"Let's wait 24 hours. If nothing happens we turn it over to Mario's people."

"Them sons of bitches love Alfredo," said Max. "They'll go up there and start smokin' people."

They might have to smoke some of their own people, I thought. I was suddenly struck by the ironic position Mario and his unit were in. By now, the whole covert world knew that the Argentine government was supporting the Bolivians. Technically, working with us to do Hurtado, they were working against the interests of both their own government and the CIA.

"I'd like to go with them," I said. At the moment I meant it.

"Twenty-four hours," Max shook his head. "I think the guy's already a goner."

"Max," I said, "if Alfredo's still alive, nothing's going to kill that bastard—ever."

At about four in the afternoon, the Marine security guard called. "A guy named Alfredo here."

"Bring the son of a bitch right up!" said Max, whooping for joy.

The "dead man" had returned! Without a word, Alfredo barged past Max and me into my office and started tearing off his clothing.

"Look at what they did to me!" he yelled. His voice was high-pitched and almost hysterical with fury. "Those *hijo de puta,* motherfucking, fathersucking Bolivian faggots. Just look what they did to me!"

His body from neck to groin was covered with welts, burns, and blisters, some of which were oozing and festering. His right eye was swollen to a slit.

"Damn!" said Max, starting for the door. "I'm gonna get a camera. I want headquarters to see this."

"Who did it?" I asked, amazed that he wasn't in a hospital bed.

Alfredo spit out the words. "The Bolivian police." Ranting and raving, throwing blows at imaginary Bolivian cops, Alfredo stalked around my office telling the story of his adventure.

After three days of torture, Alfredo had finally admitted that he was in Bolivia to do a drug deal. We later learned that what we had feared had come to pass. Gutierrez, after getting back to Bolivia, had compared notes with Hurtado. The two figured out that Mitch-ay-el and the black Cuban were one and the same. But holding out for three days might have saved Alfredo's life. "So these stupid fucking mountain monkeys think, 'Well, we poured boiling oil all over this Argentine for three days and he wouldn't even admit he's here to buy coca. Now he admits it, but he insists he was never working for the Jew DEA agent. So maybe either he didn't know the guy was an agent, or maybe Hurtado made a mistake.'"

"Hold still a minute," Max said as he aimed the camera.

"Suddenly the burro-brained idiots believe me. Now they're all looking at the famous $5 million bank letter, then they look at me, then they look at the letter," he imitated the motions, "then back at me. All of a sudden they're all smiling. I'm blinded by gold teeth. One minute these mountain monkeys are boiling me alive, the next they're fighting over me. They all want to sell me coca.

"All the fucking *Jefes* now want to have appointments with me. I swear by my mother," he kissed his fingertips, "I had appointments with Arce-Gomez himself, with Tito Camacho [head of the Bolivian narcotics police]. The narcotics police told me I have special permission from now on to come to Bolivia, to buy all the cocaine I want. I am protected. Filthy *hijos de putas.* The arrangement is $6,000 a kilo to Arce-Gomez and $500 to Camacho for every kilo I take out of Bolivia. They say it's okay to deal with Hurtado if I want—he's authorized [by Arce-Gomez] to sell. All I have to do is pay [the narcotics police] $25,000 for my release and we're all set. Can you imagine the fucking nerve of these *boludos*?"

"How the hell did you get out of that one?" said Max, grinning from ear to ear. I was grinning too at this crazy man.

Alfredo laughed, then held his side in pain. (The Bolivians had broken some of his ribs.) "*Che*, it is impossible to underestimate the mind of a Bolivian policeman. I tell them, 'Hey, I don't travel with that kind of cash.' And they say, 'But we see you have the money in the bank.' So I say, 'Yes, but the bank is in Buenos Aires.' So they say, 'But we see you have a checkbook.' So I say, 'But I don't have $25,000 in that account.' So they say, with their big donkey eyes staring, 'How much do you have?' So I say to myself, 'What's a good number?' 'I have only $10,000 in that account.'

"So the *Jefe* says, 'Okay, you write me a check for $10,000, and when you come back you pay me the rest.' Can you believe these *boludos, Che*?"

"Well, what did you do?"

Alfredo looked at me, his head bobbing and the crazy grin back in place. "I wrote him the check, what else could I do?"

Max and I were both laughing. "You're one lucky bastard to be alive," said Max.

"No," said Alfredo, his face suddenly grim. "Hurtado is one unlucky bastard that I'm alive. Because now we've got him."

"What do you mean?"

"Before I left, he calls me. He pretends he knows nothing about what happened to me. But suddenly he's friendly again. And I'm going along with it, like 'Sure, sure, my old friend Hugo.' And he tells me that it really wasn't him who had the problems with the Minister, it was his niece."

"Sonia?" I asked. "What kind of problem?"

"He didn't say, but you haven't heard the best part yet." Alfredo paused and looked from me to Max and back again. The maniacal grin cracked his face. "The *pelotudo* son of a bitch is coming to Buenos Aires on the twentieth. He wants to meet Max and do the deal."

# 4

The Hurtado operation came off with breathtaking ease. On November 20, Hurtado appeared in Buenos Aires ready to talk business again. In an Oscar-winning performance as a Texas cattle rancher-turned-drug smuggler, Max convinced Hurtado to deliver the goods. Then, on November 27, Hurtado and five female "mules" he'd used to smuggle the cocaine across the border were arrested by Argentine secret police under Mario's command as he tried to deliver 15 kilos of cocaine to an empty hotel room where he thought Max was waiting. It was not the 200 kilos Alfredo had originally bargained for, but in 1980 it was still one of the biggest cocaine seizures in Argentine history.

The case never made the newspapers. Less than an hour after Hurtado's arrest he was spirited away to one of the infamous "black holes" in Argentina from where no prisoner ever returned.

That evening, Mario, dapper as ever in a lightweight custom suit and a pair of hand-tooled Italian shoes, showed up at my house with a couple of his assistants to celebrate the case. Max and Alfredo were there, too. There would be reward money for everyone; Uncle Sam was grateful. But there was still one problem.

"I want access to him, " I told Mario. "We have important questions that only he can answer."

"We have the same problem, Miguel," said Mario, chilling me with his funeral eyes. "This man can embarrass both our governments."

I countered, "No access, no value to DEA, and no reward money."

Mario was thoughtful for a moment. "What if I can get you a tape-recording of his . . . interrogation?"

"That's the minimum, Mario. The important thing is I don't want that man killed. My government will need him as a witness in court. Dead he's worth nothing."

Mario shook his head and smiled. "Levine, you know that man will never testify in your courts."

The next evening Mario showed up at my house with a cassette.[1] "This is his interrogation," he said. "I can't promise you anything, but my superiors seem to be indicating that he will make it."

"Can I have access to him?"

"There's no way," he said quickly. "I'm already running a very big personal risk by giving you this."

After Mario left I made two duplicates of the cassette. Then I slipped one into my stereo and listened to it.

I recognized two voices on the recording—Mario's and Hurtado's, and there were at least two other "interrogators" whose voices I did not recognize. It was clear that Hurtado was being tortured, and that Mario and his partners were cool professionals and were enjoying their work immensely. It was also evident that the 90-minute cassette was not the whole interrogation, but it was more than enough.

Hurtado, at times gasping for breath and crying out in pain, described a Bolivian government that from top to bottom was involved in producing and selling cocaine destined for other South American countries, the United States, and Europe. He named many police chiefs and high-level government officials of South American countries who were heavily involved in either trafficking or protecting drug traffickers—people in ideal situations to be CIA assets. And he confirmed that the *capo* of what would become *La Corporacion* was Minister of Interior Arce-Gomez.

Hurtado said that as well as having his own personal cocaine lab and a fleet of aircraft, Arce-Gomez also received a portion of all cocaine produced in the country. All those cocaine producers who did not contribute were killed or arrested and their cocaine seized. Hurtado named the four people who worked directly under Arce-Gomez in the cocaine business—a chief Bolivian prosecutor (who later turned out to be a protected CIA asset), a high government official, a high-ranking army officer, and Hurtado's niece, Sonia Atala.

Hurtado was questioned about the 854 pounds of cocaine base

---

[1]The original tape of Hurtado's torture and interrogation was turned over to CIA headquarters, and then, at headquarters' direction, given to the Buenos Aires CIA office.

seized in the Suarez case. The undercover plane, he admitted, was loaded and refueled on Sonia's ranch, *La Perserverancia.*

"Who did the merchandise belong to?" asked Mario.

"It belonged to Alfredo Gutierrez, Roberto Suarez, Widen Razouk, and Erwin Gasser." Razouk was one of the largest dealers in the Arab world, and Gasser was a long-time CIA asset and father of Jose Gasser.

The Argentines made Hurtado recount every drug deal he had ever had anything to do with, detail by detail. "Here, theatrics don't go over very well, my friend," It was Mario's deadly monotone again. "You can eventually get out of jail, but from beneath the ground no one ever gets out."

"I will tell you everything, sir," said Hurtado. And he went on to describe a series of drug and gun deals all over South America in minute detail. Every single one of them, he claimed, he had done for his niece, Sonia Atala.

"For your niece?" echoed a disbelieving Mario. "How old is she?"

"Thirty."

"Thirty years old. Is she married?"

"Yes, sir."

"What is her husband's name?"

"Pachi . . . Walter Atala; they call him Pachi."

"What does he do?" asked Mario.

"Nothing, sir," said Hurtado. "Sonia is a very powerful woman in [the cocaine business]. She works with the Minister of Interior himself."

Mario told me that Hurtado was going to be allowed to "make it." Weeks later he told me that he'd been sentenced to eight years in prison. I prayed he was telling me the truth, but from what I heard on the torture tape, I doubted it.

# 8

# Return Receipt Requested

On Monday, December 1, I received the first reaction from DEA headquarters to Hurtado's statements precisely linking the Bolivian government and high government officials from many other South American countries to cocaine trafficking.

I was ordered to open my files to the CIA office in Buenos Aires.

During the rest of the week, while CIA agents under the command of station chief Vinx Blocker pored over the Suarez and Hurtado case files—both of which contained information on the activities of Sonia Atala—extracting and making copies of whatever they needed. The Hurtado torture tape spurred me into action. Once again I began to plague DEA headquarters about pursuing a grand jury investigation and indictment of the entire Bolivian government.

"I wonder if we'll see the day that we can go through CIA files for drug dealers," I said during a phone call with Mark Best (name changed) in the South American section.

"Are you kidding?" he said, "we'd end up indicting *them* and they know it."

Gordon Groot called a few days later. "I've been told to speak to you about your teletypes and phone calls," he said.

"So speak," I said.

"The opinion here is that you are starting to make us look bad . . . unprofessional. You've pissed off State Department people, Miami DEA, the U.S. Attorney's office in Miami, and people here in head-quarters. You're putting too much info in cables and you're talking too much over telephone lines. You're aware that State can close down a DEA office?'"

"You know," I said, feeling my self-control evaporate, "I watch the biggest drug dealers alive turned loose after I make a case on them; I stand by helpless while they murder, rape, and torture people, and then put contracts on my life; then they take over their own fucking country, with the help of my country. And all I can do is make tele-phone calls and send cables to try to stop this bullshit, and you're telling me, 'Relax, you're making DEA look bad!'"

Groot was silent. Damn! How did I get drawn into this again?

"The other reason I was asked to call you," continued Groot, as though I hadn't said a thing, "was to ask you if you wanted to be trans-ferred out of Argentina."

"Out of Argentina? Why?"

"Well with the contracts on your life, we . . . they thought you might feel safer . . ."

"Man," I said, "I don't know who asked you to call. I probably don't want to know. I asked for protection from DEA when Tanya and I came to Miami in September to testify—I got nothing. Now all of a sudden you people are concerned with my safety?" I felt safer in Argentina than I'd ever feel in DEA headquarters.

"I'm sorry you feel that way."

"So am I," I said, and slammed the phone down.

During the first three weeks of December, a torrent of "secret" teletypes flew back and forth between South America and Washington—requests for additional information on the Bolivian sit-uation, requests for Hurtado to be asked more questions, requests for verifications and clarifications. Most of the questions were answered by the interrogation tape, copies of which were furnished to every interested office. (The CIA already had their copy.) Anything not cov-ered on the tape was answered through Mario. At minimum, there was enough information to begin a grand jury investigation of the Bolivian government.

By the end of December the torrent had decreased to a trickle, and then it stopped altogether. The Department of Justice and South

Florida U.S. Attorney's office were as disinterested in pursuing an indictment against any of the Bolivians as they were the day I met with Sullivan and Miller. Absolutely no action was taken to prosecute any of the people named by Hurtado. No mention of the Hurtado case ever appeared in the media.

Just before Christmas I finally got Tanya shipped out of Argentina to her new home and identity in the United States. When she was gone, I realized that her presence—coming to the embassy every other day with the latest news from Bolivia—had been a constant reminder to me of the whole situation. With her gone I could more easily put it out of my mind.

By the end of January 1981, I was barely doing my job. I was no longer interested in working undercover, and was ducking informants and shirking investigative duties, leaving it all up to Max. I was having a hard time handling the reality of what I'd lived through. I found that the less enforcement I did, the better I got along with my bosses. All I had to do was keep my administrative paperwork up to date, send in intelligence reports, and attend meetings with Uruguayan and Argentine police officials about stopping drugs, and everyone was happy.

So for a while I was in a peaceful groove. No one bothered me and I bothered no one. One of the suits even called and asked me if I wanted to extend my three-year tour in Argentina for an additional three years. I almost asked why they wanted me to extend when six weeks ago they wanted me out of there, but I controlled myself—a totally new experience for me.

As long as I didn't let myself think about what I was doing, I was fine. But then the situation in the United States changed. Ronald Reagan had been elected President and redeclared the war on drugs. The media suddenly discovered that the cocaine economy was taking over South America and were "astonished" to learn that Bolivia was actually run by drug dealers. Reports on the subject began appearing all over the media, and I made the mistake of watching and reading.

Everything I read or saw was so completely uninformed, poorly investigated, or carefully edited not to expose special interests that it would have been better for the American people if nothing were reported. The media coverage was so incomplete that anyone watching it would come away with the impression that our leaders were really trying to win the drug war. Seeing this type of reporting made me less and less comfortable toeing the official line.

The *60 Minutes* show that revealed Arce-Gomez as the "Minister of Cocaine" and Suarez as the world's "biggest cocaine supplier" did not mention the Gassers—the CIA-connected family that had funded the Cocaine Coup. The program reported the Suarez sting operation, but failed to report Jose Gasser's arrest and subsequent release by Pat Sullivan. Americans were never told that Gasser was still traveling in and out of the United States with tens of millions of dollars in drug money every month, and that he would never be indicted. Nor would a host of other CIA-protected "assets" in the drug trade be indicted.

In no articles did the name Sonia Atala surface, nor did the names of the high-level Bolivian government officials whom Hurtado, Tanya, and Alfredo had named as cocaine traffickers.

Of all the reporting I read in the year following the Cocaine Coup, the only magazine that even came close to what actually happened was *High Times*. Its investigative reporters had heard about the Gasser arrest and what happened with the Suarez sting operation and smelled something fishy. They tried to get details from DEA, but they had touched a very delicate "special interest" nerve. In an article in the August 1981 issue entitled "Cocaine Colonialism: How the Fascists Took over Bolivia," they wrote:

> The Drug Enforcement Administration will confirm busting [Gasser and Gutierrez] on currency and conspiracy violations, but will go no further. This is curious, because it may have been *the* all-time great sting operation. . . .
>
> Both conservative industrial magnates [Gasser and Gutierrez], were duly arraigned in federal court, released on $1 million bail apiece, and promptly absconded back to Santa Cruz. *High Times* spent nearly two weeks trying to get a formal confirmation or denial from the Miami DEA about the fine points of this historic caper, but they just never answered the calls.

At the beginning of February, I read the article that pushed me back into the thick of the battle. I picked up a copy of the February 9, 1981 *Newsweek* in the embassy and turned to an article entitled "The Booming Drug Trade," by Steven Strasser and Larry Rohter. The piece was about the growing international drug problem, and countries around the world in which revolutions were funded with drug money. I wondered how many of these were backed by the CIA. Part of the article focused on Bolivia: "Ever since Garcia [Mesa] overthrew the civilian government of Lidia Gueiler, who worked to control coke trafficking and was receptive to U.S. help, Bolivia's drug enforcement has become a farce in the hands of the Minister of the Interior and Justice, Col. Luis Arce-Gomez." The article went on to accuse Arce-Gomez of protecting three major cocaine rings, one headed by Alfredo Gutierrez; another by Jose Gasser, and the third by Roberto Suarez. (The article did not mention the arrest and release of Gutierrez and Gasser.)

As I read the article, I began to wonder what the American people would do if only they were told how we had betrayed Gueiler and those heroic antidrug Bolivians; if only they knew how the Suarez case had been intentionally destroyed by the government; if only they knew the facts behind the release of Gasser and Gutierrez. The public outrage would shake up the whole government. Congress would have to begin formal inquiries, grand juries would be formed, heads would roll. Those in our government who had taken part in this violation of the American people would end up behind bars. And I could help put them there. I could no longer keep quiet.

I jumped to my typewriter, and quickly rolled official "American Embassy, Buenos Aires, Argentina" stationery into the carriage. I began the kind of letter that I had never before imagined myself writing. In three hastily typed pages, I identified myself and described our government's destruction of the Suarez case. I gave enough evidence for a team of investigative reporters to conclude as I already had—that the Bolivian drug dealers had come to power because special interests in America wanted it that way.

I did not include my evidence of CIA involvement in the Cocaine Coup, for the Agency and the Argentine secret units were just too close to me. I could easily become one of the *desaparecidos*. I felt that the *Newsweek* writers already knew of CIA involvement in drug trafficking—they had hinted at it in their article. If they contacted me, I would tell them everything I knew—in person.

I addressed the letter to Strasser and Rohter, return receipt requested, and mailed it on February 16, 1981. On March 1, I received the return receipt indicating that *Newsweek* had received my letter. I waited anxiously for someone to contact me. No one did.

By April I knew that I had made a very bad career decision. A letter like that floating around unanswered was like an unexploded mine buried on a crowded beach. In May, my real troubles began.

# 9

# Target

## 1

It was now May, and I had heard nothing from *Newsweek.* Maybe the letter had been lost in their interoffice mail, I told myself. Or maybe the article's writers had just discarded it, along with a ton of other mail about other projects. I was now regretting having sent the damn thing, but it was too late. All I could do was try not to think about it and hope for the best. A week's vacation was in order. It would be my first since becoming a federal agent almost 16 years ago.

My bosses, delighted by the low profile I had been keeping recently, quickly and cheerily authorized my vacation and I was on my way. Maybe they'd forget about me and let me finish the last eight or nine years of my career in Argentina. As long as I didn't allow myself to think about my lost ideals, my own self-betrayal, and what had happened to my cases, I'd be fine. As I boarded my flight to Puerto Rico I even started fantasizing about putting in for a promotion and having a risk-free career as a suit.

During my first night in Puerto Rico, in an incredibly comfortable bed in a room at the Caribe Hilton Hotel in San Juan, I had a dream. I was moving through the dark, deserted streets of a city I didn't recognize, although I somehow knew it was Santa Cruz, Bolivia. A woman with shoulder-length dark hair was behind me, and I was running from her, terrified. I knew that if she touched me I would die instantly. I ran as fast as I could, but she kept gaining; she seemed to glide above the ground. Suddenly I could run no more. I turned and she was right there, smiling. She reached out with her hand. I was about to die.

"Why?" I said.

"I'm Sonia."

The ringing of my telephone saved me from my dream, only to drag me into a real-life nightmare. It was Max.

"I got bad news, and real bad news."

My first thoughts were the letter, the suits, the CIA. "Don't fuck around, Max."

"I wish I was fuckin' around, Mike. I'll give you the not-so-bad news first. Somebody broke into your house. Embassy security called me. I went on up there and took some pictures."

"Broke into my house?"

"Man, I'll tell ya, Mike, there's somethin' real funny about it. It don' look like they took anything. They trashed the house up pretty good, but far 's I could see the TV and the stereo's still there."

"Nothing stolen? Are you sure?"

"Pretty sure. When you get back here you c'n check it out yourself, but it seems like most of the stuff them *rastreros* usually take wasn't touched. And what's real strange is it looks like these guys weren't in any kinda hurry. They sat around your living room and finished off some of your whiskey."

"What?"

"I ain't kiddin' Mike. We found a couple of almost-empty bottles and glasses. Looks like there was three or four of 'em."

"Anyone dust for fingerprints, or anything?" I said, feeling as though an icy hand had gripped the back of my neck.

Max laughed. "You kiddin'? By the time I got there, them security people already had their hands on just about everything."

"It'll have to wait until I get back," I said. "I'm almost afraid to ask. What's the bad news?"

Max was silent for a long moment. "I hate like hell to have to tell you this. A couple of Internal Security inspectors are on the way down here. They want you back on post so they c'n have a little talk with you."

My heart sank. The Internal Security Division of DEA, charged with investigating corruption within the agency, was not known for tact and diplomacy. In 1981 it was a much misused division, and its inspectors were considered hatchet-men for DEA's upper management, used primarily to chop down the career of any street agent deemed a "target" by the suits.

DEA street agents are administratively vulnerable to being fired at almost any time. Their lives are governed by three manuals, each the size of the Manhattan telephone directory, that include some of the most ridiculous, unrealistic, and oppressive regulations the suits have invented since the Internal Revenue Code—regulations that are clearly intended to cover the bureaucrats' asses and to keep the street agents silenced, fearful for their jobs, and under absolute control. A street agent might suddenly be charged with "unlawful use of a government car" for stopping for groceries on the way home, or "unauthorized enforcement activity" for meeting with an informer at 3 A.M. without calling a superior, or "falsifying government reports" for reporting 117 hours on the time sheet when the inspectors say they have been following the agent and counted only 115 hours. In these cases, the agent has been stepping on the wrong toes—the agent is a "target."

And DEA street agents are the easiest victims in the world. They are more terrified of losing their jobs than of charging through the barricaded doors of crack dens into blazing gunfire. For a lot of them the gun and badge become their identity—what they are instead of what they do. Perhaps the agency becomes the mother or father some agents never had, or the reason for being that many of us spend our lives hungering after. Whatever the reason, a lot of agents would rather die than have their ties to the DEA cut.

This misuse of Internal Security, thought to have contributed to the suicides of several DEA employees, eventually caused the the agency to completely revamp the system and put the investigations of corruption and misconduct more in the hands of field supervisors and the street agents themselves. But in 1981 Internal Security was the DEA equivalent of the Gestapo, and I was their next target.

"Did they say what it's about?" I asked.

"They said somethin' 'bout your undercover expenses in the Suarez case."

"When did they say they want me there?"

"Yesterday. There's two of 'em on the way down here from Miami now. They just said to pass the word on that they want your butt back on post ASAP."

## 2

Twenty-four sleepless hours later Max turned the car down Calle Enrique Sinclair and I was home again in Buenos Aires. I hadn't said a word during the half-hour trip from the airport. I was expecting the worst, and I was not disappointed.

The moment I saw the house I could feel something different about it. The fieldstone facade fronting the quiet residential street seemed like the dark, foreboding face of a stranger. The seven-foot hedge that ran the length of the property and hid the garden, the pool, and most of the house from view, giving me a sense of privacy and seclusion that I enjoyed, now seemed to isolate the house; to make it a place where anything could happen and no one would know.

Max parked the car and we entered through the garage. As we stepped into the hallway, a powerful odor of rotting food hit me. The entire main floor was littered with broken glass and torn clothing, and it was splattered with the putrefying remains of what had been the contents of my refrigerator. For a moment I was unable to move. My beautiful fortress of a house, where I had felt so safe and protected for the past two-and-a-half years, had been violated.

"The rest of the house looks pretty much the same," said Max, "but like I said, it don't look like they took anythin'; least not anythin' big."

"You find shit anywhere?" I asked. A New York City detective had once told me that many burglars leave their fecal signatures.

"Say what?"

"Shit. Did you find any shit?

"You mean like doo-doo?"

"Exactly."

"No," said Max, looking amused. "It sure looks like they made themselves comfortable though."

He led the way to the living room. Three chairs had been pulled around a minicomponent stereo that would have fetched at least $2,000 on the Buenos Aires streets and could have been carried out in one pillow case. A quarter-full bottle of Chivas Regal was on the floor near an easy chair. Piled on the floor in front of the stereo were about 100 tapes, some of which were marked "Drug Enforcement Administration, Evidence." There were three chairs around the pile and a half-full bottle of whiskey lying on its side.

"Looks like they done had themselves a party," said Max.

"Is this how you found it?"

"Exactly. I took some photos."

"Who reported it?"

"Your gardener showed up around six in the morning, heard some noise inside and hightailed it outta here. He called embassy security. They called me. Time they got here, this is how they found it."

I stared dumbly at the pile of cassettes. I had kept them hidden throughout the house. Some were only music, others were undercover conversations between myself and drug dealers. There were a few that were very sensitive to me personally—they were of conversations I had had with various suits. The intruders had evidently gone through the house collecting the tapes and then sat calmly, drinking and playing them on my stereo.

I suddenly remembered that I had left a copy of the Hurtado torture tape in a bedroom drawer. Numbly, I thanked Max and assured him I could handle everything myself. After he left I raced upstairs.

The master bedroom looked like the inside of a garbage bin. The contents of the closets had been strewn all over the room and every drawer had been dumped. Even the bed had been turned upside down. A VCR and a color television set worth thousands sat untouched. The Hurtado tape was not there.

For the next hour I plowed through the whole house looking for tapes. I found none other than what were in the pile in the living room. All the tapes involving the Suarez and Hurtado cases were missing, as well as my taped conversations with the suits.

Next I reconstructed the break-in. The intruders—since there were four used glasses, I assumed that's how many intruders there were—had entered the house through the glass veranda door leading directly into my bedroom, just feet from my bed. They had forced up the heavy wooden outer blinds and then cut a circular hole near the door handle using a glass cutter and suction cups. An almost perfectly round piece of glass lay unbroken outside the door in silent tribute to someone's criminal skill. They had chosen for their entry point the part of the house most exposed to the street. They could have easily entered from a half-dozen other places and been totally invisible.

They had expected to find me in bed, right where they broke in.

I had been assuming that whoever did the job had to know I was out of town, but only Max, Linda, and the suit who had approved my leave knew. I looked at the round piece of glass laying on a chamois cloth that had probably been used to muffle the sound as it was placed on the ground and had a vision:

Three shadows crouch in the dark outside my bedroom; one standing upright. One works swiftly and silently cutting the glass only inches below the lock. Another shines a dim light through the glass. I am fast asleep. The upright figure has something in his hand—a handgun with a long silencer. He's aiming at my head.

But why isn't he shooting?

The man working on the glass is finished. He attaches the suction cups, and then taps the glass lightly through the chamois cloth. The man with the gun tenses, and a tiny infrared dot shines on my forehead. The cutter pulls the circle of glass away and lays it silently on the cloth. He reaches inside to open the lock.

Suddenly the door is open and the men rush inside. They pin me quickly; the gun is in my face. They drag me downstairs. They have questions they want to ask me—a lot of them—and all night to ask them.

The vision ends with a picture of Mario sitting in my easy chair with a bottle of Chivas at his feet, his viper eyes studying me.

Later, in all likelihood, my body would never be found. Neither would the tape recordings that might reveal the real reason for my disappearance. There were thousands of drug dealers with motive to kill me—the perfect crime.

That night I barricaded myself in one of the smaller bedrooms and fell asleep with one 9mm automatic in my hand and another on the floor beside my bed. I would rarely be without both guns for the rest of my tour in Argentina.

On Sunday morning, Max called.

"I jest wanted to let ya know they're here," he said. "They say they don' need ta see ya jest yet. They're gonna interview me and Linda first."

On Monday morning I arrived at the embassy early. The inspectors had already commandeered a small office for their investigation, and were in the midst of a closed-door interview of Linda. Max looked at me and rolled his eyes skyward.

"What the hell are they doing with Linda? She had nothing to do with the Suarez case." I hated the frightened sound of my voice.

"I don' know," said Max, "but I'll tell you what, Mike. These boys ain't jest playin'."

I went into my office determined not to show any signs of intimidation, and locked the door behind me. With trembling hands I unlocked my desk drawer, and then I breathed a sigh of relief. The small metal box was still there, just as I had left it—copies of most of the tapes that had been removed from my house.

Hours later, the door to the interrogation room opened and Linda emerged, followed by the two inspectors.

The senior inspector glared at me for a long moment. He was a tall, gangling, bald man in his mid-forties with a protruding Adam's apple. I dubbed him "Stork." I met his rheumy, blue-eyed gaze and waited for him to speak.

"Fuck you!" said a little voice in my head that's been talking to me since my childhood in the Bronx. "I'm right here in front of you, man. Do your worst."

Stork's bald head turned bright pink, as if he were reading my mind. He said, "If you have business to take care of, why don't you take care of it. We won't be getting to you just yet."

"Sure thing," I said, forcing a carefree smile. I looked past Stork at his partner, "Barrel."

Barrel stared at me with a sort of we've-got-your-number look that he must have practiced before a thousand bathroom mirrors in cheap hotels around the world. Stork, without taking his eyes off me, motioned for Max to join them in the room.

After the door closed, I looked at Linda, who was pale and shaken. She had started out in Argentina working for the CIA, had fallen in love with and married an Argentine tennis pro—a no-no in the CIA—and had then transferred to DEA. She had been through a hell of a lot in her seven years in Argentina, and it took a lot to shake her.

"What's it all about?" I asked in a hushed voice.

"Mike," she said, her eyes on the door, "they want to know anything and everything about you."

"Honey," I said trying to sound reassuring, "you just tell them the truth. I've got nothing to hide."

Although I recognized the psychological pressure the inspectors were using, it was still effective. They were taking their sweet time before talking to me, giving me plenty of time to think about the power they had over my life. They wanted my stomach in knots, my brain scrambled, and my tongue loose by the time they got to me.

On Wednesday, May 6, after the inspectors had spent the morning interviewing the ambassador, the mailroom clerk, and a few others in the embassy with whom I had dealings, they ordered me into my office to begin their interrogation.

"Before I ask you any questions," said Stork, reading from a Miranda card, "it is my duty to advise you of your constitutional rights. You have the right to remain silent. . . ." Barrel leveled his well-prac-ticed, squint-eyed stare at me as Stork droned on. When Stork fin-ished reading, he asked me if I wanted an attorney present.

"I've never done anything to go to jail for," I heard myself say. "I don't need any attorney."

The two looked at each other as if confirming some private bet. Stork shoved a sheet of paper at me.

"Then you won't mind signing this."

I knew the document well; it was a waiver of rights. I signed it, sur-rendering my rights under the Fifth Amendment, and shoved it back at him. I was now without attorney or Constitution to protect me. But I had nothing to hide.

"This is about your expense money during the undercover work you did in Miami," began Stork. "Do you know an informant named Tanya?"

"Yes."

"Did you work undercover with her in Miami?"

"Yes, about a year ago, on the Roberto Suarez case."

"Did you have her sign Form 103 indicating she received $2,500?"

"Yes, I did."

"Well, she said that you kept the money."

"Is that what this is all about?" I asked, incredulous.

"That's what originated the investigation," said Stork, taking out a cigar that looked to be a foot long and inserting about half of it into his mouth. With his eyes going slightly crossed, he began to roll the huge stogie around in his lips and tongue, slipping it in and out, wetting it until it was a soggy mess. For a moment I watched in fascination, won-dering what he thought of as he ran that huge stogie in and out of his mouth. He finally lit it, blew a puff of smoke in my direction, and said, "But we've decided to look into a few other things while we're here."

"If you had called me," I said, "I could have saved you the trip."

"We'll see," said Stork, settling back and blowing another stream of smoke in my direction.

"Tanya is absolutely correct," I said. "When we set up the sting operation, the Miami DEA office refused to give us any cash for the UC work. In fact they did everything the could to kill the case. I called

Ralph [Saucedo] in Washington. He flew down to Miami with $2,500 cash that he had taken from PEPI [a special fund used for paying informants]. He told me to get Tanya to sign for the money and that we should use it for the undercover work.

"I followed his instructions. In fact, out of the $2,500, I was given only $700. Out of that $700 I gave a couple of hundred to the pilots and a hundred to Special Agent Lydia Diaz[1] [name changed] for their expenses. Within a day or two I was spending my own money." From the looks on the inspectors' faces, I was not telling them something they hadn't already heard.

"But you didn't have to come here for that," I said. "Ralph Saucedo could have verified it in headquarters."

I was now about to find out what Stork meant when he said he had decided to look into "a few other things."

The two inspectors began a methodical interrogation of me that lasted the rest of the week. They expanded their investigation to include every expense voucher I had written since my arrival in South America. (Later they would expand it to every voucher I had written since I had come to work for DEA.)

Expense vouchers are the detailed accounting of every penny a government employee spends on official business, from telephone calls to airline tickets to undercover meals. After one year of undercover work, the average agent can end up with several hundred pages of vouchers. If an inspector can find one single item claimed that wasn't actually paid for, or was not for official business purposes, the agent may be prosecuted for fraud and falsifying government reports—federal felonies punishable by up to 10 years in prison.

Can you imagine if our elected officials had to fill these out?

The inspectors falsely accused me of black marketeering; they went through all the embassy mail records to document the amount of goods I received through APO (a duty-free import privilege for Americans stationed overseas), and Stork interrogated all my Argentine neighbors to see if I was selling American goods imported with my diplomatic status. They checked the records of every phone call I made from the embassy, and interrogated me at length about the purpose of each and whether it was for official business. They ques-

---

[1]She is the undercover agent who played the role of my wife during the Suarez operation.

tioned many of the Argentine police officials I worked with about the "propriety" of my actions, leaving the impression I was in trouble.

By the time Stork and Barrel left Argentina for their Miami head-quarters on Tuesday, May 12, telling me that they had just begun their investigation, virtually everyone who knew me believed I was the subject of a major criminal probe and that I would soon be arrested. People from the diplomatic community began to avoid me; Argentine police and even informers would no longer have anything to do with me. The inspectors had effectively rendered me useless as an agent.

## 3

Ralph Saucedo called me. "I already told [Stork] that I was satisfied that you had only spent the money on the case. What's going on?"

"I don't know," I said. "I have a feeling they're trying to do me."

By the end of June I was hearing from agents I had not heard from in years who were all being called in and interrogated about every investigation they had worked with me and what they knew about my private life. One of the administrative officers for the South American section called to say that inspectors were checking the written records of "everything you had anything to do with." Almost everyone in DEA believed that my indictment and arrest was imminent. I had a pretty good idea that my letter to *Newsweek* had ended up in the hands of people in the DEA or the CIA, people who wanted me silenced, or discredited, or both.

My first inkling of how fast the rumors were spreading came in a phone call from Vinnie Z (name changed), a veteran New York City street agent. I was surprised to hear from Vinnie; we'd gone through a lot of New York City doors together and had gotten close, but in typical DEA fashion we lost touch after my transfer.

"Mikey," he said. "I'm glad to hear you still a free man."

"What are you talking about, Vinnie?"

"Everybody's talkin', Mikey. *Mingeh,* I can't tell you the fucking rumors that are floatin' around aboutchu; that you went bad; that the inspectors already busted you, or dat they was gonna indict you. So I says to myself, I know Mikey, I'll fucking call him direct and find out."

I was stunned. The inspectors had left Buenos Aires only a few days earlier.

"I don't believe this," I said. My head ached. "This is bullshit."

"So it ain't true, Mikey?"

"Vinnie," I said, "you can tell anyone that's interested that I haven't

114

done a thing wrong; that they're trying to 'do' me." I hated the anguish in my voice.

Vinnie was quiet for a long moment, probably wondering—as I was—if our phone conversation was being monitored.

"*Mingeh!* Those motherfuckers. Take no prisoners, Mikey. You plannin' on comin' to the Apple?"

"Sooner or later," I said.

"You need anything, Mikey, you know howta reach me."

On June 25, Stork called me from his Miami office. "We talked to the pilots—Dave Kunz, Gorman, and Vandiver. They're denying that you gave them any money."

I knew he was lying and quickly hooked my tape recorder to the phone. From that moment on I recorded every phone call I had with the inspectors.

"If they said that, it's not true," I replied. "But I can't believe they would say anything like that."

"And Lydia Diaz also denies that you gave her any expense money."

"It's hard for me to believe, but if she said that, she's not telling the truth."

He was silent for a long moment. "I think we'd like you to come in and give another statement."

"To Miami?" I said.

"Are you refusing?"

You'd love that, wouldn't you. Then you could suspend me on the spot. "Hell no," I said. "Just tell me when and where."

On the evening of June 29, I left Argentina on a Pan American flight headed for Miami and more interrogations. In the meantime my right knee—injured several times over the past 10 years during raids—had begun acting up. I didn't know it then, but blood that had pooled up inside the knee joint had formed into a hematoma about the size of a walnut. Months later I would have it surgically removed. But that long night cramped into my coach seat was torture. By the time I arrived in Miami at 7:30 A.M. On June 30, I had a high fever and was in some pretty serious pain. I had been gobbling Voltarin, an Argentinian anti-inflammatory. But for some reason the drug wasn't working now.

At 9:00 A.M., I was in a small, windowless room in Miami with Stork and another inspector, one of the ugliest human beings I had ever seen in my life. He was very fat, with a few wispy hairs scattered sloppily over his balding dome. His triple-chinned, bloated face and splayed front teeth that protruded over his lower lip gave him the permanent sneer of a warthog. His shirt, a collage of food stains, was missing a button over his bulging stomach. This was "Inspector Quasimoto."

I watched fascinated, in spite of the pain and high fever, as Stork and Quasimoto took their time getting down to business. Quasimoto placed a recorder on the table in front of me and began looking around for an outlet. In my mind I pictured a TV cop series called *Stork and Quasimoto, Crime Fighters in the War on Drugs.*

I laughed.

"Something funny?" said Stork, examining a cigar that in my delirium looked like a Little League baseball bat.

"Just a thought I had."

"You want to share it with us?" said Quasimoto, placing a mike in front of me.

"Not really."

I watched once again as Stork pushed the huge cigar in and out of his mouth until it was a soggy mess. When he lit it and the soupy smoke wafted over me, I thought I would faint. The idea that they would enjoy it if I did faint helped me to pull myself together. There was no way I would let them get the better of me.

At Stork's signal, Quasimoto turned on the recorder and began to read me the Miranda warning. It was beyond torture. The man's breath was like being downwind from an outhouse. Between the ache in my leg, the fever, the cigar smoke, and Quasimoto's stench, I was on the ropes. If they had been smart, they could have gotten me to confess to murder, treason, and necrophilia. But they were just dumb bureaucrats. The best they could do was to pull out my travel expense vouchers and go over the questions they had asked me before.

When they reached the vouchers for the Suarez sting, Stork told me again that the pilots and Lydia Diaz had denied that I had given them money.

I felt my own recorder in my pocket to make sure that it was on. "I can't believe it," I said. "I gave them the money."

"Are you willing to take a polygraph?" asked Quasimoto, his breath bringing tears to my eyes.

I couldn't hold out much longer without screaming or fainting, so I said, "Sure, let's do it now." I prayed the Voltarin would kick in.

The two looked at each other; a faint sign of triumph passed between them. My interrogation was over. Within minutes they ushered me into their supervisor's office like I was a stuffed trophy.

The chief of the Miami office of Internal Security was the suit of all suits. He had thick hair that he had pomaded and sprayed into something that looked like a lopsided dish. He was immaculately attired in Sears polyester and had a televangelist's smile. I named him "Max Headroom."

Headroom nodded to me from behind his desk. On his face was a half-sneer that I recognized. Agents reserved that look for the "dirt-bags" and "shit-heel defendants" whom they arrest.

There were two other inspectors in the room, their faces set in bureaucratic deadpans. One was introduced as the "Polygraph Technician." The other, "Nameless," was not introduced. He sat in a corner watching me with mild amusement.

Headroom, smiling at Quasimoto and Stork, quickly explained that I had the right to refuse the polygraph. We then discussed the questions that I would be asked. They were mainly about whether or not I had given the money to the pilots and Lydia Diaz.

Polygraph then explained that I could not take the test immediately; that he needed about a week to get the proper authorizations, etc. This was more bullshit; the delay was simply to get the subject unnerved, a condition that was apparently necessary for almost everything the inspectors did.

"You can spend the week in the U.S.," said Headroom. "I'll authorize it. Just call us in a week and we'll let you know if we're ready."

I left the building feeling that I had really been had; that I'd walked into a well-planned trap. The bastards had been too pleased with themselves, but I was just too sick to care. If only DEA had put this kind of effort into keeping Gasser and Gutierrez in jail. How different the whole South American drug war might have been.

By July 6, the Voltarin had finally started to work. My fever was down and I was able to walk with a slight limp. I telephoned Stork from where I was staying in New York. He informed me that they were not ready yet. The U.S. Attorney had not signed certain forms.

"When there's a possibility of criminal charges," he explained, "we've got to get the authorization of an assistant [U.S. Attorney]."

"Criminal charges," I repeated dumbly. The phrase echoed in my head throughout the rest of the conversation. "Which U.S. Attorney?" I asked.

117

"Sullivan," he said. "Pat Sullivan."

"Pat Sullivan?" I felt my heart sink. The man who released Jose Gasser was now presiding over my case.

"You know him?" asked Stork in a perfunctory tone that told me the two had already discussed me.

"Yes, I know him," I said.

Stork had no comment. The polygraph was delayed until July 14.

## 4

On Friday evening, July 10, I called on Vinnie for the favor he had offered, and he came through. He arranged a dinner for me at a Brooklyn restaurant with Ken, a pale, bookish guy who had been a polygraph examiner from another government agency. He had quit and gone professional.

"You're walkin' in there like a fuckin' lamb to the slaughter," said Vinnie. "They set a trap and you bit. I guarantee you, they already know how that test is gonna come out. Mikey, you surprise me. For a guy who's been around, you really ain't been around."

"But if I have nothing to hide," I said, looking at Ken, "how can the test hurt me?"

"*Mingeh!*" said Vinnie, slapping his head. "Tryta talk some sense inta this guy."

"If a skilled polygraph examiner wants you to fail," said Ken, picking neatly and methodically at his lobster, "you fail. I don't care how truthful you think you are."

"*Ma-rone,*" said Vinnie.

"One of the things you've got to be wary of," continued Ken, "is if they try to change the questions at the last minute—if they try to make them so general in scope that you have to fail."

"What do you mean?" I asked, my swordfish steak untouched in front of me.

"They might say, for instance, 'Have you ever taken anything that doesn't belong to you since you've been in DEA?' You could fail if you once took home some paper clips or a government pen."

"What'd I tell ya?" said Vinnie, chewing on a mouthful of lobster. "Those motherfuckers."

"Well, we already agreed on the questions," I said. "They're gonna cover every incident where another agent has contradicted me."

"Let me ask a stupid question," said Ken. "If they've opened up investigations into all these different areas of your life, and you already suspect that you're being set up, why even agree to a test that can only hurt you?"

On July 11, Stork called. "I'm calling to advise you not to take any kind of medication before the test."

"Okay," I said. "I'd like to go over the questions that I'm going to be asked again. We agreed that the questions would only encompass those areas where other agents have allegedly made statements that contradict me, correct?"

"That's right, but we'll go over that when you get here. We want you here at 8:30 A.M., and don't be late."

I walked into Internal Security in Miami at exactly 8:30 A.M. on Tuesday, July 14, like the turkey who was invited for Thanksgiving dinner, wondering how I had allowed myself to get into this vulnerable spot. An inspector I didn't know met me and put me in a small room.

At 10 A.M., Stork and Quasimoto, all smiles, came to get me. They shook my hand and led me down a long hallway to Headroom's office. Stork began to unwrap a fresh cigar.

Headroom, Polygraph, and Nameless were waiting. Everyone shook my hand—I hadn't felt so popular since my transfer to Argentina. In the morning sunlight Headroom's hair looked as if it had a shiny new coat of shellac. Everyone was smiling and flashing knowing looks at one another. They were ready to have some fun.

Then I said, "I want to go over the questions again."

There was suddenly a lot of shifting around and throat clearing. Polygraph and Headroom started to go over some of the questions, and they were different from the ones I had agreed to. The new questions encompassed my whole career and were tricky and hard to understand, such as, "Have you deceived the inspectors?" Hell, I was deceiving them that very moment by not telling them that I'd been tape-recording them.

For about 30 minutes we wrestled around with the questions, trying to make them more "acceptable" to me. As this went on, it became obvious that these people weren't after truth—truth was their enemy. They were after me. These polyester-covered sharks were circling, ready to fling themselves into a jaw-snapping, bone-crunching, feeding frenzy—and the dinner was me. As they talked, I was no longer hearing their words. I was watching the foam forming in the corners of their lips and the spray of saliva as their voices grew louder and more insistent. Headroom's mouth was set in a steely grin, and his eyes were narrowed. More than anything else in the world, I wanted to clear that smile off his face.

Suddenly I said, "I'm exercising my right to not take the test!"

The room was perfectly still.

Each inspector looked like a guy returning to the bar and discovering the girl he'd been buying drinks for leaving with another guy. The silent question "Can he do this?" floated in the air.

The bastards got this far with me only because I was afraid. Now they had gone too far and I wasn't afraid anymore.

"Well," I said, getting to my feet, "unless someone has a reason for me to stay, I'll be on my way. I've got to catch a plane back to Argentina."

Headroom's face flushed a deep crimson; his look said that I hadn't seen the last of him. He nodded his head slightly and smiled. I returned the smile and left.

## 5

By the beginning of August the inspectors were still going over everything I had ever been connected with in DEA and interviewing everyone and anyone who had had anything to do with me. They were even snooping around my ex-wife and my two children. During one of my routine calls to my kids (ever since the Suarez-Gutierrez contract had been placed on my head, I had called them two or three times a week to keep them aware of strangers), my 15-year-old son Keith said, "I haven't seen anything, but some of the neighbors said there were people around asking questions about you. But they had government identification."

"Did they say where they were from?"

"Mrs. Barr said they called themselves 'inspectors.'"

Although the inspectors had gone well over the 30-day limit for concluding personnel investigations or preferring charges, I was officially accused of nothing and the investigation was expanding.

On Monday, September 28, the first step in my forced removal from Argentina came.

DEA sent a three-man evaluation team—efficiency auditors—to inspect the operations of the Buenos Aires office. When they walked into my office I could scarcely believe my eyes—the team was headed up Max Headroom himself. The chief was doing double-duty that month as the head of an audit team. Lucky me.

"I told my boss, Terry Burke, that I didn't know if it was proper that I come," he said with his televangelist smile, "but he insisted I come."

Headroom and his men spent a week evaluating my performance as Country Attache. I was proud of my record. In two of the almost three years I'd been there, my Argentina-Uruguay office had accounted for more arrests and drugs seized than any other DEA office in South America. It seemed to me that as the week progressed Headroom grew progressively friendlier. Maybe he was realizing that I was only making DEA look good and doing some good for my country. By the time he left I thought I'd converted him.

By chance I had to go to Brazil to attend a conference. The first leg of my flight was with Headroom and his evaluation team. We bought each other drinks at the airport and chatted during the flight; when we reached Rio de Janeiro, we all shook hands and said goodbye.

"Well, lots of luck to you," said Headroom, gripping my hand firmly and patting me on the back.

Man, was I wrong about this guy, I thought. I'm glad he came. Gee, even his hair doesn't look so funny now.

Two weeks later, I learned Headroom had out-undercovered me.

On October 6, I was in Leesburg, Virginia along with all of the other DEA Country Attaches from South and Central America, to meet with the new administrator of DEA, an FBI agent named Francis Mullen. We had been told that DEA was being taken over by the FBI, although it would supposedly remain an autonomous enforcement agency. (To this day no one has figured out the exact relationship between DEA and the FBI, nor does anyone seem to really care.)

The purpose of this takeover was to "streamline narcotics enforcement by combining FBI informants and methods with DEA expertise," or so the suits and politicians told us. But narcs and street cops are the masters of bullshit; it usually doesn't take us too long to recognize when we are being sold a load of it. And when the first of the "sweeping changes" Administrator Mullen announced was that all DEA agents—unless directly involved in enforcement activities—would be required to wear "business type suits, shirts (off-white, white, or pale blue, only) and ties at all times," the reality of the new, improved drug-fighting agency was clear—more political bullshit.

"They're trying to turn us all into suits," whispered one of my colleagues from South America who'd spent most of his career tracking drugs from the Amazon basin to the peaks of the Andes. "I haven't worn a suit in four fucking years," said another. "What's a suit?" said a third. Right from the start the whole thing was a joke to most of us on the street. Unfortunately, it was very serious to the clowns who would be running our lives.

We were all waiting for Mullen's arrival when I was called out of the conference room for a phone call from Tommy Dolittle (name changed), my new boss in the South American unit.

"I've got bad news for you," said the slow-talking Texan, whom I had spoken to only on the telephone. "The results of the evaluation team have just come in. Inspector Headroom has recommended your immediate removal from Argentina."

"On what grounds?" I said, trying to keep my voice calm and even.

Dolittle rustled papers. "They've accused you of excessive absences from your post o' duty . . ."

"Every one of them was either to work an undercover assignment or testify in court," I interrupted.

". . . questionable expense vouchers . . ."

"That's bullshit. I'm being investigated for that by Stork and Quasimoto—they work for Headroom. Is he convicting me before the investigation's over?"

"Why don't you let me finish, Levine," snapped Dolittle, "then you can give me your comments." His voice had suddenly taken on a bureaucratic crispness, and his drawl had vanished. He was quiet for a moment, and then continued. "They said that when they interviewed Country Attache Levine, 'he did not know where the CIA office was located in the embassy, and had to ask his secretary'; and it says here, 'It was noted that Country Attache Levine plays loud rock music on his radio, disturbing other embassy personnel.'"

Dolittle was silent. I guessed it was time for my comments.

"That's it?" I said. "I don't know where the CIA is and I play rock music too loud, and they want to remove me from Argentina?"

"I'm not sayin' I've got to go along with this report," said Dolittle. "That's their recommendation."

"I was out of town on official business the week before they came. When I got back the CIA had moved to a different part of the building. If Headroom had just asked me why I didn't know where it was, I would've told him. Isn't it obvious what they are trying to do?"

"You don't have to raise your voice with me," said Dolittle.

"Look, I'm sorry, but they're supposed to be an evaluation team. Did they say anything about my production as a narcotics agent?"

"They mentioned that it was satisfactory."

"Satisfactory? They call the Roberto Suarez case *satisfactory*? I play my radio too loud? I don't know where the CIA office is? Look, they . . . somebody wants me silenced, discredited, and out of Argentina, plain and simple. That whole report is bullshit."

"Like I told you, Levine," said Dolittle, coolly drawling again, "I don't have to follow their recommendation. Why don't you write up somethin' with your side o' the story, and I'll make my decision."

On January 5, 1982, I boarded a plane for the United States, having been removed from my post in Argentina. Whoever wanted me out of the way had won. I was not the first agent who had stepped on the toes of special interests and been "neutralized," and I was definitely not the last. Less than two years later a DEA agent in Tegucigalpa, Honduras documented that the Honduran military—which was then helping Oliver North and the CIA to support the anti-Sandinista Contras in Nicaragua—was the source of more than 50 tons of cocaine smuggled into the United States in a 15-month period, or half the estimated U.S. consumption. The DEA suits promptly transferred that agent out of Honduras and closed the office.

In my 12-page reply to Headroom's charges, I pointed out that it had cost more taxpayer dollars to investigate my radio playing than DEA had spent to investigate the entire Bolivian cocaine corporation, and that Headroom and his men had earned more money on per diem during their stay in Argentina than the entire cash outlay for undercover expenses in the Roberto Suarez case. My memo had no affect on Dolittle's decision.

"I'm not removin' you on their recommendation," Dolittle drawled during a later telephone conversation. "I'm removin' you because o' the murder contracts on your life, and because—with all the accusations against you—the performance of your job as Country Attache has been made impossible. Do you have any preferences for your next post o' duty?" he asked.

"Anywhere but headquarters," I said, swallowing my disappointment. "I just want to stay on the street."

When my orders came through, I had been transferred to DEA headquarters. Dolittle was to be my boss.

As the plane took off from Eseiza Airport into the bright morning sunlight, I peered out my window and watched Buenos Aires sprawl beneath me as far as I could see. It was difficult to believe that more than three years had passed since my arrival as an idealistic young narcotics agent and that these were the final moments of what I had once believed would be my "new life." It was even harder to believe how much I had changed in those three years. I had come to South America full of hatred for those druglords my leaders called "our nation's biggest enemies." I had laid my life on the line believing in the virtue of the drug war.

I had been betrayed.

The war on drugs was only an illusion that I had been fool enough to believe in—a belief I might easily have died for, were it not for plain, dumb luck. And those of my brethren who were not so lucky were very much on my mind then as they are to this moment. I had found as much to hate about many of my own leaders—those so-called "good and loyal Americans" who hid behind official titles and secrecy laws—as I did about the criminals they protected.

I had been one of those for whom being a DEA agent had become my reason for living. There were agents like me all over the world, having their illusions shattered, stepping on toes, trying to lock up drug dealers who had bigger and better connections in the American government than they did. Their cases were getting destroyed, just as the Bolivian cases were; they were getting in trouble, just as I was; yet they kept on pushing, kept on butting their heads against the brick walls of clandestine agendas.

Perhaps we kept at it because we never doubted that what we were doing was right; that we were putting evil people in cages; that, we were saving lives and making life a little better for everyone; and that in the end, the rightness of what we were doing would prevail. I needed to believe this; there was nothing else in life I wanted to do.

But the war I now found myself engaged in was one I had never prepared myself for. I was on my way to a new job in DEA headquarters to work among the very people who were trying to steal my reason for living and put me in jail, and I wasn't sure if I knew how to stop them. And though I did not suspect it, my life had once again been put on a collision course with Sonia Atala and the Bolivian drug government.

# PART TWO

# OPERATION HUN

The CIA in its pursuit of intelligence and influence, often courts the same powerful figures [DEA] pursued as criminals . . . and intelligence wins precedence over law enforcement. The highly connected tuxedo-clad criminal is left in place to provide intelligence to the United States—and drugs to its citizens.
— James Mills, *The Underground Empire*

# 10

# Operation Hun

## 1

DEA world headquarters at 1405 Eye Street, Washington, D.C., sat at the edge of one of the seediest sections of our nation's capital. Headquarters was a dingy, 12-story building with no distinguishing markings, as if its planners were ashamed of what it housed. Off the main lobby of the world's lead agency in the war on drugs was a side entrance to a topless bar. Standing against the far wall of the lobby, you could look past a photo exhibit entitled "DEA in Action Around the World" through a glass door and see some anatomical action suggestive of the screwing the American people were taking under the banner of the war on drugs.

The first week of my new career as a suit was spent wandering solemn, bare hallways echoing with the sounds of clacking typewriters, gurgling phones, and buzzing intercoms; riding elevators full of tense, sallow faces eyes-front to the floor numbers; all under the constant scrutiny of dour bureaucrats who couldn't look me in the eye and who grew silent whenever I was around.

In Argentina, I had been living in a beautiful, safe haven of a home

I loved in a land where I felt comfortable with the people, culture, and language, and had spent my waking hours doing what I did best—carrying out deep cover probes designed to destroy major drug dealers. Now, because I was under investigation and could possibly be indicted, I was living in an Arlington, Virginia basement apartment with no windows; performing make-work tasks in a job that outside the government would have no reason for even existing; and working among people who avoided me like the plague.

My first headquarters job was as staff assistant in the Latin American Unit. My supervisor was none other than Tommy Dolittle. I was assigned to "service the needs of, coordinate, and oversee international investigations involving" Colombia, Bolivia, Peru, and Venezuela. "In those countries you are the eyes and ears of headquarters," said Dolittle, a cold-eyed bureaucrat whose back seemed to stiffen whenever he saw me. "I'm gonna be watchin' your performance closely," he said with his Texas drawl.

And watch me closely he could. The staff assistants of the Latin American Unit were housed in a suite of five offices—four small cubicles for the assistants and a large corner office for Dolittle. From his office, Dolittle could look up from behind his desk and see the entire outer office, where the three secretaries sat, and the entrances to the assistants' cubicles.

My little box was the last one in the row. It had bare walls and an air-shaft window, and vibrated with the hum of some nearby machinery from 9 A.M. until 6 P.M. This was where I was supposed to spend 10 hours a day—a DEA agent's work week is a minimum of 50 hours—for as long as I was assigned to headquarters—or until they fired me or put me in a real jail.

One day, over coffee at a nearby restaurant, Tony Buono (name changed) showed me the headquarters ropes. Buono was a tough street veteran who had charged through more doors in his career than a firefighter. When I had known him on the streets, he always looked like a cross between a Mafia hitman and a crack dealer. The Tony seated across the table from me now looked like a used-car salesman who was trying to look like a banker.

"You know, bein' seen hangin' out witchu Levine ain't exactly good for a career in headquarters," said Tony in his thick New York accent, glancing out the window at the DEA building.

"So why'd you invite me?"

"Hey, c'mon!" He looked me in the eye. "This is me, Tony. You think I'm serious? You ever think the day would come, Levine, when guys like you and me would be suits?"

"It's not exactly like I want to be here."

"I'm not talking about in here, Mikey," he said, pounding his chest. "You know I ain't one of these chickenhearts. But I got tired of bein' passed over for promotion and transfers. So I made a lot of cases, what did it get me? Nothing but problems. Big cases, big problems—no cases, no problems. By now, you oughtta know that better than anybody." I nodded. Going out for coffee with Tony wasn't turning out to be such a good idea.

"Believe me, Mikey," he continued, "this is a blessing in disguise. You kiss the right asses—I don't care what kinda trouble you're in—two, three years you walk outta here with a promotion. A bureaucracy got a short memory. And this is where the contracts are made."

"Okay," I said, "but what do you do every day? How do you stay sane?"

"Forget about it. This is the easiest fucking job in the world. All you do is read cables. Anything newsworthy you highlight in yellow and give it to your boss, so he can bring it up to the Administrator. He likes that shit. You get a chance, you bring it up personally—score a couple of points, and the Man himself gets to know who you are—if he don't already know."

"That sounds like a real rush."

"What you don't want to happen is some reporters calling the boss about some shit that went down in one of your countries, and you didn't send the cable upstairs."

"I don't think I could stand that," I smiled.

"Fuckin'-ay. The other half of the job is makin' up fact sheets and briefing papers—you know, statistical bullshit, how we're winnin' the war—so one of these clowns can go on TV or testify before Congress."

"Where do you get the statistics?"

Tony laughed. "Outta yer head, where else? And the rest of the job is pretty much up to what you make of it. For psychos like you, Levine, you could get as involved as you want in tracking cases; invent yourself a couple of nice trips; call meetings, conferences, anything you want; or don't do a fucking thing—no one cares. You ever heard of anyone being fired in DEA for doing nothing?"

"Nope, I can't say 's I have."

"You're only gonna get about 10 or 12 cables a day. Forget about it. You can become a brain surgeon in your spare time on this job."

"Thanks for the advice, Tony."

"Don't mention it. And Mikey . . . a word of advice." Tony was grinning and pointing at his shoes. "Wingtips," he said. He was wearing a shiny brown pair. "Get yourself a pair of wingtips. All the feebs that work for Mullen—they all wear wingtips."

"Tony, you really changed."

He pointed an index finger to his head.

"Just thinking, Mikey. It's the future. Guys like you and me? Forget about it—we're dinosaurs. We either gotta go with the times, or the times will go right over us. Wingtips, Mikey; it's the future."

My job was almost exactly as Tony had described it, except that my boss along with unseen others were watching my every move. The first sign of how closely I was being monitored came when Mike Powers, a buddy of mine who had been brought to headquarters to chill out after his wife was killed by drug dealers in Bangkok, got me to join a nearby gym. We began going over there during lunch hour, and the daily workout helped me fight off depression.

Mike had been going to the gym for several months before I arrived. He was surprised and then enraged when he found out that someone had reported us for taking more than our allotted lunch hour off to go to the gym. Although Mike couldn't figure it out, I was sure it was the inspectors, but I said nothing to Mike. I just stopped going with him. He never had another problem.

I had thought about turning to the Rabbi for advice, but during my second week I saw him on a crowded elevator. He was with two FBI suits, and for a millisecond our eyes met. I started to smile, but he quickly averted his gaze. So not even the Rabbi was immune.

On Monday, February 1, I found a new worry. My ex-wife called from New York to tell me that our 14-year-old daughter Niki was acting strangely, and that she suspected that she was using drugs. I just could not believe drugs were the problem because she didn't fit the profile I had in my mind. They were living in one of the nicest neighborhoods and school systems in the country. Niki was a great kid— pretty, smart, and popular. I had spent hours talking to her about drugs. She knew how much I loved her and how her using drugs would devastate me.

I called Niki on the phone in her room, and we were having a good talk until I brought up the drugs. She got angry at me for even hinting that she was using. "It's mommy," she said tearfully. "She hates me."

"No she doesn't, baby," I said. "She loves you so much that even the thought of you using drugs makes her crazy."

"Well, I would never do anything like that to you daddy."

When I hung up, I was uneasy, and images of my brother kept trying to force their way into my consciousness.

I sat staring at the small pile of meaningless paper that had been my day's work. I unholstered my 9mm automatic and lay it on top of the stack and put my gold badge alongside it. The odd still-life seemed to have a message in it. I started wondering what it all meant—what a person spends a life doing; what part a person plays in making his or her own destiny; what is right, wrong, good, evil. Suddenly I was thinking about all the agents I had known who had ended their lives sitting at their desks with their guns jammed against the roofs of their mouths.

I grabbed my gun and locked it in the desk drawer. Not me. No fucking way. Not me.

I had been at headquarters almost three weeks, and I felt I was losing my mind. I wasn't going to make it, and they knew it. I had to escape.

## 2

"You okay?" said a voice.

I looked up through a cloud of cigarette smoke. Looming above me on an angular 6'4" frame was a face so much the Irish cop that its owner could have directed traffic in any U.S. city without a uniform. This was the face of Special Agent Jack Rourke (name changed), and as usual, there was a cigarette stuck in it. Jack and I had been in the New York office at the same time. We never worked together, but his reputation among street agents was as a guy you would want with you when you had to go through a door.

He was tall and slim, and he should have looked good in his clothes, but his suit looked slept in, his hair was tousled, and his tie hung loose and angled. He had the look of other street agents I had known—so obsessed with their cases that their private lives became as rumpled and neglected as their clothing.

"I'd be a hell of a lot better if I could get back on the street," I said.

"It's funny you should say that," said Jack, grinning. "Got a couple of minutes?"

"The rest of the year."

Rourke gave me a knowing grin. He glanced around as if he were about to commit a crime, and then stepped inside and shut the door behind him. He sat down, lit a fresh cigarette from the butt of the old one, and blew a long stream of smoke in my direction. Then he asked, "How would you like to do a little undercover assignment?"

"Me? I'd fight Muhammad Ali to get out of this fucking place." Suddenly, a single light had appeared at the end of a very long tunnel.

"This one could be a little hairy."

"Jack, I don't care what it is. I'll do it. But what about the suits? Internal Security's been working on me for almost a year."

"I already cleared it," said Rourke. "I won't say I didn't get any resistance, but they said okay."

If the suits had okayed me for an undercover while the inspectors still had an open investigation on me, something had to be wrong. But what difference did it make? I would have walked on fire and broken glass to escape headquarters.

"What's it all about?"

"It's called Operation Hun," said Rourke, putting an inch-thick folder on my desk. "Right now, it's the most sensitive investigation in the agency. We've targeted Luis 'Lucho' Arce-Gomez, the Minister of Interior of Bolivia."

For a long moment I stared at Rourke. "The Minister of Cocaine," I finally breathed.

"None other," said Rourke.

I studied Rourke for some hint of ulterior motive. Could this be a setup? Could Rourke be working for Internal Security? Was he aware that the people he had targeted had been helped into power by the CIA and their collaborators in the DEA?

"How about Sonia Atala? Does that ring a bell? She used to sell dope for the Bolivian government."

"You're shitting me!" I said.

"Not in the fucking least—for the Bolivian government. She used to work directly under Arce-Gomez. Now she's workin' for us."

"How did that happen?"

"Mike, I cannot exaggerate how big this broad got in the dope business. She was doing deals with everyone from the Medellin Cartel to the fucking Mafia in Italy. She had her own thing going, plus she was selling the stuff Arce-Gomez was seizing and storing in Bolivian bank vaults. I mean like all the coke in Bolivia was hers.

"Next thing happens is Arce decides he's gonna put the screws to her. Some of the dope he's giving Sonia out of the bank vaults has been sitting there for a while—you know, the shit goes bad after a while and has to be reprocessed. So he gives Sonia like 300 or 400 kilos of bad stuff, and her chemist can salvage only about 30 or 40 kilos of good dope out of it.

"So now Arce and his boys claim Sonia owes them for the whole 300 kilos . . . some phantasmagorical sum, like $1.5 million. In the meantime, Sonia does a deal with a Colombian named Papo Mejia. You ever heard of him?"

"No," I said, telling him the truth. "Should I?"

Rourke paused to light another cigarette. "He's only one of the deadliest fucking killers in the cocaine business. You ever hear of Griselda Blanco, 'the Godmother'? The Cocaine Wars? The Cocaine Cowboys?"

"Sure."

"Papo and Griselda *were* the Cocaine Wars. The two were after each other for years, and ended up killing everybody but each other. This guy Papo's like a rabid dog. Even the fucking Cocaine Cowboys quake in their boots when they hear this guy's name.

"Anyway, Sonia does a deal with Papo—a bag of jewelry for . . . she promises him like 30 kilos."

"Jewelry? How come she took jewelry instead of money? That might be important."

"Will you just let me finish the fucking story, ya hump?" The people in Rourke's life were divided into broads, dirtbags, and humps. The humps were the good guys.

"Who's story is it?" I asked.

"Sonia's."

"Just her's? You got any corroboration?"

"Believe me, this broad ain't lying, Mike. She's in no fucking position."

"If you say so."

"Anyway, what's important is she gives the jewelry to Arce. Now Arce, instead of giving her the dope for Papo, says, 'Okay the jewels are part payment on the $1.5 million you owe me.' Now Sonia's left high and dry between Arce and Papo.

"Now when this guy Papo realizes that she took his jewels and he ain't gettin' a fucking thing for them, he goes nuts. This is the last guy in the world you wanna do something like that to. He's gonna kill her,

her family—she's got a husband and four kids—and the family dog. And he's got a small army to do it with."

"You mean they're looking for her right now?"

"Are they ever!" said Rourke, shaking his head.

"How did we get her?"

"Who else did she have to turn to?" said Rourke. "On top of everything else, Arce-Gomez seizes all her property and bank accounts and is looking to lock her ass up. So she contacts DEA through a couple of Bolivian cops who can be trusted."

"Bolivian cops who can be trusted?" I said. "I didn't know there was such a thing."

"Well, according to the guys down there now, there's a few."

"'Guys down there'?"

"Yeah, we're reopening the office. Didn't you know?"

"I kinda lost track. What about Arce?"

"He resigned as minister to clear his name. Right now he's the Bolivian Military Attache to Argentina."

"That's some story," I said.

There was a lot about the story that bothered me. Atala had become one of the most powerful drug dealers in the world. She was not the kind of person who would run to DEA that easily, especially not to a DEA that was pretty much a laughingstock in Bolivia thanks to what was done to the Suarez case. Sonia was also connected enough in that CIA-supported government to have protectors who were much more reliable than DEA. But I didn't express my doubts to Rourke. I wanted out of the Palace of Suits so badly I would have worked an undercover case with the devil. "Where are you keeping her?"

Jack took another deep drag on his cigarette, studying me, still deciding whether or not to trust me. People were saying, "Levine is under investigation; he's going to be indicted." At that moment I knew he had not put together my role in the Suarez case and the Cocaine Coup, nor any of the events that followed. And if I wanted to escape headquarters, I had better not tell him . . . not yet.

"We got her and her family installed in a little house in Virginia."

"Where do I come in?"

Rourke lit another cigarette. "Well, when we first got her here we thought we'd just turn her loose with an undercover and see what we came up with. You know, let people know she's back in business and see what happens. We sent her undercover to New York and Miami with Luis Alvarez [name changed]."

I knew Alvarez from New York City, where he'd done some good UC work.

"So Sonia calls up one of her old customers—an Argentine babe living in New York—to see if we can get something going. We set up a meet, but it goes bad. The Argentine broad smells something wrong, she doesn't trust Alvarez. What's worse—Sonia loses confidence in Louie and she's afraid to work with him. The case is just too important to fuck around with.

"In the meantime, I hear you just got transferred in from South America. I know you've been doing a lotta UC work down there, so . . ." He shrugged. "That's the story. What do you think?"

"I like it. I like it a lot," I said, a little too quickly. "But we should set our sights higher."

"What do you mean?" asked Rourke.

"Why not go for it all?" Rourke looked puzzled. I was surprised he hadn't seen the opportunity. "Sonia was part of a conspiracy involving Arce-Gomez and his people and Papo Mejia, right?"

"So?"

"So we just get ironclad proof that the deal actually happened and indict them all for conspiracy."

"Keep talking."

"I go undercover with Sonia, posing as her business partner, or whatever."

"Yeah . . . whatever." He looked at me with a grin.

"What's that supposed to mean?"

"Sonia's a good-lookin' babe."

"Don't even think it," I said. "If I'm gonna get involved with a woman now, it's not gonna be with a government stool who was probably putting out cigarettes on some poor slob's dick a couple of months ago. There's a small army of inspectors out there who'd throw a party if they caught me messing with a low-life stool."

"I hear you," said Jack.

"So here's the setup. Sonia's back in business; I'm her partner. We have a load of coke we're trying to sell. We get like 50 or 100 kilos of DEA's best coke out of the lab and authorization to give out undercover samples to the bad guys so that they know we're for real. The word gets around that Sonia's really back. I make myself responsible for her debt to Papo. You know, I act terrified, like 'Hey, I'm a businessman, we want to do business in peace, let's straighten this thing out.'

135

"If she's as big as you say, the whole drug world will be knocking our door down, trying to do business with us," I said, coming alive. This was what I did best. "To go fishing with bait like Sonia is really big-game fishing. You're not gonna get this kinda opportunity too many times in your career, Jack."

"I hear you," he said, dragging on his cigarette.

"We can't give out coke samples unless its the best stuff available, 100 percent pure or as close to it as we can come. Now the word spreads like wildfire. 'Sonia's back and she's got dynamite shit.' We negotiate with everyone who shows up, get it all on videotape, do a couple of reverse undercovers—with her rep we can keep locking up people till the jails are full.

"In the meantime, during the negotiations with Papo's people . . ."

"Papo's people!" echoed Rourke, laughing and shaking his head. "Levine, you *are* a hump."

". . . we're getting evidence of the original conspiracy that goes right back to Arce-Gomez and his crew. Once we can't go any further, we pay off Papo in cocaine instead of money. Everyone gets busted. We take a murderer off the street and we indict the ex-Minister of Interior of Bolivia for conspiracy." *And we fuck the CIA.*

Rourke was quiet. He lit still another cigarette.

"Is that a victory in the fucking war against the White Death, or what?" I said.

"I like it," said Rourke, getting to his feet, picking up the case folder he had never opened.

"I'm glad," I said, standing. "I think we can really do something with this." I stopped myself from thanking him for saving my life and urging him to hurry up and get me the hell out of there before it was too late. I shook his hand.

Rourke said, "Let me take it up with Ralph Saucedo."

By Wednesday, February 3, I hadn't heard from Rourke, and I figured the undercover assignment was finished or never existed in the first place. It was just part of a master plot to drive me over the edge. Inspectors were grinding away at my life; Tommy Dolittle had hardly spoken to me and could barely look at me; the suits in the twelfth-floor executive offices seemed a hell of a lot more concerned about neutralizing Michael Levine than Luis Arce-Gomez or Papo Mejia. How could they approve me going undercover on their most sensitive investigation when they were trying to put me in jail?

I was staring at a small pile of teletypes that were every bit as bullshit as Tony had described. This was now my life's work, my *raison d'etre*. Outside it had begun to snow. I had a long, depressing day ahead of me; maybe a long depressing life.

Then Rourke stuck his face in my office. "It's a go. You and Sonia are going to Miami tomorrow. You can start spreading the word about the Levine-Atala Cocaine Corporation. There'll be enough time on the way down for you to get to know each other and work out a good cover story."

"Great!" My spirits soared, then dived. I was overcome by an attack of paranoia. DEA was sending me—an agent they were trying to put in jail—to work as an undercover partner with one of the biggest drug dealers in South America; a woman I'd just spent two years of my life trying to indict? There had to be something wrong.

"Oh yeah," said Rourke, "I almost forgot. You know Lydia Diaz?"

"Of course. She posed as my wife during the Suarez case."

"Well she'll be posing as your sister tomorrow. She's flying in from California."

"Fine with me."

It was anything but fine. Inspector Stork had grilled Lydia over and over about the money I had given her during the Suarez operation. He claimed that she had called me a liar. Of all the female agents in DEA, why would they send her all the way from California for this particular assignment? But I said nothing to Rourke. Operation Hun was my only ride out of headquarters.

"Okay, we're all set then," said Rourke.

"Just one thing puzzles me," I said. "Where'd you get that name—Operation Hun?"

Rourke's eyes twinkled mischievously. "Atala . . . like Attila . . . the Hun. Get it?"

# 11

# Sonia and the Miami Nightmare

## 1

On Thursday morning, February 4, 1982, I met Sonia Atala, the woman who had reached the pinnacle of the drug world, a world that was responsible for tens of thousands of drug-related homicides, overdose deaths, and suicides. A world that costs the American economy hundreds of billions of dollars a year. A world that had already claimed my brother and was now threatening to take my daughter. She had gone higher than any woman before or after her, and her name represented everything I had spent my life fighting.

Rourke led me through the crowded passenger terminal at Dulles Airport on the way to our flight to Miami. Ahead I could see two women in business suits, silhouetted in bright sunlight, watching our approach. "There they are," he said.

The shorter of the two, with shoulder-length auburn hair and dark, penetrating eyes, had already made eye contact with me, her gaze a burning question mark.

"*Sonia Atala, aqui es Mig-wel Levine,*" said Jack in butchered Spanish.

*"Encantado,"* I said, taking her hand.

I noticed she wore an unusual fragrance. It was subtle, yet strong and unmistakable. It fit her perfectly. Later she told me that she'd had it specially blended for her. Everything about her seemed understated. She had almond-shaped eyes and high cheekbones that hinted of Indian blood, but her skin was fair. She wore little makeup and her jewelry was expensive but simple. Her two-piece business suit was perfectly tailored to her petite figure. She looked like a young advertising executive.

The Sonia Atala whom I had been hearing about for the past two years had aligned herself with mass murderers, torturers, Nazi war criminals, and the CIA. Her uncle Hugo showed unmistakable fear when he talked about her, and under torture had spoken of delivering M-16 and AK-47 machine guns to her. My Bolivian informer Tanya—herself as treacherous as they come—had called Sonia "dangerous" and a "black widow." But before me was a woman who looked like a kindergarten teacher. The only clue to what was beneath that quiet veneer lay in her eyes, which were the twin dark lasers of a predator. As Rourke introduced me to the other woman, Maria Montez (name changed), an attractive, pleasantly smiling DEA intelligence analyst who had been Rourke's translator and assistant, I could feel those eyes appraising me.

We had more than an hour before our flight to Miami, so we went to an airport restaurant. Sonia and I had to get to know each other quickly—we had a cover story to build. Within hours we might be meeting drug dealers who had known Sonia intimately for years; we might be spending hours or even days with them. The success of the case and maybe our lives would depend on our believability.

The restaurant was crowded and full of curious eyes—a difficult place to detect surveillance. Sonia and I sat across a table from Rourke and Maria. I began with small talk to get us accustomed to being close. When the dealers met us we'd present a relaxed, natural picture—not an informant working with an undercover agent. Drug dealers lay their lives on the line every time they meet a potential customer. The ones who survive are hypersensitive to even the slightest signals of danger. On the plane we'd get into our cover stories and the more intimate details about each other's lives.

"Do you speak any English?" I asked in English.

Sonia shrugged and answered in Spanish, her eyes burning into mine for a moment before darting away. "Only a couple of words.

People from the Mormon Church come to our house. They're teaching my husband and children."

"Are you a Mormon?" I asked, trying to hold her gaze.

Sonia laughed. A quick glimpse of a little girl. "No, I'm Catholic. Religion is something I don't know." She shrugged again.

As we spoke her voice became a soft hum. My mind was working on automatic—a tiny portion of it clicking out small talk while the rest was digesting everything my eyes were seeing. This is a technique that most undercovers develop after years of having to recall the most minute details of meetings and conversations on witness stands.

I noticed that Sonia also had a difficult time keeping her eyes from following the movement around us. Everyone had to be checked out, classified, watched, and then sorted away for future reference. I was certain she was cataloging me as thoroughly as I was her.

*"Miguel,"* said Sonia softly, *"permiso."* Her hand was on my arm pressing softly as she stood. Then she was by me and moving across the restaurant. I noticed that she was watching me through a mirror.

And so was someone else.

The man in the mirror had suddenly averted his gaze. He was seated across the table from another man reading a newspaper. I studied the two, half conscious of Rourke speaking as I watched. I caught the man sneaking another quick look at me. I had been around long enough to distinguish drug dealers, thugs, and hitmen from government agents, and these two were definitely agents, either CIA or inspectors. What did they expect to see? This was weird. The whole fucking setup was weird.

"Are you okay?" Rourke's voice brought me to earth. "You look like you just saw a ghost."

"I'm sorry," I said. "My mind drifted."

"It better not drift in Miami," said Rourke.

The mention of Miami brought a succession of images and sounds to my mind: my arrival in Miami with Tanya, Headroom's face, Pat Sullivan, the inspector standing in the doorway of Internal Security headquarters watching me leave, Hurtado's frightened voice on the tape-recording—"She is a very powerful woman."

"Is the Miami office going to cover us?" I asked.

Rourke shrugged. "We asked them for help, but you know how that goes. They said they're busy but they'd try to spring a couple of guys to cover us."

"To tell you the truth," I said, "I feel safer without them."

I glanced at the mirror. The two men were gone. They had vanished too quickly. I decided not to say anything to Rourke—if they were inspectors or CIA that was my problem. If I laid that on Rourke right at the outset he might drop me and get another UC, and I'd never survive headquarters.

"Well, if everything goes okay in Miami," Rourke was saying, "Saucedo wants us to set up a new base of operations in Tucson. It's a small town, safe, the situation is more controllable, and we won't have to worry about the Miami politics. We already set up an answering service there, so if you gotta give anyone a phone number, you'reset."

I could understand Saucedo wanting to avoid Miami. At one point during the Suarez case some of the Miami suits were working so hard to derail the operation that they actually denied him approval to travel there from headquarters to check on its progress. The fact that Saucedo—himself a senior manager—had stood up against the other suits to make the Suarez case, and that he was willing to work around them now, was encouraging. It told me that at least there were some among DEA's leadership who wanted to do the right thing.

"Great," I said scanning the crowd for more watching eyes. "I've never been to Arizona. Maybe we'll get lucky."

"Luck's got nothing to do with it. You oughtta know that."

## 2

Sonia and I were seated together on the plane so we could work on our cover stories. I'm not the bravest airline passenger, and during takeoff I leaned back and squeezed my eyes shut. When we leveled off, I opened them. Sonia was watching me, a faint smile on her lips. "You don't like to fly."

"No, I'll never get used to it."

Suddenly I was having a hard time accepting that this situation was real. Two years of hearing Sonia's name in whispers, two years of hell trying to put her and her neo-Nazi partners in jail, and now we were on the same side?

"That's funny," she said, and looked out the window. The "No Smoking" light went off. "Do you mind if I smoke?"

I did, but I wanted absolutely no friction between us. "No, go ahead."

She lit her cigarette and glanced around the cabin. As I watched her up close, her eyes seemed more alert and predatory than ever. "Tell me about yourself," I said.

Her eyes narrowed. "What do you want to know?" she said, studying me.

"Whatever the people we are going to meet would expect me to know."

"I thought DEA knows everything," she said, with just a hint of disdain in her voice.

"Yes, but I don't know anything. I'm supposed to be your business partner, and I'm taking responsibility for the money you owe Papo. We'll be with a lot of people who know you, and they're going to have a lot of questions about us. If we sound phony . . ." I shrugged.

She looked at me as if seeing me for the first time. She took a long drag on her cigarette, and then pushed her seat all the way back and beckoned for me to do the same. "All right. Where do you want me to begin?" she asked.

"At the beginning. Tell me all the things you would be curious about when you meet someone new."

Sonia took a deep, how-many-times-must-I-do-this breath and began. Over the next hour, I learned that she came from a poor family and was married at 14 to Walter "Pachi" Atala, who in Bolivia was a well-known race car driver. She had had four children by her early twenties. Her husband's family was rich, powerful, and politically influential, and Pachi once held a political post in the Bolivian government that had "something to do with labor." At one point, he was being groomed for the presidency. From the time of her marriage, Sonia had lived a life of luxury, with property, servants, and all the things that money could buy.

"How did you get into the cocaine business?"

"Pachi was racing cars. He goes off to Europe. I was tired of following him around the race tracks or being with the children all the time. So I began a business."

"What kind of business?"

"Importing things—televisions, stereos, those kinds of things—from Panama."

"This was before you went into drugs—cocaine?"

"Sure. And then after they took over the government, the Minister calls me and invites me to participate."

"You mean before that, you weren't in the cocaine business?"

She gave me a long, penetrating look. "No. But in my travel and business I met many who were, and the Minister knew this."

She could not have looked more disarmingly sincere. She was a flawless liar—the perfect undercover weapon, if she could be controlled. I decided not to show my doubts about anything she said, for I knew if I started questioning any inconsistencies in her story, I could say goodbye to the undercover assignment. Right now, I didn't need absolute truth from her—I wanted performance. "What happened then?"

Sonia shrugged. "I was bored, so I said 'Sure, why not?'"

"Didn't you have any trouble with men?"

She paused, and looked into my eyes. I held her gaze. "I had no trouble, because I didn't want men. I'm married. I don't cheat on my husband."

"But when you traveled and dealt with the Cubans, Colombians, and all those super-macho guys, how did you handle them?"

She smiled over some memory. "I never had any difficulties. I was under the protection of the biggest. The Ochoas [Medellin Cartel] adored me; they treated me like a queen. They would send me their cars, their drivers and bodyguards to use as I saw fit. There was nothing they would not do for me. No one would dare insult me, let alone lay a finger on me."

"Your life must have been incredible. I mean, there you are selling cocaine for Bolivia, traveling first class all over the world, wined and dined by the richest, most powerful people. You really were treated like a queen."

She laughed ironically. "Yeah, I was the Queen of Bolivia with a crown of snow, that's what people called me."

"The Queen of Cocaine."

"Yes," she said idly. An uncomfortable silence.

"When Arce-Gomez turned on you, and Mejia was hunting you, why didn't you turn to the Ochoas or some of the others for help?"

She sighed. "That's business. In this business one doesn't interfere with the business of another. Besides, Papo is crazy. Many of the others—whether they admit it or not—fear him."

"Do you fear him?"

She looked at me for a moment, as if thinking that perhaps she had been sent another idiot agent. "Only a fool is not afraid of Papo."

I heard her words, but saw not a hint of fear.

"Now this jewelry–cocaine swap you did with him, how much

*perico* was he supposed to get?" Her eyes were suddenly alert again.

"I think it was 30 kilos."

"That's more than $1 million in jewels. Did you check the stuff out? Do you know jewelry?"

"Papo said they were worth $300,000 or $400,000. I sent them to the Minister—he said they were good. Then Papo also gave me a car and some checks."

"A car? Checks?" Rourke hadn't told me about this—only about the jewelry.

"A new yellow Mercedes and some checks, but one of the checks bounced."

"And you gave all this to Arce-Gomez for about 30 kilos of cocaine that were supposed to go to Papo?"

"Sure." Her fist was clenched and she was rubbing her thumb and index finger together. At Sonia's level of dealing, all transactions were strictly cash. Agreeing to barter with an animal like Mejia was looking for trouble. It was hard to put a value on cars and jewelry. Mejia would almost certainly claim they were worth more than they were. The question I wanted to ask, but couldn't, was "Why were you looking for trouble, lady?"

The stewardess serving lunch interrupted us. While we were eating, my mind filled with images of the Bolivian coup: neo-Nazis wearing their hoods and swastika armbands and shooting and torturing people, and a dark building with heavy walls that muffled the screams of the dying. I wanted to ask Sonia where she was when the coup took place—everything she knew and everything she did—but I fought back the urge, as I would have to do many times while I was with her. I knew that if she said the wrong thing, my role in Operation Hun could end on the spot. I nervously ate everything on my tray, and even licked the jelly out of the little plastic cube. Seeing this, Sonia laughed—another flash of the little girl.

We soon returned to our conversation. "Did you give any of the things you received from Papo directly to Arce?"

Another full alert. "No, to his people, his assistants. They brought everything to him."

"How do you know that?"

"Later we discussed it, but he said I still owed him more than $1 million—he said interest. It was a debt without end."

"But you already had that debt when you were making the deal with Papo, *verdad*?"

"Sure."

"I mean when you took the jewelry and stuff you already knew that Arce was claiming you owed him all that money."

"Of course."

"So you knew Papo was never going to get any merchandise."

Sonia smiled. "Do you think I'm crazy? I thought the Minister would deliver."

"Did you tell this to Papo?"

"He said that it was my problem. And then the Minister seizes my bank accounts, my properties. What was I supposed to do?"

"Why would he do that?"

"Why?" Sonia's eyes turned cold; the vixen was cornered and dangerous. "I had introduced them to all my customers. With me out of the way they could sell directly."

More questions raced through my mind, but I couldn't ask them. I'd end up interrogating her and risking my escape from headquarters. I had to know just enough to play the role of her new man. If she knew Arce-Gomez was squeezing her out, then she had to know Papo was never going to receive any cocaine from her. She was no fool. Why would she intentionally rip off one of the deadliest men in the cocaine world? I managed to keep quiet.

We were approaching Miami, so I swung the conversation to our undercover roles. Since my Spanish has a mixed Argentine-Puerto Rican accent, we decided that I would be an Argentine who was raised in New York, a cover story I could back up pretty well. Sonia and I met through my sister, Lydia Diaz—at that moment on her way to meet us in Miami. For a while we went over our responses to other questions we might be asked, and then tackled the most sensitive question.

"What about whether there's anything personal going on between you and me. How do we handle that?"

"What do you mean?"

"I'm taking on a debt that's liable to get me killed; that's not something a man will usually do unless there's more than money involved."

"It's nobody's business what's between us."

"I know that, but we'll be dealing with people you know. Some of them know your husband. What's going to make them suspicious? What are they going to say to you in private? What are you going to tell them? I have to know so that I can act accordingly . . . so that we look real."

She studied me. "I'll tell them we're business partners. They're going to believe what the hell they want no matter what we tell them."

## 3

The landing gear hit the Miami runway and jarred me awake. I found Sonia wide awake and studying me.

*"Estas cansado?"*

"Yes," I croaked, "I'm very tired."

"Do you have children?"

"Yes, but they don't live with me."

"It must be difficult for you, Miguel."

"Yes . . . yes, it is."

There was something unexpectedly warm about Sonia. For a moment I felt a strong temptation to open up to this woman who epitomized everything I despised. I was lonely, in pain, and afraid, and there was no one in my life I could trust. From this moment on she and I would have to trust each other with our lives. It seemed so easy, so natural to talk to her. Somehow I managed to keep my mouth shut.

Sonia and I walked side-by-side toward the baggage claim without saying a word. We were comfortable enough together to fake our way through an undercover meeting, as long as it didn't get too deep and personal. I glanced over my shoulder, to check the crowd.

There he was.

The guy from the Dulles restaurant was trying to lose himself in the crush about 20 feet behind me, but he was just a little too obvious. Did he want me to know he was there?

I swung my head back naturally, as if I hadn't noticed him. Elementary counter-surveillance: never let on you know you're being followed—that way you might learn as much about the people tailing you as they do about you.

When we reached the baggage carousel, the guy had vanished.

Maybe it was just coincidence that we were on the same plane. But would anyone fly from Virginia to Miami without baggage? He had no carry-on bag, either. Probable conclusion: He followed me as far as Miami, where someone else would pick up the tail. But I was a government agent on an undercover assignment; if an agency was watching me, wouldn't they already know where I was heading? Why would they need a tail on a plane? Either they thought something would happen on the plane or they wanted me to know they were there.

As Rourke, Maria, and Sonia gabbed away at the carousel, I tried to check the crowd for surveillance from behind my sunglasses without turning my head too much—a great trick I'd heard about someplace. It gave me a headache.

"Hey, what's with you?" said Rourke. "I never knew you to be so quiet."

"She's got a few people looking for her, Jack. If someone recognizes her we oughtta be aware of it."

"Good thinking," said Rourke. "I almost forgot—we're in Papo Mejia country."

"Any Miami agents supposed to meet us?" I asked.

Rourke laughed. I remembered when Tanya and I had come to Miami to testify and the Miami DEA had refused to protect us. I also remembered the guy who was shot at the airport that day. Was Rourke laughing at the idea that the Miami suits would lift a finger to protect me, or simply at the idea that they would aid any operation that wasn't their own?

We taxied over to our base of operations, the Sheraton River House, a medium-sized hotel on an isolated canal a short way from the airport entrance. Sonia and I took a separate cab so that we would be seen arriving as a couple.

Operation Hun had begun.

The moment we entered the crowded lobby with its potted palms and hidden alcoves, the hair on the back of my neck prickled. Memories of Miami—the Suarez operation, Internal Security interrogations, Pat Sullivan, being followed to my mother's house—threatened to overwhelm me with fear and depression.

I felt a light touch on my arm. I jumped. "Are you okay, Miguel?" Sonia asked, concerned.

She had good reason to worry—I was starting to act like a strung-out druggie. She was probably picturing how I would handle myself when the two of us were alone in a room with Papo and his men. If working with Louie Alvarez had frightened her, working with me might just kill the both of us. I had to get myself together.

"I'm fine," I said. "It takes me a while to get used to the heat."

Maria and Rourke were already signing in, pretending they didn't know us. We would never be seen talking together in public.

A short time later I was finally alone in my room. I tore my clothes off, turned on the air conditioner full blast, and threw myself on the bed to cool down. Within minutes I was on my feet again, pacing the room, peering out at the street through my curtains, and acting like a fugitive working against my government rather than for it. I had to get control. If Internal Security was following me there wasn't anything I could do about it. As long as I did nothing wrong, they couldn't hurt me. That's what I kept telling myself.

A ringing woke me from my soaking bath. The water was cold and my neck was locked, yet I felt better. Looking at the clock, I saw I had been out for almost four hours. Maybe all I needed was a little more sleep. I dragged myself out of the tub and across the bed to the phone. It was Rourke. Lydia had arrived from L.A., and they were all waiting for me in Sonia's room.

Fifteen minutes later I rapped lightly on Sonia's door and Rourke jerked it open.

"Jeez, it's about time, ya hump. You don't get paid to sleep, ya know." He was only half-kidding. He had already managed to shroud the room in cigarette smoke that was settling in gray swirls over the remnants of a tray of assorted muffins and coffee.

"Well, let's do it," I said.

Lydia Diaz, the pretty Puerto Rican agent who had played my wife during the Suarez operation, sat in a corner watching me. "Aren't you gonna say hello?" I said, moving to give her a kiss on the cheek.

She gave me a blank look; her face had gone pale. Then, leaning away from me, she barely managed an uncomfortable "Hi."

"How are you doing? How's your husband?"

"Okay. Fine." She dropped her eyes and the conversation.

Lydia had been a vital part of the Suarez undercover team. She was bright, aggressive, outgoing, and fearless; she had been ready to travel undercover to the Bolivian jungle on a plane that had a good chance of crashing and killing all the occupants. But now she was different. She didn't look like a woman who'd volunteered to fly 3,000 miles to pose as my sister. I'd heard that the inspectors had been working her over pretty good; that they'd interrogated her several times about me. Could they have forced her to take this assignment so she could work on me?

Sonia, already seated by the telephone, studied us with her ever-searching eyes. She had a thick, leather-bound address book open in front of her.

"That thing reads like a who's who of the drug world," said Rourke, hooking a tape recorder to the telephone. "I'm going to have her start calling some of her Miami contacts. We'll play it by ear, just let 'em know we're back in business."

I looked over Sonia's shoulder as she thumbed through the book. Almost every page had phone numbers written all over it—scribbled in corners, on borders, and at every angle; the area codes were from all over South America, Europe, and the United States—probably a thousand names altogether. It occurred to me that if we played her right, we could put every single one of them in jail.

Sonia telephoned several Miami-based Colombian and Cuban drug dealers to whom she had sold cocaine in the past. I listened to her telephone rap. She was calm and composed; it was as if she had been playing the traitor's game her whole life. If she was that smooth in person we had half the battle won.

"Well I've had to disappear for a while . . . You know about my little problem . . . *Si, si, con el* . . . I have a new partner now—Miguel, I don't think you know him. He's been living in Argentina . . . Well, we want to straighten our problem out with Papo before we go into business. But you know how it is, we have to earn a living . . . No, we don't have any merchandise right now, but we will have, soon . . . If you want to reach us you can call us at our place in [here she had to stop and read] . . . *Took-sone,* Arizona . . . Sure you can have the number."

Sonia was using the Tucson number because the instant we were known to be in Miami, we would be vulnerable to Mejia, to whom Miami was a second home and the U.S. power base of his organization. We could not afford to underestimate him. Before we surfaced we had to be sure he knew of our intentions and hoped he would think it was good business to allow us to live long enough to repay the debt and maybe even do business with us. But we could not afford to wait too long, for in the drug world money talks and bullshit walks. The telephone rap would work for only so long before Mejia would know that either Sonia had lost her marbles or she was working an undercover scam. We would soon have to meet in person with some drug dealer and either buy or sell drugs.

Within hours our Tucson answering service was receiving inquiries. Some of the calls were from Mejia's organization, trying to vector our location. One was from a Colombian named Mario Espinosa, who had introduced Sonia and Papo, pleading with Sonia to call him. I was sure Papo had allowed Espinosa to live only so that he might eventually lead him to Sonia.

We decided that our best bet was with a trafficker connected to the top people; someone who, after seeing our act, would spread the word that the Queen was back; someone Sonia could reasonably trust not to reveal our location to Mejia until we were sure he would be coming to negotiate and not to kill.

"Ana Tamayo," said Sonia, her eyes lighting up. "She's perfect. She's a *comisionista* [a broker who puts South American dealers together with U.S.-based buyers for a commission]. Everyone knows her; everyone respects her. She has even brokered deals for the Ochoas."

"Will she tell Papo where you are?" I asked.

"Never!" Sonia looked offended by the mention of such treachery. "She adores me; we're very close. She would do nothing to hurt me."

I wondered if she knew she was about to destroy her good friend.

It was decided. Ana Tamayo would be our first unwitting participant—Operation Hun's first victim.

"Let's call her first thing in the morning and set up a meet," said Rourke.

"Ana is a warm, nice person," said Sonia, later that evening across dinner in the hotel restaurant. "She knows Papo, but she would never betray me."

The restaurant was a dark place full of shadowy corners and alcoves. Sonia, Lydia, and I were tucked into a corner table so dark that we had to read the menu by the light of the small candle on the table. Lydia had said barely a word all evening, which made me even more edgy.

"Where does Ana think you are?" I asked.

"Everyone thinks I'm hiding from Papo."

"Will she think anything is strange when you introduce me as your partner?"

Sonia grinned. "She'll adore you. She's about 50 years old, but she thinks she's a teenager. She loves to laugh and flirt," she said, laughing at some memory. "She's a lot of fun." Her smile vanished. "Will she be arrested?"

"Probably."

Sonia made a mild protest. "But she's my friend. She's only a *comisionista*." But her eyes were hard and cold.

"In this country," I said, "that can cost you 30 years in prison." It's your choice, baby.

The look on Sonia's face reminded me of my father at my brother's funeral, five years earlier. He had abandoned us when we were kids, more than 30 years earlier. He knew he should look bereaved, but it was hard for him to fake a feeling that he'd never felt.

"It's because she's your good friend that we need her," I said. "We can trust her not to tell Mejia where we are, until we're ready."

Sonia's attention was on a five-piece Latin combo that had just taken the bandstand and was playing a salsa tune. People were rising to dance.

Lydia looked at her watch and made a show of yawning. "I'm tired," she said. "I want to call my husband before I turn in."

As I watched her walk away I suddenly got paranoid. Why was she leaving? I scanned the shadows. I knew I was being watched.

As two Latino couples rose to dance, one of the men looked at Sonia. He said something and all four turned and looked at her. Then they continued on to the dance floor.

"Do you know them?" I asked.

Sonia glanced. "No. Should I?"

"They seemed to know you."

Sonia shrugged—she was used to that kind of attention. From the looks of her address book, half the drug world must know her by sight, and we were in the American capital of that world.

"Do you know how to dance to this?" asked Sonia. I nodded. "Come on. It will do you good."

As I got to my feet, I felt the eyes watching us. Wherever we went we would be on stage, and our act had to be flawless. We could end up doing a drug deal with someone who had spent a night watching us from the dark corner of a restaurant. And being out with the Queen of Cocaine multiplied that risk tenfold.

As we danced, my thoughts were quickly replaced by the pounding rhythms of the congas, bongos, and timbales as we spun, turned, slid, and swayed together until sweat soaked our clothing and notions of treachery, the CIA, and the inspectors dissolved into another world that had nothing to do with me. The band slipped seamlessly from one number to another in a medley of salsa that, for a while, let me forget who I was.

And then it was over.

The band stopped, the lights came up, and couples moved off the floor. Reality snapped back into focus, and I was staring into the eyes of Sonia Atala. At that moment she was the most important informer in DEA and perhaps in other agencies as well. I had no idea whether anyone really wanted us to make a case, or if I was just being sent on another fool's errand. The only thing I felt certain about was that whatever I said and did with Sonia would be analyzed by a hundred suits, few of whom had any love for me. There was no room for error.

"Come on," I said, leading Sonia off the dance floor. "It's getting late."

When we reached our rooms, Sonia gave me a peck on the cheek and said, "I like you, Miguel." Then she disappeared behind her door.

At 11 A.M. the next morning, our lives were put up for grabs.

Rourke, Maria, Lydia, and I sat in smoke-filled silence as Sonia called Ana Tamayo's home in Colombia. Learning that Ana was staying in Miami, just 10 minutes from our hotel, Sonia hung up and dialed the Miami number. Ana's daughter Candy, a cocaine addict in her early twenties, answered.

"Sonia! I can't believe it's you. Everyone was worried about you. Where are you?"

Sonia hesitated, and then said, "I'm here in Miami."

"Momma's going to be so happy."

"Is she there?"

"Momma's gone. She's got some business, but we expect her back in like 10 minutes. Oh God, is she going to be excited! Where are you staying? Give me the number."

Sonia read the name of the hotel—*"Cher-a-tone Reeber House"*— and phone number off a brochure. When she hung up, no one said anything. Rourke was watching me.

"Does she know Papo?" I asked. Maria translated for Rourke.

"Probably." Sonia shrugged.

"And she knows about your problem with him?"

"Of course."

"Is there a chance she'll tell someone?" I was wondering how Sonia could be so untroubled.

"I don't think so. When Ana calls I'll tell her to make sure."

I could think of nothing else to say. The Atala-Levine Cocaine Corporation was about to have its trial run. After a few moments Sonia got up and turned the television on to one of the Spanish language networks. I stared at it for a few minutes before realizing it was a *telenovela* made in Buenos Aires, and that Sonia was watching me watch it.

"You recognize anything?" she said, grinning mischievously, and I wondered just how much she really knew about me.

"Yes, everything."

"You miss it, Miguel?"

"Right now, very much."

Two hours, and no call from Ana. Suddenly, there was a loud rapping on the door. Rourke, Lydia, and I drew our guns, and Maria ducked into the bathroom. Sonia sat on the bed, amused.

*"Quien?"* I yelled.

"People on your side, Levine . . . good guys," said a voice in Spanish, with a chuckle.

Two Miami DEA agents entered the room. One was Avelino Fernandez, a veteran street agent and one of the top undercovers in the agency; the other guy I didn't know. I shook Avelino's hand warmly, and quickly brought them up to date.

"I think we should watch the front of the hotel," said Avelino. "If they think she's here, they'll sit outside waiting for her to show."

"Great," I said.

"We'll call you if we see something." Avelino left us a portable radio so we could communicate with him.

Two more hours, and still no call from Ana. Rourke grabbed the TV remote, and we were watching a barrage of daytime programming—*Wheel of Fortune, Days of Our Lives, The Newlywed Game, Let's Make a Deal.* The room gradually filled with room service trays and empty coffee cups. A dense fog of cigarette smoke shrouded us and began eating its way into our skin. I prayed that whoever had been assigned to follow me was living through something similar.

Sonia was calling our Tucson answering service every half hour. They reported only calls from Spanish-speaking people who would not leave messages.

Finally, just as Monty Hall was making a deal with a woman dressed in a banana suit who was jumping up and down and screaming, "Monty, I love you," Avelino's voice crackled over the portable. "Miami unit to hotel."

"Go ahead, this is hotel."

"There are people watching the hotel. Two cars, right out front. Three Hispanic males in one, and two in the other . . . rental cars. The only thing I can tell you is that they're not the good guys." He described the cars and the people. We had no photos of Mejia, so the only way we could know if he was out there was to have Sonia go out and look—and we weren't about to do that.

"This is a tough place for us to sit," said Avelino. "If we stay out here too long we're going to burn them. I suggest we move into the lobby in case you need close support."

"I agree," I said.

"Okay. If you need us, just have the hotel operator page Mr. Fernandez."

"Ten-four."

I was revved up; my heart was pounding. Something was about to happen—everyone in the room was energized. But we couldn't be prepared for what went down.

Ten electric minutes later, the phone rang. Sonia picked it up, listened for a moment, and said, "Somebody speaking English."

I motioned for Lydia to grab it.

"Yes," Lydia answered. Her face lit with surprise. "This is Lydia Diaz."

I was stunned. This was Sonia's undercover room. Who the hell had the nerve to call here looking for Lydia and use her real name?

"Yes . . . Yes . . ." Lydia's olive skin went sickly pale before my eyes. She grabbed a pencil and paper. "Go ahead." As she took the information, her hand trembling, I got sick. She was writing down Inspector Quasimoto's name and number.

"Okay," said Lydia, "I got the message." She hung up and looked directly at me for the first time. "That was Miami DEA. They said I have to call Internal Security immediately."

"I cannot fucking believe this!" I looked at Rourke, who shook his head and turned away. "These guys want me dead!"

The obvious surveillance, this phone call—now I understood their game. They wanted my nerves as jangled as possible. If I had to do an undercover meet right then, I'd blow the case and maybe my life. Then they could put my obituary up over their desks like a trophy. (An inspector in New York had allegedly done this when an agent he was investigating committed suicide.)

I fought the urge to crash through the door and start running and screaming until someone put me in a nice, warm, padded place. I noticed Sonia observing me closely. She didn't seem surprised by what had happened. Feeling dizzy, I told Lydia to call Quasimoto.

"Mike," she replied, her face pale, her hands shaking, "they're trying to use me to get you. They've already interrogated me three times.

They tried to get me to change my statement about how much money you gave me. They wanted me to say it was possible you gave me less. I don't want to talk to these people anymore. My husband Johnny (name changed) said next time they've got to talk to our lawyers."

For an undercover who daily lays his life on the line enforcing the law, to accept that his own government would break those laws to hurt him is devastating.

"Lydia, you'll be doing me a favor if you call them." I knew that if she didn't call they'd find a way to blame it on me. "I'd like to know what they're up to. Besides, if you don't, they'll find about 15 violations of the Manual you committed by not calling as ordered."

This got Lydia. Her hands were trembling so much that she had to try three times before she dialed the correct number. I felt my heart hammering as she asked for Quasimoto.

"You ordered me to call?" Lydia spoke into the phone. She listened, and then said, "Well, what's it about? . . . I thought that was over with a long time ago." Listening, she grabbed a pen and scribbled down an address I knew well—Internal Security headquarters in Miami.

Lydia hung up. She was as pale and shaken as I was. "They want me to report to their headquarters for more questioning."

"What's it about?" I asked.

"When I asked him, he said, 'The same thing as before.'" Lydia was suddenly on her feet. "Look, I'm sorry. I'm going home."

"Lydia, if you leave, they're gonna try to blame that on me, too."

"I'm sorry, Mike. I'm out of here. They're going to have to go through our attorney."

Rourke was watching, speechless, as Operation Hun crashed before takeoff. "I'm sorry, Jack," I said. "There's no way I can do any undercover work under these conditions. You can see that."

Rourke shrugged. "You gotta do what you gotta do. By the way, what are you going to do?"

"What am I going to do? I'm getting the first fucking flight out of here. There are bad guys watching the hotel, inspectors watching me—I can't even think straight."

Moments later I was in my room grabbing clothes from hangers and drawers and throwing them into my bags, then pacing the floor like a maniac. I was under attack—there had to be a way I could fight back. I tried to think rationally about my next course of action, and decided to call my headquarters supervisor, Tommy Dolittle.

"I'll call Dick Johnson [Deputy Chief Inspector]," said Dolittle after I had given him a rambling account of what had just happened. "You sit tight and I'll call you back." I thought I could hear a smile.

I continued pacing the floor for the next hour, pausing from time to time to bang my head on the wall. When the phone rang, I snatched it off the hook before the first ring was finished. It was Rourke calling to say he was shutting down the operation, and that the men watching the hotel had disappeared. "At least the Miami guys are gonna stay with us to the airport," he said.

If the inspectors' goal was to screw me up so badly that I forgot about my safety, they had succeeded.

About 20 floor-pacing minutes later, the phone rang again. This time it was Dolittle. "Johnson said that Quasimoto is investigating a matter that has nothing to do with you."

"Nothing to do with me?" I repeated dumbly.

"His exact words were 'a matter unrelated to Levine's,'" said Dolittle impatiently. "I take that to mean nothing to do with you."

"But when Lydia asked him, he said it was 'the same matter as before!'"

"Hey, what do you want me to tell you?" snapped Dolittle. "Johnson's the man's boss, and he said it was unrelated."

I sat down on the edge of my bed, feeling totally defeated. "Okay. Thanks," I said. "I'll see you in headquarters."

Dolittle had already hung up.

Within an hour, what had been the Operation Hun team had gathered at the airport. I had decided to fly into National Airport in D.C. instead of accompanying Rourke, Maria, and Sonia to Dulles. I felt the walls closing in on me, and I had a terrible need to be alone.

"You are in trouble?" asked Sonia.

We were alone on plastic airport seats. Rourke, Maria, and Lydia were busily telephoning whomever to reconnect with the real world.

"Yes," I said.

"Does this mean you will no longer work with me?"

"Yes," I said.

Sonia smiled ironically and shook her head. "I don't understand your government," she said with neither regret nor sorrow. It was a simple statement of fact; probably the only candid expression of her feelings I'd heard since I met her.

"Neither do I," I said.

An hour later I was alone in the crowded airport terminal. I was sure

I had plenty of company, but this time I didn't want to spot the tail. I might do something I'd regret, and that would be just what they wanted to happen. They knew—unless they got someone like Lydia to lie—their investigation of me was going nowhere, so they were trying to make me crack. I had to hold myself together.

An hour before my flight I went to the check-in counter. I was armed and needed clearance forms to carry my gun on board.

The clerk looked at my identification just a moment too long. "I don't have the forms out here," she said, and she disappeared through a door with my credentials. I'd gone through the routine so many times that I knew it by heart. This was not usual procedure. In a couple of minutes she returned with my credentials and the multicopy form. She was nervous.

She was watching me as I filled out the form. When I was finished, she asked me if I wanted to check my bag.

I had one overnighter and an attache case. I never checked the bag. "No, thanks. I'll carry it on board."

"I'm sorry," she said quickly, "we're booked and the Captain's requested that everything bigger than hand luggage be checked."

Alarms went off in my head. They wanted a free no-warrant peek in my bag. "I was just thinking, miss. There's still an hour left before my flight—maybe I should check my bag just before I go on board. I don't want it to get lost."

"I'm sorry sir, it's our regulations," she said, and she reached through the space beside her counter and snatched my bag. "Don't worry, you've got a direct flight. I'll make sure it gets there." Click, clack, snap, pop—I had a claim ticket in hand, my bag was on a conveyor belt, and I was watching it disappear behind a curtain.

I knew how easy it was for bureaucrats with badges to get bureaucrats in uniforms to do special things, like leaving a suitcase unwatched on an airport tarmac or in some out-of-the-way room where it can be quickly searched. If nothing is found, no one is wiser. If something incriminating is found, the facts can always be adjusted to fit the circumstances. The ends always justified the means for those in power. And to get an "out-of-control" agent like me, any means seemed to be okay.

My flight landed at National Airport at 8 P.M. At 9:30, I was still standing by the baggage carousel, watching a crate of Florida oranges going around and around.

My suitcase never arrived.

# 12

# The Drug War Machine

## 1

On Sunday, February 7, Eastern Airlines finally delivered my bag to my furnished room in the Virginia suburbs of Washington, D.C. Inside, my clothing was in jumbled and knotted balls; some of it was damp and soiled. Not only had the bag been rifled but it had been done outdoors, probably right on the tarmac. I remembered at least one tropical downpour while we were at the Miami airport on Friday.

Months earlier, when I had first suspected that the inspectors were trying to coerce agents into making statements that would incriminate me, I had contacted the Federal Criminal Investigators Association for support. I was a member of the union, and was supposedly eligible for legal assistance for all job-related matters.

"There's really not much we can do until they fire you or take some legal action against you," said a representative of the firm that handled the union's legal work. He said he could make a few unofficial phone calls for me and perhaps write a letter of inquiry. But if I wanted a full-fledged legal counterattack charging DEA with harassment, negligence, and unlawfully endangering my life, and suing for damages, I would have to hire the law firm privately and pay for it myself.

I then consulted with two attorneys with big reputations in defending government employees against their own agencies—an expanding and lucrative specialty. Each of them assured me that I had a great case. Each of them wanted a $25,000 retainer.

"I've got a four-man office," said one. "You can bet the government will put a dozen attorneys against me. I couldn't do it for less."

In 1982, $25,000 might as well have been $25 million to me. The only asset I owned outright was my motorcycle. But I had to strike back. I had a couple of weapons left.

On Monday morning at 5 A.M., I raced my motorcycle to work along the slippery black pavement of Virginia's Route 50, trying to gather my scrambled thoughts and shake myself out of depression. Even the shock of the icy predawn air had no effect on me.

By 5:30 I had parked the motorcycle in the headquarters underground parking garage and sealed myself off in my sterile little office.

There on my desk were my weapons: an IBM Selectric typewriter and the Manual—the suits' version of the Bible. In the inspectors' heated pursuit of me, they had not only stomped all over my constitutional rights, they had also violated some of their own regulations. Now I was going to fight them with those same regulations.

The inspectors had been taking potshots at me for months; now I was going to unload on them. I figured I had nothing left to lose. Whatever I wrote had to pass through the hands of at least one fair-minded person in authority; at least one person who would see that not only were these people violating my rights and exposing me to inordinate danger, but they were turning the entire war on drugs into a sham.

I turned to the Manual—three huge books, totaling some 1,300 pages: the DEA Personnel Manual, the DEA Administrative Manual, and the DEA Agents Manual. These books contained the rules and regulations governing virtually everything a DEA enforcement agent did during every moment of his career, both on and off duty. What I had to do was find the specific rules and regulations the inspectors had violated when they were trying to crucify me. It was not going to be an easy job.

I was a typical agent in that I hated and feared bureaucratic manuals. I had always counted on some suit consulting the Manual to tell me what I could or could not do; and that had always been fine with me. It left me free to concentrate on the street.

Whenever there was a shooting, an injury, or an ugly incident aris-
ing from enforcement of the drug laws, the suits would embark on an
orgy of Manual consultation to help them fix the blame on whichever
street agent or group supervisor had sinned. If there was a culprit to
be named, some Manual regulation would unerringly lead to that
street agent's or group supervisor's discovery. The sinner was never a
suit.

A collateral—and frequent—use of the Manual was as a terror tool
to keep street agents in line. Its rules and regulations made all street
agents vulnerable to termination at the whim of the suits. To enforce
narcotics laws and not violate some of the morass of interlocking rules
and regulations on an almost daily basis was an impossibility. When
the suits "throw the Manual" at a street agent, it means they are after
his job, and there's usually not much the agent can do about it.

Thus, for a street agent to use the Manual against the suits bor-
dered on lunacy. However, I saw that as my only possible route. So I
pored over the bureaucratic mumbo jumbo for hours—through index-
es and appendixes that referred to manual supplements and administrative memorandums that referred to notandums, written opinions,
and decisions of the DEA and other government agencies—searching
for some category that would cover my rather unique position. I eventually narrowed my choices to misconduct, misuse of office, and about
a half-dozen other possible violations. But was I making an oral grievance, an informal grievance, a formal grievance, or something else? I
knew that if I chose the wrong format or wording, my grievance would
be rejected without a read—"agent's complaint does not conform with
manual requirements"—and I would have to start all over again.

By 9 A.M. I could hear the clacking of typewriters and teletypes and
the gurgling of telephones outside my door, and the machinery outside my window had begun vibrating my office. The Drug War
Machine had sputtered into action for the day, and I had not written
a thing.

But then something clicked. I felt my insides swell, and my fingers
began stabbing at typewriter keys as if operating on their own.
Addressed to Tommy Dolittle, my supervisor, the final heading was
"Informal/Formal Grievance (Additional Act and/or Acts Perpetrated
by Internal Security with the Intent to Harass, Intimidate, and to
Continue Its Campaign Aimed at Ruining My Career, Health, and
Reputation." In the six-page report, I fired all my guns. I detailed my
undercover work on the Suarez case, the suits' attempts to destroy

that case, the mysterious release of Gasser and Gutierrez, the drug dealers named in the Suarez case starting the Bolivian revolution with the help of our CIA, and my letter to *Newsweek*. I included the contracts on my life, my Buenos Aires home being ransacked, the inspectors tearing up my life with an investigation that had far exceeded the 30-day limitation prescribed in the DEA Personnel Manual, Inspector Quasimoto's call to the Miami undercover room, and my rifled luggage. Finally, I accused the inspectors of coercing agents into changing their testimony in an effort to incriminate me, and stated that I had recorded my conversations with the inspectors as proof.

I ended the memo this way:

> I further request that the Administrator be made aware of this entire matter. I feel that grievous harm has been, and is being done me by these men's actions and that the Drug Enforcement Administration's negligence is permitting this to continue.
>
> . . . Is this how the Drug Enforcement Administration repays hard work and sacrifice?

When I finished I was soggy with perspiration, and as drained as if I'd just run a marathon. I reread the memo, cringing at the emotion that showed through, at the errors in bureaucratese, and at passages that now sounded almost hysterical. But I was through being cool and professional. I was fighting back.

"If you gotta fight a big guy," my streetwise father used to say, "no matter how bad he whips you, you make sure you hurt him somewhere—his eye, his leg, his knee, his big toe. While he gets his dinner, you get your fucking breakfast. Nobody likes to get hurt; nobody messes with a guy who always gets his breakfast."

I quickly gathered the roughly typed pages and stapled them together. I had to put them in Dolittle's hands fast, or I might change my mind. If I did that, something inside me would burn out and I would never have the nerve to do it again. I was throwing down the gauntlet, challenging the big guys who had been beating me up every day. It was time for my breakfast.

I stepped out of my office into the secretaries' area, and the silence was eerie. Through the window I could see snow drifting and swirling in the darkness. It was 7:30 P.M.—I had spent over 13 hours in the office without speaking to anyone. (I also failed to do my cables.)

I crossed to Dolittle's office and tried his door. It was locked. I started to shove the memo underneath the door when I saw I had forgotten to date it.

I thought, God's giving you a second chance. Remember what happened with the letter to *Newsweek*? Tear this thing up and forget about it. If the inspectors get a hold of this, you're really done for!

Huh, you think they're going to get tougher with you after they read this? You think they're holding something back? Jerk! If they could hurt you any worse they'd already be doing it.

I found a pen on someone's desk and scribbled the next day's date on the first page. I shoved the memo under Dolittle's door.

That night I had my first restful sleep in a long time.

## 2

"Come in and close the door," said Dolittle, staring up at me from behind his desk with his cold bureaucratic eyes. It was 10 A.M. Tuesday. I closed the door and sat down.

"You wanted to see me?" I said.

"First, I wanted to advise you that I've forwarded your memo upstairs," Dolittle drawled.

"Thank you."

"The reason I called you in here," he said, opening a green, hardbound, government notebook, "is to tell you that I'm unhappy with your work performance." He made a notation in his book. I waited for him to stop writing.

"I've only been back a month and . . ."

"Your head just doesn't seem to be in what you're doing. Yesterday, for example, you didn't even bother checking cable traffic."

I recognized what Dolittle was doing. He was giving me "official notice of unsatisfactory work performance"—the first step in a series of procedures detailed in the Manual that would lead to me being fired.

"I'm doing the best I can. I've been under investigation for over a year. I just started this undercover assignment and . . ." I stopped. Dolittle wasn't listening. He was making notations in his book.

After a few moments, Dolittle looked up and said, "You'll be getting a memo about this conference. You've been advised."

When I got back to my office, I closed the door behind me and leaned my face against its cool metal. I could hear the Drug War Machine and feel the vibrations in my cheek. I felt like I had been caught in its gears and was being ground into hamburger. I had made some of the biggest drug cases in the agency and was about to be fired for substandard performance as a narcotics agent.

I stayed shut up in my office, unable to compose my thoughts. I was waiting for something to happen—the phone to ring, a knock on the door—I didn't know what. I wondered how long I would be allowed to stay closed up in my office before people in white uniforms shot me full of tranquilizer and led me drooling to a rubber room in an old mansion, to be forgotten by everyone except my kids.

My kids! I had been so caught up in my life that I'd forgotten theirs. I could always get another job, but I couldn't replace my kids. I dialed New York. Niki answered the phone.

"How are you doing baby?" I asked.

"Fine," she said curtly.

"Is there anything you need, honey? I know I haven't spoken to you in a couple of days. Is everything okay?"

"Everything's just wonderful!" she snapped.

"What's wrong, Niki?"

"There's nothing wrong!" she said, her voice rising in anger. "I've got to go."

"Come on baby, what's wrong?"

"I already told you—there's nothing wrong. Everything's great!"

"Then why are you raising your voice at me?"

"Because you keep asking me dumb questions! You're driving me crazy!"

The unthinkable—drugs—flashed through my mind. No! Not my kid. I pushed the thought from my head and changed the subject.

"Look, I miss you a lot, honey. I don't want to fight with my only little girl on the phone."

She was quiet. "I miss you too, daddy," she said. I was suddenly talking to my sweet little girl again.

"How about if I come up this weekend and we do something?"

"Nah—not this weekend, daddy, I'm gonna be busy." The little girl's voice was gone. "I've got to go."

I wanted to ask her where she was going and what she was doing, but that would only drive her into a phone-slamming rage. "Sure, honey," I said. "Is Keith there?"

Now she was impatient. "Keith went to karate."

"Okay, baby. Just tell him I called."

"Sure," she said and the phone clicked.

"Hello? Niki?"

The phone clicked again and I was listening to the dial tone.

I spent the rest of the day in my office with the door closed. I spoke to no one. When I heard footsteps outside my door, I would sit upright expecting someone to come in. Instead, papers were slipped under the door—cables, manual addendums, interoffice memos, and government envelopes—the goop on which the Drug War Machine ran.

I was being left alone.

The pile by my door grew until there was more paper than I'd seen in any three days prior. That's the way it was done. People had been assigned to document my "poor" performance, and they were doing it quantitatively as well as qualitatively:

> Observations of Special Agent Michael Levine, February 9, 1982: By physical count S/A Levine was given 12 cables, 13 reports of investigation, and 5 interoffice memos, all of which required administrative action. Levine took no administrative action whatsoever and remained in his office for the rest of the day with his door closed. It should be noted that this lack of performance came after Acting Regional Director Tommy S. Dolittle advised him of his prior substandard performance. S/A Levine's behavior may be a result of too many years of undercover work. Observations will continue.

If I tried to take "appropriate administrative action," I would fail no matter what I did. The suits would find a violation in anything I did. When the suits wanted to "do" someone, they had all the cards, and those who set the dirty work in motion were always shielded behind three or four layers of bureaucracy.

When the time came to confront me with my "unsatisfactory" performance—if the inspectors were unable to get me indicted—Dolittle would hand me a report the size of a Sears catalog that would prove beyond doubt that I was unfit to continue as a DEA agent, and I would be fired.

I was well acquainted with the suits' methods. In 1975, when I was Acting Group Supervisor of a unit of street agents in New York City, an agent fresh out of the academy was assigned to me. My suit supervisor called me just before his arrival: "Headquarters wants us to get rid of this guy."

"Why?" I asked.

"The academy said he's dead wood—one of those dumb Democrats that slipped through." (*Democrat* was the code word for *black*.)

"Well, how come they passed him on to New York?"

"I don't know," said my boss. "I'm just passing on the message."

"Hey, if he's dead wood, his performance will speak for itself," I said. "But if he's not, I won't hurt the guy."

"Like I said," continued my supervisor, "I'm just passing on the message."

The new agent, a young black guy hired from a local New Jersey police department, turned out to be an exceptional agent, and after six months I rated him outstanding. Not long after, I was removed from my position, and was not promoted again until I threatened to sue.

On Wednesday, February 10, I was in my office before dawn after another sleepless night mulling possible defenses. I allowed myself the hope that when Administrator Mullen saw my memo and realized what the destruction of the Bolivian cases had done to the South American drug war, he would at least investigate the matter. He had to do *something*, I thought.

I needed sleep badly. Tony had advised me to get a pair of dark glasses and to practice sleeping sitting up. "Just in case some suit with a hard-on for you sticks his head in your office while you're catching some z's." So I slipped on a pair of sunglasses with heavy black side-panels used as eye protection at the pistol range. I laid the DEA Agents Manual open on the desk before me, propped my head on my hands, and fell into a deep sleep.

A loud knocking on my door awoke me. I was sprawled across the desk, the sunglasses bent and twisted beneath me.

"Yes," I croaked, bolting upright, wondering how long they'd been knocking. "Come in." I struggled to my feet in time to see a memo slipped under the door. They wanted to make sure I saw this one.

The memo was from Administrator Mullen himself. He had seen my memorandum and was taking swift action. Addressing himself to "All DEA Employees, Worldwide," the Administrator said that he had just been made aware that "certain DEA employees" were record-ing their conversations with other DEA employees. "This will no longer be tolerated," said the Administrator. Any agent found surrep-titiously recording a conversation with another agent would be fired.

The phone rang. Tommy Dolittle wanted to see me immediately.

# 13

# A Shooting
# in Colombia

The Arabs have a saying: Any day is a good day to die. But on the quiet tropical evening of February 9 in Cartagena, Colombia, death was the farthest thing from the minds of two DEA agents on assignment in the beautiful resort town. But as Charlie Martinez and Kelly McCullough were about to learn, the saying was one that DEA street agents should keep in mind at all times.

At 11:50 P.M., both agents were reading in their room in the Don Pas Hotel when there was a loud banging on the door. Neither man had a gun—an unfortunate error they would soon regret. The suits who had sent them on the assignment had not instructed them whether they could carry firearms in Colombia and the two agents, who were primarily pilots, assumed that they could not.

"*Quien?*" asked Martinez, a native Spanish speaker.

"Colombian National Police," answered a gruff voice.

The agents were suspicious. Earlier in the day—following orders from the suits at DEA's Bogota headquarters—they had made inquiries at the hotel concerning the whereabouts of a fugitive Miami-based cocaine trafficker named René Benitez. Thus, if these really were police outside their door, they had to know they were dealing with DEA agents. They could have just called and asked the agents to come to police headquarters. Why would they be banging on the door in the middle of the night?

Martinez telephoned the front desk, while McCullough listened to furtive whisperings on the other side of the door. A clerk told Martinez that the visitors were indeed Colombian National Police. Martinez still wasn't convinced. The clerk sounded tense, and Martinez knew he was in a country where drug traffickers had more power and protection than any DEA agent. He asked the clerk to call the local police, but the clerk refused, saying hotel security was being sent to the room.

Now the agents knew something was wrong.

They looked at each other, and the same thought occurred to both—without guns they didn't have a chance. They had no DEA backup, nor were they furnished instructions about what to do in emergency situations.

After a 15-minute standoff, a man later identified in DEA files as Ivan Duarte slipped a police identification card beneath the door and warned that if the door wasn't opened soon, the men outside were going to break it down. It was later revealed that Duarte was an ex-Colombian National Police officer. Thus, the identification might have been legitimate, but nothing else about the visit was.

Unarmed and unable to call for help, the agents reluctantly opened the door, and Duarte, a hefty, sweating Colombian, stormed into the room followed by five men. The agents knew immediately that these were no policemen. Duarte began interrogating Martinez in Spanish about their assignment in Cartagena. His main interest was why they had made inquiries about Benitez.

After a few minutes, a dark, angry Latino entered the room waving a gun. He jammed it into the side of Martinez's head. "I'm René Benitez."

Martinez and McCullough were led from the hotel at gunpoint and forced into a small Toyota parked out front. Martinez was wedged in front between Benitez and the driver, and McCullough in back between Duarte and another man. The agents noticed that they were being followed by a second car with five or six men in it.

For the next hour they were driven through the dark streets of Cartagena as their kidnapers made sure they were not being followed. Finally, the cars headed away from the city into a remote area. After traveling for about 20 minutes over an unpaved jungle track, the two cars halted in a clearing.

Except for the chittering of insects, the night was still. Then a thunderclap and a scream tore through the dark. Benitez had shot Martinez in the thigh.

Charlie writhed in pain. "Don't worry about it," snarled Benitez. "DEA shot me in the leg and I'm okay."

Taking advantage of the distraction, McCullough dove headlong past his captors and started running, with Duarte and an unknown number of men chasing him.

Benitez backed out of the car, aimed, and fired at Martinez again, hitting him in the right shoulder. Now Benitez aimed at Martinez's head and pulled the trigger, but the gun misfired. Martinez leaped for Benitez, and the two began to struggle for the gun.

In the meantime, Duarte had opened fire on McCullough. The first bullet grazed his left knee; the second hit him in the buttocks and knocked him off his feet. As McCullough lay wounded on the ground, Duarte stood over him, aimed, and fired into his neck. He left McCullough for dead to join the pursuit of the now-fleeing Martinez.

The three slugs had not killed McCullough. Semiconscious, he heard Martinez scream and more shots fired. Then it was quiet. McCullough struggled to his feet and stumbled in the direction of the last signs of people—a church steeple he remembered passing. He felt blood pouring from him. Pain tore through his body, but he couldn't stop. Charlie might still be alive out there in the dark; he had to get help.

At 3:30 A.M. Father Guillermo Grisales, priest of the parish of Santa Catalina de Alejandria, on the outskirts of Cartagena, was awakened by his mother. "Someone is outside calling," she said excitedly.

Father Grisales got quickly out of bed and rushed to the front door. There he saw the bleeding McCullough, hunched over and gasping for breath. Luckily Father Grisales spoke a little English and had a car.

Within minutes the priest was driving McCullough to the local police station. When a doctor examined McCullough's wounds, the priest was incredulous. The bullet to his neck had passed through his chest and exited below his arm. It seemed miraculous that the young American was alive.

Suddenly there was a skirmish. The American fought to get to his feet. Unbelievably, the young man was refusing treatment and was demanding to be taken back to where he had left his companion. He would let no one touch him until his friend was found.

The doctor, the policeman, and the priest loaded McCullough back into the priest's car. After a long drive, they found the clearing where the shooting had occurred. Once again Father Grisales was astounded. The desperately wounded American, who had walked five kilometers to get help, was now calling out his friend's name and struggling to get out of the car to search for him.

McCullough, the priest, and the doctor searched for Martinez for more than an hour before giving up. The policeman, in mortal fear of the Colombian Mafia, would not move, telling the priest, "This smells like Mafia. Maybe it is an ambush to kill policemen." McCullough continued to refuse treatment until hours later, when he was told that Charlie too had survived and was already in the hospital.

Father Grisales had truly been witness to a miracle. In a letter to the U.S. Ambassador to Colombia, he wrote, "How could a man so beaten and wounded who left so much blood on the upholstery of my little car, managed to have even reached my house? What formidable training men like these must receive in the United States. It amazed both me and the doctor. . . . I would like this letter to be forwarded to Kelly's great mother for having raised with such feeling, such an incredible son."

I opened my office door to a South American Investigations section of DEA that was like a swarming ants' nest. The drab hallways echoed with the sound of typewriters clacking away insanely; phones rang, intercoms buzzed, and secretaries raced back and forth carrying cables; suits gathered in small whispering groups or hurried around with file folders. I had never seen that many people at work so early.

I stepped out into the secretaries' area. It seemed that all eyes were upon me as I crossed to Dolittle's door. I felt a sinking sensation. Today's the day. I've been indicted and now they're going to arrest me.

"I'm givin' you the McCullough-Martinez shooting," snapped an angry Dolittle before I could say a word. He had an outraged expression on his face.

"What shooting?" I sputtered, still looking over my shoulder for approaching inspectors.

"You don't know what happened?"

I tried to calm my racing heart as Dolittle filled me in on the shootings. "I'm sendin' you down to Colombia as the Latin American Section's representative in the hunt for Benitez. That appeal to you?"

The suits couldn't make up their minds whether to fire me, jail me, or use me like a disposable tool. "Just tell me when," I said.

"I'm catching the next flight down there. You have a visa for Colombia?"

"No."

"Get one right away. You don't have much time. And you better pack a bag with enough stuff for a coupla weeks, maybe more. You're gonna stay until the job's done."

"That's fine with me," I said. "If you all happen to forget about me and just leave me there for good, that's fine too." Dolittle smiled at me for the first time since I'd met him.

"Just get yourself squared away and I'll get back to you." His phone buzzed. He picked it up and turned his back on me. I was dismissed.

When I headed for the door, I noticed a packed suitcase near the wall. Dolittle didn't even speak Spanish—why was he rushing off to Colombia like a fireman? Why wasn't he rushing me down there while the trail was hot, memories fresh, and witnesses still available?

I later learned that the reason for Dolittle's rush to get to Colombia was to find out how two DEA agents could have been sent into such a hazardous situation unarmed and with no backup. His investigation resulted in a report absolving the top suits in Colombia of all blame, in which he would state—contrary to Charlie Martinez's statement—that "the fact that [the agents] were unarmed may have actually worked to [their] advantage." Once again the incompetence and boobery of DEA's leadership, which would soon lead to other agents being tortured and killed, was covered up, as it has been to this day.

I wasn't about to say anything that might change Dolittle's mind. Getting out of headquarters and back to the South America that I loved was like receiving a pardon just as they were strapping me into the electric chair. And at a time when my life seemed without purpose, going after a killer like Benitez seemed like God's work.

The suits had promised the media that DEA wouldn't rest until Benitez and his men were captured. Now it was up to the street guys to prove the suits men of their words. I knew if they really did turn me loose, I'd have Benitez fast. I had a quick vision of Benitez and me in a room together with no guns—just man against man. Taking people like him out was why I'd become an agent.

By the next morning I had gotten my visa, arranged for my bills to be paid, and called my kids. I was sitting in my office with my bags packed, ready to go, when Jack Rourke called.

"Well, you ready for phase two of Operation Hun?"

"Are you kidding?" I shouted. "After what happened in Miami, didn't you get another undercover?"

"Nobody told me anything like that," said Rourke. "We just ain't goin' back to Miami. In fact, ya hump, we just rented you and Sonia a luxury house up in the foothills of Tucson. We're gonna have you set up with a whole undercover Mafia family, like the Suarez case."

"Don't even mention that," I said.

"Forget Miami," said Rourke quickly. "This time the whole thing's gonna be handled by Buck Turghid [name changed]. He's the Tucson RAC [Resident Agent in Charge]. Supposed to be a real good man. The Tucson answering service is buzzing. Everybody's hot for Sonia to get back into business."

"That's no surprise. Shit, doing an undercover coke case with the Queen of Cocaine is like fishing with dynamite. But me undercover?"

"C'mon, ya hump. Sonia's got a lotta confidence in you. She thinks you can bring it off." I saw Sonia's eyes—eyes that trusted no one.

"I'd love to help you, but I can't," I said, relieved that I had an excuse. "Dolittle just assigned me to the McCullough-Martinez thing. I'm going to Colombia."

"Nope, you ain't escapin' that easy, ya hump. I just been on the phone with half the bosses in the agency. Operation Hun is top priority. You're goin' to Tucson."

"You're telling me this is definite?" I said, my heart sinking.

"Absolutely. In fact, they want us to get started right away. Ralph Saucedo and some of the other bosses want Sonia to start reaching out for Benitez."

"What do you mean?"

"She knows him well. She did dope deals with him. She spent a lotta time with him. In fact, once you and her establish some credibility, she'll stand a better chance of findin' that piece of shit than anybody. Which reminds me. I'm gonna need you with me at her house tonight. I want her to make some UC calls." I didn't reply. "You're comin' with me, right?"

My role still reeked of a setup. I had just been reassigned to pose as the partner of a beautiful drug dealer; to live under the same roof as her with a large amount of government cocaine at our disposal. Sonia's supposed allegiance was now to the same DEA bosses who were trying to put me in jail. The odds of my coming out of this a free man had to be 100 to 1, but it was clear I had no choice. "Why not," I said.

"Great. You're gonna love Tucson."

# 14

# Tucson

*To betray you must first belong.*
—Harold Philby

## 1

Rourke parked the G-car in front of a nondescript frame house in the middle of a long block in an Arlington, Virginia neighborhood. When we knocked, Sonia, dressed in jeans and a work shirt, opened the door and without a word stepped back for us to enter. For a brief moment her eyes swept the dark street. Behind her a short, husky, good-looking guy stood waiting to be introduced.

"Miguel, my husband Pachi; Pachi . . . Miguel," said Sonia. And there I was shaking hands with another name from the Hurtado torture tape, Sonia's husband, Walter "Pachi" Atala.

Walter's appearance, like Sonia's, could not have been more deceiving. There was an innocence, almost a guilelessness about him. I could easily picture him as an erstwhile race car driver, but it was impossible to imagine him as the Undersecretary of Labor for one of the most brutal dictatorships in Bolivia's history. Sonia had told me that he was being groomed for the presidency before all the trouble started.

Sonia led Rourke and me into a small living room where her four children sat on the floor at the feet of a clean-cut, middle-aged couple dressed in jeans and sweaters with toothpaste smiles. The man smoked a pipe. "The Mormons," Sonia whispered.

"Hello," I said.

"Hello," the couple said almost in unison, looking at us curiously. Pachi took a seat at their feet, looking like one of the kids. The kids, all beautiful and dark-eyed with fair complexions, ranged from about eight to the early teens.

I noticed Walter watching me closely. As Sonia led us from the room, she and Walter exchanged apprehensive glances.

Sonia led us to the telephone in a small, cluttered bedroom. The plan was for her to call Mario Espinosa in Colombia to let him know we were still in business and what our intentions were. His reactions would give us a feel for Papo's plans for us.

"Are you okay, Miguel?" asked Sonia, as Rourke attached the recorder to the phone.

"I'm fine," I said, wondering what she knew about my troubles.

Within minutes Sonia was talking with Espinosa's family in Colombia, who said he was away and would be back in the morning. They were suspicious and pressed Sonia about her whereabouts. Sonia said she would call back in the morning.

When Sonia hung up she was troubled. She had been in contact with Espinosa over the past months, stalling him. Papo was probably pressuring Espinosa to either find Sonia or make good the debt himself. For the first time, Sonia felt Espinosa might be ducking her.

The following morning we were back at Sonia's house calling Colombia from a kitchen phone. While the rest of her family slept and Rourke chain-smoked, I listened to Sonia play cat-and-mouse with someone who was trying to find out where she was calling from. Espinosa was "traveling." No one knew when he would return.

"I'm getting a house in Tucson," said Sonia. "Tell Mario that I will call him when I'm established."

"It's odd," Sonia said when she hung up. "I'm sure he was there. He always talks to me."

"How long have you been stalling him about the debt?"

"On and off for about six or seven months."

"No wonder," I said. "This guy Papo isn't waiting anymore. You can only talk so much without doing something before you make these guys foaming-at-the-mouth crazy. Sometimes you're better off not having any contact until you're ready to do something."

"Of course, but he told me to call," Sonia nodded at Rourke.

"What's going on?" said Rourke.

I translated the conversation for him and said, "My opinion is Papo doesn't believe a fucking thing she says. He just wants revenge."

"What are you saying?" asked Sonia.

"I just translated what I told you," I said.

"What'd you just say?" asked Rourke.

"Hey cut this shit out. I can't translate every sentence. She just asked me the same thing."

"Okay, ya hump, just take it easy," said Rourke. "It doesn't matter anyway. You're gonna make believers outta them . . . in Tucson."

## 2

On Wednesday, February 24 at 8 P.M., American Airlines flight 619 skimmed into a smooth landing in Tucson. I hoped the landing was a sign of things to come. Phase two of Operation Hun—the deep cover phase—had officially begun.

In the terminal, Rourke, Maria Montez, Sonia, and I picked up a rental car and headed for the Marriott Hotel in downtown Tucson. The undercover house would not be ready for a couple of days, so the hotel would be our first base of operations.

I was thankful for the silent ride into downtown Tucson. I had never been in the desert. I expected it to be hot, but it was pleasant and cool, and all the people we'd dealt with so far were friendly. That too, I hoped, was a sign of things to come.

Before leaving headquarters, we had two weeks of meetings and conferences with various suits who stressed that the principal operational target would be Arce-Gomez, now Bolivia's Military Attache to Argentina, along with several of his aides, all of whom had worked closely with Sonia to sell huge quantities of cocaine destined for the United States. Another objective was arresting Papo Mejia and immobilizing his organization. A separate target was René Benitez.

What we were not told was that one or more of our principal targets were paid and protected CIA assets.

Since Sonia had done countless drug deals with all these people, her corroborated testimony in a federal conspiracy trial would be enough to convict them all for about 1,000 years' worth of drug trafficking felonies. But without corroboration, her testimony wouldn't convict a Bowery bum for jaywalking, let alone Bolivian government officials of drug trafficking. Thus our primary goal had to be the independent corroboration of Sonia's statements about our targets.

And what better corroboration for a jury could there possibly be than a secret film of a bunch of dopers in the middle of a drug deal, talking about their old drug deals and confirming everything Sonia had said? Once we had that, nothing would stop us. For once, *60 Minutes* might have a real drug story.

At about 10:30 P.M., Sonia, Maria, Rourke, and I were huddled in a booth in a dark corner of the hotel lounge, too keyed up to sleep. The dimly lit, thickly carpeted lounge, with red velvet drapes and black leather booths surrounding a small dance floor, was about half full. A four-piece combo was playing a slow number, and three couples swayed to the music looking like they'd fallen asleep.

"The whole house is gonna be wired for sound and video," said Rourke, still in the rumpled blue suit that he was wearing when we left Washington. "Sonia gets 'em talkin', it'll be devastating. There won't be a jury in the world who won't believe her."

"Why stop there?" I said. "Remember her address book? While we're proving the conspiracy we can also do everyone in that book."

"Don't you think I know it, ya hump."

Rourke drained the rest of his beer. He and Sonia, who was also chain-smoking, had built a smoldering mountain in the ashtray, and the smoke was getting to me.

"The setup is gonna be really important," I said. "There can't be any doubt about us, Jack, or the whole thing is shot, along with both of us."

"What are you worried about? We got you a fucking luxury house in the foothills. Turghid says it's gonna knock your eyes out. Headquarters said this is number one priority; we get anything we want."

We stopped talking when a smiling waitress appeared to clear the table. Sonia ordered a vodka, and though it was her sixth or seventh, she didn't show any effects. I ordered a diet soda. I hadn't had a good night's sleep in weeks and felt that as much as one beer might put me into a coma. Rourke and Maria were getting ready to leave.

"It's the details I'm worried about," I said, "all the little details that count. Like the dope; it's got to be the best—the purest available."

"Relax, it's being done," said Rourke.

"And all of us, right now, sitting here in this place."

"Whaddya mean?"

"I mean, this is a small town. Next week we could be doing a deal with people who are right now sitting somewhere in this joint, and they might remember seeing me and Sonia here with you . . . and you look like a traffic cop. Or that waitress that just left could be waiting on Sonia, me, and Papo next week."

Rourke looked around unhappily. "You're right. Why don't you and Sonia stay down here a while and spread a couple of bucks around. Lydia will be here tomorrow."

"Lydia's still on this?"

"Yeah."

"After what happened in Miami?"

"Evidently, headquarters wants her." Rourke shifted uncomfortably and looked at his watch—Miami and Lydia were not topics he wanted to discuss. When Sonia and Maria went to the bathroom, he said, "So why you think we haven't heard from Mejia's people?"

The answering service had been getting messages from several traffickers, including Ana Tamayo, but no calls from Mejia's people.

"I'm sure he's aware of everything we did from the time we arrived in Miami," I said, looking around the lounge. The room was getting crowded, and I was worried about too many people seeing us with Rourke.

"Then why isn't he calling?"

"Put yourself in his place. Sonia vanishes from Bolivia, and as far as anyone knows she's flat broke, right?"

"Yeah," says Rourke."

"Sonia's been selling dope all over the world without ever getting involved with any men, right?"

Rourke raised an eyebrow.

"Allegedly," I added.

"Allegedly," Rourke repeated.

"And she's part of a crew that took over Bolivia; a crew that might even be hooked up with the Agency [CIA]." I paused and watched Rourke for his reaction.

Operation Hun and the Atalas presented too many frightening question marks to me, not the least of which was their connection to the CIA. Sonia and Pachi had been too powerful in Bolivia for the Agency not to be interested. After the Argentines arrested Sonia's uncle Hugo, I had been shocked when the suits ordered me to open my files to the CIA. And now, with Operation Hun aimed at the same Bolivians, the CIA's silent presence was ominous. Their support of Nazis and drug dealers was not something they wanted public. There had to be people among our targets who could expose them. Thus, I reasoned they had to maintain an iron-fisted control of the direction of Operation Hun. There had to be CIA plants in DEA, and some of them, I was sure, were very close to this operation.

Rourke ignored the comment. He had on his best police deadpan.

So I continued: "She disappears off the face of the earth for a couple of months and then suddenly surfaces in Miami, with a new man as her partner. Then—thanks to the inspectors—she just as suddenly disappears again, only to resurface three weeks later in Tucson. Mejia would have to be nuts to jump at that kind of bait. This guy's no dope. Right now, he's sitting back waiting to see if we're for real before he makes his move."

Rourke watched the dancers silently. I wondered if my CIA comment had upset him. The combo started a lively salsa number, couples moved toward the dance floor, and Sonia and Maria returned.

"I don't know about you guys," said Maria, "but I'm tired and I want to call my husband before it gets too late."

"Yeah, I need some shut-eye, too," said Rourke. "You two hang out a while; throw a couple of sawbucks around, but don't make it too late."

After Rourke and Maria left, I called the waitress and ordered two more drinks. When she brought them, I dropped a $20 bill and told her to keep the change. She was the first of many Tucson waiters and waitresses who wouldn't forget us.

Sonia and I sat in silence listening to the music. The place was now almost full. I scanned the room, with its shadowy corners and dark alcoves. I was suddenly furious at the notion of gun-carrying men being paid by my government to work on me. They probably considered themselves working undercover. They'd have some great stories for their grandchildren. I wondered what kind of "undercover expenses" they were running up. Here I was working on drug dealers, they were working on me, and the American taxpayer was footing the whole ridiculous bill.

"Well, do you want to dance or not?" Sonia was on her feet, waiting. Suddenly I was leading Sonia toward the dance floor. Okay you bastards, I thought, you do your job—I'm going to do mine. You can sit in the shadows and play with yourselves for the rest of the night for all I care.

Sonia and I began to move with the salsa, and in a moment I was lost in the music. The combo went from one number to the next—salsa, rock, merengue, foxtrot, tango—and we kept dancing. From time to time I glimpsed Sonia's face. Her lips were set in a faint smile; her eyes, flicking and darting around the room, missed nothing. She was in total control and utterly unknowable.

We stayed on the dance floor for most of the next two hours. By then, the soothing effect the music had on me had long worn off. Finally, the lights came up and the combo began to pack up. Cocktail waitresses rushed about settling tabs, and Sonia and I were left alone for an awkward moment in the middle of the dance floor.

That's when I noticed them.

Two men in suits, with haircuts that tax collectors would have been proud of, watched us from the bar. They were so damned obvious. Didn't these bastards ever try to blend in with real people? As we walked toward our table, I saw one of them pay the bartender while the other watched us.

"Is something wrong, Miguel?"

"No. Why?"

"You have this strange look."

She has to see them, I thought. Why isn't she saying anything?

"I guess it's late," I said. It was 2 A.M. Tucson time, which meant it was 4 A.M. for our bodies.

"I'm not tired," said Sonia. "I thought we were supposed to make ourselves famous in Tucson? Maybe there's someplace else we can go to dance."

I glanced over at the bar, and the two men were gone. I was sure they hadn't gone far. Good! You bastards are really going to earn your money tonight.

"Okay, if there's someplace open, we'll go."

"Great!" said Sonia, grabbing her bag.

I left a $50 bill on the table, the kind of tip that would get Sonia and me recognized and treated like royalty (or drug dealers) wherever we went and hopefully, help impress the real drug dealers when they were our guests. And I didn't mind a bit if it got the inspectors' bureaucratic balls in an uproar.

A Chicano bellhop directed us to an after-hours club. "Just walk up West Broadway; it's the first hotel you come to," he said in Spanish. "You can't miss it; it's kind of a beat-looking place." He spoke with the singsong Mexican accent that I'd been hearing since we arrived. I found it melodic and pleasing to my ears. He looked us up and down and grinned. "You know the crowd is kind of rough, *ese*."

"Great!" I said, slipping him a $10 bill. "Sounds perfect."

"Where you folks from?"

"I'm from Argentina and she's from Bolivia."

He grinned knowingly and gave us a thumbs-up. Sonia laughed and we headed out into the cool desert night. We headed up West Broadway, Tucson's main drag, which was now dark and deserted. Maybe the two tails thought we were finished for the night, and went home.

At the first intersection, the sound of an idling engine caught my attention. The car was parked in shadows about 50 feet to our right. All I could make out were two dark forms in the front seat. Sonia acted as if she hadn't noticed a thing, and so did I.

The bellhop's description of the after-hours crowd hadn't done it justice; it wasn't "kind of rough," it was junk-yard-dog mean. At the far end of a dark, cavernous room lined with cafeteria tables and benches, six musicians dressed in sparkling cowboy outfits and huge sombreros blasted Tex-Mex border music at a dance floor packed with stomping, shouting Mexican laborers in work clothes dancing with heavily made-up women bursting out of brightly colored, sequined evening dresses. The stale beer, cheap perfume, sweat, and urine combined to form an odor so pungent that it forced my eyes wide open.

"I like this place," said Sonia, grinning and taking my arm.

"I need a drink," I said.

Our view of the room was suddenly blocked by a gargantuan body with a head to match. Murderous little eyes raked us up and down. "Ju wan somsing here?" he said, his voice comically high pitched.

"We just came to dance and have a couple of drinks," I said, slipping him a $20 bill.

The doomsday face flashed a broad white grin. *"De donde son ustedes?"*

*"Somos de Miami."*

He motioned for us to follow him. His bulk shoving aside those who didn't move quickly enough, he led us to a spot at one of the long tables near the middle of the room. He motioned to a waitress, who quickly cleared us a small space in the forest of beer bottles, pitchers, and glasses. The nearby men and women studied us with hostile curiosity. Sonia's conservative skirt and silk blouse and my best Miami Vice outfit spelled slumming gringo tourists.

As our huge host turned to leave, I stopped him. "Do gringos in suits ever come here?" I almost had to shout into his ear above the music. He looked at me curiously.

"Gringos don't come here. Why do you ask?"

"When I see gringos in suits I get nervous." I shoved another $20

179

into his hand. Another flash of white teeth, a knowing look, and he was moving away through a crowd that parted before him like the Red Sea before Moses.

Sonia was on her feet, pulling me toward a dance floor packed as tight as a sardine can. I was suddenly squeezed between the beer-covered table and a short, wide woman in a glow-in-the-dark red dress. The band was playing a bouncy Tex-Mex song in Spanish about a man who wished he could find a woman as loyal as his dog. Sonia got right into the spirit, bouncing to the music, unmindful of the horde of slam-dancers around us.

I attempted an up-and-down motion. In the middle of an up, Red Dress jolted me in the ribs with her shoulder and I sprawled headlong over a tabletop, knocking beer bottles and glasses to the floor. One of the bottles exploded. I looked around. No one had noticed. Red Dress was slamming away in another direction and Sonia, her back toward me, was bouncing up a storm.

I righted myself back into my narrow slot on the dance floor and stood there dazed, my right sleeve soaked with beer, trying to gauge my territorial limitations. Red Dress came out of nowhere and rocked me again, but I managed to stay upright. As long as I kept both feet planted I was fine, although this limited my motion to a frightened little jig. I decided to expand my territory a little.

I made my move when Red Dress slammed off in the other direction. Timing my move to hers, I slammed my entire weight against her. A row of people toppled away from me like dominos. There were some grunts and a curse, but mostly everyone laughed. Red Dress didn't even glance back. This was a dance floor that could have been used as an NFL training camp.

Sonia, laughing, said "These people are such fun, aren't they, Miguel?"

"Great!" I said, nodding and smiling with as much enthusiasm as I could muster. Sonia resumed her happy bounce and I my up-and-down motion, keeping a wary eye on Red Dress. It was then that I noticed the huge host blocking the entrance and almost obscuring two gringos in suits.

It was the two guys from the Marriott.

This was not coincidence—they had to be following me. I started off the dance floor, intending to shove my badge and gun in their faces and make them identify themselves. If they were inspectors or CIA, I would be on the next plane for Washington. But I quickly stopped myself. If I showed my badge, everyone in the place would know I was the law. There had to be 200 people there. I'd blow our cover for good.

Suddenly it was all clear—they wanted me to blow the case. I squeezed back onto the dance floor and watched the host do his stuff. Sonia, still bouncing, hadn't noticed a thing.

The bouncer was exchanging heated words with the two gringos. He pushed his finger into the chest of the bigger guy, shoving him back toward the doorway. Even across the room I could see the tall man flush the color of a dying ember.

Cops and agents hate to be treated less than reverently in public; in fact, it drives them wild. And the bouncer was treating these guys with pure contempt. If they were "on the job" their badges and guns would be out and the bouncer would disappear into a back room where his head would be reshaped by their pistol butts. Instead, the two turned and meekly left.

The bouncer turned, his eyes seeking me out in the gloom. I waved, acknowledging that I owed him; the service was worth $50. I gave it to him on the way out and we were buddies for life.

Shortly, I was back in my room nursing bruised ribs and a swollen elbow. This undercover work was some dangerous shit.

In the morning Rourke called. "I'm taking the car. I gotta go over to the Tucson office. Turghid wants to go over some things with me."

"How long you gonna be?" I asked, sensing his discomfort. The fact that he had not asked me to come along hung between us.

"I, uh, I'm not sure . . . probably a couple hours."

"And what about Sonia and Maria?" I said, feeling the paranoia but unable to bring myself to say anything.

Turghid must have made a point of telling Rourke not to bring me. Normal procedure was that the undercover be included in all planning sessions and discussions affecting the operation. I had never met the man, so I assumed any animosity he felt toward me was the result of the inspectors' investigation. I'd already suffered a deep wound; every additional rejection was like rubbing salt in it, making my position a little bit more uncomfortable than it already was.

"I, uh, Sonia's gonna be on the phone trying to get a lead on Benitez."

"Then I'm gonna take off for a couple of hours and find a gym."

"Good idea. Why don't you do that."

Twenty minutes later I had my workout clothes jammed into a hotel laundry bag and I was in front of the hotel hailing a taxi. Something inside me was screaming for me to escape. But escape what? My life? Soon I was signing in at a gym that accepted my Holiday Spa membership from Washington, and five minutes later I was on the gym floor ready to beat whatever was shrieking inside me into submission.

The gym, all chrome, carpet, and mirrors, was crowded with mostly young people in designer workout gear. Soft rock music came over hidden speakers. The high-tech workout machines in the main room were all occupied. I decided to begin with a couple of sets of pushups and situps, and looked around the room for a clear patch of floor. The only one available was next to three old guys in sweats who were just standing and gabbing.

As I began my pushups, they gave me just enough room to work out at their feet. I was going to say something, but then I figured the last thing in the world I needed was a hassle over a piece of gym floor. I threw myself down and began driving my body hard. I was trying to keep time to the music, only I couldn't hear it because of the three guys' talking.

"So how do you know he died in de seddle?"

"How do I know? Because Kranz, who lives two doors down, heard the ambulance guy say it."

"I don't believe it."

"Vy not?"

"Dis is a man whose putz only gets hard ven he looks at his bank book. He's gonna pay for a prostitute?"

"Maybe ven she gave him de bill, he had a stroke?"

"Den dat don't count. He didn't die in de seddle."

"You know John Garfield died in de seddle."

"Ven I vas a kid—ven ve first came here—someone in de building dropped dead shtupping his vife, and dey couldn't get dem apart. Dey had to take dem to de hospital togedder."

"Oy, such a liar. You see. Now you're doing it again."

"Vat you mean I'm doing it again? Vat de hell . . ."

"Shhhh. You're boddering de man, he's trying to do pushups."

"I saw mit mine own eyes, she vas screaming and he vas dead and dey vas carrying dem out, and a liar you're calling me?"

"Morris, Morris, Morris. *Gornisht halfin.*"

I couldn't go on. I sat there on the floor laughing while the three old guys stared down at me.

"You see, schmuck, you're boddering de man," said the shortest one, who was bald and had "Sam" embroidered on his bright red sweatsuit.

"No, no," I said, getting to my feet. "I'm fine—don't worry about it."

"You're from New York?" said the tallest one, who was slightly stooped and had thin white hair and a mustache. This was Morris, according to the name embroidered on his lime-green sweatsuit.

"Yeah," I said, and next I was talking about the Bronx, where Sam and Morris had both lived for many years, until it "changed." Both had come to the United States from Poland as young men, just one jump ahead of Hitler's march across Europe. Both had worked for many years in the garment district, and now both were living in a retirement village nearby, where they had met for the first time. Sam was a widower, and Morris was still married to his wife of 50 years but never mentioned her. The third guy, Izzie, had coke-bottle eyeglasses and never spoke a word. "He's from Chicago," explained Morris. These guys made me feel safe and warm, like I was with my own family.

"So, you're Italian?" asked Morris.

"Oy," said Sam. "Such a nosybody!"

"No. My last name's Levine."

"Levine?" they repeated in unison, looking at me differently. "You're Jewish?"

"You ever hear of a Levine that wasn't?" I said.

A strange feeling of relief and freedom washed over me. I was actually talking to strangers and telling them my real name.

The truth ended with my name, of course. I told them I was in town looking for business investment opportunities and lied about everything else. I spent the next hour with my new friends, talking about everything from the sex lives of movie stars to the Israeli army.

A couple of hours later, after a long workout, I was on the way back to the hotel in a cab wondering why I had taken the idiotic chance of telling three strangers my real name. I had no idea what situations I would be in during the next several weeks, and I could easily run into the guys anywhere. I could be at a restaurant entertaining a table of drug dealers. Suddenly, "Hey, Levine, ve didn't see you in the gym."

I no longer understood my own actions. I was under too much stress and getting careless. I had to get myself under control before I blew my cover, my career, and maybe my life.

# 15

# The Setup

## 1

On Friday morning, I met Rourke, Maria, and Sonia in the Marriott parking lot. It was 9:30 and the sun was already a blinding glare. We were on our way to the DEA office for the first meeting of the Operation Hun undercover team. Rourke had spent a whole day at the office and had not said a word about it.

Rourke wheeled the car out into the early morning traffic. On the way to the office, I kept checking the sideview to see if we had picked up a tail. Sonia suddenly tapped the back of my head.

"*Preguntale, Miguel,*" she said.

"Ask him what?"

"What I did yesterday," she said proudly.

"Translate," ordered Rourke, looking hot and uncomfortable in his regular blue suit.

"What did she do yesterday?"

"She's really hot shit," he said, shaking his head and looking at her in the rearview.

"Well, what did she do?"

"She got a lead on Benitez."

"You're kidding! So fast?" Why did I have to pry it out of him? "How?"

"She called some of her old customers in Colombia, said she's back in business. Starts asking around for Benitez—he used to be one of her customers. And she finds out he's bein' protected by some Colombian military guy—a colonel—and he's hidin' him out in the boonies someplace."

Sonia tapped me again. *"Te esta diciendo?"*

"Yes, he's telling me," I said without turning. "Does it sound real?" I asked Rourke.

"Well, headquarters was pleased. They think it's on the money. Now it's a matter of findin' him."

"Ju see," said Sonia in English, rubbing her fingertips on her lapel in mock pride.

"Yes," I said, "you did real good. *Hiciste muy bien.*"

We arrived at the DEA office, a one-story concrete building surrounded by a cyclone fence just inside the Tucson airport, at about 10 A.M. Its only distinguishing feature was a flagpole atop of which Old Glory hung limp and ragged in the still desert air. Rourke parked in the midst of abused cars, trucks, and vans that looked like they'd been raced over unpaved country roads and through swamps and then never been cleaned. I can spot a DEA parking lot anywhere in the world. We trooped silently into the building.

"They're all waiting for you," said a receptionist, buzzing us through the outer door into a narrow corridor. Rourke led the way. As I passed one room I recognized an agent I'd once worked with. He quickly looked away.

At the end of the corridor, we entered a large space where about 20 men and two or three women lounged on office furniture. Most wore guns on their hips or in shoulder holsters and had handcuffs hanging from belts. As we entered the room the hum of conversation ceased.

A big, barrel-chested, redfaced man in his late forties, wearing jeans, cowboy boots, and a guayabera shirt, stepped out of an office to greet us. This was the Tucson RAC, Tyler "Buck" Turghid.

"Heard a lot aboutchu," said Turghid, eyeing me coolly.

"I hope some of it was good," I said.

Turghid ignored the comment. He said something to Sonia in a rapid Tex-Mex Spanish that made no sense. Sonia smiled politely and nodded. When he turned his back, she gave me a quizzical look and shrugged.

"Why don't ya'll step inta my office, and I'll explain the setup." Feeling awkward, I smiled dumbly and followed. Turghid's office was neat and well organized without so much as a stray paper clip in sight nor a piece of paper that wasn't perfectly squared away in an "in," "out" or "pending" box. On the wall were photos of DEA Administrator Mullen, Attorney General Edwin Meese, and a smiling President Reagan. Mullen and Meese seemed to stare at me disapprovingly.

Turghid leaned back in his chair, putting one of his feet up on the desk, showing off his fancy boots with hand-tooled scrollwork. I took a seat along a wall to the right of his desk. Sonia sat beside me, her face as stoic as a cigar store Indian's. Maria sat opposite us. Rourke remained standing.

"Shut the door, wouldya?" said Turghid.

Just as Rourke reached for it, two men slipped into the office and shut the door behind them. Each was in his late twenties, of medium height and slim build. Both were dressed in identical forest green Izod shirts, cotton slacks, and brown penny loafers—with pennies inserted. The men inside the perfectly matched clothing were as different as a hare and a hound. One was as fair as wheat, with light brown curly hair; the other was as dark as mahogany, with straight black Indian hair.

"This here's Special Agent Oliver South, Jr. [name changed]," said Turghid. "I'm designatin' him case agent for this operation. And that there's Sergeant Rudy Herrera [name changed]. He's the supervisin' officer of the sheriff's deputies." Both men nodded. South was eyeing me nervously enough to pique my curiosity.

"Headquarters wants this case top priority," Turghid said directly at me, "and that's 'zactly how it's gonna be. Yer gonna find that I don't run things like they do up there in New York." Turghid spoke quickly, his voice a low monotone with a cowboy twang. "I got technicians out to the UC house, settin' up video and recording equipment. Ya'll can probably move in in a couple days. The UC plane'll be here on Monday. We rented three Lincoln Town Cars—your Mafia fleet. By Monday we gonna have the plane and cars wired for sound."

As Turghid spoke I studied him closely. All I'd heard about him was that he was one of the oldtime Border Rats; a hard-as-nails group of ex-Customs agents who had worked the Mexican border before the formation of DEA, when dope cases were made drinking in border saloons and life was a series of cross-border car chases and shootouts. Buck Turghid looked the part. He had the expressionless face of a professional poker player. His skin was cracked and craggy from too much sun, and he had narrow eyes that at one instant were focused with suspicion and the next darting and furtive.

"I got people doin' the paperwork right now," Turghid was saying, "to get you 50 kilos of DEA's best cocaine. We're gonna flash the stuff in the UC plane; you can bring dopers out to see it, sample it, or whatever. You can have as many people you need coverin' you, working UC with you, or whatever."

The meeting was suddenly interrupted by Turghid's secretary—he was needed elsewhere in the office. The moment he stepped outside, Ollie South edged over to me. With one eye on the door and speaking low, he said "You're gonna need UC drivers and bodyguards; Rudy and I would, kind of, like to work together."

I didn't like this. I was the same grade level as Turghid and had been a group supervisor, commanding men on the street. The last thing in the world a supervisor wants are agents who go through the back door to weasel around your orders.

"You speak Spanish?" I asked.

"I do," said Rudy.

I looked at the unlikely duo. My first instinct was to agree—the last thing I needed was hard feelings between the case agent and myself. But there was something bothering me about South other than the fact that he was backdooring his supervisor. He was staring at me with the "fearbiter" look.

When I was in the air force, I had been a sentry dog handler for two years. The experience had taught me a lot about both dogs and people. In both cases, the ones that feared me were the most dangerous and unpredictable. A frightened dog has a way of looking at a handler with its head ducked low that was a warning. What others call a hangdog look handlers call the fearbiter look.

One of the sentry dogs at Plattsburgh Air Force Base, a German shepherd named Vitz, gave me that look one day as I was trying to feed him. He attacked me, taking three healthy bites and breaking bones in my arm and hand.

There's never a problem if a fearbiter—human or canine—has room to run, but if it even senses it's being cornered, you have a serious problem. Over the years as a narcotics agent, I had seen a lot of people look at me that way, and I had managed to steer clear of them all. But I couldn't see any way of avoiding South.

"I don't know if I've got the authority to say anything," I said.

"Buck is going to leave it up to you," pressed South, speaking quickly, his eye checking the door. Sonia was watching us closely.

I was in a difficult spot. As case agent, South would be charged with keeping the operation running smoothly—that all legal procedures were followed, that reports were written and that they were up to date, that recorded conversations were translated from Spanish to English for the prosecutors, that investigative leads in other jurisdictions were followed up on, and that we were supplied with everything we needed from money to bullets. These duties alone, in an operation the size of this one, should have kept South busy for 18 or 20 hours a day. Why did he want to work undercover, too?

On the other hand, I was under investigation. Seeing the way the agents and cops outside the door had looked at me, perhaps it wouldn't be a bad idea to have the case agent feeling like he owed me one.

"Sure," I said. "If it's okay with Buck, it's okay with me."

"If I tell him you said so, it'll be okay with Buck," said South. He had a tentative, sneaky smile that annoyed me. Then he turned and huddled with Rudy for a moment. Sonia leaned over and said, "What did he want?"

Just then, Turghid returned, crimson-faced. Someone had pissed him off. "Sorry 'bout that," he said resuming his seat. "Some people are so damned stupid." He spat the last word with venom. "Where were we? Oh yeah." He focused on me again. "I wanna hear what Levine's thinkin' is."

"My thinking?" I looked from Turghid to Rourke. Rourke looked at me deadpan.

"Yeah, where you think we're goin' with this."

"I'll tell you where I think we can go," I said. "Sonia's the biggest informant we may ever have working for us. She's the kind of bait that will attract a football-stadium-full of class-one drug dealers. We just pretend we're real dopers until we get the stadium full, then slam the gates shut and lock 'em!"

I could see the words *pushy Jew-Yorker* written on Turghid's face, and I let my voice trail off.

"And what about Mejia?"

"As soon as he hears we're for real—we got coke and we want to pay the debt back—and he decides it might be good business to let us live, we start negotiating the debt with him, get him on camera admitting everything. We stall him until it looks like we've gone as far as we can with Operation Hun, then we give him the coke he originally ordered and lock his ass up."

Turghid's face showed no reaction. "And what about the target of this whole thing: Arce-Gomez?"

"Once we corroborate Sonia's statement we oughtta have enough to indict the whole Bolivian government for conspiracy. I can't see it any other way.

"But who knows? I mean once we get this thing rolling and people think we're for real, we don't have the slightest idea what's gonna happen. We could end up back in South America doing a direct deal with him."

"Who you think we oughtta invite out here first?" asked Turghid.

"Well . . . ," I said, looking at Rourke for help. He averted his gaze and blew a long stream of smoke at President Reagan. We had discussed it for hours—why was he keeping his mouth shut now? "Rourke and I thought it ought to be a *comisionista*. They'll spread the word fastest. We were thinking either a Colombian, Ana Tamayo, or an Argentine, Monica Garcia [name changed]."

Turghid was silent, his eyes still fixed on me. Finally, he nodded his head slightly and said, "Well, let's do it." He got to his feet and started toward the door, "C'mon, I wantchu to meet the rest."

I got to my feet numbly. I didn't have a clue about what he was thinking. He didn't say whether he liked the plan or didn't like it.

Sonia tugged my sleeve. *"Pobrecito, Miguel,"* she whispered. "He doesn't like you too much, does he?" She was grinning mischievously.

"We get along fine."

Still grinning, she said, "I don't think he knows it."


# 2

In the big room Turghid introduced Sonia and me to the waiting crew. Some would work undercover as our "employees" when needed, and the rest would be used for surveillance, protection, and any investigative work that had to be done on the spot. In appearance they were a perfect cross-section of Tucson's populace—bikers, cowboys, insur-

189

ance salespeople, college students, and gangsters; about a third were Spanish-speaking Chicanos.

Later that afternoon we had a small dress rehearsal. Oliver and Rudy, in identical mirrored sunglasses, assumed their undercover roles and drove Sonia and me to lunch at El Torito. In spite of the preppy clothing, the two were credible as bodyguard-drivers. Rudy wheeled the big Lincoln to the front door with an attention-getting chirp of tires; South opened our doors. The two preceded us into the restaurant and secured us a private table, then got a separate table of their own just in front of ours. Sonia fell comfortably into the game, which was no surprise—this had been normal behavior for her for many years.

From the furtive glances and whispers of the other diners and the extraordinary service from the staff, I figured our ensemble was a hit. About an hour later, after a heavy lunch and some heavier tipping, I signaled and Rudy moved out smartly for the car while South called for the check. Within minutes the bill was paid and the car delivered to the front door. The place grew silent and every head in the restaurant turned as South led the way to the exit. None of the restaurant help would forget us, which was exactly what I wanted.

We did pretty good with a bunch of waiters and parking lot attendants, I thought. How will we do under the close scrutiny of the real thing?

Our next stop was to check out the UC house. "The zoning laws here don't permit building homes above a certain level in the hills," explained Rudy as he drove us toward the northern foothills. "It takes away from the scenic beauty. We rented you guys one of the highest homes available. It's a real beauty."

Rudy was enthusiastic and had an engaging smile that would get him over with the bad guys. South, on the other hand, sat tense and uneasy in the passenger seat, saying nothing unless asked. He radiated the kind of tension that was contagious.

As we drove toward the mountains, I noticed a car with two men in it swing onto the highway behind us. I couldn't quite make it out because the desert heat had turned the road to a shimmering blur and the car never drew up close enough for me to get a good look.

"Hey Rudy," I said, "there's a guy behind us. Is he one of ours?"

"No," said Rudy, "I've been watching him."

We drove on for a few more minutes in silence.

Rudy made a sudden skidding left onto a road called Skyline Drive and gunned the powerful engine. Dust billowed up behind us. I twisted in my seat and watched the intersection until it was out of sight. The car never reappeared.

We continued along a ribbon of road that skirted the edge of the mountain. After about 10 minutes, Rudy made another hard right onto a road so dusty that I couldn't tell if it was paved. It seemed to go straight into the mountain.

"We're here," said Rudy.

The house, a sprawling desert ranch with a circular driveway, sat about 100 yards from where the road abruptly ended. It felt as if we were at the very edge of the world. Above and behind us was nothing but desert and mountain, and spread out below us was Tucson, looking like a mini-model city.

Sonia and I stepped slowly out of the car into the oven heat and absolute stillness of the desert. I looked across the vast open landscape, and a certain tranquillity came over me that I had thought I would never again feel. The car doors slammed, and the feeling quickly ebbed.

There were two cars in the driveway and a pickup truck parked in front of a large attached garage. "The tech people are still working on the house," said South as he and Rudy led the way to the front door. It was the first time he had spoken since we had left the restaurant.

"This is home," I said. "What do you think, will this work?"

Sonia shrugged. "It will do."

Rourke and Maria were already there watching the DEA tech men installing a hidden video camera inside a large-screen TV that sat in a corner of the main living room.

"That's hot shit," said Rourke, crouching in front of it. "It can cover everything in this room."

"Even when the TV's on?" I asked.

"Just don't turn the volume up too loud," said a tech man from behind the television set. All I could see was his baseball cap. "We installed mikes all around the room. But if you wanna get real good quality, keep the volume down."

"There's one more little item," said his partner, a heavy-set guy with a bunch of tools hanging from a utility belt. "The picture is being transmitted to a video recorder in the pool house on one of the UHF frequencies. So if you're watching television with the dopers, make sure you don't turn it to the last UHF channel."

"What will happen?" I asked.

"Stand in front of the set," said Baseball Cap. He clicked something and the big screen flickered to life. In a moment I was staring at myself on screen. "That's what happens."

"Could be embarrassing," I said.

"Yeah," said Baseball Cap. "But I wouldn't worry about it; it's the last UHF channel. Who watches UHF anyway?"

We toured the rest of the house. The master bedroom, which was also to be wired for sound, had a picture window looking out on the desert. It would be Sonia's room. A sliding glass door led to a rear patio and pool. Just off the master bedroom was a huge bathroom, including a sunken Jacuzzi, that overlooked the desert and Tucson. We stepped out the sliding doors onto the concrete patio that surrounded the free-form swimming pool. The whole rear part of the house was separated from the desert by an adobe wall.

Then I checked my room out. It was large, with a comfortable queen-size bed and a nice desk. Lydia's room was across the hall from mine; Sonia's room was on the other side of the house. I closed the door behind me so I could be alone. The door had no lock on it, which I didn't like. I'd have to get a cheap chain lock and install it myself.

The other thing about the room that bothered me was that it was too busy—too full of paintings, pictures, bric-a-brac, and places to conceal microphones and cameras. Not that a lot of furniture was needed to hide spying devices. A state-of-the-art spy camera had a lense the size of a pinhead and could be hidden in just about any appliance or piece of furniture. I had to assume there wasn't a place in the house that I would be safe from observation.

Otherwise, the setup was fantastic. The house exuded a feeling of understated wealth. The walls were lined with expensive artwork, and the record library was stocked with everything from Tito Puente to Beethoven. The refrigerators, bar, and pantry were fully stocked, and everything looked lived-in, as though the place had never been vacant.

Later, South led Rourke and me to a heavily padlocked utility shed beside the pool. "I'm the only one with the key to this," he said.

The shed was filled with video and sound recording equipment. South flipped a switch and two video monitors flickered to life, showing Maria, Rudy, and Sonia in the living room. Sonia looked ill at ease;

she was hugging herself and staring off into space. I wondered what she was thinking.

"I can operate all the equipment from here," said South. "When you're in the house with the bad guys, I'll slip out here like I'm working around the pool and turn it on. I can lock myself inside."

"Looks good," I said, taking in the jumble of wires, gauges, screens, and dials and wondering where else the images were being transmitted and why South never looked me in the eye.

"When's it gonna be ready for us to move in?"

"By Monday. Tuesday the latest."

"All I can say is that in all my years of doing this shit, this is probably the best setup I've ever had to work with."

"Yeah, well, Buck really wants this to go well," said South, playing with some dials and looking uncomfortable.

"Nice, huh?" I said to Rourke, who had been silent.

"Looks real good," he said without much enthusiasm.

Something was bothering Rourke. In Washington he'd been excited about the whole setup. Now, even though it looked like we would get everything we had hoped for, he was deflated. Something had happened. I cornered him in the kitchen before we left to go back to the hotel. "Is there something wrong," I asked, "something I should know about?"

Rourke looked indecisive. Then he said, "Just do your job, ya hump, and there won't be anything wrong."

I wouldn't let him off the hook. "You're not telling me everything, are you?"

He shook his head impatiently. "What do you want me to tell you? You know everything you need to know, Mike." He brushed past me and headed out the door.

## 3

On Saturday night I almost lost it. I was crossing the hotel lobby when I noticed a man glance at me over a newspaper. I'd seen him only hours before at the El Parador restaurant where Sonia and I ate dinner.

I picked up a couple of tourist pamphlets, opened one, and stood there watching him. After a moment he lowered his paper to glance at me again. I smiled and winked, and he ducked his face behind the paper. I had a sudden impulse to kick the paper out of his hands, spit in his face, and scream at him like a raving lunatic. If he was an inspector or CIA, what would he do? Blow his cover and identify himself? Arrest me? Or maybe I should just dropkick the son of a bitch across the fucking lobby, handcuff him to the front desk, and go find Rourke and Turghid and tell them the guy was following me.

I was moving across the lobby toward him before I began to think clearly. What if the guy is an insurance salesman from Phoenix who didn't know me from a hole in the ground? I changed my course slightly and swung past the guy, slamming the newspaper from his hand with my arm.

"What the hell!" he reacted, reaching down for the paper.

"You say something to me?" I said, standing over him.

The guy looked up, his face flaming. I had planted my feet, ready to front-kick his head if he even looked like he was reaching for something. I was giddy—a hair from losing control. I was just a threatening motion away from letting two years of pent-up rage explode on this guy's head.

A thin smile appeared on his lips. "No, you must be mistaken," he said, calmly gathering his paper. He rose slowly, keeping his eyes on me, smiling all the time, and then headed across the lobby and out the front door. If pushing me to my limit was their purpose, I had arrived.

Over the weekend our answering service was deluged with phone calls from prospective drug customers, but there was still no word from Mejia's people. Both Ana Tamayo and Monica Garcia had called a half-dozen times. Sonia called them back to tell them our house would be ready this week. We would have preferred Tamayo as our first house guest; she was the closest to Sonia, the least likely to sense anything wrong with our act, the least likely to betray us to Mejia, and the most likely to spread the word about us.

But Ana was busy. She was finding customers for 150 kilos of cocaine that a Colombian trafficker named Pacho Cuervas (name changed) had just smuggled into Miami. So it looked like Monica Garcia, an Argentine *comisionista* working out of New York City and Miami, would be our first guest. She was to arrive Tuesday afternoon, and the plane carrying our 50 kilos of cocaine was to arrive Tuesday morning. We'd be cutting it close.

On Monday afternoon Sonia and I moved into the undercover house. Lydia, who was supposed to have arrived the same day we did, had delayed coming until the last possible moment, and wouldn't arrive until late that evening. Officially, DEA never forced anyone to accept an undercover assignment; however, I know of at least one agent who was pressured into an undercover assignment and paid with his life. Remembering how frightened and anguished Lydia had been after the inspector's phone call in Miami, I could only believe that she was now being forced to work with me.

On Monday evening Rudy and South, in matching Izod shirts, cotton slacks, and topsiders, whisked Sonia and me off to dinner at one of Tucson's better restaurants. We had perfected our entrance and exit routines all weekend at some of the best restaurants and clubs in Tucson, so that when we returned with drug dealers as our guests, waiters would be fighting each other to light their cigarettes and hold their chairs. There's nothing phonier than a so-called big time drug dealer having to stand in line for a table at a restaurant. Sonia was treated as a queen in South America, and her customers would expect nothing less here.

After Sonia and I were seated, I sent our bodyguards off with instructions to pick us up in an hour. I wanted to go over the scenario with Sonia one more time—everything she and Monica knew about each other; Monica's likes and dislikes, and any weaknesses we might exploit in getting over on her; what we would and would not tell her about ourselves. If there were any obvious flaws in our preparation, this would be our final chance to correct them.

"Monica is very much the coquette," said Sonia, putting a cigarette to her lips. A flame appeared before her instantly. She lit her cigarette, paying not the slightest heed to where the flame came from. She smiled a mischievous smile. "I think she's really going to go for you." For a moment her eyes stopped darting around the room and focused on me.

"You mean I'll be in danger around her?" I asked jokingly.

"Only if you want to be," she said, her eyes still probing.

"What's she going to think about you and me?"

Sonia looked annoyed. "I already told her you're my business partner."

We'd been over it before, but I wanted to hear it again. I wanted no surprises when Monica was under the same roof with us. "Will she believe you?"

"She's no fool. She'll believe whatever she wants to. Most of all she's money-hungry; that's her first love. And she has always made money with me."

"How did you meet her?"

"A few years ago she came to Bolivia—she heard the cocaine prices were better than in Colombia. But if you don't know the right people you get eaten alive. To the narcotics police she looked like a fatted calf. They didn't know whether to eat her for dinner or to sell her to the Indians." Sonia laughed with the memory. "But they weren't sure whom she really knew—she kept mentioning the names of all the big Colombian traffickers—so they arrested her and stuck her in jail.

"It was almost Christmas when I heard about her. I felt sorry for her. So I got her out." Sonia laughed again. "She kissed my hands. There's nothing she wouldn't do for me."

*So you had the power to get people out of jail. How did you do it? Who did you call? Arce-Gomez? The CIA?*

"So she really trusts you," I said. "She ought to be easy pickings for us."

"Easy?" Sonia considered the word. "That's not a word I would use to describe Monica. She's like radar. She'll miss nothing."

"Is she that sharp?"

Sonia laughed. "When Lydia and the other one—I don't remember his name—went to New York with me to meet her . . . what's his name?"

"Louie Alvarez."

"Yes, Alvarez. When Monica met them, she took one look and wouldn't say a word in front of them."

"Why?"

"Why? I don't know . . . maybe she sensed something was wrong." Sonia took a deep drag on the cigarette and smiled wryly. "You have to admit, she was right."

"Then she may already be suspicious of you."

"No. When we were alone, she told me everything she was doing. It was just them. She must have seen something that bothered her. If she was suspicious she would not be coming here."

"She might if she were working for someone else," I said. "Someone like Papo."

Sonia focused on me again. It was the first time I thought I saw fear in her eyes. "I don't think so."

"Does she know Papo?"

"Sure. Everyone knows him."

"And you don't think it's possible that he would send her to check us out?"

"Everything's possible. I just don't think so."

The waiter came with a dessert menu. We both ordered coffee. A piano player began to play a soft ballad. Sonia had slipped into her own private world. She chewed her bottom lip unconsciously and stared off into space.

Was this a crack in Sonia's armor? There was so much hidden about this woman. I'd spent most of my adult life working with informants, getting to know them intimately, understanding what motivated them to betray their loyalties, understanding what made them tick. After spending almost a week with Sonia I was sure of only one thing—all I knew about her was what she wanted me to know. This had never happened to me before with an informant.

From the little I'd learned about Sonia while I was stationed in Argentina and during the past week, in Bolivia she had been doing million-dollar coke deals like they were going out of style. She owned at least three homes in Bolivia, along with a huge cattle ranch and cotton plantation; she had apartments and offices in Brazil, and her husband Pachi had come from wealth before she got into the cocaine business. The $1.5 million she owed Arce-Gomez should have been small change. I couldn't believe that such a threat was enough to make her trade her life as a Bolivian cocaine queen for that of a DEA informant living in a frame house in the suburbs of Washington, D.C.

"Sonia," I said, "did your husband Pachi know Monica?"

Her eyes narrowed; they were once again the eyes of the threatened predator backed into its den. "Sure he met her. She stayed with me."

"Yes, but did he know what business you did with her?"

Her eyes sparked fire. "I don't know what he knew. What he knew was his business."

"He knew what business you were in, didn't he?"

Now the fangs were showing. "I already told all this to Jack and the other one. What I did was my own business."

She put another cigarette to her lips. A flame appeared. In the glow I saw an anger in her eyes that I'd never seen before. If I pushed any harder my undercover partner would become an enemy. The last thing I needed was another enemy.

"There's no doubt about it," I said with the biggest smile I could muster. "You were the queen."

She looked at me and smiled. "Yes, I was."

# 16

# Strange Cocaine

W hen I opened my eyes on Tuesday morning, bright sunlight was flooding the room. It was late in the morning and no one had awakened me. The house sounded like it was humming with activity.

By the time I was showered and dressed it was already past 11 A.M. South and the technicians were in the house going over the bugging equipment, and a couple of undercover cops and agents were lounging in the driveway. Rudy was making coffee in the kitchen, while Rourke was on the kitchen phone speaking with headquarters.

"You want some coffee, boss?" asked Rudy.

He had on a little apron and a big grin. I was really starting to like him. He had started out being very quiet and careful around me— with the rumors that accompanied me, I could hardly blame him. Lately he'd been loosening up a bit, which was more his nature.

"Sure," I said, "but aren't we running late?"

"Nah," he said, pouring me a cup. "Monica called. She can't make it until tomorrow."

"Great. We can use the extra day. What about the dope?"

"It's already at the airport."

*"Fenomino,"* I said. I could see Lydia and Sonia out beside the pool. "Lemme go say hello to Lydia."

I stepped through the sliding glass door onto the patio. The heat blasted me.

"Good morning, ladies," I said, standing over Lydia. Sonia mumbled something, and Lydia raised her sunglasses and squinted up at me.

"Oh. Hi." Immediate tension.

"How was your trip?" I asked.

"Fine." She lowered her glasses and lay back.

"I guess your husband's not too happy about it."

"Well, no, he's not."

I stood there awkwardly. Ever since the day Quasimoto had tried to interrogate Lydia in Miami, I'd been tempted to call her. But Tommy Dolittle had told me that the Chief Inspector himself had said the matter had nothing to do with me—a thinly veiled warning to butt out. I figured that if I did try to contact Lydia the inspectors would use it to charge me with "interfering with an investigation" or something else. The Manual was full of possibilities. I already suspected that they'd try to accuse me of influencing her refusal to be interrogated that day. I didn't want to open another bureaucratic door for them to attack me through.

It probably wouldn't do me any good talking to her anyway, for what could I do with her information? I had recorded the inspectors trying to frame me, and the suits had made recording of DEA employees illegal. If the inspectors did have something unrelated against her, maybe they had used it to flip her so that she'd work undercover against me. Maybe the reason I could no longer detect surveillance was that it was now Lydia doing the watching.

In the afternoon, the whole crew headed out to an isolated corner of the Tucson airport, where we were met by two old friends—DEA pilots Dave Kunz and Dave Gorman, who had flown the Suarez mission to Bolivia.

Since that fiasco, I had heard that the inspectors had interrogated them several times about their involvement with me, and that the questioning had been rough. After surviving that kamikaze mission to Bolivia and then being forced to undergo a half-dozen tough interrogations, I didn't think they'd be too anxious to hear from me again.

But as we rolled to a stop beneath the wings of a Beechcraft Queenaire, a medium-sized propeller craft, I was happy to see that both Daves were grinning at me from the plane's doorway.

"I see you're still with us," said Kunz as he helped Sonia up the last two steps of the stairway and through the little door, eyeing her appreciatively.

"Don't even think about it," said Rourke, on the steps behind me.

I slipped into the tight, cluttered cabin and shook hands with both of them. Gorman punched me on the arm; Kunz clapped me on the back. It felt good.

"They can't fire you for thinking," said Gorman.

"Don't bet on it," said Kunz.

I introduced the two Daves to Sonia in Spanish as the only gay lovers ever hired as a team by DEA, and she laughed.

"What did you say, Levine?" asked Kunz, a tall, blond Texan who loved to brag about being happily married to Sue, his wife of at that time 14 years.

"That you were two of the bravest guys I knew."

"I'll bet," said Gorman. "Levine, you'll never fucking change."

"They wire the plane already?" I asked, glancing around, looking for visible indication of recording devices, the way I knew a doper would.

"It's all set," said Kunz. "They wired it up this morning. Me and Dave will turn on the recording equipment the moment we see your car coming. The switch is up in the cockpit."

I nodded, wondering whether someone in some nondescript office was listening to us at that moment.

After the whole undercover team had squeezed into the aircraft, Kunz hefted one of two Samsonite suitcases that had been stacked by the wall just behind the cockpit. He laid the heavy suitcase on a seat and unzipped it. Twenty-five kilo bags of cocaine were packed neatly inside.

"What it is," said Gorman.

"There's 25 keys in the other one, so that's about $2 million worth," said Kunz. "All we need's about an hour's notice and we'll be ready with it here, just like ya see it."

Something about the cocaine looked wrong. I picked up one of the bags and held it up to the sunlight just inside the doorway. "The stuff looks kind of yellow," I said.

"That's the best we could get from the lab," South said too quickly.

"Well, I hope it checks out as close to 100 percent pure as possible. We're not gonna be dealing with any fools. The stuff look okay to you?" I asked Sonia.

She took the bag and examined it in the sunlight. She shook the bag up and down and held it up to the light again, squinting at the powder with one of the most practiced eyes in the Americas. She had done this many times during countless drug deals in many countries. Watching her do this was like watching Martina Navratilova take her practice swings before a match.

"I don't like the color," said Sonia, "and I don't see any rocks." She handed the bag back to me. Even street dealers knew that a lot of rock-like crystals in the powder indicated a higher probability that the cocaine was pure.

"They said it's 100 percent pure."

"If it tests pure it will be all right. If it's not, everyone will know."

I put the bag back into the suitcase. Kunz zipped it closed. DEA had tons of the world's purest cocaine stored in its Evidence vaults to choose from. There wasn't a doubt in my mind that the stuff would test out pure.

At midnight, Sonia, Lydia, and I were alone in the undercover house, sitting around the big-screen Evil Eye in the living room. It was tuned to a Spanish movie that none of us was really watching. We sat apart, staring blankly at the moving images, each lost in thought. I had been told that the monitoring equipment in the house would be off when no drug dealers were present, but I didn't believe it. I couldn't shake the notion that the camera in the TV was on. I had to do something to relax. I got to my feet.

"Where are you going, Miguel?" asked Sonia. She was seated on the large, soft couch wearing a bathrobe, her legs curled up under her.

"I'm going to try the Jacuzzi," I said, directing my words as much at the television as toward Sonia.

I turned out the lights in the bathroom, turned the Jacuzzi on full, and slid my tense body into the bubbling warmth.

At night, the view from the whirlpool was spectacular. The lights of Tucson formed a carpet of gold below me, stretching into the distance and ending somewhere below the horizon in a thick strip of desert blackness. Beginning at the horizon, the night sky swept overhead like a black velvet sheet encrusted with sparkling stars.

I was suddenly overcome with the spectacle of that desert night.

My thoughts drifted from my problems to the immensity of the universe and the unknowable intelligence that it implied. Operation Hun suddenly seemed at once laughably minuscule and monumentally important. It seemed to me that there was a beautifully crafted order to the universe; that every particle and every event had its precise role to play in the overall scheme of things. Every one of the trillion points of light overhead was exactly as and where it should be. If any one of them changed position, size, or temperature, it would set off a chain reaction of events that could potentially affect me, that submicroscopic organism bathing in a Tucson Jacuzzi. Once again I had that warm, confident feeling about life and my role in it. I was exactly where I was supposed to be, doing what I was destined to do. My mind finally let go, and I felt the tension drift out of my body and into the swirling waters.

I awoke with a start. I found my watch—it was 3 A.M. I quickly dressed, listening for some noise in the house, my breathing unnaturally loud in the glass-and-tile enclosure. I could hear nothing else.

I stepped into the coolness of the dark living room and was halfway across when a lamp clicked on. I yelped and jumped back.

Sonia laughed. "I frightened you." She was sitting almost directly in front of the TV.

I started across the room.

"Miguel, wait a moment."

"Yes?"

"Come, sit down here with me for a while."

"What is it, Sonia?"

"I just wanted to talk to you about something . . . about that coke, in the plane."

"What about it?"

"It . . . it reminded me. It looked like the merchandise I used to get from the minister."

"This stuff is pure."

She said nothing. Her eyes glittered in the lamp light.

"We'll talk about it tomorrow," I said, my thoughts now on the strange yellow cocaine, peace and tranquillity slipping away from me like quicksilver.

# 17

# Monica:
# La Argentina

## 1

Monica was scheduled to arrive on the noon plane. The plan was that Lydia, Sonia, and I would meet her in two Lincolns with a cadre of bodyguards. A really strong first impression, I thought, would win her confidence. After she saw the undercover plane and sampled some of our coke we'd send her off to her New York and Miami buyers thinking she'd just visited the biggest thing to hit the drug world since the hypodermic needle. From there the word would spread about us across the dope world, and we'd be off and running. At least that was the plan.

As I dressed, it hit me that for a big-time drug dealer I was wearing some pretty cheap jewelry. My watch was a knock-off of a gold Rolex. It was a decent copy that I had paid $75 for in Argentina four years earlier, and it had withstood the short-term scrutiny of many a drug dealer. But if Monica was as sharp as Sonia said she was, she might notice that the second hand moved in jerks as opposed to the smooth sweep of a true Rolex.

It was one more seemingly minor detail that could blow the whole case. Jewelry among Latino drug dealers was very important. In a business without a Dun & Bradstreet to check someone's credit rating and business bona fides, it was one of the important outward signs that you were genuine. To pose as the business partner of the Queen of Cocaine, a $12,000 Rolex was a minimum requirement.

"You two meet Monica at the airport," I told Sonia and Lydia. "Rudy, since you speak Spanish, you drive their car; South, you follow in the other. Take along a couple of undercovers as bodyguards, and make sure the recorder is on in the car with Monica. On the way back to the house, you guys in the backup car check real close for a tail. You got it?"

"Got it," said Rudy, eagerly. To my relief he had discarded his preppie uniform for a black silk ensemble. South, wearing his forest green Izod shirt and penny loafers, nodded sullenly. "You want us to blindfold her on the way back here?" Rudy asked.

I hadn't considered this. Ominously, there had been no word from Mejia's people, and for all we knew Monica was already working for them. I asked Sonia what she thought.

"If something is wrong, I'll know in an instant," she said coolly.

"I'm sure you will," I said, "but if you even think something might be wrong, signal Rudy. Sit so that he can see you in the rearview, and nod. Rudy, if she signals you, you pull over and blindfold Monica."

"Right."

"Apologize," I said to Sonia. "Tell her it's your partner Miguel's fault. He's a very cautious man."

"I'll know what to say," said Sonia, irritated. "There's nothing to worry about."

Five minutes later I was heading for Tucson's main shopping drag going over all the preparations in my mind. Had we forgotten anything? No, the UC team had done great.

Suddenly, my head started to ache fiercely. I pulled into a Mini-Market, bought a bottle of aspirin and a Diet Coke, and gobbled down four pills. I rested my pounding head against the steering wheel. When I came to, I was slumped over the steering wheel, bathed in sweat, dizzy and nauseous. My headache was gone. It was 1 P.M.—I had been unconscious for almost two hours. Monica was probably at the house already, and I hadn't even gotten my jewelry.

I stripped off my sopping wet shirt and hustled back into the Mini-

Market. All they had were sleeveless T-shirts, and I bought a red one that said "Save the Whales."

Big-time drug dealer.

Next I found a pawnshop in the Old Town section. I figured the owner would be happy for the rental money and I'd be able to get some real flash for less money. I wasn't sure that the suits would approve the rental, so if I wasn't saving the government money, I was saving my own.

The moment I walked through the door the owner stared at me suspiciously from behind a heavy wire cage. He was an old, thick-bodied Chicano with a heavy mustache and tattoos crawling up his neck from beneath his shirt. His hands were out of sight, which made me nervous. "Where'd you do time?" he asked, staring at the tattoo on my left arm.

I'd had the tattoo done in Vera Acuña, Mexico when I was in the Air Force in 1959. At 19, I really thought I was hot stuff. The tattoo was done with a filthy needle by a drunken bartender who wiped the blood off with a rag dipped in whiskey. The result was less than spectacular, looking more like a crooked, flying banana than the propeller and wings it was supposed to be. It was so poorly done that it looked like a typical self-inflicted jailhouse tattoo. Over the years it had helped me get over during undercover deals, but there were times—and this was one of them—that it was a problem.

I ignored the man's question. "You rent me some jewelry?"

At first the guy looked at me, stunned. Then his face cracked into a nasty grin. "What kinda fuckin' scam you tryin' to run on me, man?"

"No scam," I said. "I need some flash to impress some people on a business deal." I pulled out my American Express card. "All you gotta do is write up the value of the merchandise on a credit slip and keep it as security."

The guy turned mean, as if I'd insulted his mother. "Get your fuckin' ass outta here before I call a cop." As I hit the door, he was yelling, "I'm sick an' fuckin' tired of you scam artists. . . ." This was just not my day.

After being turned down by two more pawnshops and a jewelry store, I decided I'd have to identify myself at the next place. If I was still refused, I'd have to make do without the jewelry.

I drove into the first fancy shopping mall I saw and picked out the most expensive-looking jewelry store. Incredibly, it was managed by the ex-wife of a DEA agent. For a modest rental fee, a large credit card deposit, and a vague explanation of what I needed the jewelry for, I was on my way with a gold Rolex, a zircon ring that looked like a five-carat diamond, and a gold bracelet heavy enough to sink me in rapids. Before leaving the mall I ran into a clothing store and bought a pow-der-blue silk shirt to match my pants and shoes, put it on my credit card, and wore it out the door.

Twenty minutes later I pulled up to the house. Both Lincolns were parked in the driveway, along with a third car I didn't recognize. South and two undercovers watched me park. As I passed, one of the under-covers, a Chicano, said, "Lookin' clean, my man."

"Where you been?" asked South, looking at me suspiciously. "We were getting worried about you." I'll bet you were.

"Everything going okay?" I asked him.

He shrugged. "I don't speak Spanish. They're in the living room waiting for you."

I walked into the house, concentrating on my entrance. Don't be hesitant! This is your house; your employees. You are the boss. I had to assume the unmistakable manner and bearing of a man entering his own home. It would be Monica's first impression of me, so it had to be right.

Sonia, Lydia, and Monica were seated around the Evil Eye, drinks in hand, while Rudy hovered attentively.

*"Como estan todos?"* I said, going over to kiss Sonia and then Lydia on the cheek, aware of Monica studying me carefully through tinted glasses. "Please forgive me for not being here to greet you," I said, moving toward Monica. "I had some unexpected business."

She started to rise.

"No, no. Please—relax." I leaned over, took her hand, and kissed her cheek. "Enjoy your drink. I'm only sorry I'm not a better host."

Monica was full-bodied, a little on the heavy side, but very attrac-tive, with fine features and dark hair worn high. She wore a gold Rolex, the women's version of the President model that I had on. Her eyes, however, were pawnbroker's eyes, seeming to make emotionless appraisals of everyone and everything. At that moment they were checking me from head to foot like a computerized scanner. Shoes—*beep;* pants—*beep;* shirt—*beep;* Rolex—*beepbeep;* diamond ring—*beepbeepbeep.*

"Don't worry," said Monica in heavily accented Argentine Spanish. "Sonia and Rudy are taking excellent care of me." She had omitted

Lydia. It was not the kind of unconscious omission an Argentine would make.

"Please excuse me," I said. "I just want to clean up." Before I said another word, I had to be brought up to date on what had been said. Also, I felt the dull throbbing returning at the base of my skull. I made it to the bathroom, filled the wash basin with cold water, and stuck my face in it. My hands were trembling. What the hell was happening to me?

There was a light tapping on the door.

"Yes?"

"It's me," said Sonia softly. I opened the door. She looked at me anxiously. "Are you all right?"

Water dripped from my hair onto my shirt. "Why? Don't I look all right?"

"You look pale."

"Did Monica notice anything wrong?"

"No, nothing at all. You made a good impression."

"Great! Is she talking?"

"She won't say anything in front of Lydia. I don't know what's wrong with her. She doesn't say a word, she just sits there. But Rudy's perfect, he's polite, he's funny—Monica really likes him."

"Did she say anything else?"

"She's studying everything, even the paintings and furniture, everything. And she's not shy, believe me." Sonia looked over her shoulder. "I'd better get back."

When I returned to the living room the stereo was playing a soft Spanish ballad, Rudy was serving drinks, and Monica was examining a magnificent oil painting of an Indian seated at a desert campfire.

"Ah, Miguel," she said. "What an interesting painting. Sonia tells me that you picked it out." Her unblinking, emotionless eyes studied me.

I had to change the subject quickly. The painting was unsigned and no one had been able to tell me anything about it. It was just one of many possible trouble spots that we had to work with. "Do you know anything about Indians?" I asked.

"We have Indians in Argentina, you know," said Monica, facing me fully. She was an imposing person.

"*Had* Indians in Argentina," I said. "The Argentines did all they could to wipe out their Indians, just like the Americans."

"Sonia tells me you are Argentine."

"I was born there, and lived there for a few years. I had some business interests there. But I was brought up here."

"You have an interesting accent," she said, eyeing me curiously. "You pronounce some words like a Puerto Rican, some like an Argentine, and some with no accent. How odd."

"I think it comes from traveling and living in different places."

"How interesting," she said, her pawnbroker's eyes trying to peer into my brain.

Monica was in no rush to talk drugs. She had come to Tucson to do a drug deal, so if she wasn't talking business, she had a reason. I decided to wait her out.

We sat around the living room talking for a tense hour with Rudy, joined by another Chicano undercover cop, serving drinks and snacks. Sonia had been right about Monica—she didn't miss a thing, and if she was curious about something she wasn't shy about asking. She questioned me about Argentina—what section of Buenos Aires I had lived in, the kind of businesses I was involved in there, my family connections and friends there. She kept comparing Lydia and I suspiciously. I was grateful for the similar complexions and features that Lydia and I had.

"Miguel," said Monica suddenly, "how strange it is that your sister is pure Puerto Rican and you are Argentine."

I was ready. "We have the same father but different mothers," I said. That was explanation enough—embellishment would cause more suspicion. Let Monica figure out the rest.

"How odd."

"Not in America," I said.

I was developing a strong dislike for this woman with eyes that never blinked. That was dangerous; inner feelings have a way of flicking out at unguarded moments through a look or a slip of the tongue. As Undercover Tactics 101 taught, the key to winning confidence is to get your target to like you. Like equals trust. Without trust, your case is going nowhere.

I signaled Rudy. Moments later the phone rang and he called me away. I excused myself and headed for the bedroom. Rudy followed.

"Did she say anything on the way from the airport?"

"A little bit," said Rudy. "I heard them talking about Bolivia. I couldn't hear everything, but the recording device must have picked it all up. Damn! She's one cautious lady, isn't she?"

"You said it. We gotta keep the act going. She knows Mejia. When she leaves here she's gotta believe us or the whole operation is screwed."

"You mind if I make a suggestion?"

"Shoot."

"Why don't you invite her to see some of the sights. I'll do the guided tour. We can go out to Old Tucson where they shoot all the cowboy movies. She'll enjoy it and it'll keep her mind occupied."

"Good thinking," I said. "Get the word to the others that I just want Sonia, you, and me on this trip—nobody else. I want Monica relaxed and happy by dinner time. But it can't be obvious that we're trying to make her happy."

Rudy laughed. "Anybody ever tell you you got a devious mind?"

"My mother."

The sightseeing trip went well. By late afternoon the Argentine *comisionista* was relaxed and smiling, and had stopped her probing. When Sonia suggested Rudy take our pictures, Monica grinned happily for the camera and snuggled against me as I put my arms around her and Sonia.

At dinner that evening, everything seemed to come together. Rudy had taken a more dominant role in supervising the rest of the undercovers. South sulked but said nothing.

As our cars wheeled up to one of the restaurants we had spent the week cultivating, I fought to keep my mind on my performance. With Rudy and our bodyguards leading the way, we were ushered to our tables like visiting royalty. Waiters rushed to place chairs delicately beneath our royal derrieres. Sonia and Monica took out cigarette packs and flames appeared before them before they could get the cigarettes to their lips. Monica inhaled deeply, blew a long stream of smoke, and gave me a satisfied smile.

"You seem to be very well known here, don Miguel," she said, for the first time using the honorific.

"In America, you spend money you're well-known," I said. "But I try not to be too well-known."

We sparred this way throughout dinner, talking about everything except drugs. I was beginning to think that perhaps this cagey Argentine had our number and was backing out. Being a slick undercover meant knowing when you're in a trap, but never letting on until you've maneuvered yourself out of it. And Monica Garcia was slick.

Over after-dinner drinks, Monica leaned close to me and said, "I'm working with some Cubans, between Miami and New York. They've heard a lot about Sonia and are very interested in doing business. Of course, it depends on the quality and price of your merchandise."

"Of course," I said. "I didn't think you came here to see the sights of Tucson."

"Oh, I don't know," she said. "I'm always curious about new places . . . and new people."

"Unfortunately, you're visiting us right in the middle of some troubled times," I said. "You know Papo Mejia?"

"Yes."

"Then you know about our problem."

"Yes."

"Well, then you know it's difficult for us to go into business on the level that Sonia was before without first resolving this thing."

"Of course," said Monica, her eyes glancing around nervously. Papo was not a comfortable topic for her.

"I only tell you this because I want to lay all my cards on the table with you. If your people turn out to be good customers, I don't want to lose you. We're looking forward to doing a lot of business. The problem is, right now, I only have 50 kilos of merchandise left. We have several hundred ready for us in Bolivia, but we can't go there until the problem is resolved. You understand."

"Perfectly."

Good—that was the information that I wanted Papo to hear.

"How much merchandise are you prepared to buy?" I asked.

"All you have."

Once Monica started talking, there was no stopping her. By the time we got back to the house late that evening, we had learned that she was no longer just a *comisionista*—she was a full partner in a group that regularly trafficked cocaine from Miami to New York, carrying as much as 50 kilos a trip in cars equipped with hidden traps. *La Argentina* was a solid class-one drug dealer. And with the information she was giving us, it didn't matter whether we could con her group into coming to Tucson or not. With a little investigation—perhaps putting a bug on her New York telephone—DEA's New York and Miami offices could easily identify the rest of her organization.

And we could do the same thing with everyone in Sonia's address book.

❖    ❖    ❖

That night, Monica and Sonia shared the master bedroom. As it turned out, it was nothing new for them; they'd shared beds before. But I doubted that those beds had had as many hidden microphones around them as this one had.

The moment Sonia and Monica closed their bedroom door, I telephoned Rourke and told him what we had so far. For the moment I had forgotten the Bolivian fiasco, the inspectors, and all my life's problems. I was doing what I did best and it looked like no one was stopping me. I felt good.

"We got Monica's New York phone number," I said. "All we gotta do is check her telephone tolls, then set up a pen register and we'll know everyone she's involved with. We follow it up with a Title 3 [wiretap] and we close down her whole operation. She won't have a clue where it came from."

"Right," said Rourke. "I'll pass the information on to New York and Miami. Just keep it up."

I slept good that night.

2

On Thursday morning, March 4, I awoke early. Rudy was already in the kitchen making coffee, along with Lydia and another Chicano undercover named Hector. Through a rear window I saw South in a lime-green Izod, chinos, and his penny loafers shuffling toward the pool shed. South looked, dressed, and acted more like a CIA agent than many of the CIA agents I had known. I simply could not believe that the only place receiving our images was that pool shed.

Sonia suddenly appeared, looking as excited as when she got the lead on René Benitez. "She talked with me about everything."

"What did she say?"

"Everything I told Rourke and the others," she said. "It's all true. They can hear it themselves."

"Did she mention names?" I asked. "She talked about Arce-Gomez and his people?"

"She said everything," said Sonia gloating, her eyes burning in triumph. "I hope it's all recorded."

"Did she mention the names of her current partners?"

"Yes, and she even described them. She said everything, everything, everything." Sonia suddenly looked worried. "It was recorded, no?"

211

I looked at Rudy. He nodded. "Yes," I said, "everything was re-corded."

"Is this enough for her to go to jail?"

"More than enough."

Sonia returned to the bedroom, and I headed out toward the pool shed. The door was ajar. Inside, South was staring at the screens. If I had been Monica wandering around, Operation Hun would have ended at that moment. South's gaze remained focused on the screens, and he began fidgeting with some dials.

You just can't look me in the eye, can you? I thought.

"What's happening?" I said.

"Not much."

"You know there's gold on the recordings from Sonia's bedroom. Not only did Monica corroborate Sonia's whole statement about Arce-Gomez and everyone, but she talked about everything she's doing currently. Sonia said she even described her partners."

"Sounds good," said South absently, continuing to fiddle with the equipment.

"With the information she's giving, us we might be able to get a Title 3 on her phone in New York and nail her whole operation."

"Sounds good," repeated South.

I was losing my patience. "I already told Rourke last night, but I know how these things can get lost in the cracks. You're the guy that has to reduce everything down to sixes [DEA-6, the form for investigative reports]. I just wanted to make sure the info got to New York and Miami ASAP."

South looked directly at me with his fearbiter eyes. "I'm turning all the tapes over to Turghid," he said. "He's got to assign someone to translate them, then I write the reports."

I met his gaze, and he turned back to the machine. I felt like smacking him in the head. Where was the guy who was so anxious to work undercover that he backdoored his boss?

I started toward the house, and then turned back. "Hey, somebody's liable to wander out and see that stuff."

The shed door slammed shut.

I telephoned Rourke and told him about my conversation with South. "Look," I said, "we're undercover one day and we've got a major operation identified. But if the info doesn't get to where its needed quickly, it's worthless."

"Will you stop pushing," said Rourke, annoyed. "I'm right on top of this thing with Turghid—it'll get done."

"Jack, the last thing in the world I wanna do is get involved in any more problems. But if this operation goes the way I think it will, this same scenario might happen 50 times over the next couple of weeks. If we don't get off on the right foot, we're gonna be dead in the water with the dopers laughing at us."

Rourke was quiet. "Look," he said finally, "I'll call Turghid today and talk about it."

"Okay," I said, "and I promise you I won't bug you anymore." God give me the strength to keep that promise.

"Just relax, okay, ya hump? You'll be a lot healthier."

I pictured him with his head in a cloud of smoke. "Thanks for the advice."

### 3

When Monica awoke she was all business. She wanted to see our merchandise. A little past noon, Rudy drove Monica, Sonia, and me to the airport, followed closely by South in the other car with Lydia and a couple of bodyguards, checking for a tail. Kunz and Gorman had been notified and were waiting for us.

As we neared the airport, our backup car parked on a side street. We had to be careful that our Mafia show didn't arouse the attention of the local police, the FBI, or some other federal agency that might raid us. With the intense competition for headlines in the drug war, we would be a juicy target, and that would be the end of Operation Hun. Thus, an important part of our bodyguards' job was to watch for law enforcement surveillance and intercept any police action before it got started.

As we drove through the small rear gate and onto the airport tarmac, Kunz lowered the stairway of the Queenaire. Moments later we were all on board.

"Open both suitcases," I ordered.

Both Daves moved quickly and professionally. They had done their drug pilot act so many times for so many audiences that they probably could have qualified for Actor's Equity. Seats were slammed down, and the suitcases were laid across their backs and zipped open. Monica's pawnbroker's eyes darted hungrily over the merchandise.

"*Ai,*" she breathed softly. "*Esto,*" she said, selecting a package, "*esto, y esto.*"

Gorman took the three packages of cocaine that she had selected and lay them on a seat in front of her. Monica fished a little pocketknife out of her handbag and made an expert incision in the first bag. She then sifted through the powder with the knife blade, avoiding the rocks, and carefully extracted a bladeful of powder, which she held up and examined in the light. She was a seasoned dealer. She had avoided the few rocks in the package because they almost always test out purer than the powder; the powder might be "mix,"—cocaine that has been diluted with some other substance.

"It seems to have a yellow tint to it," she said. "Has it been sitting around for a long time?"

"No," I said, praying that South had told me the truth about the coke. How incredibly futile it would be to attempt an operation like this with anything less than 98 or 99 percent pure.

"Look for yourself." Monica held the powder up in the bright sunlight of the doorway. I examined it, and my heart sank. It looked even more yellow than I remembered.

"I've already sold 50 kilos of this batch without a complaint," I said.

"It could be an imperfection in the process," she said, "but I'll have to test it before I call my people. *Tienes una bolsita de plastico?*" she asked Kunz.

He fished out a plastic bag from somewhere and handed it to me. I held it open, and Monica dumped the bladeful of powder inside. She would test it thoroughly at the house in front of the camera. The Daves gave me meaningful looks. Monica Garcia was as cool as we had ever seen.

Monica repeated the process with the other two bags, examining the powder carefully and shaking her head. "How odd," she murmured. Finally she took a pinch of cocaine and rubbed it between her fingertips. "It feels a little moist," she said. "It could be that it was stored for a long time, or it was stored in a damp place. We'll see how the tests come out."

"Of course," I said, looking at Sonia, whose face betrayed no emotion.

At the house, Rudy set up an electric thermometer on the table directly in front of the Evil Eye. Alongside of it he placed two clear glass tumblers—one half-full of water and the other half-full of Clorox—that Monica had requested. With the camera rolling she went to work testing the cocaine.

Her unblinking eyes first examined the cocaine's reaction in Clorox.

She dropped a pinch of powder into the Clorox; about half of it sank to the bottom and dissolved—a bad sign. Pure cocaine will float to the top and dissolve, leaving a tan, oily slick. She then placed a pinch of powder on a glass slide and laid it carefully atop the electric thermometer's hot plate and turned the temperature knob to its highest reading. Pure cocaine will begin to melt down at 130°C, and when fully melted will leave a yellowish, oily slick. The powder began to break down well below 130° and was leaving dark smoking crusts.

"It's definitely not pure," she said, holding out a glass slide stained with crusty black residue. "Look for yourself."

"I don't sell cut stuff," I said. My heart was in my mouth. The cocaine had been cut, and Sonia had promised her the best. That's what the Queen of Cocaine was famous for.

"Or, if it isn't cut then it's been stored for a long time," she said with finality. "Let's just say it's not the best quality I've seen." She looked at Sonia, who flushed crimson. "How much do you want per kilo?"

"Forty thousand," I said.

She thought for a moment. "That's $2 million; a lot of money for that quality."

"Why don't you call your partners and discuss it with them?" I said, knowing that if she made the call from the house we'd have their phone numbers almost immediately.

"I'm waiting for their call. It should come between seven and eight this evening. I can tell you right now, if you would agree to give us the merchandise on consignment, I'm sure there'll be no problem."

"Monica, as much as I like you, I can't do that. We need the cash to settle with Papo and to pay for the merchandise waiting for us in Bolivia. Besides, this is our first transaction with you. After we've done some business, we can do everything on credit, but now . . ."

"But Sonia knows me for many years," said Monica, looking from Sonia to me. "She will tell you. My credit is good."

Sonia shifted uncomfortably. She was used to running deals. Now she had to keep silent.

"But I'm responsible for her debt. Suppose something unforeseen happens with you and your partners—an arrest, lost merchandise, one of your customers is slow in paying—and our payment is delayed. We could have serious problems."

Monica was silent. There was nothing left to say.

But even without a deal, Operation Hun was an unqualified success as far as Monica went. She had already said and done more than enough to get herself convicted for conspiracy, possession, possession with intent to distribute, and three or four other crimes I hadn't thought of. On top of that, during the night Monica had corroborated on tape much of Sonia's statements about Arce-Gomez and his stooges, whom she'd met while she was in Bolivia doing business with Sonia. We could lock Monica up anytime we were ready. If she flipped and testified before a grand jury, it would be a giant step toward indicting Arce-Gomez and his mob—exactly what I'd been trying to do since I first arrived in Argentina four years earlier.

But as far as the rest of the operation went, the yellow cocaine was a serious problem. I doubted that Monica's partners would come to Tucson with $2 million for beat cocaine, and if the word got out that we had inferior dope, the honey would be gone from our trap and the risk on our lives would be doubled. If Mejia heard about it, he might decide just to kill Sonia, and me with her.

And then there was the question of who was responsible for the bad cocaine in the first place? Whoever it was had to be highly placed in DEA and involved in Operation Hun. Whoever it was had no qualms about putting our lives in jeopardy.

At exactly 7 P.M. the phone rang and a male caller asked for Monica. She took the call in the bedroom. While she was on the phone I went out to the pool house and tapped lightly on the door. South opened it and I slipped inside.

On the television monitor I watched Sonia and Lydia sitting in silence. Monica's telephone conversation could not be monitored, because it would have required a court order that we didn't have. Turghid had not thought one necessary.

"I forgot to ask you," I said, "what's the quality of that coke?"

"I told you the lab said it's pure," said South, studying the screen.

"Yeah, but how pure? Dopers are businesspeople. The exact purity can mean a lot to them."

"I think they said 89 percent. I've gotta check the paperwork."

"Wait a minute. The stuff didn't even test out to 89 percent. And even if it had, why didn't they give us something better? Do you know how this is handicapping us?"

"You know how that works," he said, keeping his eyes on the little screen. "I put the request in to Washington; they sign off and tell us which coke to use."

I had no reply. South was claiming that out of all the tons of pure cocaine in DEA's labs, headquarters had decided to furnish "the most important operation in the agency" with beat yellow garbage that I'd have had a hard time selling on a street corner as an undercover prop to fool some of the biggest drug dealers in the world. On top of that, the cocaine had not even tested out anywhere near 89 percent pure. If it had been cut, as Monica's tests indicated, it could only have been for one of two reasons: either someone stole part of the original 50 kilos to sell it, and then replaced the stolen coke with mix; or someone wanted to make sure Operation Hun failed.

I realized that both theories rested on whether the drugs were actually cut, so I knew I had to be extremely careful about the topic. Before I opened my mouth I had to be 1,000 percent sure I was right, and Monica's tests were not conclusive. The only way to get absolute proof was to put in a complaint to Internal Security. That would cause the immediate shutdown of Operation Hun and focus DEA's investigative force on those of us working the case. How convenient if they could somehow lay the blame for the diluted coke on me.

Monica returned from the bedroom, her face unreadable. "They will take the merchandise only if you send it to New York."

"They want me to front it *and* send it to New York?" Sounding incredulous was easy—they'd gone farther than I thought they would.

Monica shrugged. "They said speak to the gentleman."

"I'm sorry," I said, thinking that at least she wasn't trying to con me. "I don't think we can do business; at least not this time. But we'll stay in contact—perhaps in the future."

"Yes," said Monica. "I'm sure one day or another we will do business. By the way, Miguel, Sonia tells me that Ana is coming on Saturday. Do you mind if I stay with you a few more days . . . just until she comes? It's been so long since I've seen her."

"Of course," I said. "My house is your house."

I didn't want Monica around for a moment longer than necessary— she was too curious and too sharp. We'd have to sustain our act without the cover of doing business, and Monica would expect to see another side of our Mafia family's behavior—a group of people relaxing and enjoying each other's company. We hadn't practiced that.

That night, after Monica and Sonia had gone to bed, I telephoned Rourke and told him about the cocaine.

Rourke was upset. "Are you sure she ain't fuckin' with you, just tryin' to get you to front the stuff?"

"I'm about 95 percent sure."

"Why don't you call Turghid?"

"Jack, I haven't heard a word from the guy since the meeting. I don't even know if he's interested anymore. Besides, even if the stuff's what South says it is, why are we using yellow, bullshit, 89 percent cocaine if this case is so fucking hot?"

"Fuck! Lemme talk to Turghid in the morning. I'll get back to ya."

That night was a sleepless one for me, and in the morning I went to the gym. I peeked around before I went inside; I didn't want to run into Sam and Morris. Sometimes I could handle them, but not that morning. I put myself through a two-hour, mind-numbing workout and headed back to the house. When I got there I was relieved that Rudy had taken Sonia and Monica shopping and sightseeing. I would have had a hard time keeping up the act right then.

Rourke called.

"I spoke to Turghid and he said the stuff's 89 percent; that's what the lab papers say and he's got no reason to doubt them. Lemme ask you somethin'. Are you sure it's not?"

"Of course not, how can I be? All I saw was Monica's test."

"That's what I mean. Don't jump to fuckin' conclusions so fast."

"Jack, I don't want to. But even if the stuff is 89, why don't we have 99 or 100? Why do we have any problem at all?"

Rourke was quiet. "Look, this is his show out here, you know that. We're lucky we're gettin' the kind of cooperation we are."

I let Rourke convince me that "maybe" Monica's test was a slick ploy by Monica who "maybe" didn't have the cash and was "maybe" just trying to con us into fronting her the drugs; and that while 89 percent coke wasn't the best stuff in the world, it certainly wasn't the worst. To insist that the coke was as bad as I truly believed it was meant forcing the matter into the hands of Internal Security, killing Operation Hun, and giving the inspectors another shot at me. That was the last thing in the world I wanted to happen.

Monica staying over paid an unexpected dividend. As we all sat around the living room in front of the Evil Eye later that evening, I overheard Monica questioning Sonia about a German drug customer. Sonia said she couldn't remember him, although Monica insisted that she had to.

Later, when Sonia and I were alone I asked her about the German. "Just someone I met," she said evasively. "But I met a lot of people."

# 18

# Ana: *La Comisionista*

## 1

When I got out of bed on Saturday morning, Sonia was already in the kitchen with Rudy, laughing and in a good mood. Monica and Lydia were still sleeping.

"Miguel, you're going to love Ana," said Sonia. I sure hope I don't, I thought. "She's so much fun, you'll see. I guess I didn't realize how much I missed her."

Rudy gave me a wry grin. Ana Tamayo was due in from Miami on an afternoon flight. I still wasn't quite sure how to handle Ana and Monica in the house at the same time. My instinct was to get out of the way and let Sonia and the listening devices do the job.

"You all going to sleep together in one bed?" I said.

Sonia laughed coquettishly. "Sure, why not? I've shared beds with each of them, why not all together?"

"That oughtta be one hell of a recording," said Rudy in English.

"What did you say?" asked Sonia. "What did he say, Miguel?"

"He said, 'Is there any room for me in there?'"

Sonia laughed like it was the funniest thing she'd ever heard. I'd never seen her in such a good mood.

"I think I'm gonna stay out of the way today," I said. "You go to the airport with Rudy, Monica, Lydia, and a couple of the bodyguards; let everyone get real relaxed and I'll show up later tonight. Tell Ana Miguel is out with customers for our merchandise . . . please forgive me . . . you know."

"Lydia doesn't have to come," said Sonia, lowering her voice. "She doesn't say anything anyway. Monica is nervous around her. You want them to talk . . ."

The phone rang. I picked it up. It was the answering service—a Mr. Pineda had called from Miami. He left a callback number.

"Who's Pineda?" I said to Sonia. For a moment she went pale.

"That's Eduardo . . . from Papo."

"They must have heard something," I said.

"I'm sure," said Sonia, no longer smiling. "What do we do?"

"Call him back, tell him we're here; we want to settle the debt; but first we have to discuss how much it is and see if we all agree. But they'll just have to have patience until we're ready."

"What if they want to come here?"

"Tell them we're not ready yet," I said. "You've got a partner now and he's responsible. They've got to deal with me."

As I suspected, the number was an answering service. Sonia left a message that she was in Tucson; that everything was going well and that she would be calling again.

"That's fine," I said when she hung up. "Now they know we're not trying to run away. They can wait until we're ready."

Papo was finally making his move.

In the afternoon everyone else went to the airport to pick up Ana. South was moping around out at the pool shed. I took one of the cars and made my almost daily visit to the gym.

"Hey, Levine," yelled Morris. "Ve vas just talkink about you." He and Sam were standing in exactly the same spot where I had first met them, between a row of Lifecycles and a treadmill.

"Yeah," said Sam. "Ho boy, do ve have a goil for you." He held his hand to his shiny bald head, his eyes rolling toward the treadmill where a sun-kissed blond in exercise tights tried not to hear him.

"So, woddya tink, Levine?" said Morris, jerking his head toward the now-blushing woman.

"When I switch back to women," I said.

For a moment they looked puzzled. "Ahh," said Sam uncertainly, "he's pulling our leg."

"Where's Izzy?" I asked. "I don't see him with you guys anymore. You didn't do something you shouldn't have, did you?"

"Izzy? Vots an Izzy?" said Sam.

"Sam don't trust people vot don't talk."

"Maybe it's because you never let him get a word in edgewise."

"He's from Chicago," said Morris, "so woddya expect?"

I spent about an hour and a half talking with Sam and Morris before I finally began to work out. I was becoming attached to them. They'd become an important part of my Operation Hun survival mechanism. After a two-hour workout, I called the house and spoke to Rudy.

"What's happening?"

"Everything's going great, boss. We're getting ready to take the three of 'em to dinner."

"They talking freely?"

Rudy laughed. "Ana is something else."

"A talker?"

"Like there's no tomorrow. You can't shut her up. I think she got Monica a little nervous."

In the background I could hear a woman's voice chattering away in Spanish.

"Is that her I hear?"

"None other."

"Wow," I said. "They miss me?"

"Not at all," said Rudy. "Oh, by the way. Monica got a call from some guy . . . real mysterious. After she hung up she said she has to leave the first thing in the morning."

"Where's she going?"

"Miami. I heard her make the reservations."

"You got it covered?"

"No problem," said Rudy. "Me and South will take her."

"Hey, do me a favor. Either go alone or take a Spanish-speaking undercover with you, okay?"

Rudy was silent for a moment. I had to remember that he and South had been good friends a long time before I got there, and they'd probably continue as friends long after I was gone.

"Whatever you say, boss," said Rudy.

"Okay, I'm gonna show up tonight after you take them to dinner. Just give them my apologies; I'm out doing business."

I arrived at the house about 8 P.M. to find it empty. I took the opportunity to call my kids in New York. My father had abandoned my family in New York when I was 13, and I never saw or heard from him again until I tracked him down when I was in my twenties. I promised myself I'd never lose contact with my kids. Now, life was racing by.

"Where are you dad?" said my 17-year-old son Keith. "We tried to call your apartment in Virginia, and your office. All they would say is that you're out of town."

"I'm in Arizona son. I can't give you a number here, but if you need me, call DEA headquarters and tell them you're my son and it's an emergency. If they give you a hard time, tell them you want to speak to Jack Rourke. He'll get to me. Okay?"

"Okay."

"What's going on? How's your karate coming?"

"It's a crazy house here, dad." The anguish in his voice made my heart ache.

"What is it?" I closed my eyes.

"It's Niki. She's acting crazy. You can't even talk to her without her screaming and cursing at the top of her lungs."

"I'll talk to her."

"You're only here every other week, Dad. What am I supposed to do, let her talk like that to mommy?"

"Keith, you can't play father with her. Just as soon as I can get out, I'll be there."

He was quiet. "I gotta go, dad." His voice was just audible.

"Everything's gonna be okay, son. Don't worry."

"Sure."

"Son?"

"Yeah, dad?"

"I love you."

"I love you too, dad."

All thoughts of my problems and Operation Hun vanished, replaced by thoughts about my kids. I was pacing the floor and talking to myself.

My first impulse was to drop everything and fly to New York. But if I did, I'd be gift-wrapping myself for the inspectors. They'd fire me on the spot for leaving my post without authorization, dereliction of duty, taking leave without a proper request and authorization, conduct unbecoming an agent, and a dozen other charges. And if I asked to be removed from the case, I'd probably be blamed for whatever became of Operation Hun, the strange cocaine, and Sonia Atala.

Suddenly I had to get out of the UC house. Once again I felt like running—where was unimportant.

Five years earlier, right after my brother's suicide, I felt as though my life was coming apart. I had jumped on my motorcycle in New York to take a ride. I kept on riding until I ended up three days later on a South Florida beach at 4 A.M., staring out at the ocean. I had run away almost as far as I could, but all my problems were still with me. I couldn't run away from myself.

Now five years had passed and I was still running away to nowhere.

I raced the big, smooth-riding car aimlessly over desert roads, a cassette of salsa music drowning me in sound. I had no place to run, but the act seemed to dull the pain of living in constant stress and fear.

Sometime before dawn I slipped into the undercover house weary enough to collapse into a black, dreamless sleep.

## 2

I awoke to the sound of a woman's voice chattering away in machine-gun Spanish. I pulled myself out of bed, shaved, showered, and dressed, and the voice was still going. It had to be the television; no human could speak in sentences that long without pausing for breath. I started toward the living room. Rudy met me in the hallway.

"Ana's here," he said, nodding in the direction of the voice, "and Monica's on her way back to Miami."

"Everything going all right?"

Rudy smiled and shook his head. "She's some piece of work. She had Sonia and Monica up all night."

"Anything good?"

"Christ, dope is all she talks about. She must have mentioned 100 names already."

"Sounds good."

"You better get in there. She's waiting to meet don Miguel."

When I entered the living room, I immediately came under the power of Ana Tamayo. The tall, big-boned woman with long black hair tied in a ponytail was holding court before Sonia and Lydia from a large easy chair directly in front of the Evil Eye. When she saw me, she stopped speaking and smiled warmly, her dark eyes searching mine.

"This must be don Miguel," she said rising to meet me.

"Yes," said Sonia, studying me worriedly.

*"Encantado,"* I said, crossing to Ana and kissing her on the cheek.

"Please forgive me for not being here last night. I had some last-minute business."

"Don't trouble yourself, don Miguel," she said, squeezing my arm. "Sonia, your beautiful sister, and the enchanting Rudy have been taking wonderful care of me."

Her smile was the most infectious damned thing I had ever seen. She just seemed to bubble over with wonderful life. I found myself grinning back at her.

"Why do I feel as though I know you?" I asked her. This was none of my undercover jive. There was a warm familiarity about the woman that made her feel as though she were family.

"I know," she said. "I have that feeling, too."

"Please, sit down and relax, Ana." I asked Rudy to bring me some coffee, and he disappeared into the kitchen. I sat next to Sonia.

"My God!" Ana held her hands together. "What a beautiful couple you make!" She grinned at Sonia, who looked annoyed.

After an hour with Ana, we had become friends. She was supposed to be about 50 years old, but she had the youthful energy and enthusiasm of a teenager. She used heavy makeup and wore too-tight pants that she had to keep adjusting. It was intended to be sexy, but the combination of her appearance and her personality made her seem more like a gangly school girl dressing up like the big girls rather than a dope dealer.

As Ana chattered nonstop about her husband's laziness, the price of television sets in Miami, the sexuality of certain movie stars, and huge drug deals, it occurred to me that it would be hard to find two women more opposite than Ana and Monica. Where Monica was calculating and secretive, Ana was warm and trusting to the point of guilelessness. Without any hesitation she told me and the Evil Eye that she had just finished selling 145 kilos of a 150-kilo load of cocaine; enough of an admission to get her 45 years in prison.

"The shipment belongs to Pacho Cuervas," she said.

"Who?"

Ana suddenly lowered her voice as if she were afraid to be overheard. "He's only the biggest in Colombia."

"Bigger than the Ochoas and Escobar?" I asked.

Ana was supposed to have brokered deals between Sonia and Jorge Ochoa and Pablo Escobar (the Medellin Cartel). The idea of Sonia being a source for the men DEA and the world press had accredited with supplying as much as 80 percent of the cocaine consumed in the

United States was mind-boggling. It was verification that Sonia was the back door to the very heart of the cocaine empire, and Ana would underscore this many times on tape.

"Bigger," insisted Ana. "Sonia . . ." She shook her head, unable to find the words. "You cannot imagine."

Sonia looked at me. Her eyes seemed to sparkle with the unspoken words, *Didn't I tell you she was amazing?*

"I still have five kilos left in Miami," continued Ana. "I just had to rush over here the first moment I had free to see my *Soñita.*" She beamed at Sonia, who beamed back. "As soon as I sell them—which may be next week, because I have some gringos coming—and take care of some family matters, I will get to work finding you customers.

"*Ai, Dios mio,*" she said suddenly, putting her hand to her forehead, "and I have two babies who can't do anything without their mommy waiting for me in Miami. *Aiii,* Miguel, there's no rest."

"You have two children?"

"No," she laughed, "not children—babies. My husband and my daughter Candy." She threw her hands up in mock despair.

Sonia laughed. "So everything's still the same."

"*Aii, Soñita,* I swear they can't go to the bathroom without me."

"There's no rush," I said. "We've got some customers coming. If we sell out before you return, there'll be much more, I hope."

"*Ojala!*" said Ana, raising her eyes to the heavens. Rudy was grinning at me from across the room, and I had to look away. Even Lydia was smiling. "By the way, don Miguel," she said, her voice dropping again, "you know that I am a *comisionista,* no?"

"Yes, Ana. Sonia already told me."

"My fee is $2,500 a kilo."

"*Que Dios te bendiga, Ana,*" I said.

"Thank you, don Miguel."

"Do you like to dance?"

Ana beamed. "I would love to."

I put on a hot salsa tape by El Gran Combo de Puerto Rico, and we danced around the floor with Sonia, Rudy, Lydia, and the Evil Eye gawking in silent wonder.

For the next two hours we danced, told jokes, and had a few drinks and a lot more recorded conversation. At one point I stepped out of the room for a minute to take a break. The kind of energy an undercover uses up in even the simplest of scenarios is something few suits understand. It's like juggling balls and balancing spinning plates on poles at the same time. You have to be two people functioning in one brain—an actor performing for an intimate audience and an investigator who can memorize detailed descriptions and hours of conversation and then testify flawlessly about them at trials that take place months or even years later.

When I returned Ana was talking to Sonia about the German.

"You must remember him," Ana was saying. "He was obsessed with you. *Ai, Dios mio, chica,* he sent you tickets to come to his house in Hawaii, and you don't remember?"

"How am I supposed to remember?" said Sonia, shrugging and glancing at me nervously. "A lot of men were inviting me everywhere." Ana and Monica remembered this guy vividly and Sonia didn't?

"Who is that?" I interrupted. Ana smiled impishly.

"Just a customer of Mejia's," said Ana. "He's somebody who . . ." Ana saw Sonia glaring at her and stopped.

"A German, right? I think Monica was saying something about him."

Ana flared suddenly, "Miguel, I don't like to talk about people, but Monica is not . . . you shouldn't listen to everything she says. And you can ask Sonia, I never talk about people."

"I just thought he was somebody we could talk business to. But if he's in Germany . . ."

"No, no, not Germany. He spoke with a German accent, but he lives in Miami," said Ana, glancing at Sonia, who was looking away.

"Didn't you say something about Hawaii?" I insisted.

Now Ana was really uncomfortable. "I really don't know Miguel. Somebody said he had a house there." She stopped; Sonia was glaring at her again.

Later, during dinner at one of our best-cultivated restaurants, Ana and I toasted our wonderful fortune in meeting. Ana leaned over and said, "Miguel, I cannot tell you how happy it makes me to see Sonia again, and to see her with a gentleman like you." I thought I saw a tear in her eye—she was a refreshing bundle of emotion. She squeezed my hand. "I know everything will turn out well for both of you."

"Thank you, Ana," I said, suddenly feeling sad. "I hope so."

## 3

Late that evening, back in our living room, Ana opened the door to the Colombian drug world for DEA with an offer I did not think the agency could refuse. Sonia and I had spent an hour or so pumping guileless Ana about the whereabouts of René Benitez. During the conversation, I was surprised to learn that Ana had introduced Sonia to Benitez and that Sonia and he were a lot closer than just having done a few minor drug deals. In one case, the two had spent a couple of days together in Panama negotiating a major deal. I have since learned that Benitez has claimed that Sonia also wanted him to kill some Bolivian politicians for her; that she had claimed to be arranging the assassinations on behalf the Arce-Gomez government.

"I thought if anyone would know where he is," said Ana, "it would be you. Why are you so anxious to find him?"

"I have some important business I want to talk about," said Sonia.

"Ana, you know about our problem with Papo, no?" I said. Just the mention of his name was enough to frighten Ana. Her eyes opened wide; her voice dropped to just above a whisper.

"You know he killed Hernan Carini and his whole family?"

"I heard," said Sonia.

"Who's that?" I asked.

"They were his competition in Colombia," said Sonia.

"Yes, but they also did business together," said Ana, glancing wide-eyed at the dark shadows around the room, like a Campfire Girl about to tell a horror story. "Papo owed Hernan a lot of money. It's just as dangerous to have him owe you money as it is to owe him, my darlings . . . more dangerous. He didn't want to pay so he decides he's going to, you know, kill him. But Hernan has a big family and all of them were traffickers, so Papo knows if he kills one, they're going to come after him." Ana pointed at her forehead. "He thinks like that; like a devil.

"He waits until the family is getting together for, I don't know, a celebration, and all the time, they say, he was acting so friendly. And then he comes with his men and machine guns. He kills them all, even the women and babies—even the dogs."

"I heard one survived," said Sonia matter-of-factly; she seemed little affected by the story.

"Yes, Hugo."

"Who is Hugo?" I asked.

"The old uncle," said Ana. "He escaped into the forest. Nobody ever saw him again, but Papo's men are still looking for him."

"Papo must have made himself lots of enemies," I said. "Doesn't he fear being killed himself?"

Ana shivered. "He is like a poisonous snake. The only sure way to kill him is to cut off his head."

"Now you understand why we have to resolve this thing before we can really feel safe about doing business," I said.

"Of course," said Ana. "How about the other one that had problems?" she said to Sonia.

Sonia shot a warning glance at Ana. "That was all taken care of."

"What other one?" I asked quickly.

"My uncle mixed sugar with some merchandise that went to Colombia and I had to pay."

"That's not going to be a problem for us, is it?" I asked.

"No," said Sonia coolly. Was she telling the truth, or would I find out she was lying in a hail of bullets?

Ana had flushed crimson and looked like she wanted to crawl into a hole. I had to get her off the hook. I wanted her speaking freely.

"Ana, you see what I mean?" I laughed. "With this business I can take no chances."

"True," said Ana. "*Aii, Dios!* Why didn't I think of this before?" She leaned toward me excitedly. "Miguel, you spoke earlier of doing a large marijuana deal in Colombia, true?"

During dinner, mixing truth and undercover fantasy, I had told Ana of a marijuana deal that I had done in Argentina with a Colombian named Eagleman. Max Pooley and I had negotiated for 27 tons of marijuana with a diminutive, jewelry-laden Colombian by that name who Max had conned into coming to Argentina. The Argentine undercover cops who were covering the meetings had gone nuts over the little drug dealer's jewelry—particularly his watch. It was all Max and I could do to convince the kill-crazy Argentines to let the guy leave the country alive. Somewhere in Colombia there's a drug dealer named Eagleman who will probably never know how high a price he almost paid for wearing his diamond-studded Rolex.

"Well, right now, Pacho has 17 tons of yellow, high-grade marijuana sitting near a landing strip with no customer."

"Where?"

"In Colombia, where else? Near Cartagena."

"I don't know, Ana . . . grass. I haven't done . . ."

"You don't have to pay until you sell the merchandise, Miguel. You have nothing to lose. Pacho knows all about Sonia, and I will vouch for you. All you need to do is send a plane to pick it up. When it's sold, you can pay me right here."

She had caught me by surprise. Seventeen tons of Colombian marijuana was going for about $20–$25 million dollars, and she was offering it to me free.

"Well, I don't know," I said, stalling. I wasn't sure what to say, but I didn't want to let the opportunity go. "We haven't settled with Mejia yet. I'm a little afraid of going to Colombia until our problem's resolved."

"Don't worry about him," said Ana, almost bouncing with enthusiasm. She took me by the hand and said, "I feel so much like I know you, Miguel. I trust you. I will vouch for you with Pacho. While you are his guest, no one will harm you, not even Papo. I cannot tell you how powerful he is. And he has something else that might interest you. Did you ever hear of little pills they call 'Kawasaki?'"

"No, what is it?"

"Tiny little tablets—doses of morphine. They came into Colombia stashed in hollow fishing rods from France—Marseilles. Pacho never had it before, and he asked me to find some customers. If you like, I'll tell him that you will try and sell it for him."

"How much does he have?"

"A million doses, maybe more; they're tiny," said Ana, pinching her fingers together. "One little box holds . . . I don't know . . . maybe 10,000 pills. When you come for the marijuana you can take the pills back with you. Whatever you don't sell, you send back to Pacho. What's to think about? All you need is a plane and a pilot. What do you have to lose?"

I was speechless. Because of her friendship with Sonia, Ana was offering me $35–$40 million in marijuana and morphine fronted to me by someone she described as the biggest drug trafficker in Colombia. This was the chance to uncover a morphine connection between Marseilles and Colombia—an undercover's gold mine.

So why was I hesitating? Because I wasn't sure that my own agency wouldn't turn on me the way it had during the Suarez case and the Bolivian investigations.

Ana appealed to Sonia. "What is there to think about? Tell him he has nothing to lose." Sonia looked at me, waiting for rescue.

I made up my mind—this was an opportunity that no agency that called itself the Drug Enforcement Administration should miss. "Ana, it's not that I'm hesitating. The thing with Papo has me a little worried. You can tell Pacho yes. We'll do it as soon as I get rid of the merchandise we've got here. Then it'll take me a week or two to get a pilot and plane. Of course, we'll have to come there first to check out the landing field and make refueling arrangements."

"Pacho will take care of all that for you," said Ana quickly.

"I'll need at least a week or two," I said. That ought to be long enough for the suits to make a decision.

"Wonderful!" said Ana, excited. "The landing field is a dirt strip 2,000 meters long. It's flat and hard. Anything can land on it."

"The pilot will have to see for himself, Ana."

"Oh, but of course, my darling. Pacho will roll out the red carpet for you both. We'll have a party. I have such a wonderful feeling about this." She hugged Sonia and then came into my arms and kissed me.

"So do I, *mamita*," I said.

## 4

After everyone had gone to sleep, I lay awake in my bed listening to the hum of the air conditioner, trying to clear my mind of all thoughts. Someone had told me that was the key to meditation—if you could blank your mind for 10 or 20 minutes and totally relax yourself, you could have the equivalent of a whole night's sleep. It was also supposed to relieve stress. But the effort to blank everything out turned out to be just one more stressful ordeal for me.

The phone rang, and I picked it up in the darkness. *"Hable."*

"Michael, is that you?" It was my ex-wife, Liana. Then I heard a click on the line.

"Is there someone else on the line?" I asked.

"Not on this end," she said.

*"Esta en la linea, alguien?"* Silence. "How'd you get this number?"

"You told Keith if there was an emergency to call DEA. I did."

"Okay. I'm right in the middle of an undercover, so we're probably being recorded."

"Niki's on drugs," she blurted.

The words rocked me. Would drugs destroy everyone I loved? "How do you know?"

"How do you think I know? I'm her mother—I live with her!"

I was suddenly furious at my daughter. I was a narcotics agent; I had talked to her about drugs any number of times. How could she do this?

"Put her on the phone!" I snapped.

"She's not here."

"Christ, what time is it?"

"I don't know . . . 3:30."

"She's only 14. What the hell is she doing out at this time of night?"

"You think I don't think about that?" Liana screamed. "Do you think I let her out, you son of a bitch? You think I can control her? She's stronger than me—I'm afraid of my own daughter! Face it Michael, your daughter's a druggie, just like your brother! And it's your fault. It's all your fault!"

Her words penetrated deep inside me. The breath went out of me and an immense weariness fell over me like a heavy blanket.

"Don't you have anything to say, Michael?"

"If I leave here now, I'll be fired for sure," I said, holding my head in my hand.

"That goddamn job of yours," she said. "I can't tell you how much I hate it. You're supposed to be a narcotics agent—well, come and do something about your own daughter."

"If you can hold it together for just a couple of days . . ." I began. Liana slammed the phone down.

I turned the lights on. I felt I had to get out in the open, out in the desert so I could think clearly. I dressed hurriedly, trying not to think of anything but each article of clothing as I put it on.

But as I left my room, I heard sounds in the living room. Coming out, I saw Ana crouching in front of the television, now alive with images and light. Ana looked at me with a start and stood. I saw that the unthinkable had happened—she had turned the selector to the forbidden channel. On the big screen I could see Ana turning to face me as I entered the living room.

"Miguel," she said, putting her hand over her heart, "you frightened me. I couldn't sleep and . . . Look at you. You are crying."

I had to keep her turned toward me. "I just got a call from my ex-wife. My little girl's on drugs," I blurted, realizing that this wasn't something I should be telling a drug dealer, against whom I would soon be testifying in court and whose life I would eventually destroy.

"*Aii, pobrecito,*" said Ana taking me in her arms. I held her, keeping her back to the TV. "I've got the same trouble with my daughter," she said. "Children can wrench the life from your chest."

"Ana, please don't pay any attention to me," I said, positioning myself between her and the screen. I changed the channel and switched the set off in one motion, praying that she didn't notice.

I had been told that the hidden video camera could function only when South operated it from the pool house. He'd gone home hours ago. Someone was still operating it, and not from the pool house.

"I didn't mean to get you involved in my problems," I said as I faced Ana. "I'm sorry. Did you want to watch television?"

"Please don't trouble yourself, Miguel," she said, sitting down. "We're awake for the same reasons. Life is not easy."

We sat together talking until the sky grew light. Ana told me about her cocaine-addicted daughter and alcoholic husband. She was the sole support of her family, and dragged them everywhere with her. At the moment both husband and daughter were awaiting her return to Miami. The weight of having to provide financial, moral, and psychological sustenance for her family was wearing her out.

I told her about my brother's heroin addiction and suicide. "Sometimes, Ana, I think that maybe God is trying to get even with me for all the years I have been in this business."

"Don't think that way, Miguel. With all the guns and bombs the gringos sell all over the world, does God strike their children down with guns and bombs? It's the gringos themselves that want *perico*. It's their problem. And as long as they want it someone will always be around to provide it—whether it's you and I or not. And that's life."

"Thanks Ana. I needed that."

She laughed and gave me another hug. "Miguel, I really like you."

"And I feel the same about you, Ana," I said, meaning every word.

After Ana left for Miami on Sunday, I tried to reach Rourke at his hotel, but he was out of town until Monday morning. I decided to wait for his return to hit him with Ana's invitation to front us more than $30 million of Pacho Cuervas's dope. This would be a major deep cover operation involving foreign travel authorization and coordination between several DEA fiefdoms, the State Department, and possibly the CIA. Headquarters would have to handle it. I decided not to tell Turghid. Cartagena was a long way from Tucson and Turghid's fiefdom. Why take a chance on muddying the waters?

Later that day Sonia and I were lying side-by-side on beach chairs by the pool, alone. The more I was around Sonia the more questions I had about her. How much English did she really know? I'd seen her reacting when English was spoken in a way that showed she understood a lot more than she let on. How much information had she withheld from DEA? When Ana and Monica had brought up drug dealers like the German or Pacho Cuervas, Sonia seemed to tense the way suspects do when agents executing a search warrant open the closet door where the drugs are hidden. If anyone mentioned Pachi and cocaine in the same sentence, she turned to stone. What about her and Pachi's involvement with the CIA? And what was this mysterious deal where Colombians got ripped off by Sonia's uncle?

"You never told me about having trouble with other customers," I said, sitting upright and looking at my reflection in her sunglasses.

"What trouble?" she asked.

"You said your uncle stole some cocaine from a shipment and replaced it with sugar. At least that's what I thought you said."

"Oh, that trouble."

"Yeah, that trouble. Are these people in the U.S.? I mean, is there anything we have to be afraid of, or am I going to walk into a shopping mall with you one day and while the bullets are flying you say, 'Oh, there was a deal I forgot to tell you about, Miguel?'"

"They were Cubans and Colombians from Miami. But there's nothing . . . it was resolved."

"Why didn't you tell me before?"

"I told Rourke," she snapped impatiently. "I can't remember to tell you everything I tell him and the others. Why doesn't he tell you?"

I said nothing; I had no answer. Sonia stretched back on the chair and said, "Why don't you relax, Miguel? You're always so serious."

"I'm trying," I said, my voice coming out dry and croaky. Once again I realized how vulnerable I was to this woman. Internal Security was still digging for anything they could use against me. Anything derogatory Sonia said about me would be accepted as fact.

I leaned back and closed my eyes against the blazing Arizona sun. I didn't trust Sonia at all. Whatever her game was, I figured her last allegiance was to DEA. I wanted to at least trust Rourke, but I doubted that he'd go out of his way to help or protect me. At least he seemed sincere in wanting to make the most out of Operation Hun.

The blast furnace sun baked us both into silence.

"Wasn't Ana special?" said Sonia finally.

"Yes," I said, "very special."

"She's only a *comisionista*."

"Yeah, I know."

"It's a shame, with all this . . . to put someone like that in prison."

I tried to decide whether or not it really was a shame, and just couldn't come up with a clear feeling about it one way or the other. I guess I'd just seen too much of the "real" war on drugs to say that it wasn't, and had believed in it for too long to say that it was.

# 19

# Off the Target

## 1

**M**onday morning I awoke to the ringing of the phone.

"Don Miguel?" It was Ana calling from Miami. She'd wasted no time arranging the huge morphine-and-marijuana deal with Pacho Cuervas. She must have just gotten off the phone with Colombia. She was breathing in quick, short breaths.

"All you have to do is tell me a date when you and your pilot will come. Everything is set. Do you understand, Miguel?"

"Ana, I just woke up. Please forgive me."

"No, forgive me for calling so early. I wanted to make sure . . ."

"You know I still have to finish this business here first."

"I know all that, but this is important, Miguel. This is a very big opportunity. I didn't want you and Sonia to lose—not something like this. I spoke to Pacho himself and he's very enthusiastic. He knows all about Sonia, and I told him about you. He's anxious to meet you."

I thought about how long it might take to get the suits to understand the operation, let alone support it. "What I'm saying . . . I just don't want him to be upset if I'm a couple of days late."

"No, he'll understand. All he needs is the date of your arrival. He'll have his own plane waiting to meet you. They'll take you right there."

*"Tremendo, Ana. Fenomino,"* I said. "We'll do it."

Ana laughed. "Pacho wants to have a party in your honor."

"I'll be there, Ana," I said. "Let me just take care of the business here and I'm on my way."

"Please don't fail me, Miguel. I vouched for you personally, you know what that means? In their eyes you're already accepted."

"Don't worry Ana," I said. "You won't be sorry."

Ana, like the good *comisionista* she was, was busily laying the groundwork for me with a lot of traffickers—not just Cuervas. There was no telling how far into the Colombian drug world our trip to Cartagena might take us.

"I know, Miguel. *Un beso grande, mi amor.*"

"*Un abrazo, mamita.*"

"*Aiii,* wait Miguel. I have someone here who wants to say hello."

"Miguel?" said a young woman's voice, with a lilt of laughter. I'm Candy. I don't know what you did to my mother, but she can't stop talking about you," she said in lightly accented English.

"Well, she did the same to me, Candy."

"You sound like a sweet guy. I'm looking forward to meeting you."

"Me too," I said, my throat going tight.

The instant I put the phone down it rang again.

"Sir, I'm looking for someone named Erica," said a woman's voice in English. Erica was one of Lydia's undercover names, and we had used it for the answering service.

"What's it in reference to?"

"Sir, are you one of the people who have the answering service?"

"Yes," I said, "what's this about?"

"I just wanted to tell you that our Spanish-speaking operators are getting some upsetting calls; the callers are abusive and . . ."

"Are those the calls from Miami?" I said, cutting her off.

"Yes, I believe they are. A Mr. Pineda."

Pineda had been calling leaving progressively angrier messages. In his last one he had said, "This isn't something that will go away."

I promised the woman I'd take care of it and hung up. We couldn't stall much longer.

By late morning, none of the Tucson agents had appeared; Sonia was at poolside sunbathing; Lydia, as usual, was staying in her room.

Rourke called. He was still at headquarters and wouldn't arrive in Tucson until the next day. I quickly brought him up to date on the

Mejia phone calls and the Cuervas situation.

"You shouldn't have told her you were coming," said Rourke.

"Jack, how could I call myself a drug enforcement agent if I turned down a shot at the biggest violator in Colombia?"

"Levine, don't break my balls. You know who I'm dealing with."

"Well, don't break my balls. I'm supposed to be a drug dealer, not some fucking bureaucrat. If I'm real, I can't refuse an offer of $30 million of dope out front so easily. And if I do refuse and it gets back to Mejia, he'll know we're phony."

"Just take it easy," he said. "I'll have to talk to some people here about it. I don't suppose you wanna call Turghid?"

"What for? This has nothing to do with Tucson. Besides, he hasn't even been out here since this thing began. Why change anything?"

"I'll call him," Rourke said tiredly.

Fifteen minutes later, Rourke called back. "Turghid wants all of you in his office."

"What about the Cuervas deal?"

"I'll get on it as soon as I hang up."


Early in the afternoon, Sonia, Lydia, and I arrived at Turghid's office. The moment we entered, I could feel that something was up. The normally friendly receptionist buzzed us through without looking up. Agents looked the other way. Turghid glared at me from behind his desk. South, sitting in Turghid's office, didn't even look up.

"Whyntchu put 'er somewhere!" snapped Turghid, his words coming low and fast. He indicated Sonia and eyed me like he was John Wayne facing down some gunslinger.

"Why?" I noticed that Sonia was already edging toward the door. Did she understand what he said?

"She's an informant. I don't have no 'formants sittin' in on plannin' sessions."

"I'll sit with her," said Lydia, looking relieved to get out of the room. South shut the door after them.

I took a seat across from Turghid and laid a small bag of cassettes on his desk. They were my taped telephone conversations with Ana. "These are gold. They're Ana Tamayo talking about everything from the Medellin Cartel to this new guy Pacho Cuervas."

"I wantchu to know I'm against you goin' to Colombia. Our target's Arce-Gomez. Far 's I'm concerned, goin' to Colombia's offa the target."

"Ana says Cuervas is bigger than the Medellin Cartel," I said. "Sonia says Ana knows what she's talking about—she deals for the Cartel. How can possibly the biggest doper in Colombia be off the target?"

"You'll have to take it up with headquarters," snapped Turghid. "Meantime, that scumbag Benitez's still out there; they want Sonia to keep reachin' out for him. Now I wanna know whatchyer plannin' to do with Mejia's people."

I tried to keep my voice flat and unemotional. "I was gonna try to bait Mejia out here for a sitdown to discuss Sonia's debt, then stall the shit out of him. I figure while we're stalling him and getting him on tape admitting everything, we squeeze in as many dope cases as we can—maybe even the trip to Cartagena."

"I already toldju what I thought about that."

I shrugged. Then, being as deferential as I could, I said, "I'm just gonna report it the way it's happening. Headquarters might think it's worth the shot."

"Do whatchu gotta do." Turghid glared at me, his hands resting flat on the desk as if he were about to launch himself at me.

"After Mejia gets here—and we got enough on tape to indict him— I was gonna to tell him that we're goin' out of town for a couple of weeks for a load or some other bullshit, and that we'd settle up with them the moment we got back."

"You say shut down the whole operation?"

"That'd give some time for the word about us to spread to more dopers, maybe even Arce-Gomez himself." I doubted that would ever happen—Arce-Gomez was safely tucked away in Argentina and not about to risk leaving to do a dope deal with anyone. But Turghid was using Arce-Gomez as if it were his trump card to keep Operation Hun anchored in Tucson; so why not play the same card against him? "Then we disappear for a couple of weeks. By the time we come back, it'll be just a matter of deciding how long we wanna run with this thing, how many people we want to indict, how much evidence we want to gather against Arce before we start busting people.

"Buck, if we play with this thing right, we can have half the fucking dopers in Sonia's address book busted right here in Tucson, maybe 100 class-ones. Who knows?"

Turghid's tiny eyes clouded with thought. His face softened. One hundred class-one dopers arrested in his district could mean the Attorney General's Award.

"Okay. You go ahead 'n call Mejia's people," Turghid said. "But I'm gonna tell ya this one mo' time: Operation Hun's got one main tar-get—Arce-Gomez. I don't wantchu getting offa that target. Think y'understand that?"

"Perfectly," I said.

## 2

The drive back to the house was in complete silence. Lydia stared out one window and Sonia stared out another. I had become accustomed to this from Lydia, but Sonia was obviously pissed about something.

When we got back to the house, Lydia was jumpy and agitated. "I'd like to just take off for a couple of hours. Mind if I take one of the cars?" she asked me.

"Hell no," I said as lightly as I could, but the look in her eyes fright-ened me. "What's up? You okay?"

"I'm fine," she said dully. "I just wanted to do some shopping and get lost for a while."

I was once again overwhelmed by an attack of paranoia. Where was she going? Why was she upset? Was it related to me?

After Lydia left I called Rourke at headquarters to give him a quick summary of my meeting with Turghid.

"Well, I got tentative good news for you, ya hump," said Rourke. "Ralph liked the Cuervas deal. We've been running it down to the powers that be, and so far they like it."

"Jack, we don't have a hell of a lotta time for them to play around."

"Jesus! Here I think I'm givin' you good news, and you're off again."

"I'm sorry, Jack," I said quickly. I couldn't afford to alienate him. "Just let them know about the time, okay? I told Ana two weeks."

"Believe me Mike, I'm pushing as hard as I can."

"What about the Mejia thing? Is everyone in agreement? I try to have a sitdown with him, and then stall?"

"What'd Turghid say about it?"

"Jack, I swear to God I can't tell what he's saying, other than this bullshit about me not getting off the target. All I could tell for sure is he didn't say no."

"Jesus! Fucking Levine. Lemme get back to you."

I sat by the kitchen phone for a few minutes lost in thought. Looking up suddenly, I saw Sonia standing behind me and watching me with a look on her face that made me thankful she no longer had a Nazi death squad under her control. Her face was a tight-jawed, coal-eyed mask of rage. "Am I some kind of joke?" she said, looking as if she were about to strike me.

"What . . . what are you talking about?" I said, realizing we were alone and wondering how long she'd been standing behind me. I glanced quickly toward the pool house—for once I would have been happy to see South.

"You put me in a room because I'm some kind of low-life, a dirty informer, and then you laugh about me?"

She *had* understood Turghid. Had she been eavesdropping on all my conversations?

"Sonia, you're mistaken." She was coming toward me and I was backing away. Whatever was about to happen, I thought, her word would be taken over mine. "Turghid is the boss here. I had nothing to do with that. And who was laughing?"

"I heard laughter."

"You didn't hear me laughing. Did you see those people around me? Do they look like they're my friends?"

She looked me in the eyes. "I know what I heard. I'm not stupid."

"You didn't hear me laugh at anything!" I said, letting some of my own anger spill out. "Nothing in my whole damn life is funny!"

We stood facing each other, and then Sonia's features suddenly softened. Was it doubt, or was it all an act?

The phone rang and I grabbed it. It was Rourke.

"Right on time," I said.

"What's that supposed to mean?"

"Nothing . . . you had to be here. What's up?"

"I just called to tell you to go ahead with the plan. You're gonna have a sitdown with Mejia's people, then shut down in Tucson for a while, right?"

"Yeah, and hopefully go down to Colombia."

"Okay. You think you'll be shut down by the weekend?"

"The way things are going, I hope we're alive by the weekend."

"Very funny, ya hump. I wanna know if I'll be home by then."

"I wanna get out of here, too," I said. "I got some family problems in New York. I'd like to take a day or two up there if I can."

"Yeah. Go ahead. So it looks like we'll be down by the weekend?"

"It all depends on how Mejia's people react when Sonia calls."

"Okay. I should be out there sometime tomorrow night."

"Have a nice flight Jack."

When I hung up I looked around. Sonia was gone.

# 20

# Eduardo: *El Teniente*

## 1

Sonia dialed Miami for the third time in an hour. Pineda—just as we were doing—would leave nothing but an answering service number. Drug dealers use answering services to protect themselves against undercovers, stool pigeons, and other dealers with murderous intentions. They pay the service fee in cash for many months in advance and can be reached only through a pager that the service rents them. They never leave an address, either, so there is just no way to find them. Our first goal was to play phone tag until Pineda broke down and left a number where he could be reached directly. That would put us a step closer to having him located for an arrest.

"Mr. Pineda's wire," said a woman's voice.

"Please tell him that Sonia is returning his call."

"Just a minute," said the woman, "he's right here."

Sonia looked at me and rolled her eyes. Mejia had probably ordered him not to leave the switchboard until Sonia called.

"Sonia?"

"*Hola,* Eduardo, it's so good to hear your voice," said Sonia.

"So what's this I hear that you're married again?"

"I made that mistake once, Eduardo, why should I make it again?" *The word about us had gotten to them.* "I have a new business partner; that's all."

"And what about that matter?"

"Well, you know the position that I've been in . . . and the troubles in Bolivia. I wanted to make good for every cent."

"I understand that."

"So I'm here working very hard. I've been waiting for some rugs to arrive here before I got in contact."

"In Tucson?"

"Yes . . ." I signaled Sonia to pass me the phone. ". . . yes, I have a partner, you know."

"So you told me."

"And we want to straighten it out. Maybe it's better you talk to him." She passed me the phone.

"I'm Miguel."

There was a long silence. I was afraid he would hang up. "So you're Sonia's partner," he finally said in a flat tone.

"Yes, I am," I said, matching his tone.

"You've inherited quite a problem. The gentleman I work for is very upset."

"I understand," I said, "and I'm anxious to resolve it as soon as possible. You know we're working hard now, trying to build up business."

"So I've heard," he said.

"I can see a lot of mutual benefits for the gentleman to consider doing business with us on a continuous basis—that is, once we've resolved everything."

"Everything is possible," said Pineda. "I only hope there are no more delays."

"I am sure there won't be," I said. "It's just a matter of agreeing on what's fair. You won't have any problems with us."

"Good. The gentleman would not like that."

"Look . . . what's your name?"

"Eduardo."

"Eduardo, we're not running anywhere. I want no problems with . . . Mr. Mejia," I said, in order to make it clear on the tape exactly whom "the gentleman" was. "I just want to straighten it out and do some business."

241

"A good idea," said Pineda. "We'd like to do it as soon as possible. I think we have to meet face-to-face."

"Perfect," I said. "We're in Tucson."

"We'll leave tomorrow."

"Okay," I said, "call the service as soon as you arrive and we'll meet you."

"Let me speak to Sonia."

"Sure." I passed the phone to Sonia. "Papo," I whispered, "ask him about Papo."

"Yes?" said Sonia.

"So I'll see you soon."

"Yes. And Papo . . . he'll be here?"

There was a long silence. "He's in Medellin, but I'm in contact with him."

"I, uh, thought I'd see him. Send him my best."

"I'll tell him. So . . . until we see each other?"

"Sure."

When Sonia hung up, she was upset. "What happens if Papo doesn't come?"

"Well, by the time we start arresting everyone, we'll at least know where he is. He's the one that's got to agree on the final terms, right?"

"Well, the others took part."

"But he's *el jefe*."

"Yes."

"Then how can he settle this thing without exposing himself?"

Sonia looked at me. "He's very clever."

"Sure," I said, "but Sonia and Miguel are a little more clever, right?"

"We'll see," she said.

Forty-eight hours later our answering service called to report that a Leo Rodriguez had arrived at the Holiday Inn in Tucson. He left a room number. South and a team of agents had been posted at the airport for the previous 24 hours, checking all known names and aliases used by the Mejia organization against the lists of passen-gers on all incoming flights. Pineda and God knows how many others had slipped by unnoticed. For all we knew, Mejia himself was in Tucson with a small army.

At 6:30 P.M., I telephoned the Holiday Inn and asked for Leo Rodriguez's room.

*"Hable!"* said Pineda.

"This is Miguel, Sonia's partner. How was your trip?"

"I thought we're going to meet," he snapped.

"Of course."

"When and where?"

"How about the cocktail lounge, right there where you are?"

"When?"

"In about an hour and a half."

"Eight o'clock," he said. "I'll see you then." He hung up.

At 7:30, Sonia, Lydia, Rudy, and I set out for Pineda's hotel. Lydia was wearing a flashy, form-fitting, black evening dress; Rudy was dressed from head to foot in black silk. I was all in white, which has always been a lucky undercover color for me. Only Sonia, who wore a simple white blouse and a conservative pair of slacks, didn't look like a South American drug dealer. Before we left, South had told me that there were 20 undercover agents already in and around the Holiday Inn, and that backup teams with shotguns and assault rifles were positioned nearby.

We were all edgy. I'd had some second thoughts about bringing Lydia, who seemed to bring tension wherever she went. But she was a beautiful woman, and her presence might break Pineda's concentration, put him a little more at ease, and keep him from noticing too many watching eyes. More importantly, Lydia was one more loaded gun, right beside me where it might be needed the most. It had been more than 18 months since Sonia had ripped off Mejia for several hundred thousand dollars in goods—18 months of stalling, lying, and hiding. There was a good chance that Mejia had long since forgotten the money and was coming to Tucson for vengeance.

I took the time in the car to go over the jewelry deal with Sonia. It was still fuzzy to me, principally because Sonia had never given a clear accounting of it. She was not much more forthcoming now.

"So the original agreement was for 30 kilos of coke for the jewelry?"

"No," said Sonia, her eyes on the distant city lights. "It was for 100 kilos."

*"Dios mio,* am I glad I asked! You better explain how it happened again, so it's fresh in my mind."

Annoyed, Sonia began. "Papo wants 100 kilos. So he gives me the jewelry, a car . . ."

"The Mercedes?"

"A yellow Mercedes . . . and some checks."

"What kind of checks?"

"Some—what do you call them?—cashier's checks, and some private ones."

"How much in checks?"

"I don't know," she said impatiently. "There were maybe a dozen or more, some for $20,000, some for $50,000 . . . I don't remember."

"Well, altogether how much?"

"The checks?"

"Everything."

"Well the checks came back without funds."

"All of them?"

"I think so . . . I don't remember."

Why was she playing dumb? She knew that no one was going to prosecute her. Maybe she never intended to give Mejia the drugs in the first place. It would be just like Sonia to plan to rip off a man like Mejia and then put the blame on her enemies. I should have been on top of this before. The worst thing in the world I could do now was to interrogate her 15 minutes before an undercover meet.

"Sonia, I just need to know, more or less, how much you got in value. Otherwise Pineda will see right through the act."

"I got nothing!" she snapped. "It all went to the Minister's people."

"I know that. What I mean is, how much is Papo claiming you owe him?"

"I don't know what he's claiming now."

"What about the 30 kilos? Where did you get that number?"

"That's what Papo said it was worth. He says I owe him the whole world. He says the jewelry was $300,000, the car was $100,000, and I don't know how much he's claiming for the checks. But the jewelry was only about $150,000, the car maybe $50,000, and the checks were worthless."

"They were all worthless, even the bank checks? Are you sure?"

"I already told you—I don't remember."

"But the last number Papo told you was you owed him 30 kilos?"

Sonia stared out her window. "Yes."

I could push no further. Actually, for my purposes, the situation wasn't so bad. The whole transaction was so vague and confused—intentionally or not—that there was no way we'd ever be able to settle it in one meeting, even if I wanted to.

As we turned into the parking lot of the Holiday Inn, Sonia touched my arm and said, "Papo must have sent more people than just Eduardo."

"Nothing's going to happen," I said. "There's an army out here protecting us."

## 2

The desert night was hotter than usual as Sonia and I entered the hotel, The hotel's air conditioning was broken, and the lobby seemed 20 degrees hotter than the street. As we crossed the lobby toward the lounge, I turned on the minirecorder I was carrying in a small man's handbag.

The lounge was like a noisy, crowded sauna. The jukebox was blasting country music at a beer-drinking, boots-and-jeans crowd. Sonia and I paused in the doorway. Pineda sat alone at a table near the exit. The bushy-haired Colombian was the only man in the room wearing a jacket—a heavy wool tweed.

As we approached the table I saw that his face was covered with sweat. A dozen pairs of eyes glanced covertly in our direction from nearby tables. I recognized two or three undercovers; the rest I wasn't sure about. I felt the adrenaline surge and my heart hammering in my chest. Pineda rose stiffly—very stiffly—to kiss Sonia on the cheek, his right arm staying close to his side. He looked like he was packing an Uzi beneath his jacket and not doing much to conceal it. Sonia glanced at me significantly.

"*Eduardo, te presento a Miguel. Miguel, Eduardo.*"

"*Mucho gusto,*" I said, extending my hand. Pineda shook it without a word. His eyes darted to the doorway, where Rudy and Lydia were just entering. Wisely reacting to Pineda's tension, Rudy nodded at me and then led Lydia to the table next to ours instead of joining us.

"My sister and one of my people," I said.

Pineda, who looked like he was in his early thirties, was short and slightly built. His handsome, clean-shaven Latino face had something mean-spirited about it, which was perhaps accentuated by his pale complexion and bushy hair style. His eyes were like glistening black olives ringed with bands of white—there was fear in them. While we sat, he kept one of his hands under his jacket.

It occurred to me that Mejia and his crew were probably as fearful of Sonia as she was of them. Sonia was not only one of the most powerful drug dealers in the world, she was also believed to be involved in gun-running and political assassination. In Bolivia she had had the power to order people murdered half a world away. A whole detachment of Klaus Barbie's Nazi mercenaries had been placed at her disposal, and her husband Pachi had been a rising star in one of the most brutal political regimes in Bolivia's history. Mejia—a man whose survival depended on staying one jump ahead of his countless enemies—had to assume that Sonia's resurgence also signified some renewal of killing power. And Mejia must have known what others knew about him: in the drug world, being owed money is often more hazardous than owing money.

Sonia immediately went to work to soften the tension. "It's so good to see you again, Eduardo," she smiled warmly. Whatever fear I thought I saw in her before had vanished. She sensed the danger and acted to take care of it—a natural undercover.

She was all over Pineda with questions about his family, friends, and associates, touching his hand affectionately; acting as though she was overjoyed that the problem between her and Mejia was finally going to be settled; acting as though she really gave a damn. She seemed to know him a lot better than she had let on.

Pineda, only half-listening, answered her curtly. For the most part, he was studying me and occasionally looking over the crowd, among which I now picked out at least six undercovers. I also noticed three Latinos—two at one table and one by himself—who were watching us closely. I was not sure who all the good guys and bad guys were in the room. All I knew was that a lot of people seemed to be aware of what was going on, and that if anyone drew a gun, when the smoke cleared it would be hard to find a stick of furniture without a hole in it.

We ordered cold beers, which did nothing to cool Pineda off. He was drenched in sweat.

"So what are we going to do?" he asked finally, looking from Sonia to me.

"Eduardo, it's a real simple thing," I said. "I'm a businessman, not a gangster. We've got merchandise waiting for us in Bolivia, and customers waiting for it. I can't do business and have to be afraid. Wherever we go in South America, everyone knows about it."

Pineda seemed pleased.

"And I'll tell you the truth, Eduardo, I know Mr. Mejia's reputation. Honestly? I'm afraid. If we can, I'm ready to settle the whole thing right now."

This was the last thing in the world I wanted to do. My goals were to find out as much as I could about the Mejia organization; con Mejia himself into coming out into the open; get as much recorded evidence against them as possible, including whatever they knew about Arce-Gomez; and not give them a damn thing.

"We've got 50, uh, rugs that we're in the process of selling. It's my understanding that the debt is something like 30."

"But that's not what it was," Sonia broke in angrily. "The checks Papo gave me bounced." I put my hand on her arm to calm her, but I didn't want to discourage her. Her reaction was natural; that of someone really concerned about the money, not an actress in a sting operation.

"Papo really should be here," I said.

"First of all," said Pineda, "let me give you some advice. Don't ever call him Papo." He paused to let the significance of this sink in.

"Everyone used to call him Papo," said Sonia. "I always called him Papo."

Great! The man can't decide whether to kill us or do business with us, and she wants to call him Papo.

"No one ever calls him that to his face," warned Pineda. "Now . . . he is called Guacho."

"Guacho," Sonia and I repeated almost in unison.

"You see," I said, "this is not a man I am going to take any chances with. I have to insist on assurances that he is aware of everything that is going on here."

Pineda suddenly glanced around the room. I wondered for a moment whether Mejia was nearby. No way—for Mejia to have survived as long as he had, he had to have the instincts of a jungle cat. He would never allow himself to be within a thousand miles of anything that had the slightest hint of a trap. And up to this point Operation Hun had been as subtle as two garbage trucks in a head-on collision. If we didn't get some direct evidence against Mejia—a face-to-face meeting or a recording of his voice acknowledging his part in the jewelry-for-coke transaction—we would never convict him.

"Don't worry," said Pineda. "You'll get all the assurances you need."

"You must understand, Eduardo," I said. "As I told you, I'm a businessman . . ."

"I understand."

"The way I figure it," I continued, "the original deal between Sonia and . . . Guacho was for about $600,000; correct?"

"Okay," said Pineda.

"So we can do one of two things: You wait until I sell the stuff we have now at a much higher price than we would charge Guacho, and I pay you cash. Or I give you 10 kilos now, which would be roughly $400,000 delivered here. You wait until we're back from Bolivia with our next shipment. I give you the additional five. We shake hands as friends. We're even."

Pineda thought for a moment. I wondered why he hadn't rejected the offer outright—Mejia was clamoring for over $1 million.

"Why don't you let us sell the stuff for you?" he finally said.

"What do you mean?"

"We've got a big organization not far from here, in Los Angeles. We'll sell it for you."

"That's an idea I never thought of."

"My brother is the biggest in California. I make a call tonight, a special truck is on the way by tomorrow. It's got hidden compartments that carry 25 kilos at a time. We make two trips."

"You mean you sell the whole 50 for us?"

"Sure," said Pineda.

"That's something to consider," I said.

Now I understood Pineda's marching orders. Mejia figured that if we were coming looking for him to pay off the debt it was either a trap or we were frightened suckers. It was Pineda's job to figure out which of the two. And he had obviously decided on the latter. Fifty kilos was worth about $2 million and he was going to take it all. I could see it in his hungry little eyes. We were starting to look like "easy meat" to him. If he got away with the 50 kilos, it would be just the beginning, and when they felt they had bled us dry they would take our lives.

"You know, Eduardo," I said, "this could be good for all of us. I've got a good feeling about you. Once we have this debt out of the way, we have another 150 kilos waiting for us in Bolivia. And we have been assured as much merchandise as we can handle."

Pineda's eyes suddenly ceased roving and focused on me. "Listen, it will be a good thing for you to work through us. Our organization stretches from Colombia to Miami and New York across to California and it's growing." He clicked his fingers. "My brother is the biggest dealer in California. The German, just a single customer of ours in Miami, bought 1,200 kilos last year, and this year, so far, he has taken 400 . . ."

"A German?" My little heart was going pitter-patter. It seemed that everyone but DEA knew this German—or did they? Roberto Suarez

248

DEA Special Agent Michael Levine undercover as "Miguel" in Operation Hun (1982).

Levine and Agent Pooley receiving an award from the Argentine Federal Police for making a record number of undercover cases and drug seizures in Argentina (1981).

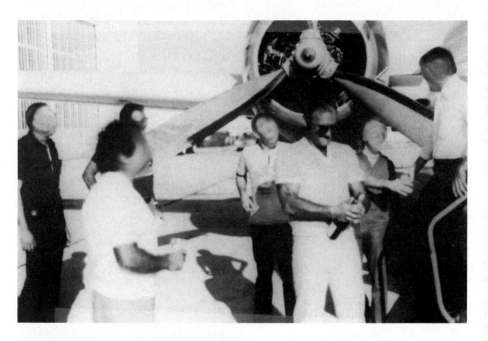

Levine and other DEA undercovers celebrate the conclusion of the Suarez sting operation, in which 854 pounds of cocaine were seized (1980).

Michael "Pat" Sullivan, Miami Assistant U.S. Attorney who released drug trafficker Jose Gasser, indirectly leading to the Cocaine Coup in Bolivia.

Luis Arce Gomez, a leader of the Cocaine Coup in Bolivia, also known as the "Minister of Cocaine" for his part in the Bolivian government's drug trafficking.

THE MIAMI HERALD

Roberto Suarez, considered to be one of the world's most important cocaine traffickers in the 1980s. The sting of his organization set up by Levine in 1980 set in motion the events that would culminate in Operation Hun.

AP/WIDE WORLD

Klaus Barbie, called the "Butcher of Lyon" for his bloodthirsty rule of the French city during the Nazi occupation in World War II. He escaped to South America, and later advised various South American police forces, including the Argentines and Bolivians, on interrogation and torture techniques.

During the Cocaine Coup (1980), troops supporting the new Bolivian government killed citizens savagely and indiscriminately. Here, students carry a man who was killed when troops fired on an opposition crowd in La Paz.

Oliver North, Jr., aide to President Reagan,
suspected of involvement in drug
trafficking to fund the Contra rebels
against the leftist Sandanista
government of Nicaragua.

Below, Francis Mullen (standing next
to President Reagan), Administrator
of the DEA during the time of
Operation Hun.

Levine during Operation Hun, in Tucson with Monica Garcia (left) and Sonia Atala. Garcia has never been indicted, and Atala is in the Witness Protection Program, so their faces have been obscured.

Ana Tamayo, *comisionista* and target of Operation Hun, after her arrest and extradition to the United States in 1989.

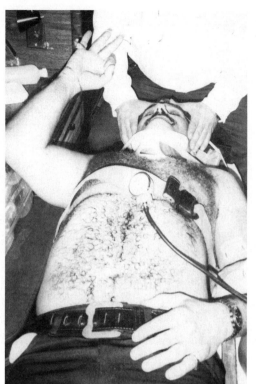

In 1989, Levine suffered career-ending injuries during a crack raid in New York City.

Miguel Perez, who stabbed Papo Mejia 10 times with a bayonet.

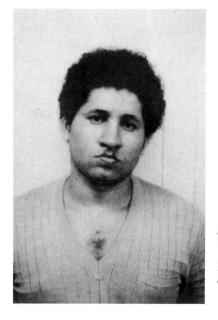

The murderous Columbian drug lord Papo Mejia, target of Operation Hun, after he survived bayonet attack of Miguel Perez.

Levine's marriage to Laura Kavanau (1991). From left to right, Levine's son Keith (a New York City police officer who was killed one week later), Levine's daughter Nicole, Levine, Kavanau, and Levine's mother, Caroline Goldstein.

Levine's brother David, who commited suicide in 1977 after 19 years of heroin addiction. His last words were, "I can't stand the drugs any more."

hadn't been in the computer. "Didn't you know a German?" I asked Sonia.

"Sure Sonia knows him," said Pineda. "Don't you remember, you met him at that party in Panama?"

Sonia flushed. "No," she said, "I don't remember him."

Pineda insisted. "Sure, you remember . . . the guy went crazy over you. He sent you tickets to come to his house in Hawaii."

"How lucky you know him," I said. "I wanted to look him up."

Pineda laughed. "It would have done you no good. That man is loyal to Guacho . . . to us. He's been doing business with us for eight years. He loves Guacho. Some *hijos de putas* from Colombia who we sometimes bought merchandise from tried to go around us and do business with him. They went to his house in Miami and said, 'Why pay so much to Guacho and Eduardo when you can buy direct from us?' The man excuses himself for a moment and telephones me. I went right over there. You should have seen these bastards' terrified faces. Right in front of me he told them, 'Next time you want to deal with me, you call Eduardo first.' That is the kind of man he is."

"May God surround me with loyal people like that," I said.

"Let me tell you something," said Pineda. "One customer like him can make an organization. His customers are judges, district attorneys, theater people, and sports figures, not street junkies. He is completely protected."

"Eduardo," I said. "I consider Sonia's debt a stroke of luck. It is because of it that we met. I can see a great future for us working together."

"By the way," said a much more relaxed Pineda, "the way we do business is that before we accept your merchandise and sell it as ours, we have our own chemist check it and reseal it. I personally initial each bag. From that point on the merchandise carries my personal guarantee of purity."

"I only have the best," I said, my stomach going a little queasy at the memory of Monica's test and the realization that he might have already heard about it. Monica knew Mejia, and she had flown directly from Tucson to Miami.

Pineda smiled shrewdly. "You won't mind, then, if I have our chemist check it."

"Of course not," I said.

I invited Pineda to join us for dinner. Grinning like Little Red Riding Hood's wolf, he accepted. He wanted to get a real good look

249

at what the Atala-Levine Cocaine Corporation was all about. The sweating little man expected to leave Tucson with $2 million worth of cocaine—not a bad return on an investment of a couple of hundred thousand dollars in jewelry. But there was no way I was going to let that happen. I would have to stall him while at the same time keep him believing our act. The trouble was I had no idea how I was going to accomplish that.

# 21

# How Not to
# Trap a Killer

## 1

The waiters at La Fuente Restaurant did everything but carry us from the entrance to our tables. Pineda smiled for the first time. Happily, the air conditioner functioned perfectly, because he never took off his heavy jacket. At a prearranged signal Rudy appeared to tell me I had "urgent business" elsewhere. For once it wasn't for show—Rourke and Turghid were waiting at the office for an update.

When I rose to leave, Pineda stood and shook my hand. "I want to congratulate you on your organization," he said. "You've got good people."

"Thanks," I said.

"I need a favor, if you don't mind."

"Sure."

"Can you lend me a car and driver tomorrow?"

"No problem. Take care of it, Rudy."

"Sure, boss."

I moved around the table to kiss Lydia on the cheek and then Sonia.

"Where are you going?" said Sonia in my ear.

"Just some business," I said. "I'll talk to you about it later."

Sonia looked worried as I left, and with good reason. She was a woman with many secrets, and she was learning that when you become an informer you surrender the right to choose what you reveal.

Fifteen minutes later I was in Turghid's office repeating everything Pineda had told me, including the information about the German. Turghid sat watching me with a barely concealed scowl, his thick fingers drumming the desk in front of him; Rourke wrote down the specifics; and South sat staring at his hands.

"The things we gotta move on fast, in my opinion," I said, "are identifying the German; Pineda's brother in L.A.; and right now, Mejia's whereabouts."

"That ain't your worry!" snapped Turghid. "We're takin' care of that."

"You guys identify anyone else in town with Pineda?" I asked.

"We've been out there 48 hours," said South, staring at his hands, "and we haven't seen anybody."

"The man's alone," said Turghid.

"Sonia doesn't think so."

Turghid slammed his fist down. "Fuck! I don't care what some goddamn informer thinks! What's yer plan for right now?"

I looked at Rourke for support, but he avoided my gaze. "I think we've gotta make locating Mejia and getting him on tape a priority," I said. "He's either smelled the trap, or he's just too cagey. The man does not intend to come out in the open. And if he doesn't, we have no case on him—all we've got is Sonia's word."

Turghid, still drumming, looked at South. Rourke, tense and unhappy, puffed on his cigarette. Tucson was Turghid's empire—there wasn't much Rourke could say. "Okay," Turghid said finally. "But I wanna be kept up to date."

"No problem," I said. "What about this German? He oughtta be easy for Miami to identify. How many politically hung, dope-dealing Germans can there be in Miami?"

"I'll make sure Miami gets the info," said Rourke before Turghid could say anything. "You just concentrate on Mejia; that oughtta be enough for you, ya hump."

I wanted to bring up getting better cocaine as a prop and the deep cover trip to Colombia, but the look Rourke was giving me said, "Keep your mouth shut."

* * *

252

Rudy showed up at the UC house at about 6 P.M. the next evening with a wolfish grin. He had spent most of the day chauffeuring Pineda on a shopping and sightseeing expedition and had so ingratiated himself that Pineda bought him an expensive silk tie and shirt and offered him a job with the Mejia organization. Rudy, no doubt thinking of his civil service tenure in the Pima County Sheriff's Department, politely declined. While Sonia was busy on the phone hunting René Benitez in Colombia, Rudy told me about the day.

"I'll tell ya boss," he said, "This guy expects to get paid. He's got the whole Mejia organization mobilized from coast-to-coast."

"What do you mean?"

"He had those phone lines buzzing. He's got people coming here from everywhere. He said he wants you to give him a call."

"Okay, as soon as Sonia's off the phone."

"So what are you gonna tell him?"

"Rudy, I've got two surprises for Señor Pineda: one, we're leaving town and he's not getting a damn thing until we get back; and two, I'm demanding a face-to-face with Mejia, or there's no deal. The trouble is, I'm not really sure how to break the news."

After I finished with Rudy, I went to Sonia's room to see if she was still on the phone. I was about to knock when I heard her angry voice through the door.

"Why did you trust him? . . . I told you Pachi, he was no good . . . No! He'll never pay! . . . You don't know these people; I do!"

I rapped on the door.

"Yes?"

"It's me. Are you going to be on the phone long?"

"I'm not on the phone."

"Oh, sorry. I'm going to call Pineda now."

"I'll be right out."

I stood there a moment longer, listening, but Sonia didn't say anything more. She must have hung up the instant I knocked. What the hell could be going on? The first thing that came to mind—that she was dealing drugs again—just couldn't be. No one could be that crazy . . . or that sure of themselves.

Moments later I dialed Pineda's room.

"When can we meet to talk about the details?" he asked, his voice tight with anxiety. Mejia must have been increasing the pressure.

"How about dinner tonight? We'll pick you up at 8:30."

"Fine." He hung up.

Rudy drove Sonia, Lydia, and me up to the front of Pineda's Holiday Inn, and then went inside to call Pineda on the house phone. In a minute he was back.

"He wants you to come up to the room."

"How's he sound? Upset? Nervous?"

"I couldn't tell. He only said, 'Tell Miguel to come up to the room.'"

Moments later I rapped lightly on Pineda's door. Pineda opened it quickly, dressed in slacks and an undershirt. "I'm on the phone," he said, "come in." As I entered, he glanced up and down the corridor before closing and locking the door; something was up. He rushed back to the phone. "They're here, now," he said. "I'll call you back."

He hung up. "Excuse me. I've been on the phone all evening making arrangements." He was sitting stiffly on the edge of the bed, eyeing me nervously.

"No problem," I said, sitting in a chair across the room. The room looked pristine. The pillow just behind him on the bed looked slightly mussed. He probably had his gun there.

Pineda got right to the point.

"I spoke to Guacho. There were some things I never considered, when we were speaking yesterday."

"I don't understand."

"Guacho said the debt should be more like a million and a quarter."

"You have to be joking."

"What we . . . what you were saying yesterday didn't take into account all the time we were put out, all the money that our money could have earned. We didn't consider the inconvenience."

"Brother," I said, measuring my words and getting slowly to my feet, "I was afraid of this. There's no way we can reach an agreement without Mr. Mejia sitting down face-to-face with us."

Pineda paled. "Look, the way I understood you last night, you were going to give me $750,000 worth of merchandise right now, and the remainder when you came back from Bolivia."

"Wow," I said, holding my hand to my head. "I thought we agreed the whole thing was $600,000. I've been holding off a sale just to resolve this thing. I delayed our trip to Bolivia. I've got people waiting for me in New York for a deal right this minute."

"What are you saying?" demanded Pineda, his eyes wide. "You're not going to pay?"

"Of course not," I said. "I'm a businessman. I don't want any trouble; I want a fair settlement. You can't go from $600,000 to over $1 million in 24 hours and call that fair. Sonia tells me that even the $600,000 isn't fair; that checks Mr. Mejia, or whoever, gave her bounced; that the jewelry wasn't worth what you said it was."

"That's a lie! None of those checks bounced. She said those checks bounced?"

"That's what I mean; there are areas that are open to dispute."

"So you're not going to pay."

"Why would I call you if I wasn't going to pay? Whether we're going to pay or not isn't what we're discussing—we're discussing how much we're going to pay, which will be impossible to decide unless Sonia and Mr. Mejia agree."

"I told you, that's impossible."

"Look," I said. "We've got people in Bolivia waiting for us with 150 kilos. I can't go down there without money. I can't let you just take our merchandise and run off to California without leaving me a *centavo*. I have a business to run."

Pineda's eyes bugged out. He looked at the pillow, and I leaned forward slightly and slid my hand along my leg toward my 9mm in my ankle holster. Ten thousand hours in hotel rooms like this one were telling me he was going for it, and I was praying that he wouldn't. I didn't want to have to use my gun.

Pineda turned back. "Let's just say," he hissed, "that you never said those words."

"I didn't mean to offend you," I said quickly, "but I'm under a lot of pressure. If I let you take everything, we're out of business."

Pineda relaxed a bit. "I thought we understood each other. I called my people—everyone is on the way. Now what do I tell them—go back?"

"Be reasonable, Eduardo. How can we settle a debt when we haven't agreed on the amount?"

After a moment, Pineda said, "You want to talk to Guacho yourself?"

"I'd love to," I said, "but under better circumstances. It's he and Sonia that have to come to terms."

"Where is Sonia now?"

"Outside in the car."

"Come on," said Eduardo, springing to his feet and grabbing for a shirt. "I want to talk to her."

## 2

As Pineda and I walked out to the Lincoln, I could see Sonia's eyes, round with surprise. We piled into the back seat with her, with Rudy and Lydia up front.

"Drive!" ordered Pineda.

Rudy looked at me. "Just drive us around slowly while we talk."

Within 60 seconds, Sonia and Pineda were locked in a no-win argument over numbers, just as I had hoped.

"Miguel is saying it's something like $600,000," said Pineda, "and I remember back then it was close to $800,000, and we have to consider time—how much the money would have earned."

"But none of the checks turned out to have sufficient funds," said Sonia.

"That's impossible!" said Pineda. "I wrote them myself. They cleared the bank."

Sonia reared up. "Do you have proof?"

"In Miami, I have the canceled checks."

"You have them in Miami?" Sonia looked worried.

"Two $50,000 checks are from my own account, and there are the monies that were sent to you in Panama."

"We'll go tomorrow," said Sonia, "we'll go to the house and figure out the amount. You telephone Papo. I will speak with Papo."

It occurred to me that Sonia might have intentionally used the name Papo to anger the hot-tempered Pineda.

"Okay!" said Pineda, throwing his hands up in disgust. "That we can do tomorrow. What I want to know is this. Do I tell the people not to come? That's what I want to know, nothing more. Some are already on the way with the car. And there are others who will be leaving tomorrow morning. I don't want that they should get here and I have to tell them . . ."

"They can see the merchandise tomorrow," snapped Sonia.

"What?" said Pineda.

"They can see if they like the merchandise, or if they don't like it. Yes or no?" pressed Sonia.

"Yes . . . yes," said Pineda.

"Wait a second," I said. "We don't have an agreement yet on what the debt is. I have to leave for New York on Saturday the latest . . ."

"It doesn't matter," interrupted Sonia. "The fact that you're leaving is no problem. In the next couple of days they can look at the merchandise and select the cocaine they like."

Sonia had suddenly taken control of Operation Hun, and I had almost missed it. She was trying to push the case to a climax tomorrow. If Pineda's men tried to leave with any cocaine, they'd be arrested and the operation would be over. I had to regain control, so I steered the conversation back to how much Sonia actually owed Mejia.

"The accounting," said Pineda, "when we did the transaction in Cali, was that we gave Sonia around $800,000—counting $300,000 in jewels and the $500,000 in checks."

"But a lot of the checks came back because of insufficient funds," said Sonia looking at me.

The anguish I saw in Sonia's eyes was plain—she wasn't looking too clean. She had always been vague about how much money in checks she had received from Mejia, claiming it didn't make a difference since the checks bounced anyway. DEA had bought that story. But it didn't make sense for Mejia to give Sonia bad checks as front money for drugs—especially not when he'd already given her jewelry and a car. The checks would have bounced long before delivery was due on the cocaine. So where was the half-million dollars?

"I was never told any of the checks were bad," said Pineda. "Maybe the bad checks were those issued by *Los Pablos.*"

"Yeah," said Sonia.

Highly unlikely, since *Los Pablos*—Pablo Ochoa and Pablo Escobar—were two of the biggest traffickers in Colombia. Mejia buying checks from their "legal" corporations to disguise drug payments was another tentacle in the conspiracy that Sonia had opened up for us. DEA could have a field day with this information.

"The only way we are going to resolve this thing," I said, "is if Sonia and Guacho agree on a number. How many kilos will it take? Whatever the number is—so the two of you are satisfied. A fair number."

"Exactly," said a worn-looking Pineda. "Then lets . . . I will speak to him right now."

"Then we'll go directly to the house and wait for you to call," I said.

It was perfect. I had everything I wanted—the delay and direct contact with Mejia. "Is that okay with you?" I asked Sonia.

"Why not settle this tomorrow?" she said. "You take a sample of our merchandise; you do all you have to do. I will come, I will talk with Papo. We decide—yes, now! It is done. Everything!"

"Okay," said Pineda, confused by the sudden change.

"Tomorrow in the morning then," said Sonia. "What time do you want to do it?"

She was again forcing the end of the operation so quickly that I couldn't react without stepping out of my role.

"Early," said Pineda, brightening. "I'll be here waiting for you at the earliest it can be."

Sonia forged ahead. "You be here at ten. Is that all right?"

"That's fine," said Pineda.

Sonia had just pushed me out of the picture and taken complete control. I wanted to throw her out of the car, but that might have been just a bit out of character for my role. Instead I leaned forward and again demanded, "How can we do business when we haven't even agreed on the amount?"

Silence. Sonia glared at me, seething.

Pineda finally shook his head in defeat. "Exactly . . ."

Sonia began to speak again, but I cut her off sharply—"We have to reach an agreement!"

Pineda agreed to arrange a phone call between Mejia and Sonia. By the time we left Pineda he had all but given up hope of getting any dope this trip. He was disappointed, but he still believed in us—exactly the condition I wanted him in.

As we drove back to the house, Sonia stared at the distant lights of Tucson.

"Sonia," I said, "you can't do that."

"What?" she said angrily, glancing sideways at me.

"I'm running the show," I said as quietly as I could. "If you had your way tonight this whole case would have been over tomorrow. That's not what we want."

"Whatever you say," she said, and she turned away from me again.

I had considered telling her that she had better watch her ass—that if she pulled one more stunt like tonight's I'd personally feed her to Mejia. That's how informants must be handled, at least in the unwritten Agents' Code. But I didn't because I had no idea how far we had left to travel together, and when I might be vulnerable to her. She had more hidden agendas than a CIA retirement party. She was as much my enemy as were Suarez, Mejia, or the inspectors, but in her case my future and perhaps my life were inextricably linked to hers. I couldn't afford to drop my guard again around her for an instant.

## 3

When we got back to the house, I called Rourke and told him that with any luck we would have a direct telephone conversation with Mejia and possibly a phone number where he could be located.

"He's supposed to be in Miami," I said urgently. "The guy is very cagey and very deadly. The minute we get his location we've got to get him under surveillance and keep him there until it's time to bust him."

"Just get me a phone number," said Rourke. "I'll have Miami DEA standing by."

"This may be our only chance to get this guy, Jack. We don't even have a photo of him. Tell Miami to at least make sure they get a photo of him while he's on the phone. Pineda mentioned something about his wife being in Miami to give birth. Maybe they can ID her or something. Anything!"

"Just get me the phone number, ya hump."

The next afternoon, Rourke and Turghid were standing by at the office. An army of Tucson cops and agents had the Holiday Inn under surveillance. No suspicious activity had been noted, and Pineda had not left his room.

At about 3:45 our phone rang. I answered it. "Mr. Pineda would like Sonia to call the Holiday Inn," said the answering service.

I hustled out to the pool to get Sonia. "I think this is it," I said. She got to her feet without a word and followed me back to the kitchen. I hooked the recorder to the phone, plugged an earphone jack into it so that I could monitor the call, and dialed the Holiday Inn. I handed the phone to Sonia, my hand trembling.

"He's waiting for your phone call right this minute," said Pineda, and he gave the number, with a Miami area code.

When Sonia hung up, I called Rourke and gave him the number. "We can't stall too long," I said. "If we wait too long, he's gonna smell something and book right out of the country."

"Gotcha."

"This call may be our whole case against him."

"I hear ya."

"Jack! Please make sure Miami knows how many people this guy's killed."

"Believe me, they already know."

"Just make sure, will ya Jack? If anything makes this job worth it, it's putting a guy like this away."

"Well, you just get the fuck off the phone so I can call them."

I figured Rourke's call to Miami would take a minute. It would then take the Miami agents about 90 seconds to get Mejia's location from telephone company security. Within three minutes they'd be radioing the location to DEA cars already on the street. Within about six minutes, undercover cars would be speeding to wherever Mejia was waiting for Sonia's call.

In my mind I saw Papo as he'd been described to me—short, bulldog-like, with killer's eyes—standing by a lone phone booth on a little side street near the beach, pacing nervously. His stomach had to be twisting the way mine was. He had to suspect something wasn't right—he knew what Sonia was all about. She had stolen almost $750,000 from him, and had been successfully hiding and lying for a year and a half.

Would a woman like that roll over so easily?

Now I saw the undercover agents parking cars, slipping up alleys, crawling over rooftops with cameras and radios; maybe Metro-Dade Homicide was there, too—Mejia had to be a suspect in at least a dozen homicides. They wouldn't be able to arrest him on the spot without blowing our cover, but at least they could follow him to wherever he was staying so he could be grabbed when the time was right. Maybe they'd even get a photo of him at the precise moment he was speaking to Sonia—it would be devastating evidence, not to mention the only known photo of him.

Seven minutes had gone by since I spoke to Rourke. They had to be close to Mejia by now. My shirt was drenched with perspiration. I began to dial the number. I could feel Papo's tension 2,000 miles away, waiting for the phone to ring. He had to be leery of the phone call; he had to know 100 dealers who had been put away for 20 or 30 years for saying one word too many on the phone. His instincts were probably screaming for him to run. I hoped his desire for revenge against Sonia was stronger than those instincts.

The phone rang once . . . twice. I had waited too fucking long!

"Hello," said a man's voice.

"Papo?" Sonia said.

"You're talking to him."

She used "Papo." Was she trying to piss him off?

"This is Sonia. How are you doing?"

260

"I'm doing fine. How are you?" he said gruffly.

"I'm calling to find out if you're in agreement," said Sonia, "if you knew what we were doing here with Eduardo?"

Her eyes were wide and her face was flushed crimson—she was terrified. I was glad.

"What?"

"That, I'm calling to find out if you're in agreement, about . . . what we're arranging with Papo, with Eduardo." She was so frightened that she was confusing the names.

"Yeah," said Mejia, undoubtedly trying to decide whether to just hang up. He hadn't said anything incriminating yet.

"We agreed to 25 kilos. You're aware of that?"

"Yeah, he told me more or less the same thing," said Mejia, sniffing at the bait but still not biting.

"I only wanted to know if you knew," said Sonia. She had to grip the phone with two hands to keep it from shaking.

"What?" snapped Mejia, still sounding on the verge of hanging up.

"I only wanted to know if you knew . . . and now I know," said Sonia, now ready to hang up herself.

Mejia was silent for a long moment. He still hadn't said anything incriminating. Finally, he continued. "You have to know Sonia, that whatever Eduardo says is all right. But you also have to consider that this was a double-cross. You cost us two years."

He had taken a firm bite, and had said enough to convict himself.

"No, it's not that," whined Sonia. "At the beginning I wanted to resolve the situation, but later I was so sick, I know that you . . . It's that I was in such a bad situation that I wasn't even able to call. That's why I'm calling now. Please accept my apologies. I realize you've lost a lot; that I left you holding the bag, but from now on I'm going to try and straighten it out. I only wanted to know if you were in agreement, so that arrangements can be made with Eduardo."

Sonia was almost blubbering, begging for him to accept, but accept what? We hadn't agreed on anything. What the hell happened to the whole story about bounced checks? Where was the negotiating?

"Listen Sonia, when is this deal going to take place?"

Sonia looked at me, pale with fright. "Two or three weeks," I whispered.

"You'll get it in eight days," she said, looking straight at me.

"Then why not make it 30 kilos?" said Papo.

"You'll be getting 25 in a week," said Sonia.

"What?" said Mejia, as confused as I was.

"You'll be getting everything in eight days . . . the whole thing."

"What?"

"You'll be getting the 25 in eight days," said Sonia.

"I said why don't you make it 30, Sonia? You gave me a lot of problems."

"Exactly. Uh, I understand . . . I know that you are in . . . well, that you are exactly right, well . . . yeah . . ." She was spouting gibberish.

"Let's say 30 and the whole problem is squared," insisted Mejia.

"You want 30?"

"It's fair."

"Yeah?"

"You'll be doing the right thing. I'll come off well. And we'll be as if nothing had ever happened."

"Well, all right. Then we agree on 30."

What a tough negotiator she was.

"Yeah," said Mejia.

"I'll arrange it with Eduardo."

"For sure?"

"Absolutely for sure," said Sonia, "I'll deliver everything, 10 days at the latest, and we'll be friends again."

"Okay, perfect. Talk to Eduardo and you can rest assured that it's the same as if I were there."

Perfect! The jury would see it that way, too. "Try to keep him talking," I whispered. Sonia nodded.

"Since I was vulnerable, and everything, I wanted to at least hear your voice . . . to know that the deal . . . that I'm doing right."

"You have to let yourself be seen, so that we can talk," said Mejia.

"Sure," said Sonia, growing bolder, "from here on, we'll be seeing each other."

Mejia also relaxed, and now seemed in no rush to get off the phone. He started asking Sonia about different people they both knew. I was overjoyed. I pictured agents hiding all around him, taking pictures, getting ready to follow him. Nice job, Miami!

"You've had a lot of problems," said Mejia.

"Yeah, but they're all solved," said Sonia, looking at me.

"What about that bad guy, what's his name?

"Which one? Which one of them?"

"That guy Willie."

"They're all bad people," said Sonia, trying to get off the subject. This was undoubtedly another drug dealer she had screwed and failed to tell DEA about.

"Well, this guy Willie is filth," said Mejia. "He refused to talk to me."

"And Lucho," said Sonia, switching to a safe topic, "the great Minister Lucho Arce, who ruined me, and after all I did for him. You saw, you were right there. You knew that all the people with me were his representatives."

"Of course, of course . . . it was a whole world of people who were no good. But I couldn't do anything, to me Bolivia is a foreign land. I was really upset, because you disappeared so suddenly. If you had just spoken with me, I'm a reasonable person, but I do have my ways."

"Listen to me, something else," said Sonia, looking at me significantly to show that she was keeping him on the phone. "We're going to have about 150 rugs, then we'll see if, after I make the delivery, if we can do business with the balance."

"Of course, there's no problem with me. You know I'm a sincere person."

"Yeah."

"We'll settle the account first, then we'll reach an agreement for the rest. You know I'm living in the California area. I only came here for the birth of my son. He was born two days ago."

"Congratulations."

Mejia then brought up Pachi, and Sonia, in a panic to change the subject, almost made a serious error.

"And Pachi, is he in the military here, or in a university?"

"He was there about six months," said Sonia, her hand suddenly trembling violently again. "They wanted to kill him; they were looking to kill me, too."

"That's what I was told. I became aware of many things, all the problems you had."

"I know I left you looking bad. The Minister took all the jewels, all my houses and left me with nothing. I'm trying to recover the houses . . ."

"But you don't have any more problems in Bolivia?" interrupted Mejia, sounding incredulous.

"No," said Sonia, "the main thing is that now I'm fine with you."

"Ah, no, no, no, that problem, of course, will be done away with," said Mejia, but I could hear doubt in his voice. How could Sonia be going back to Bolivia after she had just barely escaped there with her life?

Finally, Sonia tried to bait Papo himself to Tucson.

"Look, the day that we make the delivery, you come, you take a sample, and if you like, we'll do business for the balance."

"Ah, well, fine, perfect," he said, but his voice was tight. "If there's anything, you talk to Eduardo about it."

"When we settle everything," said Sonia, "we'll have no problems. It's that I heard all kinds of things—people were telling me that you were going to kill my daughter. It frightened me."

"You know, Sonia, we all have problems, but until you fix things you cannot go on calmly. You pay me what you owe me and I will immediately let it be known to all those under me: 'She paid me and we're at peace.'"

"Well, now I am more at ease," said Sonia, looking anything but.

Suddenly there was a clicking on the line. Who the hell was playing with the phone?

"*Ola?*" said a startled Sonia.

"Hello? Hello?" said Mejia.

The clicking stopped.

"So we'll speak when the delivery is made?" asked Sonia.

"Okay," Mejia said brusquely.

"Is that all right?"

"All right, Sonia," he said, more tersely. He had to suspect something now.

"Okay, then when we make delivery," said Sonia, "I'll call you at the answering service and you can agree with Eduardo."

"Okay."

The costliest conversation in Papo Mejia's life was over. He had been on the phone a little over 15 minutes.

"We did it!" exclaimed Sonia, her face flushed.

I quickly dialed the DEA office and asked for Rourke. "Well?" I asked him.

"Well what?"

"Did Miami get him?"

"Are you kidding? I could barely get them to check out the fucking phone number."

# 22

# On the Edge

From the moment Rourke told me that Miami DEA hadn't lifted a finger to cover the Mejia phone call I had been in a daze of disbelief. I sleep-walked through the 36 hours following the call, doing as I was ordered and saying little to anyone.

Members of Mejia's organization had arrived in Tucson from Miami and California, bringing with them a four-wheel drive jeep with hidden compartments for transporting the drugs. Pineda called me to ask if I could safeguard the jeep at the house until we returned to Tucson. This was the kind of thing that should have had my investigator's heart racing with joy. It was an opportunity to trace the license plates and chassis numbers of what was virtually a rolling drug container; whatever fingerprints could be lifted would enable even a rookie agent to trace and identify whomever was connected with the car; cocaine residue, almost certain to be found in the hidden compartments, would lead to enough additional criminal charges to put those people behind bars for an eternity; if anyone in the organization flipped, it was an entree into the Hollywood drug scene at the source level. The possibilities all registered in my mind out of habit, but I really didn't care. I sent Rudy and another undercover to pick up the jeep, and then put it out of my mind.

Ana called a half-dozen times to tell me that Pacho Cuervas was ready and waiting for me in Colombia, but I could barely get up the energy to talk with her. My ex-wife called to tell me that Niki had stayed out all night. I told her I was coming and hung up. Someone from headquarters left a message at Tucson DEA that the inspectors were going through my personnel records again. I suspected the inspectors themselves had left the message, but I couldn't even get angry at that. And when Rourke called and said he had to stay an extra day in Tucson, and would I please accompany Sonia to her home in Virginia, I said, "Sure, why not."

So it was that at 4 A.M. on Saturday, March 13, I was alone with Sonia in the darkened cabin of American Airlines flight 452 bound for Washington. Sonia had been fast asleep from the moment the plane took off at 2 A.M. Having Sonia and I travel alone didn't make sense; too many people wanted us dead.

I lay awake, staring at the dim lights at the end of the cabin. Thoughts about my life, my daughter, the Suarez case, the Bolivian revolution, and Operation Hun fluttered through my brain like crazed bats. When I looked at Sonia snoring lightly beside me, I had visions of neo-Nazi paramilitary units dragging limp bodies into a house with thick walls as faceless men in suits watched in the background. I had never seen Sonia's infamous house of torture, but I knew it was hers. I was afraid. My head began to throb with pain again.

I pressed the call button and asked the stewardess for some aspirin. I gobbled down a whole tinful in one gulp, closed my eyes, and laid my head back. Perhaps I slept.

Finally, a gray light began filtering into the cabin. The plane suddenly came alive. As the crew served breakfast, Sonia awoke, stretched, and began to eat without saying a word. How could she be so cool? Although the throbbing in my skull had dulled somewhat, I couldn't eat. I knew I should see a doctor about the pain, but I couldn't even do that. If the suits found out about it, they'd push for a fitness-for-duty examination—more ammunition for firing me.

What is it about cops and street agents that makes us face blazing guns without hesitation but quake in our boots before a suit with the power to take our jobs away? Why are grown men and women so intimidated that the suits count on their silence and complicity in whatever lie they utter or fraud they perpetrate?

For 17 years my job had been my life's purpose; it was all-consuming, leaving neither time nor energy for anything else. But I had believed in it, and that made the sacrifice acceptable. Now, with my belief faltering and my purpose taken away, the thought of the void I faced was terrifying. Maybe that was why the few street agents who made it to retirement died within an average of five years. I could feel the job killing me, yet it kept its iron hold on me.

When we got off the plane, I rented a car. We passed the half-hour trip to Sonia's house in silence. When we turned into her quiet, tree-lined, one-way street, we passed the car.

At first the car didn't bother me, but then I noticed that it was parked with its rear bumper flush to the front of a truck. It was an old surveillance trick—on a one-way street the car was harder to spot. In the rearview, I glimpsed two men sitting low in their seats.

"Did Jack or anyone put people out here to watch your house?" I asked Sonia.

"No."

I parked in front of her house, the mystery car now a small spot a block behind. It was a few minutes before 10 o'clock and the small frame house was shuttered and silent.

"I have to go in," said Sonia, her voice suddenly warm. "I'm going to miss you, Miguel." She put her hand on my arm and leaned toward me, expecting a kiss.

I didn't respond—I couldn't take my eyes from the rearview. Why the hell was she all of a sudden so friendly? And how did they know we would be back this morning?

When Sonia got out and slammed the door, I woke up. The last thing I wanted was this woman to be pissed at me. "Sonia!" I called, but she went inside without looking back. Son of a bitch!

I pulled away from the curb, my eyes fixed on the tiny dark spot in my rearview. It didn't move—that would be too obvious. They were just clocking us in to see if there was too much time between the plane landing and Sonia's arrival at home. I could see the report:

> On March 14, 1982, Special Agent Michael Levine and a female CI arrived at Washington National Airport at 9 A.M., where Levine rented an automobile. The pair was next

seen arriving at the informant's residence three hours later. The drive between the airport and the residence is only half an hour.

Maybe that was why Rourke put me on a plane alone with her.

If they were inspectors and Sonia was working for them, she could accuse me of anything they told her to. There wouldn't be a jury in the world that she couldn't convince with that angelic face. The inspectors had tried to get the pilots and Lydia to lie about me; why not a drug-dealing informant? They probably had photos of the two of us arriving together. Maybe that was why she wanted a goodbye kiss—they wanted a photo.

Suddenly my fear turned to anger. If I didn't strike back these bastards would never leave me in peace. I remembered an old-time street agent telling me about how he had plotted to kill two inspectors who were dogging him day and night. "Hey, I'm a narc," he had said. "I see a car following me—I got all kindsa enemies that wanna kill me—so I try to check it out. I sneak up behind it, see two bad-looking dudes. I bang hard on the car with the butt of my gun. They turn quick—it looks to me like they're reaching for guns. I empty my two guns, 26 fucking rounds, into their heads. Then I say, 'Gee, I'm sorry . . . I made a mistake.' Prove me a murderer!"

Then I thought, They're not inspectors, they're CIA.

"He is embarrassing your government and mine," Mario had told me in Argentina. That was his explanation for why Sonia's uncle Hugo had to die. Mario was doing it for the CIA then, and now I'm still threatening the same people: Arce-Gomez, the German, Pacho Cuervas, or maybe even Mejia himself. If the CIA protecting drug dealers was cause enough to kill Hurtado, why not me? The blame would go right to Mejia or any of a thousand guys I'd put in jail.

I reached the corner and swung a hard right. I was no longer thinking about what I was doing—I was out of control. I raced to the next corner, slid into a turn, and floored it again. I reached down and pulled my 9mm from my ankle holster and held it in my hand. I always kept a round chambered and the safety on. I rested my thumb on the safety release; just a downward flick and it was ready to fire.

I'm an undercover narc working on the most sensitive case in DEA, the biggest drug dealers alive have put a price tag on my head, I just spotted two suspicious men watching me—*prove me a murderer!*

I slid to a quiet stop just before the last corner. I could just see the tail end of the truck. I didn't want them to hear me. I'd come up behind them on foot.

*Yes, your honor—I slipped up on them because there appeared to be two or more men in the car. I couldn't let them get the drop on me. I saw one of them reach for something . . .*

Then I was out of the car and moving, my gun in my hand. Somewhere deep inside me a faint voice cried, "Stop! Think about what you're doing!" I reached the corner, ducked into a low crouch, and headed swiftly toward the truck, my rage building to an incredible peak.

I was now on automatic. My body's trained response system had bypassed the decision-making part of my brain. I could hear my pulse swishing in my ears. Black spots floated before my eyes. Perhaps I was what some legal minds might call "temporarily insane." I was completely aware of what I was doing, yet I was unable to stop myself. I sprinted around the side of the truck, vaguely aware of the safety lever clicking beneath my thumb. I might have been screaming. I think I remember hearing a scream.

The car was gone.

I stood in the middle of the street, my heart banging, trying to pull myself together. I was isolated, vulnerable, and under attack. I had to do something to defend myself.

I've often thought about what I would have done had the car been there. I would like to think that after a career spent trying not to kill murderous, gun-toting criminals, I would have just pointed my gun at them and carried on like a wild man until they identified themselves. But the car was gone, and I'll never know.

# 23

# Mission Improbable

## 1

Late Monday afternoon, March 15, I crossed the Fourteenth Street Bridge into Virginia on my motorcycle, feeling somewhat renewed. The 500-mile round trip to New York, alone with the roar of the engine and the icy wind, plus the two days spent with my daughter, made me realize that there was some life for me outside DEA. There was nothing I could do to alter the course of whatever the suits, the inspectors, or the CIA had planned for me. But there was plenty I could do to affect the course of my daughter's life.

She had sworn to me that she wasn't using drugs. I wanted more than anything in the world to believe her. But I was sick with worry, and uncertain about what to do. I didn't know it yet, but I had begun what would later become the most important drug war of my life—the one to save Niki.[1]

On the ride back to Washington my feelings about how to approach my remaining time with the agency swung between two modes: sur-

[1]The full story of this war is told in *Fight Back* (New York: Dell Publishing, 1991).

vival and fighting mad. The former was that I would just do my best to get through Operation Hun and the Internal Security investigation, doing as I was ordered, making sure not to antagonize anyone. The latter was that whoever tried to protect drug dealers, for whatever reason, ought to go to jail, and I was gonna show the bastards up. By the time I reached Virginia I was firmly in the fighting mad camp.

When I got inside my cluttered room, it was already dark. The little red light on my answering machine was blinking—I had half a dozen messages, all from Rourke. His last one was, "Where the hell are you? Do you want to go to Colombia or don't you?"

The next morning at 6:00, I rode into the DEA basement parking garage wearing my black leather jacket, jeans, and boots. On the rack behind me I had my packed overnight bag. If I had to travel, I was ready.

The roar of my bike awoke the security guard. I flashed my badge and whisked by him. I was thankful that he didn't get a look at my New York license plate, expired since I took the bike with me to Argentina four years before. I'd have to do something about it soon, or it would end up as another charge against me.

The cavernous, multilevel garage was dark and empty. Most headquarters employees didn't arrive before 8:30. I liked the solitude of the morning; I could iron a suit and have some coffee and a little quiet time before the Drug War Machine clattered and hummed to life.

I pulled the motorcycle into a dark corner behind a pillar, just beyond the first turn. I stripped off my jacket and sweater, beneath which I was wearing a sleeveless T-shirt, and began covering the motorcycle with a nylon tarp that locked beneath the wheels.

I had just padlocked the nylon cover when I heard the electric garage door click and whine. For a moment I was blinded by the headlights of the arriving car—one of the brand-new Chevrolets DEA had just bought. As the Chevy whipped past me, I caught a glimpse of the close-cropped head and square recruiting-poster jaw of the new boss of DEA, Francis "Bud the Suit" Mullen himself, and realized with a start that he was craning his neck to get a look at me. He screeched to a stop about 50 feet past me, and started backing up.

I had heard that Mullen went absolutely livid when he saw an agent dressed in anything but "proper business attire"; and worse, that he believed that people who rode motorcycles were basically criminals. And there I was, impaled in his headlights, with my tattooed arms, jeans, boots, and T-shirt, obviously having just arrived on—horror of horrors—a motorcycle, in that holiest of holy places: the DEA garage.

I was sure he hadn't recognized me. I'd been stationed in head-quarters only a short time. I suppose I could have stopped and iden-tified myself, but why should I walk into more trouble if I could avoid it? After all, I was working for an agency that had just made formal charges against me for playing my radio too loud in an American embassy. How could I take the chance of any kind of run-in with the Administrator of that agency, a man who had made an important part of his life's mission the dressing of DEA agents in suits?[2] So I grabbed my bag and, shielding my face with my helmet, hustled toward a door-way that led up into headquarters.

An hour later, now dressed in a suit and tie, I left headquarters through the front door and headed toward a coffee shop. I bought a large black coffee and began looking for an inconspicuous table from which I could watch the street.

"Yo, Mike!" It was Tony Buono. In true New York narc style, he was already seated in the most out-of-the-way corner table in the place. He shoved a seat toward me. "C'mon, keep me company."

"What's new?" I asked, sitting down.

He laughed and opened his suit jacket. "Brooks Brothers." He slid one foot out. "Wingtips. I am totally with the fucking pro-gram." He shook his head. "Ain't they something? Hey, you were in South America; were you at that meeting with Mullen at the Xerox Center?"

"Yeah," I said. "I didn't know it was famous."

"Is it true that he said he looked at DEA wives and couldn't tell them apart from FBI wives?"

"Yeah."

"You see," Tony guffawed and pounded the table, "it's like a fucking disease. It spreads. Next thing you know your son's gonna wanna buy wingtips and your daughter will be dropping a dime on you. 'Hello, I wanna report my daddy for unauthorized use of a govern-ment car.'"

I laughed with him and told him about my encounter in the DEA garage.

"Holy shit!" said Tony, wide-eyed. "You have not heard the end of that."

"Are you serious?"

[2] The suit fixation continues to this day. A June 1993 article in *New York Newsday* revealed that the New York City agent in charge, Felix Jimenez, had to reissue orders for the agents to wear "proper business attire."

"Forget about it. Mikey, these guys are squirrels. And you? You already got inspectors comin' outta yer ears."

"But what'd I do?"

"Woddya mean *do*? You don't have to do nothin'. You can't make sense outta these suits. You hear about the so-called desk concept yet?" This, after the dress code, was the second major change that Mullen was bringing to the DEA.

"Big deal. So they change a couple of names and titles. Nothing's gonna be any different."

"Then you ain't heard," he said, laughing. "Forget about it. We're gonna be totally reorganized. There's gonna be a Heroin Desk, a Cocaine Desk, a Marijuana Desk, and a Dangerous Drugs Desk in charge of everything else. And each one's gonna be run like a separate little kingdom . . . just like the FBI."

"But that's like the AMA telling doctors they have to specialize in the right or left side of the body!" I said, incredulous.

"You got it," said Tony. "And it's already been approved by the Attorney General's office."

I immediately thought of Pacho Cuervas, a cocaine dealer offering to front me marijuana and morphine. Under the new organization, the investigation could conceivably be managed by three different desks. It was hard enough getting one suit to make a decision; to get a decision out of three would be like defying the law of gravity. "When's it start?" I asked, suddenly concerned.

"Within a coupla weeks is what I hear," said Tony, grinning from ear to ear. "Hey, you look like you just seen a ghost."

"It's been a strange morning, Tony."

"Forget about it, Mikey. It's time to stop taking this shit so serious. Relax. Get yourself some wingtips and climb on for the ride. It oughtta be fun."

## 2

By 10:20 of my first morning back at headquarters, I felt as trapped as I did the day I left for Tucson. Just when I was beginning to think that pushing for the Cuervas case had been a foolish error and that I'd never leave headquarters again, Rourke showed up in my office.

"Where the hell you been?" he asked, taking a seat and lighting a fresh cigarette. "You ready to go?"

I studied him. "Is this for real, Jack?" I was looking for some indication of deception, but saw only clear blue policeman's eyes and an unwavering gaze.

"Hey, we've been given the green light. You want to go or don't you?"

"Of course," I said. This wasn't the DEA I knew—approval had come too fast.

"I don't know," said Rourke, "you sure don't sound too anxious."

"Believe me, I'm plenty anxious."

"Good, because Ana Tamayo doesn't stop calling. I'll tell you what . . . she musta gone way out front for you with this guy."

"He's the real thing, Jack," I said, my own words for some reason chilling me.

"Well I'm a believer. Sonia told Ana you'll be coming as soon as you finish your business here. So let's get you going."

During the next hour Rourke and I attended a planning meeting with Marcellino Bedoya, a staff coordinator with a lot of experience working in South America; and Tom Kennedy, a Special Operations Officer. I respected both of these men. Also at the meeting was Ed Grey (name changed), assigned liaison duties with the CIA and other intelligence agencies. (Many DEA agents believed he was actually CIA.)

During the session I was told that Dave Kunz had agreed to accompany me to pose as my pilot. He would get either a South African or a Canadian passport, and I would get an Argentine passport and identity papers. We would fly into Mexico City using our official passports. In Mexico we would meet with an undercover DEA agent who would relieve us of any papers identifying us as American citizens. We would then surface in our drug dealer identities and travel to Cartagena, where one of Cuervas's pilots and private planes would fly us to his hidden ranch. From then on, we were on our own. It was really simple.

Only I was scared shitless.

If this was a real drug war run by people who knew what they were doing, I would have no problem with the Cuervas undercover. But sitting there in the Land of Squirrels, Fruits, and Nuts and thinking about the suits upon whom my life might be depending, I began to question the sanity of taking this case.

No case was worth your life was one of the undercover commandments I had taught to thousands of young cops and agents. If your intuition tells you something is wrong, don't get involved! There will always be another drug case, but you only have one life. Yet here I was, minutes after the planning session, staring at the phone in my office, about to violate the commandment.

But Operation Hun wasn't just another drug case. Like the Suarez case, it was one of those rare cases that—if it were fully exploited— might really make a difference. After 17 years of trying to penetrate the top of the drug world, it was suddenly within reach. I had come too far to turn back now.

I dialed the number that Grey had given me to arrange for my Argentine passport. It was a Washington, D.C. number, not one of the exchanges in CIA headquarters in Langley, Virginia.

"Hello," said a male voice.

"I'm Mike Levine. I was told you'd be expecting my call."

"Yes," said the voice. "Are you free Thursday morning?"

"Sure," I said.

"Can you be at the Foggy Bottom Metro station at precisely 10 A.M.?"

"Yes."

"It's right in front of the university. I'll be wearing a blue nylon jacket. I have a beard, and I'll be carrying a blue rucksack."

"I'll be there," I said. "I'll be wearing a full-length black leather coat. I've got a mustache and . . ."

"I know what you look like," he said, and hung up.

The next morning, thinking about the incident with Mullen, I took the subway to work. My instinct was dead on. At 9 A.M. my phone rang— a suit I didn't know. "Someone told me you come to work on a motorcycle, Levine."

"I only used it once or twice," I said. "I've been away . . . undercover in Tucson and Miami."

"Yes, I heard," he said, sounding unimpressed. "You weren't by any chance in the basement garage yesterday at about six in the morning, were you?"

"Why? What's up?"

"The Administrator thinks security was breached by an outlaw biker."

"You're kidding."

"No, I'm not. He's got the FBI investigating it."

The bike had been in the garage all day; if they were that worried about me, they could have just waited until I left and stopped me. No, by 7 P.M. these guys were all home, no matter what. Maybe they had gotten my license plate number by feel through the cover. If they did, the bike hadn't been registered in almost five years; they'd have to go to Albany to find out who owned it. They wouldn't go through all that, would they? Oh, yes they would.

Later, I passed Tony in the hallway. He laughed and said, "Want me to recommend a lawyer, Mikey?"

"Why do I need a lawyer when I got friends like you, Tony?" I said, wondering how he had heard so quickly, and if he was going to rat me out. It kind of went with his sense of humor.

"Forget about it. You better get with the program," he said, and pointed at his wingtip shoes.

## 3

At precisely 10 A.M. Thursday I stepped out of the Foggy Bottom subway station into the bright sunlight. The street on the edge of George Washington University teemed with students, about half of whom were bearded and carrying rucksacks. Standing there in dark glasses and leather coat, I felt about as subtle as a Gestapo agent at a Hadassah meeting.

I had spent the better part of an hour riding the D.C. subway system pulling every doper move I knew to detect surveillance. I got on and off subway cars just as the doors were closing; I exited subway stations only to turn around and reenter; I randomly changed platforms, running for trains and then stopping dead in my tracks as if I'd forgotten something. Nothing happened that was even remotely suspicious.

By 10:10 I had seen four bearded men in blue nylon jackets with rucksacks. I made eye contact with each. Three had averted their gazes and kept walking; the fourth passed me by, then stopped and edged back toward me, smiling.

"Do you go to school here?" he asked, looking me up and down.

"I think you've mistaken me for someone else," I said, feeling foolish.

"Hmmm, that's too bad," he said.

He moved off, glancing back as he did. I turned to look the other way and noticed an attractive woman watching me from a bus stop about 40 feet away. She started toward me, smiling.

"Mike?" she said.

"Lucky guess," I said. "What gave me away? Wait, don't tell me—I was the only guy on the street without a blue rucksack."

She laughed politely, took my arm, and led me toward one of the university buildings. "We can talk in relative privacy in there."

"Fine," I said. "What's your name?" I had the feeling if I didn't ask she wasn't going to tell me.

"Elaine."

"Hi, I'm Mike."

"Yes, I know." She smiled.

Elaine led the way into the university library, where she blended a lot better than I did. She had short, neat blond hair and wore a conservative two-piece business suit. When we sat down at a rear table, her manner swiftly became all business. She had the whole undercover thing of smiling, nodding, and laughing as though she were having a delightful chat, while speaking *sotto voce* of things like deep-cover identities, forged documents, levels of backup for phony IDs, and cover stories down pat. It was a marvel of deception.

"We'll need 20 or 30 exemplars of your signature," she said, "using your undercover name. Also, a half-dozen black-and-white passport photos facing the camera at a 45-degree angle. That's how Argentine passport photos are taken." She laughed, as if she'd just heard the funniest thing.

"By when do you need the stuff?"

"I understand you're leaving very soon." She smiled brightly, her eyes crinkling up. Her teeth were perfect tiny white cubes, and she knew more than I did. "Can you get me everything by tomorrow morning?"

"No problem."

"Fine," she said. "How about meeting here again at the same time?" Her mouth held the smile, while her eyes, suddenly cold, studied me. I felt a chill.

"Great," I said, but she was no longer listening.

Her eyes were already checking the people around us. She stood and offered me her hand. I took it and started to rise. "No," she said, dropping her voice and flashing the toothpaste smile. "Why don't you wait a few minutes."

After Elaine left I sat watching the people outside through the library window, picking out a smiling, unconcerned face here and there and wondering what the secret was. The minutes stretched to half an hour, and people started to glance at me. I had to get going; I had to get the passport photos and there was a lot of planning to be done, but I just couldn't move. I was really afraid.

By the next day I had managed to block out all negative thoughts about the Cuervas operation and was able to approach it as though nothing could go wrong—a point of view most experienced street agents would describe as "lame-brained optimism." I felt that once I got to Colombia and away from the control of the suits, I would make the case work. If I could convince Suarez's people to deal with me in spite of the suits, I could do the same with Cuervas. I had spent much of the night drawing up a plan to use Cuervas's offer to disrupt the dealers. Even if the plan turned out to be only 50 percent effective, it would have devastating effects on the drug world.

Kunz and I would go to Cartagena and pick up the 17 tons of marijuana and the million doses of morphine. We'd store the drugs in Tucson, where Sonia and I would use a portion of them to pay off Mejia. After Mejia's men left Tucson with the drugs, agents would follow them and arrest them in another state. It would be a long time before they realized that Sonia and I were working for the government. To maintain our cover we would even pay for their attorneys.

With cover and reputation intact, we could continue Operation Hun in other directions, selling Cuervas's drugs to the biggest distributors in the United States, then arresting them and reseizing the drugs. We could pay Cuervas with seized doper money and reorder more drugs to keep the operation going.

If we happened onto dealers whose arrest might blow our cover, we'd simply give them samples, conduct secretly filmed negotiations, and then find some excuse not to consummate the deal. When we decided that we had squeezed Operation Hun for all it was worth, everyone we negotiated with—perhaps hundreds of class-one dealers—would be arrested and charged with conspiracy. By that time we would have enough evidence to indict everyone in Sonia's black book, which included directly or indirectly every top drug dealer in this hemisphere, including the Medellin Cartel.

The plan wasn't going to win the drug war—we had damaged it too much already when we turned Bolivia over to the Suarez/Gasser organization—but it was an opportunity to cost the bad guys billions of dollars, and it would create paranoia in the minds of traffickers that would wreak havoc on the drug economy for many years. And it wouldn't cost the American taxpayer a cent—it would all be paid for by the drug dealers.

After a quick meet with Elaine to turn over the items she had asked for, I was on my eager way to headquarters. She told me that my passport would be ready the following Wednesday (March 24). Once again I felt like an agent.

DEA wouldn't go this far if they weren't serious. Maybe I'd been dead wrong about the FBI takeover; maybe the Bolivian debacle was an anomaly, a single incident where the CIA had somehow managed to prevail. DEA would never let that happen again.

## 3

Monday morning, March 21, was bright and cheery, and I walked out of headquarters at 7:30 dressed in my best three-piece suit and headed over to the coffee shop. I'd had a couple of great telephone conversations with my daughter and was feeling really hopeful about her. I hadn't had a single headache all weekend, and I had spent Sunday evening with some old South America friends without once talking about the drug war. I had managed to completely push the inspectors, Buck Turghid, Oliver South, and my outlaw motorcycle from my mind.

All the suits who'd seen the Cuervas operational plan had approved, but to make certain there were no future problems I had spent a good part of the weekend going over all the possible pitfalls I could think of, listing their solutions on paper. Yeah, I was feeling good; I was ready for anything.

Tony Buono was already at his corner table, grinning like he'd won the lottery.

"C'mon, I saw you leaving the building and got you a cup," he said.

"Thanks," I said sitting down. I was glad for the company. Since the inspectors began working on me, few agents would risk socializing with me.

"I see you're taking my advice," he said, admiring my suit. "Where'd ya get it, Montgomery Ward?" He laughed at his own joke. "How many pollies did they havta kill for all that polyester?" He guffawed again.

I smiled politely and sipped my coffee.

Suddenly, he lowered his voice and glanced around like a street-corner dealer checking for cops. "Did you come in on the bike this morning?" He had a mischievous gleam in his eye that made me uncomfortable.

"What bike?" I said.

He laughed. "Well," he said grinning like a devil, "as an old friend I just thought I'd warn you. Forget about it. The fucking FBI is closing in on you. I told you you didn't hear the last of it."

"What do you mean, 'closing in on me'? I thought by now you would have ratted me out, anyway."

Tony laughed and pounded the table. "Yeah, I was thinking about ratting you out, but this is too much fucking fun. I heard there were two FBI guys—grade-fucking-15s—down in the garage trying to get the license number off your bike. You had it all covered, right?"

"Yeah."

"Well, they couldn't get the numbers without ripping your cover or something. Forget about it. They had a whole fucking top-level meeting about whether they had the right to rip your cover or not—being the thing was technically on government property—and I heard they even called the chief counsel's office for an opinion. Can you fucking believe it?" Tony was laughing and pounding the table again.

"How do you know all this?"

Tony grinned slyly. "I got my sources. So how could I rat you out Levine, and miss these clowns runnin' around like mice in a maze? Forget about it. Not for all the fucking money or brown-nosing points in the world."

"Don't leave yet," said Ralph Saucedo, Deputy Regional Director of South American Operations. "The Administrator wants to talk to you."

"The Administrator wants to talk to me?" My first thought was that it had something to do with the motorcycle. Saucedo was punching numbers on the phone.

I looked at Rourke, sitting across the office from me, his collar open, his tie askew. He shrugged and blew a smoke ring. We had just finished an entire day of conferences with a half-dozen suits about the Cuervas operation. It still appeared to be going full speed ahead, unless that damn motorcycle screwed it up.

"I've got Levine here," said Saucedo into the phone. "Okay, we'll be right up."

"What does he want to talk to me about?" I asked.

"About the operation," said Saucedo, a big, soft-spoken man with dark hair and intense gray eyes. He had been the driving force behind the Suarez operation, defying most of the other suits to push the case as far as it went. He was a quiet, studious man of Mexican-Anglo extraction and a devout Mormon. I suppose the best way to characterize our relationship was respectful, mutual distrust. Yet here we were a second time fighting out of the same corner.

"Isn't that unusual?" I asked, still suspecting that the motorcycle might have something to do with it. I had been the undercover agent on a lot of big cases, but I had never been asked to brief anyone higher than a division leader or a staff assistant.

"That's what the man wants," said Saucedo, leading the way out of his office toward the elevators. He would say nothing more. Whatever the plots and politics unfolding around Operation Hun were, none of them would be shared with me.

Minutes later Saucedo, Rourke, and I were ushered through the thickly carpeted DEA executive suite into the office of the "main man," the *capo di tutti capo* of the war on drugs—the Administrator of the DEA.

To my great relief, Mullen was out of town; in his place was Acting Administrator Fred Monastero. There were two other blue-suited men seated on either side of the biggest desk in drug enforcement; they both seemed to be trying to skewer me with bureaucratic eyes. Each nodded slightly without smiling as he was introduced.

"I really only had one question, Mike," said Monastero. "Do you feel safe doing this assignment . . . going undercover to Colombia?"

I was stunned. Something wasn't kosher. Everyone knows undercover work is not safe anywhere. DEA agents are constantly working undercover all over the world, and rarely is an agent asked if he or she feels safe. In my 17 years in DEA, including four or five working for Monastero in New York, I had never been asked that question by any supervisor. It was an understandable, albeit rarely voiced, concern of street-level supervisors who were directly responsible for the safety of the men and women under their command. But for the head of the whole agency to call an agent to his office to ask that question was entirely out of character for DEA. He had to have been specifically instructed to ask the question, and with some high-level witnesses present.

"I feel completely comfortable with the setup, Mr. Monastero. I couldn't feel more confident," I said. I wasn't giving them any excuse to cancel the operation. "This is the kind of thing I have been doing for 17 years, sir," I added, meeting the gaze of one of the FBI men and smiling. He did not smile back.

Monastero looked around the room. Everyone was quiet. Then he smiled and stood and said, "Okay, Mike, good luck." He offered me his hand. "You've got my approval."

That was it? That was the whole thing?

I shook his hand and looked at the other faces in the room. I felt dizzy, as though I were standing on the tip of a piece of ice jutting up from the ocean and realizing that I was on a gigantic iceberg that was moving farther and farther from land.

On Wednesday morning, March 24, I met Elaine the spy at the George Washington University library. When we sat down at the rear table, she said, "Get a book," and fixed me with the same unreadable smile.

"What?"

"Get a book . . . from the shelf," she said as if talking to a slow-witted child, her smile frozen in place. "To examine the passport."

I pulled the first large book I saw from the nearest shelf, brought it back to the table and opened it in front of me. Elaine, still smiling her cheerleader's smile, pushed a manila envelope across the table to me. I placed it in the open book and removed the envelope's contents—a worn-looking Argentine passport.

I thumbed through the pages—it was a work of criminal art. I had seen enough bona fide Argentine passports to know that I was looking at the real thing or a good enough facsimile to fool any professional. The pages showed that one Miguel Antonio Rubino had traveled extensively between Argentina, Mexico, and the United States—a nice route for a drug trafficker.

"You'll notice," said Elaine, in her grinning *sotto voce*, "that you are at this moment in Mexico. The passport shows you arriving in Mexico City two days ago. You have a two-week visa, which means you have another 12 days to travel to Mexico using your official passport, leave your official identity at the American embassy, and then resurface as Miguel Rubino."

"Very impressive," I said.

"Do not leave Mexico using that passport on Tuesday or Thursday of next week. The immigration official whose signature appears on your arrival documents [these were attached to the pages of the passport] is working on those days, and might recognize that it's not his signature—although it is pretty close. But, no sense taking chances.

"And if anyone calls Buenos Aires to check on you, they'll find a Miguel Rubino living at that address, whose vital data matches everything in the passport. Do you have any questions?" Elaine looked at me with her incongruous smile. I had a dozens, but not one I dared ask.

She stood and offered her hand. "Good luck, Michael," she said. For some reason her sudden use of my real first name made me grin.

"Thanks," I said, taking her hand. Before I could say another word she had turned and was walking away.

I watched her pass through the library turnstile and out the glass doors, where she slipped into a wave of people heading toward Pennsylvania Avenue. Her smile had vanished.

I opened the passport again and examined it. It was a magnificent job; the result of enormous effort involving covert agents—CIA agents—in three countries. It was a document that said I'd be picking up $30 million worth of dope within 12 days. Maybe I'd been wrong all along; maybe the drug war was real after all.

I mean, why go through all this trouble if it wasn't?

That night I went to my room and packed a suitcase for Colombia, carefully selecting what I'd need for the role, making sure that most of the things I packed were items bought in Argentina. I prepared a special wallet with phony Argentine identification the Argentine cops had provided me with while I was stationed there, along with business cards showing a Buenos Aires phone number—an embassy undercover phone. It had been arranged that if anyone called looking for Miguel Rubino, they'd be told I was "out of town."

In the morning I brought everything to the office. I locked the wallet and passport in my drawer and stowed the suitcase under my desk. The suitcase stayed there for 10 maddening days full of unreadable cables, humming machines, clacking typewriters, dour faces, and averted gazes; 10 days under the cold, documenting eyes of Tommy Dolittle; 10 days that passed like 10 lifetimes; 10 days that it sat rubbing angrily against my shins, as if it were as anxious to go as I was.

# 24

# April Fools

## 1

"**M**ind if I come in?" said Ed Grey. I looked up from my desk and saw his head poked in the doorway. A nervous little smile seemed to suggest that he was expecting a negative reply.

"No, not at all." I was immediately ill at ease.

Grey, a very tall, angular man who wore horn-rimmed glasses, long-sleeve white shirts, and pale spotted ties, entered my little space cautiously, looking around as if he were thinking of buying the place but suspecting structural damage. No one knew whether he worked for DEA and liaised with the CIA or vice versa. He folded into a seat across from me, crossing a long leg and a huge foot over his knee. He had on the biggest pair of wingtips I'd ever seen in my life.

He just sat there smiling, not saying a thing. He was the sort of guy who could do that and make you feel that you owed him an explanation for something.

"What can I do you out of?" I asked.

"I just needed to pick up your, uh, Argentine passport," he smiled. "I was told that you weren't going to be using it."

For a moment I stared at him blankly. Then I quickly said, "Oh . . . sure," as if I had been expecting him all day.

That the Cuervas operation was killed was no surprise to me—but the way they were letting me know was. I had marked yesterday's date, April Fool's Day, in my calender as the last possible day that I could leave for Mexico before the phony visa expired. When the workday had passed with no mention of the operation and another verbal reprimand from Tommy Dolittle—noted in his green ledger—for my "lack of enthusiasm and initiative," I gave up all hope.

For 10 days, no one had said a word to me about the trip, and I, determined to play my role as a good soldier and not antagonize anyone, just waited for orders. If the suits were going to let an offer of $30 million in free dope die without a word, I wanted to see it happen. They had not disappointed me.

I found the little blue booklet with *ARGENTINA* emblazoned across its cover in the righthand corner of the drawer, exactly as I'd left it 10 days earlier. I passed it to Grey.

"The Agency's kinda ticklish about these things," he said, opening the passport to examine it, then folding it into his shirt pocket.

Grey sat there, smiling. I smiled back, feeling dull and empty, waiting for him to say something, wanting badly to be alone.

"Well . . . ," said Grey, getting to his feet and moving to the door. He opened it and the office noises invaded. "You want it closed?"

"Yes," I said." He left.

As he closed the door, the Cuervas operation officially closed, too. The man Ana had called the biggest drug dealer in Colombia would never be investigated, nor would his name ever be entered into the DEA computer. It would be as though he never existed.

## 2

On Tuesday, April 5—after the weekend and a day of sick leave—I was back in the office. I figured that Operation Hun had probably gone the way of the Cuervas operation—"disappeared" without a trace into the CIA's black hole of special interests. A year or two down the line I might hear something about it, or I might not. It didn't matter. Right now my only concerns were my kids and my survival.

By 10 A.M. I had all my morning cables read, highlighted, and sorted in Dolittle's in-box. A cable from Panama actually required action beyond just filling out a form and putting it in some suit's in-box or rerouting the cable to some other DEA office for action. It was a request for headquarters to help locate an informant, and it required a couple of phone calls. I was in the midst of trying to figure out how I could stretch an hour's work to lunchtime when the phone rang.

"Levine? This is Terry Burke. Can you stop by my office?"

Burke was one of a group of 15 or 20 CIA agents (no one knew the true number) who had transferred into DEA. Many in DEA believed they were still working for the CIA. I didn't know Burke other than to say hello to him in the hallways. He was the only member of upper management that always smiled at me—a smile that made me very nervous.

I had no idea what Burke wanted, but he was upper management, and he had sounded friendly enough. As I swung past Dolittle's open door, he gave me a look that said, "Mister, your number is just about up."

Burke's secretary sent me right into his office without looking at me. "Have a seat," said Burke, as I closed the door to his immaculate office behind me. As usual, he had a big smile on his clean-shaven, corporate face. I noticed that his set of DEA manuals, stacked neatly on a credenza behind him, were dog-eared and indexed.

"How are you doing?"

"Fine." I was sure he knew I was doing anything but fine.

"Good, good. I called you here because . . . well, you know you're going to be working for me on the Marijuana Desk, don't you?"

"No, sir."

"Oh . . . I thought Dolittle advised you."

"No, sir."

"Well, no matter," he said, the smile frozen in place. "I just thought it fair to tell you—before you came to work for me—that I was Headroom's boss when he recommended your removal from Argentina. I was the one who insisted he do the inspection."

He paused, waiting for my reaction.

He had just told me that he was responsible for sending Inspector Headroom to audit my office while Headroom was trying to put me in jail on a separate investigation; that he was responsible for my forced transfer from Argentina because I supposedly played my radio too loud and a half-dozen other ridiculous charges. And he was sitting there grinning at me like a Cheshire cat.

"I don't know what to say," I said, sensing that I was just one rash statement away from the end of my career.

"I just thought it fair that you be aware of it before you came to work for me," he repeated, his smile starting to unnerve me.

"How am I supposed to fight that report with you being my boss?" I asked, suddenly beyond caring. I was doomed; if the inspectors and Dolittle didn't get me, Burke would.

"Don't let that stop you."

I ran into Tony in the hallway. "How much you wanna bet," he said, his voice low, turning his head to check the hallway, "that any day now the suits are gonna ring a fucking bell and we're all gonna have to change offices, like musical chairs?" He chuckled.

"No bet," I said, not feeling any laughter inside me.

"Forget about it. By the way—you got New York plates on the motorcycle, right?"

"Yes."

"The word is they got a couple of numbers off the plate, by feel, and now they got the FBI in New York running it down."

"I guess they got me," I shrugged.

Tony looked at me seriously. "Mikey, you look like a whipped dog. I never thought I'd see the day."

"You see it, my friend," I said, getting into an elevator and leaving him in the hallway. "I give up."

Back in my little cell, swallowed up by the noises of the Drug War Machine, my mind wandered to fantasy.

> I was watching the front door of headquarters. I had learned of a secret conference between the suits and the CIA to finalize a plot to crush communism in the Western Hemisphere by putting drug dealers in charge of every South American government. I had the Administrator's conference room wired with C-4 plastic explosives, and a transmitter disguised as a ballpoint pen was in my hand. A push of the button and the entire executive suite would go up in smoke. A black stretch limousine arrived, and William Casey, the director of the CIA, was escorted into the building by a phalanx of bodyguards. With him was a woman in a black veil. It was Sonia Atala.

The ringing phone brought me back to the real world.

"Hey, ya hump," said Rourke. I hadn't heard his voice in more than a week. "We're goin' back to Tucson!"

## 3

Rourke barged into my office, a pile of case folders under his arm, as if the Cuervas mess and almost eight days of silence had never happened. "I need you to make a call to Ana Tamayo," he said. He looked weary, harried, and as gray as the ash on the end of his cigarette.

"You gotta be kidding," I said.

"The broad is beside herself. You really fucked her up with Pacho. Sonia's been making excuses all week, but she's insistin' on talkin' to you direct."

"I can't believe my ears. Are you telling me there's still an Operation Hun?"

"Come on, Mike. Don't give me a harder fuckin' time than I'm having. I know what you're gonna say."

"No, Jack, I'm not gonna say a fucking thing. Lemme just ask you one question—why was the Cuervas operation killed?"

"You know, you're a grade-14, ya hump. I'm a grade-13. You think it was me that canceled it?"

"I don't have the slightest idea."

Rourke flicked his ash into the wastepaper basket. "All I know is that someone upstairs said it wasn't safe."

"Come on, man, you think anyone's really looking out for me? Monastero himself knows there's undercovers doing hairier bits in the Bronx and Brooklyn. No one could care less."

"And Turghid came out heavy against it."

"What's he got to say about it? He's the RAC of Tucson."

Rourke shook his head. "He told someone he didn't want any pill cases."

"Bullshit!" I was on my feet. "Fucking bullshit! Man, I swore to myself I'd never again let a case get to me. I fuckin' swore to myself! But this just makes me sick."

"I know, Mike, I know. I'm trying to keep the thing together myself, and these people are drivin' me nuts, too. I don't know what I'm knockin' myself out for anyway. I'm gonna be on the Marijuana Desk and Burke already told me he doesn't want me working anything that's not grass. You don't wanna call Ana, I can't make you." He got up and started toward the door.

"Wait," I said. "Sit. Lemme just get a couple of things straight."

"If you're gonna start the same shit . . ."

"No, I'll make the call for you, but I don't know what's happened. Bring me up to date. Besides, it looks like you and me are gonna be on the Marijuana Desk together."

"You're kidding."

"I wish I was," I said.

"It's a fuckin' conspiracy," said Rourke, taking a seat. When he was settled he began. "Sonia's been on the phone for the past two weeks with everyone in the world."

"Let's start with Mejia," I said. "Almost three weeks ago she told him he'd have his dope in eight to ten days the latest."

"She's got them under control. You've just been delayed by business. She said you'd be back in Tucson some time next week."

"And they're buying it?"

"So far."

"You sure they ain't so pissed now that all they want is a chance to whack us?"

Rourke looked thoughtful. "I doubt it. He still sees a good chance of collecting."

"She's talking direct to Papo?"

"No. Mario Espinosa's in from Colombia. It looks like Papo's makin' him responsible."

"Why?"

"Espinosa's the guy who first introduced him to Sonia."

"Nice guy, that Papo. Do we have any idea where he is?"

"Somewhere in Colombia."

"And what about Miami? They ever find out anything at all about him? Where his wife gave birth, where he was staying? Anything at all?"

Rourke exhaled smoke and shook his head. "All they know is he took the call in a public phone booth."

"What about poor Ana?"

"Woddya mean 'poor Ana'?"

"I like her Jack. So we bust her—that's the way it goes. But we don't have to torture her." I hated the thought of screwing Ana around more than necessary. She had become more than just another doper to me, a feeling that Rourke didn't share.

"Well, Sonia told 'poor Ana' that you got tied up with business. She is fucking pissed, and wants to hear it from you."

"And that's it?"

"That's it."

"So what's the bottom line? Are we going back to Tucson?"

"As of this moment, we're going back next week. More than that I can't tell you."

I hooked my tape recorder to the phone and dialed Colombia. A woman answered. As soon as I said who I was, an angry Ana came on the line.

"Why aren't you here? Why didn't you call?"

"Ana, please forgive me. It was impossible."

"I waited here for you, Miguel, all this time. In front of Pacho and the others I look very, very bad."

"Please, Ana," I said, "I cannot tell you how terrible I feel about this. Things happened. I now have more rugs than I can handle . . . 150. But if you can help me find customers I can resolve the situation quicker. Tell Pacho that you're helping me sell some merchandise; that we'll be there the moment it's taken care of." I thought the promise of more than $1 million in commission might take some of the anger out of her.

There was a long silence, and then Ana said, "I can leave this week."

"*Este semana?*" I covered the phone and whispered "This week?" to Rourke. He shrugged. The call was mine—no one could predict how quickly the suits would move.

"Yes, because there's a holiday here," said Ana.

"Ah, then you mean, more or less, next week?"

She agreed. Ana said she already had some customers in mind. She even promised to try to bring a sample of Cuervas's morphine pills with her. But she was changed. For the first time I heard distrust in her voice.

"Where are you calling from, Miguel?"

"From New York," I said, praying that she didn't ask for a phone number.

"What is the weather like?" She sounded like a woman who'd found lipstick on her boyfriend's collar.

There had been a late snowfall in Washington, and the news that morning said New York had gotten some of it. "It's snowing," I said. "I hate the snow. I can't wait to get back to Tucson. I can't wait to see you again, *mamita.*"

Another long silence. Then, in a strange voice, Ana said, "I'll be in Miami on Sunday. I will call you the moment I get there."

After I hung up, I played the tape back and translated it for Rourke.

# 25

# Stone Killers

## 1

"**N**ow here's the way it's gonna be, . . ." said Turghid, glaring across his desk at me. It was an oven-hot Wednesday morning, April 14, and I was back in Tucson, almost a month since I had left. On my arrival at the UC house the night before Lydia could barely look at me—if anything, she was more tense around me than before. To the Tucson agents I was still the man about to be jailed. South was still skulking and cowering, and Rudy was still friendly but reserved. Only Sonia had changed.

"Guess what!" she had announced excitedly moments after I arrived at the UC house. "They got him."

"Got who?"

"René Benitez." She grinned at me, waiting for a reaction.

"You did it?"

"Of course," she said proudly. "I promised Jack I would deliver him on a platter, and I did."

"Nice work."

I talked with her for a while. She showed no sign that there had ever been any friction between us. I soon understood that her good mood was not just from handing over Benitez—everything was going incredibly well for her. Sonia had become very confident in her role as an informant. And why not? She was now in complete control of Operation Hun and her destiny.

She had spent the past two weeks successfully stalling Mejia's men on the phone; she had conned them into coming to Tucson in a few days to collect their drugs and be arrested. She had been promised that Mejia himself would be present, which meant that with Arce-Gomez out of power in Bolivia, the biggest remaining threat to her was about to be eliminated. She was going to accomplish this without jeopardizing a single one of the hundreds of class-one drug dealers in her black book.

When she had tried to rush Operation Hun to an early finish with Pineda, I had suspected that one of her hidden goals was to protect the names of her customers. Now I was certain of it. If Operation Hun ended with the arrest of Mejia in a few days—as it now appeared it would—Sonia would have managed to be a DEA informant without—in the eyes of other dopers—really being an informant. She had informed only against those who had first harmed her. She would have lost no face by her dealings with DEA; her reputation and contacts would be safe for future use. And her husband Walter, whom I believed had to be deeply involved in her drug trafficking, would never even be mentioned in a single DEA report.

The only possible glitch in that nice, neat picture, was Ana Tamayo, who just wouldn't give up trying to help us. Ana had called to say she was coming to Tucson from Miami with one of her biggest customers. They were arriving in 48 hours.

". . . So this time, we're not gettin' offa the target," finished Turghid.

"What about Ana Tamayo?" I said.

"What about her?"

"She's coming here the day after tomorrow with a customer. What am I supposed to do with her?"

"She shows up with the fuckin' money, jail the bitch."

"I asked her to bring morphine pill samples from Pacho Cuervas. What if she brings 'em?"

"She gets busted. That's it. When Mejia's people come we want this thing wrapped up, shut down, and over. You got it?"

"I got it."

"Got some good news for you," he said, smiling. "I had the coke rewrapped in nice new bags."

Old dope in new packages—that would really fool 'em. "That's fine," I said, again glancing at Rourke, who still didn't look at me. "Just great."

*I, Michael Levine, do hereby surrender all my dreams, goals, and beliefs to reality. I surrender my balls and declare myself a perfect government eunuch. All I want in return is to be left alone and be allowed to survive.*

Later, in the brutal heat of the afternoon, I wandered alone inside the UC house, trying to get acclimated to being surrounded by hidden microphones and cameras and wondering how I'd ever been able to do it before.

We had 48 hours of down time before Ana arrived. Normally down time for an undercover operation is used to perfect the operation, time to go over all the what-ifs the team can think of. But for the first time in my career, I was trying my best not to think about the case. Sonia and Lydia were lying side-by-side in silence by the pool, so I put on a bathing suit and joined them. If you ever want to stop thinking, sit in the desert sun for a while. Within minutes it had baked my brain into blissful submission and my body into molten rubber.

From somewhere I heard the distant sound of a door sliding open. "Can I have a word with you?" said the cheerful voice of Ollie South. Through eyes blurred by sweat, I made him out standing in the patio door. He had a large paper bag in his hand.

"Sure thing," I said, groggily getting to my feet. I joined South in the cool darkness of the house. He had placed the bag on the living room table and stood over it watching me, a thin smile on his lips.

"These are for you," he said.

I opened the bag and saw that it was half-full of cassettes. "What's this all about?"

"While you're doing nothing else," said South, blinking a lot but looking at me directly for the first time, "Mr. Turghid wants you to transcribe these and translate them into English."

The bag contained all the tape-recorded conversations Sonia and I had had with Ana Tamayo, Monica Garcia, and Eduardo Pineda—about 50–60 hours of conversation. South removed a DEA 12—Standard Receipt form—from his shirt pocket and slid it across the table.

"Mr. Turghid wants you to sign for them," he said, his thin smile threatening to turn into a grin. He placed a government ballpoint pen on top of the form and watched me expectantly.

Turghid and I were both grade-14s. Ordering any undercover agent on assignment to do clerical work would be insulting, but doing it to one of my grade and experience went beyond insult—it was an open challenge. Aside from the fact that it was senseless folly to have cassettes marked *DEA Evidence* lying around an undercover house, it was a dangerously distracting task. If you wanted to make an undercover agent's performance as far below optimal as possible, just make the agent spend down time transcribing recordings.

As much as Turghid disliked me, I was sure he wouldn't have issued such an order on his own. It had to have been "suggested" by someone at headquarters, someone who was anticipating that I would refuse, in which case they'd slam shut a bureaucratic trap and charge me with failure to obey a lawful order.

"Let me get this straight. I'm in the middle of UC work on what's allegedly DEA's top-priority case, and Turghid wants me to transcribe recordings?"

South was ready for me. He straightened to his full height, his smile flickering on and off like a faulty light bulb, his eyes blinking rapidly, and said, "I don't know anything about that. My orders are to bring you the tapes and get a receipt. Are you refusing to sign?" He had already retrieved the form and the pen.

"Hell, no," I said, taking the form out of his hand, signing my name across the bottom, and sliding it back to him. He stared at my signature, his lips parted as if to speak. I had not reacted as he had been told I would. His response had been programmed, but I had short-circuited him.

"Well, you got what you came for. Anything else?"

He flushed and picked up the form. "You know," he said, suddenly apologetic, "I just follow orders."

"I know how that is."

He retreated toward the door.

"Wait a second," I said. He paused with his hand on the door handle. "There's one thing I need."

"What's that?" he asked, watching me suspiciously.

"I need one of those secretarial tape-recorders with the foot pedal. If I'm going to do the secretary's job at least let me have the right equipment."

"I'll tell Mr. Turghid," he said as he started out the door.

I watched through the drawn blinds as South got into his government car. As he started the car, he reached for his radio mike. He was speaking on it as he drove away. Someone had been waiting for his report.

An hour later he returned with the machine.

I sealed myself in my room all night, listening to Sonia and myself conning, manipulating, and lying to Ana Tamayo, who sounded naive and vulnerable; Monica Garcia, the shark, who sounded even more suspicious and wary than I remembered; the frightened Mario Espinosa, the man who had first introduced Sonia to Mejia; the sinister Eduardo Pineda; and the lethal Papo Mejia. I carefully wrote all their words down in longhand, first in Spanish, then translated into English. Anyone who's ever said talk is cheap never spoke to an undercover agent—each of the people on our tapes had said enough to earn a possible 45 years in federal prison.

It was a sobering experience listening to myself manipulating these people, getting them to trust me while planning to use that trust to destroy them. What is sleazier than that kind of treachery? Informants who do this are called "stool pigeons," "rats," and "snitches." Most street cops and agents who work with informants at best tolerate them and at worst loathe them—but always mistrust them.

The undercover agent hangs carrots before his target's noses—the money, power, or revenge they hunger for, or the terrors they most fear. He maneuvers his targets into saying the things he wants them to say for secret recorders, doing the things he wants them to do, and then, in their most vulnerable moment, revealing his badge and his treachery and so devastating the target that the final surrender in court is but an afterthought, like the dagger thrust that kills the fighting bull as he lies defenseless, bleeding from a hundred wounds.

Undercover agents are always surprised to learn that in most civilized countries around the world, their work is considered illegal and immoral. We're also surprised when we learn that our own bosses don't trust us. This knowledge astounds us because most of us believe that our professional immorality has nothing to do with our real moral values. We are comfortable with our actions because we believe in the rightness of what we've been asked to do and in the virtue of those who have asked us to do it—for the most part, the bureaucrats and politicians who trust us the least.

In the early morning hours of that long night of listening to myself in action, I thought of words from Hemingway's *Death in the Afternoon:* "What is moral is what you feel good after and what is immoral is what you feel bad after." For the first time in 17 years I couldn't stand the sound of my own voice.

## 2

On Friday night at 9:30, I was alone in the UC house, pacing, waiting for Rudy to call. It had been almost three hours since I sent a two-car caravan to meet Ana and her customer at the airport. They were to take them to one of our heavily seeded restaurants, where, when everyone was nice and relaxed, don Miguel would make his appearance.

I'd been dressed and ready to go for over an hour, but I was nervous and uneasy about the whole thing. Words from my Undercover Narcotics lecture came back to me: Never work undercover when your heart's not in it—your concentration is off, you make errors, and then bad things happen. My heart was anything but in what I was doing. I was trying to rev myself up, but all I was doing was wearing out the carpet.

The phone rang and I jumped. I was standing in front of the Evil Eye. I saluted it with my middle finger and grabbed the receiver.

"We're here," said Rudy. In the background I could hear a piano playing above tinkling glassware and the hum of conversation.

"How'd it go?"

"Pretty good, I'd say. Ana showed up with two guys."

"Two guys?"

"The main guy and his bodyguard."

"Anything I should know?"

"I, uh, think this guy has a real thing for Sonia."

"It look like a problem?"

"Well . . . not yet. But she's got him heated up pretty good."

Half an hour later I drove up to the restaurant. The valet, recognizing me, sprinted for the car and opened my door before I put the transmission in park—$5 tip. The maitre d', seeing me over the heads of the crowd waiting for tables, dropped everything to lead me to our tables—a $20 bill vanished as though sucked from my hand by a vacuum cleaner.

Now Rudy was standing next to me, speaking in my ear. "Everything okay?" he asked. Beyond him I could see the two tables of our little entourage. Sonia, Lydia, Ana, and two Latinos in guayabera shirts stopped speaking and watched me from a table cluttered with plates and a small forest of bottles and glasses. South and two tough-looking Chicano undercovers in dark glasses sat at the next table. The fair-haired South, looking out of place as usual, eyed me sullenly. He made a comment to one of the Chicanos, who nodded expressionlessly.

"Everything's fine," I said, aware of intense scrutiny from the Latino just to Sonia's left. "Anything else I should know?"

"You see it, boss."

I moved past Rudy and circled the table greeting everyone. I kissed Lydia on her cheek, and then Ana jumped to her feet and gave me a big hug and a warm kiss. There was nothing put on about her; all was forgiven. I leaned over and kissed Sonia on the cheek. *"Ola,"* she said, her eyes on the Latino now standing beside her chair.

"Sorry I'm late," I said.

"Forget it, Miguel," said Ana, "we understand." She aimed me at the two men. "Allow me to present my old friend Roberto."

Roberto, balding and with a grin that revealed jagged teeth below dark, malevolent eyes, extended a jewelry-laden hand in my direction. I guessed he was sporting about $50,000 worth of gold and diamonds on his hands and neck, which would just about pay for the dental work he needed. Drug dealers are so damned predictable.

*"Mucho gusto,"* I said, shaking his hand; his grip was powerful. I judged him to be in his late forties, about 5'8" and about 170 pounds. He didn't let go of my hand right away, feeling my knuckles and the texture of my skin. Street people think you can tell a lot about a man by the condition of his hands.

"Don't trouble yourself," he said. "Sonia and your beautiful sister have been taking great care of us." His words came in short, staccato bursts—unmistakably Cuban. His breath was so foul that I couldn't breathe. "This is Carlos," he said, introducing me to a tall, rawboned man beside him.

"What's your name? I'm sorry, I didn't catch it," said Carlos. His Spanish was pure Mexican. He grabbed my hand in a big-knuckled hand that could do some damage.

"Miguel."

"Miguel," he repeated. He was as tall as me, with thick, wavy, salt-and-pepper hair and a heavy, dark mustache. He looked to be in his late forties. He was studying me closely, in a way that made me uneasy. "Don't I know you from somewhere?" he asked.

"That could be," I said. I moved past him toward the empty seat.

297

"No, no," said Roberto, "take my seat . . . sit next to your lady."

"No, brother, relax. Everyone's comfortable; no need to move."

Carlos scooted over a seat. "Sit here so you two can talk," he said. Now I was wedged between the two of them.

"Hey!" Roberto snapped his finger at a waiter. "How bou' soam fockeen service, meng." There was a sudden hush around us, and the waiter flew toward us.

"Yes, sir?"

"Wha'd I tell ju meng, when I coaming een?" Roberto was flushed, twisted in his seat like a hooded cobra ready to strike. Was he a psycho?

"But sir, I, I . . ."

"Just get another round for everyone, John," I said, cutting Roberto off and deciding I was going to thoroughly enjoy locking his ass up. "And get me a diet soda."

"Yes, sir." He spun and vanished in the crowd.

"That guy's usually very good," I said, "right on top of you."

"Well, sometimes you've got to stay right on people's asses," said Roberto, switching back to Spanish. He was pissed at me for cutting him off.

*Fuck him!* I didn't care if he lived or died. Let him go back to Miami if he wanted to—this mess would be over that much sooner.

"Come on! Time to go to the john," Roberto said to Carlos. "We're gonna go have a little toot. You want to try some of ours?" He was holding a Baggie about half-full of glistening white powder below the table. A psycho *and* a cokehead.

"No, nothing for me."

After Roberto and Carlos disappeared toward the men's room, Ana leaned across Sonia. "Miguel, he's a little crazy, I know. But in Miami he's very big. He's always been 100 percent with me."

"Ana, after what happened with us, you could bring me a gorilla. If you tell me he's your friend, I'll treat him like he's my brother."

Ana looked at me like she was going to cry. "*Aiii,* Miguel," she said, and reached across Sonia to take my hand.

I felt like a heel.

More than an hour of small talk and heavy drinking by Roberto and Carlos—including another half-dozen trips to the john—passed, and there was still no mention of business. Roberto's dark, angry little eyes darted all over the place, picking up movement at another table, studying our bodyguards, shifting suddenly to study Lydia and then me. I was afraid he was hitting the coke too heavy; he was taking on the cornered rat look of all heavy users.

Sonia was very touchy-feely with Roberto—gently touching his forearm when he said something amusing, giving him fleeting seductive looks, "unconsciously" brushing against him. But Roberto was not responding. He was still wary of me.

During a lull in the conversation, Roberto leaned toward me. "I've been in the business a long time. How come I never heard of you before?" Carlos was listening intently.

I turned slightly so that I was facing Roberto, my back to Carlos. "I should ask you the same question. But Ana brought you here; I trust her. But if you don't . . . no problems, no hard feelings, we just say goodbye."

Roberto's face was close to mine. His ragged teeth slowly came uncovered. And then something odd happened to me.

I looked into Roberto's eyes; they were the same lifeless, tombstone eyes of Mario, the Argentine cop. I could see my own death in them. I turned back toward Carlos. He was hunched forward, watching me with the same stone killer eyes.

From that moment on, my heart was back in the job. This was personal. These men meant more than just drugs to me; they had to do with serial killers, the mass destruction of the Jews, the killing fields of Cambodia, Argentina's "dirty war"—things that could never have happened were it not for men like these. Stopping them had nothing to do with the bullshit war on drugs; it was God's work. I wanted them in cages as badly as I'd ever wanted anything in my life. And I felt almost giddy with the knowledge that I had the power to do it.

"I don't mean to offend you," said Roberto, "but you can't blame me for being cautious, can you?"

I angled myself between them again and noticed that Carlos's right hand was behind him, out of sight, and his eyes were on my bodyguards. Rudy was watching us; South and the other two were deeply engrossed in conversation. Had anyone checked these men for guns? Something else I had gotten careless about.

"That doesn't make sense," I said. "I'm the one in the vulnerable position. I'm trying to sell merchandise, not buy it."

"True," said Roberto, "but DEA does that; they pretend to sell merchandise and then bust you and take your money."

I forced a laugh. "I don't believe it!"

"It's true," Roberto said, his smile vanishing. "I know two guys who went down that way." He looked past me to Carlos. "What was his name . . . Loco? The guy in Miami?" Carlos nodded, his attention on the bodyguard table. "And the Italian in New York a couple of years ago, Charlie something . . . DiPalermo, Charlie DiPalermo."

Charlie DiPalermo, a Mafia *capo*, was the first reverse undercover case ever done. It had been masterminded by Billy MacMullen, my group supervisor in the New York DEA office in 1974. DiPalermo was part of the old French Connection mob. Two Sureté agents from Paris posed as heroin smugglers and conned DiPalermo into showing up at Point Lookout, Long Island with a $150,000 down payment for 10 kilos, where we arrested him and relieved him of his money. The case was ancient and had received very little publicity. How did Roberto know about it?

"In this country I can't believe they let the police do something like that," I said. "It doesn't sound legal."

"It's true," said Roberto. "Man, I'm not lying to you."

"I believe you. I just never heard of it. Look brother, I have nothing to hide. I was born in Argentina and grew up in the South Bronx. What else you want to know?"

"Ah," Roberto nodded, "so that's how you got that little Puerto Rican accent."

"Yeah, I suppose so."

"I was trying to pick up on your sister's accent, but she doesn't say much, does she? So, how come I never heard of you?"

I shrugged and tried to sound nonchalant. "I had trouble in New York about seven, eight years ago. Everybody I knew was getting busted by the feds—for conspiracy or something like that—so I went to Argentina to chill out. I came back a few months ago and my sister introduces me to Sonia. When I found out who she was—no way I was going to let the opportunity get by me—I became her partner."

"Who did you do business with?" asked Roberto. His arm slid back and rested lightly against Sonia's. She didn't move.

"Well, a lot of years ago I used to do some *teca* business with a big black Cuban in New York. He had one eye . . ."

"Bennie One Eye!" Roberto was surprised. "You did business with Bennie One Eye?"

"Yeah," I said casually. "Then he got busted and I started working with a guy who said he was his cousin, El Indio; and later another guy who was with Spanish Raymond's people, named Chino."

I had actually arrested Bennie One Eye in the early 1970s. Later I heard rumors that he had died, but even if he were alive he had sold so much dope to so many people that he'd never be able to place me. Spanish Raymond was another guy I had worked on but was never able to arrest—he never knew I was an agent. And there had to be hundreds of Chinos and El Indios in the New York-to-Miami drug world.

"I know those people," said Roberto, eyeing me coolly. He wasn't fully convinced, but he was a little more relaxed. Time for me to turn the tables.

"Now what about you?" I said, focusing on his eyes. He blinked for the first time. "I'm getting ready to show you merchandise, I answer all your questions, and I don't really know who you are, do I?"

The jagged teeth jutted out and the lusterless eyes flicked toward Carlos. "He doesn't know who I am, Carlito." He laughed, a cross between a cough and a wheeze; his head and neck craned around as though trying to detach themselves from his shoulders—he was doing the cokehead herky-jerky. It was about time for another trip to the john. "Tell the man who I am, Carlito."

Carlos, who'd been leaning close to me, his hand still out of sight, moved uncomfortably. Before he could speak, Roberto dropped his head close to mine and said, "You heard of the French Connection, right?" His breath was a warm rolling wave of toxic gas. "I was one of the youngest guys working with them. I used to work with Carlos Rojas. In fact, I did business with the old man."

"Old man?"

"Yeah, Carlo Gambino."

I nodded noncommittally, but I was excited. So that was how he knew Charlie DiPalermo and Benny One Eye—both had ties to the infamous French Connection syndicate of Italian and French drug dealers. DiPalermo was listed in DEA's intelligence files as part of the Gambino crime family. This wasn't information Roberto could have guessed. The man with breath from hell was beginning to sound like he could be as big a fish as Ana said. While I had him on a roll, I decided to check out something else.

"Did you ever do business with the German in Miami?"

"The German?" He looked more suspicious than puzzled.

I glanced over at Ana, who was still deep in conversation with Lydia and Sonia. I didn't want my continued inquiries about this man to arouse her suspicion. "You know Papo Mejia, right?"

Roberto tensed. "I heard about him," he said.

"You know about our problem with him?"

"Ana mentioned something."

"Well, according to what I hear, his biggest customer is a German who lives in Miami. He's supposed to be connected with judges, district attorneys, politicians—you know what I'm saying?"

Roberto displayed his shark's grin. He understood my interest now. Mejia was squeezing me, so I wanted to steal Mejia's customers.

"I know who you mean," he said. "The guy's no German—he's a Jew. I think he was born in Germany, or something, but he's definitely a Jew. He owns a lot of shopping centers, real estate, that kind of thing."

My mind was racing. Maybe I could use Roberto as a springboard for an introduction to the German. After the inexplicable release of Jose Gasser and Cutuchi Gutierrez, the justice system in Miami had become a frightening enigma to me—an enigma that could be solved through the German. "You know him?" I asked.

"I don't know the man personally. I just heard about him."

"Too bad . . . I'd like to meet him."

Roberto nodded knowingly. "So would a lot of people." He glanced over at Carlos. "Carlito, it's time for a trip to the men's room."

Carlos nodded and slipped something into his back pocket. Whatever Carlos was carrying was well concealed beneath his shirt. I glanced over at the bodyguards—Rudy was watching the two men, South was watching me.

"Please pardon us, ladies," said Roberto with a broad wink at Sonia. She smiled at him, her eyes a sparkling invitation. Roberto moved behind me and then leaned his face next to mine. "You sure you don't want a taste?" His breath smothered me. "It's prime material. I hope yours is as good." He laughed, his eyes still on Sonia. Then he rotated his head like a fighter and moved off through the crowded restaurant following Carlos, who cleared the way like a one-man Secret Service. Roberto had just won himself a date with the Evil Eye.

I didn't actually need a televised performance to bust him for conspiracy—I already had enough. If I wanted to, I could even take him down for the coke he'd been offering me. But I wanted to make sure he was really nailed and facing heavy time so that we had plenty of leverage to flip him, and nothing would do that more effectively than grabbing him with a couple of million bucks in drug money. Monica, Ana, and Pineda could all identify the German and had all said and done more than enough to be convicted for several federal felonies; once we finished with Roberto we would have in our hand four of a kind. If we could convince any one of them to identify the German, we had his ass, too. It would be interesting to see the names the German had in his little black book and hear the tales he had to tell about judges, district attorneys, and politicians, some of whom I suspected already.

"Don Miguel," said Ana, leaning across the table. "What do you think?"

"He's a great guy. I like him a lot. I hope we can do business."

"A toast," said Sonia, picking up her glass, her eyes sparkling. She was enjoying herself immensely.

"Yes," said Ana, raising her glass. "To friends and how wonderful it is to be among them."

## 3

When Roberto and Carlos returned from the john we got down to business. I told him I had 50 kilos of top-quality cocaine available for immediate delivery at $43,000 a kilo, and that the deal—once he had tested the merchandise and was satisfied with its quality—had to be done quickly, *dando y dando* (cash and carry). Sonia, now tuned into our conversation, sat close to Roberto.

"No problem," said Roberto, conscious of Sonia and so charged with cocaine that his head and neck twitched. "But why Tucson? My people don't like to let their money go that far." He paused suddenly to leer at Sonia. "Miguel," he said. "I want to congratulate you on your woman."

"Don't embarrass me," said Sonia, her hand resting for a long moment on his bare arm. He reacted like a landed fish—flopping around, his mouth moving and his eyes bulging. Sonia smiled radiantly and met his gaze without batting an eyelash; a remarkable feat, considering the man's breath.

"I chose Tucson," I said, "because nothing happens here. It's beautiful—DEA, the FBI, they don't even know it exists. Here I have family connections and everything with the police is controlled. On the other hand, Miami is hot in every sense of the word. There are armies of police investigating our business."

"Let me tell you something," said Roberto, struggling to focus his attention on me. Sonia's arm, resting lightly against his, looked as if it was burning a hole through him. "With my people you'll be safer in Miami than here or anywhere else. We own the police."

"That may be, my friend," I said. "But, right now it's more risk than I am prepared to take—especially with our problem with Mejia."

Roberto gulped down a full glass of champagne and poured himself another. "Fock heem!" he said. "He's a fockeeng snake. Fock heem and hees mother." Carlos laughed a nasty laugh behind me. Roberto glanced from Sonia to me and switched back to Spanish. "Why don't you just kill him? You think because you pay him he's finished with you?"

"You know him personally?" I asked.

"Well enough. There's only one way to handle a son of a whore like him—right Carlito?"

"*Si, jefe,*" said the angular Mexican, raising his glass. "*Como todos los serpientes; hay que cortarle la cabeza.*" The two men laughed and swigged down more champagne.

"Isn't that right, *mamita*?" said Roberto, turning to Sonia.

"Sure," said Sonia, bestowing a wicked smile on both of us. Roberto filled Sonia's glass and emptied the rest of the bottle into his. I motioned for the waiter for refills; he nodded and disappeared. Carlos swigged down what was left of some brandy. I motioned to another waiter hovering nearby to refill all the glasses on the table and he darted off behind the first.

"You know what they pulled on Sonia?" I said.

"I heard something about it," said Roberto.

"Well, then you know what an injustice the whole thing is; that Arce-Gomez is the one that should be paying Mejia—not us."

"Lucho? You know I met him."

"You met him?" said Sonia, suddenly interested.

"Sure, in Miami. He used to do business with Loco. I saw him over there, but I didn't have anything to do with him. He doesn't impress me. *Soñita,* you say the word," he said, covering her hand with his, "I'll take care of Papo."

She left her hand in his.

I felt a big hand on my forearm.

"You think he's kidding?" said Carlos. I turned to face him. "I have been with that man for many years," he said, slurring his words. "That is a man, like no other man I have ever known. If he's your friend . . . all your enemies are his. And they won't be enemies for long." His eyes bore into mine and seemed to almost glow in the half-light.

"Don Miguel," he said, suddenly lowering his voice, leaning close to me, still gripping my forearm. "I have a feeling you're a man who knows what it is to kill. Well, I've killed many for that man . . . 12 men. And he has killed for me."

I turned my head and stared off into a distant corner of the restaurant. I didn't want to hear what I knew would follow. I'd heard enough stories of people like Carlos and Roberto to last 10 lifetimes, and I didn't want my feelings to affect my act. Later I would bring him to the house and he would repeat everything for the microphones anyway.

Carlos's voice broke through. ". . . the guy was laughing at me. Roberto comes up behind him smiling, and the guy keeps laughing. He was stoned out of his fucking mind. I didn't even see the gun come out. Boom! His brains go flying over everybody and Roberto is laughing. The guy's still alive, he's down on the floor jerking all over the place, and Roberto is kicking him and slipping and sliding on his brains. 'Now you think my friend is funny?' he says, and we both look at each other and start laughing."

I tried to tune him out as he rambled on about death, bloody death, gory death, death by gun and death by knife—his favorite tool—but his droning voice kept filtering in.

"I like to look them in the eyes. I want to see their eyes."

I glanced behind me. Roberto was huddled close with Sonia; across from me Ana spoke with Lydia, but her eyes were on me; Rudy watched silently from the bodyguard's table while South and the two undercovers stared in morose silence at their drinks.

"At the moment of death—I mean the exact moment—you can see the eyes change, like the eyes of a fish."

Why was this man telling me these things? Carlos's voice faded and seemed to blend with the background noise.

". . . you know I used to be a contract hit man before I met Roberto . . . 15 years ago . . . nothing we wouldn't do for each other . . ."

This wasn't like me. I should have been mentally recording his words like the professional undercover I was, ready to recite them verbatim to a stern-faced judge and a gawking jury. But you need space to store that, and I was out of space.

Waiters appeared with champagne, cognac, and wine and began filling glasses. I picked up someone's drink and gulped it down—it might have been cognac. I smiled at Carlos and tried not to listen. I wanted to scream, but somehow I just kept smiling and nodding.

\* \* \*

It was almost 1 A.M. when our caravan wheeled up to the Smugglers Hotel, where Rudy had reserved rooms for Roberto and Carlos. We arranged to meet in the morning to go to the airport so Roberto could sample our merchandise. Afterward they would be honored with a trip to the undercover house and a televised appearance that would seal their futures behind bars. I couldn't conceive of Turghid turning the plan down.

Before leaving us Roberto opened Sonia's door, performed a court- ly bow, and kissed her hand. "Don Miguel," he wheezed, "once again I congratulate you on your woman." He held her hand tightly in both of his; I saw my death in his eyes. Sonia was grinning alongside of him; I saw it in her eyes as well.

At about two in the morning I was sprawled on the couch. I had decid- ed to stay in the living room until I was sure Ana was asleep. I didn't want to chance her wandering out and seeing herself on television again. I was toying with the idea of somehow putting the thing tem- porarily out of commission when Ana suddenly appeared.

"Ah, good, you are awake," she said. She padded barefoot across the living room and sat beside me. "Miguel," she said softly, taking my hand in hers, "how is your daughter?"

"I'm worried about her," I said. "How's Candy?"

"*Aiii!*" she exclaimed, her hand to her forehead. "May God help me. Between my husband's drinking and her drugs . . ." She shook her head woefully. "May God help us both, Miguel." She paused, and then said, "I didn't have a chance to speak with you before. A lot of people were disappointed. I looked very bad."

"A lot of people?"

"I told a lot of people about you—the biggest. They all wanted to meet you. It could have been very good for you and Sonia."

"Ana," I said, suddenly feeling too tired to keep the act up. "I can't tell you how sorry I am. Maybe when we finish this business you and I will go there together." I remembered the morphine tablets. "By the way, did you bring me those samples?"

"I couldn't take the chance. I've never seen the situation so tight. For the first time in my life when I passed through the customs in Miami they grabbed me. They not only searched my luggage, they brought me into a room and made me take my clothes off."

I couldn't believe what I was hearing. Searched for the first time

306

in her life? Someone had to have put her name on SOUNDEX—a Customs list of suspected drug smugglers. Someone wanted her caught with the morphine tablets and eliminated from Operation Hun. Ana's arrest would kill any chances of an undercover probe into Pacho Cuervas and whoever else she had waiting in Colombia to meet me. And only the suits and the CIA knew she might be returning to the United States with drugs on her.

The phone rang. I picked it up.

"Miguel, I'm sorry to call so late," said Ana's daughter Candy, "but I have to speak to my mother."

"Don't worry about it," I said, noting an urgency in her voice, a tone of self-made crisis that was disturbingly familiar. I passed the phone to Ana.

"What is it now?" said Ana into the phone. She listened for a few moments and then said, "But you promised. You swore to me that you wouldn't see those people." There were tears in Ana's eyes.

I got to my feet and went to my room; I didn't want to hear anymore. I thought that I should be with my daughter, not here. The 17 years that I'd spent believing that what I was doing helped kids like my daughter suddenly weighed me down. They had all been lies. As I closed the door to my room, Ana's voice echoed through the quiet house.

"Why are you doing this to me?"

# 4

Early the next morning I went to brief Turghid. Being Saturday, the office, except for Turghid and Rourke, was empty. The big man was reclining all the way back on his chair, feet up on his desk. He fixed me with his hardest John Wayne stare as I placed a box of cassettes and a stack of handwritten transcriptions on his desk. He couldn't hide his surprise.

"I didn't want to keep these in the house while the drug dealers are there," I said. Rourke coughed.

"Why don't you just bring us up to date," Turghid said gruffly.

"Okay." I decided to stay on my feet. "The main guy's name is Roberto. I don't know his last name, but it ought to be easy to check out. He's bragging about being hooked up with the old French Connection crew. Claims he was the youngest."

Rourke pulled out a pad and began taking notes. It took me almost half an hour to run down the highlights of the evening. As I spoke, Turghid watched me and impatiently drummed his fingers on his knees. When I finished he took his feet off the desk and leaned forward, but said nothing.

Rourke whistled. "I think I know who this guy is already. He sounds like Roberto Torrez [name changed]."

"Well, whoever he is," I said, "his bodyguard's bragging about how many people the two have sent to a better place. We lock them up we'll end up solving a half-dozen homicides. He also knows who the German is, and he met Arce-Gomez at another drug dealer's house— he's like a walking who's-who of the drug world."

"Damn!" said Rourke, looking at Turghid, who just glared at me.

"I think it's worth the risk," I said, "bringing these guys back to the UC house with samples and letting 'em perform for the camera."

"What about Mejia's guys?" said Rourke.

"We stall 'em until we finish doing Roberto."

"I don't give a damn who he is," snapped Turghid suddenly, his voice low and mean. "I already told you, I don't want you gettin' off the target."

I suddenly felt an overwhelming weariness. Arguing with bureaucrats is like arguing with an automatic toll machine—it does what it's been programmed to do, and no amount of talking, teeth-gnashing, or hair-pulling will change a thing.

"Does that mean you don't want me to go any further with Tamayo and these guys?" I asked matter-of-factly. I wanted him to know that I didn't give a damn one way or the other; that I would do as ordered, but that the responsibility for what happened was all his. But trying to get a suit to accept responsibility was like trying to trap liquid mercury with your thumb.

"Did I say that? All I told you was that headquarters and me don't want you gettin' offa the target."

"Look," I said, "the guy's on target. He places Arce-Gomez in a doper's house." I looked at Rourke for support; he looked out the window.

Fighting a losing battle with my temper, I continued. "You wanted me to transcribe fucking tapes—I did it. I'm undercover, I'm a grade-14, but I did it anyway. If you want me to keep doing tapes today, I'll do it. You give me yellow, second-rate coke to use, I use it. Just tell me what you want me to do and I'll do it."

Turghid's face had turned blood red. He seemed to swell. He

hunched his shoulders as if he were getting ready to launch himself at me. "Now I'm gonna repeat myself one mo' time," he said, his voice just above a whisper. "Headquarters says they want you ta concentrate on provin' the case against Arce-Gomez . . . that's it!"

"Does that mean," I said as quietly as I could, "that I am to quit working on Roberto Torrez and Ana Tamayo?"

"I'll make it real clear for you, Levine. It means go 'head with your game plan, but don't leave Tucson for nothin'; you don't go outta your way for nothin' or nobody 'less it's targetin' Arce-Gomez. Got it straight now?"

I had it anything but straight.

"Yes," I said getting to my feet. "I read you loud and clear." I started to leave.

Turghid's squinty little eyes opened as wide as they could. "Where you goin'?"

"I'm taking them to the airplane to get samples, then back to the house so they can test the stuff, and maybe talk about some of their murders on camera."

Turghid nodded. "Just don't forget what I said."

"I won't," I said. "Believe me, I won't."

I raced back to the undercover house. Rudy was waiting for me, as usual, in the kitchen, his easygoing but unreadable smile in place.

"You okay, boss?"

"Never better," I said. "Why, I look bad?"

"You look a little beat." His smile vanished. I had the feeling he wanted to tell me something. I liked Rudy. I had watched him closely on the different undercover sets; he was cool and reliable, a thorough professional. What a relief it would have been to have one ally, one person I could trust in this madness.

"Just getting a little old for this," I said. "Anything new?"

"Roberto called the house a couple of times. They're ready to be picked up anytime."

"Okay. Where's everybody?"

"They're all out by the pool."

"Be ready in a minute," I said, heading across the house toward the pool.

As I stepped out into the hot sun I noticed South locking the pool house door. Sonia, Lydia, and Ana were stretched out on lounge chairs. They shielded their eyes to look up at me.

"Ana, I'm taking Roberto to sample the merchandise. You want to come?"

"*Aii, no querido,*" she said. "But I'm going back to Miami, so in case it doesn't work out with Roberto bring me some samples for some of my other customers."

"Sure," I said. "How much do you think you'll need?"

"Give me a little in three separate bags, only please, don't say anything to Roberto."

As I started back toward the house, Sonia got to her feet. "Can I talk to you a moment?"

We stepped inside the house, just inches short of being on camera. She stood close to me.

"Roberto's called three times today," she said, her eyes searching mine. "You know he's after me, don't you?"

"I noticed," I said. "You want me to say something?"

"No," she smiled wryly. "I have no problem handling him, but it's what he thinks of you that I'm concerned about."

"What do you mean?"

"He's made remarks."

"What kind of remarks?"

"He was hinting that maybe you weren't so much of a man."

"Did you tell him that you and I were just business partners?"

"Of course, but he asked me if there's something strange about you."

"Strange? You mean like I'm gay or something like that?"

"I don't know . . . maybe," she said, her eyes challenging me.

"I don't care what he thinks, as long as he doesn't get too far out of line . . . and at the end of this thing he ends up in a cage."

"You don't have to get angry. I thought you should know."

"I'm not angry at you," I said, quickly putting my hand on her shoulder. I couldn't risk any more friction between us. "You did the right thing in telling me, and I appreciate it." She glared at me. "Are you sure you can handle him?"

The wicked smile flashed. "Very sure."

As we drove up to the Smugglers Hotel, Roberto and Carlos were standing in the middle of the parking lot under the blazing noon sun, shading their eyes and peering nervously around them. Carlos was dressed in gleaming white from head to foot, while Roberto was resplendent in a salmon-colored guayabera with matching slacks and shoes. The gold on his hands and neck glittered brightly in the sunlight. If there was a fashion magazine for drug dealers, they could have been models for the cover story—"Proper Attire for a Desert Drug Deal."

They got into the rear seat without saying a word. Rudy wheeled sharply out into traffic, and Carlos twisted in his seat to peer out the back window. We drove several minutes in silence when I was suddenly overwhelmed with the fear that the Nagra recording device hidden in a compartment just behind the driver's seat might be discovered. It was only inches from Roberto's face. They probably had guns. I had to keep them occupied. I turned in my seat. "So, how did you gentlemen sleep?"

"I always sleep good," said Roberto, his eyes scouring the car's interior. Carlos was still looking out the rear window.

"What do you think of Tucson so far?"

"Not much," said Roberto. He pulled his plastic bag of cocaine and a little gold spoon from the pocket of his guayabera. Holding the bag just below window level, he spooned up a hefty mound of powder. He raised the spoon slightly and angled his head downward. Whoosh! A comet's tail of white flashed upward, disappearing into his nostril. The man was a human Dustbuster.

He exhaled sharply, closing his eyes; when he opened them, they glistened wetly. He took a deep breath and let it out slowly; I winced at the rancid smell. Beside me Rudy shook his head slightly. For a moment Roberto stared blankly; his body twitched and I thought he might go into convulsions—I'd seen it happen before—but he quickly recovered.

"You want?" he said, offering me the bag.

"Please put that away," I said. Carlos suddenly twisted back to face me. "This isn't Miami. I'm taking you to see 50 fucking kilos. One gringo traffic cop stops us—I lose everything."

Roberto stared at me, the bag still extended in his hand. Carlos was poised beside him like an attack dog. I was half-turned on the seat, my 9mm inches from my hand in my ankle holster. If either had a gun I'd see some movement toward where it was concealed, but I'd wait until I saw the gun before I opened fire. My gun carried 13 bullets. Thirteen quick taps on a hair trigger and the world would be just a little bit healthier, I told myself.

"No problem," said Roberto, slipping the bag back into his pocket. "No problem at all." He smiled that piranha smile while he studied me.

We rode on in silence, a salsa tape by El Gran Combo de Puerto Rico playing softly on the stereo. I relaxed. At least part of the pretext was over—I didn't like them and they didn't like me. We were together for business, and that was all.

Both Daves were watching us from the doorway of the Queenair as we approached. As Rudy parked near the wing, I saw Kunz duck out of sight to turn on the recording equipment. I let Carlos and Roberto precede me up the ladder so that they wouldn't have the chance to see the gun on my ankle. When we had squeezed on board, Gorman folded over two seats and lay one of the Samsonite suitcases across them.

Moment of truth, I thought as I opened the suitcase.

The cocaine—Turghid's new plastic bags notwithstanding—had taken on an even more yellowish hue. I held my breath as Roberto reached into the suitcase and withdrew one of the bags. He hefted it in one hand and raised it to the sunlight.

"The stuff looks funny," he said. "It looks yellow."

"I think it was something in the process," I said. "This batch might have been dried by the wrong kind of artificial light."

This strange explanation just came to me; I knew enough about how cocaine was made to know that it was plausible.

Plausible but not convincing. "Yeah," said Roberto, eyeing the yellowish powder suspiciously. "Maybe."

"It's top quality," I said. "Come on, we'll take some samples back to the house and and you can test it yourself . . . you'll see."

"Yeah," said Roberto, still studying the powder, "we'll see."

Roberto randomly selected four kilo packages. He took a small sample from each, depositing the powder in separate plastic bags. He passed the bags to Carlos, who tied them off and shoved them into the pocket of his guayabera.

Possession, I thought, and possession with intent to distribute; you gentlemen each just violated 30 years' worth of federal statutes. I suddenly felt real good.

"Is it okay if I take a little for my head?" asked Roberto. "I'm running out of my own."

"Go ahead." I watched him scoop about a half ounce of yellow U.S. government cocaine into another plastic bag, twist the top, and shove it into his pocket. He patted it and grinned at me.

I instructed Kunz to put about a gram of cocaine in each of four bags in a voice that I hoped was loud and clear enough to be picked up by the recording devices. In a little while I would be handing the four bags to Ana on camera, closing the chain of custody from the plane to her hands. I wanted to make sure that there was no doubt that I had zero opportunities to take any of the drugs myself. If there was the slightest doubt, the inspectors would skewer me with it.

"These are samples for other customers," I said to Roberto as I stuffed the little bags into my small leather handbag. "If you don't act fast I can't guarantee I won't sell out."

"Let's check the stuff out," said Roberto, "then we'll talk."

On the way back to the UC house, Carlos thought he saw a car following us. "Is that your people?" he said. I turned in time to see a dark gray car veer off into a shopping center.

"No," I said, "none of my people are with us. What did you see?"

"Two gringos. They made three turns with us," he said, still watching the traffic.

"You want me to go back and check 'em out?" asked Rudy, trying to show the appropriate concern.

Mistake! A drug dealer wouldn't do that. "No, we've got merchandise in the car," I said.

At about 1:45 we arrived at the house to find the women waiting for us. An assortment of sandwiches and booze had been laid out in the living room along with the electric thermometer and other drug-testing gear, right in front of the Evil Eye. South's car was out front and he was not in the house, so I assumed he was inside the pool house making sure the recording equipment didn't miss a moment of what was about to happen.

By 5:30 the drugs had been tested and Roberto and Carlos were in great spirits. The two had finished off all the cocaine they had come with and were now into the government's supply. Their performance before the camera could not have been more spectacular. Roberto was alternately leering and mooning at Sonia. He bragged about his prowess as both drug dealer and killer. Carlos was right there to verify and embellish most of his stories. Ana had even witnessed some of the drug deals.

They spoke of deals from Colombia to New York; of dealing with the most notorious drug barons of South America and the United States; of murders that they knew of, witnessed, or had carried out both individually and as a team. With a little coaxing I even got

Roberto to repeat what he had told me about the German and Arce-Gomez. It would be a fantastic tape for a jury—a confession complete with witnesses and accomplices all wrapped up in one session.

Sonia rewarded Roberto lavishly with long passionate looks, brushing by him closely now and then, and here and there a quick little touch. She was playing Roberto like a phonograph record, getting him to talk his life away, and all the while flashing wicked little smiles at me to let me know how easy it was. She had complete control and he didn't know it. Then in a moment she was beside me, coquettishly smiling up at me. Her hand brushed my cheek. Roberto's smile vanished.

Sonia had just created a love triangle that didn't exist; a love triangle that could cost me my life.

It's no coincidence that bullfighting is dear to the hearts of Latino men and that the bullfighter is among the most revered of national heros in Latin America. The event and the man exemplify the ultimate expression of machismo: the fight to the death. Machismo, the exaggerated sense of masculinity and its attributes—courage, virility, aggressiveness, and the domination of women—extant in many men but somehow a little closer to the surface in Latinos, was something Sonia knew well how to manipulate for her own ends.

How many had died without ever knowing they'd been had?

Roberto, sitting with Sonia at his side, bragged of having an arsenal at his home in Miami. Carlos verified it. "He's got a bunch of Uzis fitted with silencers," said the Mexican hitman, holding an imaginary submachine gun in his big hands. "They're beautiful. All you hear is *Brrrrr*, and everything in front of you goes *poof*."

Roberto said, "If you decide you want to handle Mejia the other way, I can let you have a couple. Just send some of your people to Miami to pick them up."

"That's something I might take you up on," I said, thinking of the 25-year penalty for possession of a machine gun. I immediately realized I'd made a mistake. If word that I was even thinking that way reached Mejia, the results could be disastrous.

"Or, if you like," he turned to Sonia, "I'll take care of that son of a whore myself." Sonia rewarded him with steamy smile. "It will be a present to you; to a magnificent hostess and a beautiful woman."

"I appreciate the offer, don Roberto," I said, "but I'd rather settle the debt and continue doing business peacefully."

"Yeah," muttered Sonia in a voice just loud enough for me to hear, "business, business, business . . . he lives and breathes it. Nothing else interests him."

Roberto shrugged and whispered something to Sonia. They both laughed.

The cocaine testing did not go over anywhere near as well as the socializing. Roberto was a thorough professional. "Are you sure this stuff wasn't stored for a long time, maybe in a damp place?" he asked, examining some of the yellowish powder under a lamp.

"No way," I said with a lump in my throat. "This stuff is right off the plane from Bolivia."

Roberto seated himself on the couch facing the camera and began by dropping a pinch of the yellowish powder into a glass of Clorox. About a third of the powder settled to the bottom, which meant the coke had been cut by as much as 35 percent.

"What do you think?" I said.

"Let's see."

He put some powder from a separate sample on a glass slide and then lay the slide on the hot plate of the electric thermometer. But as the instrument began heating up, the digital gauge began fluctuating wildly. I had the feeling someone had tampered with it. The broken thermometer made us look phony as hell.

Roberto didn't even flinch. "Looks like this isn't working." Grinning at Sonia, he put a pinch of powder on a strip of aluminum foil and heated it with a cigarette lighter. The room was quiet as we watched the powder melt and burn. It was a replay of Monica's test—the powder burned black and crisp instead of clean and oily. The cocaine had been heavily diluted. All hopes that Monica's test had been a fluke, that a couple of bags had gotten damp from storage, went up in smoke. Sonia was watching me with a curious expression on her face, as if she had known beforehand how the test would turn out and wanted to see my reaction.

"I don't think this stuff is any more than the mid-seventies," said Roberto, plainly unimpressed. From the way he was looking at Sonia, I guessed that his estimate was charitable.

"Hey, you're getting high on it right now," I reminded him. "How bad can it be?"

"I'm not saying the stuff is that bad," he said. "But you know how people are—they like to see the stuff nice and white with lots of little rocks. I'm not a street dealer. Yellow powder won't be easy to sell."

*   *   *

Later, Rudy drove Roberto and Carlos back to their hotel to shower and change. We would be picking them up for dinner and a night on the town. After they left I sat Ana in front of the television set and gave her the four little bags of cocaine I'd brought from the airplane.

"I'm going back to Miami," she said storing the bags at the bottom of a large handbag. "I have more customers for you, darling."

"What about Roberto? He said he'd probably take it all."

"He's good," said Ana. "I've done seven deals with him—big ones. But just in case," she added with a doubtful shrug and a sigh, "I'll contact a few more buyers."

Ana was a businesswoman; she had no time to waste. She already knew what I was beginning to suspect. Roberto wasn't going to buy our stuff. If he'd been doubtful about bringing money to Tucson when he thought we had top-quality cocaine, he certainly wouldn't risk it for inferior drugs. But cocaine was still cocaine and this was the United States. If the stuff was good enough for Roberto and Carlos to get high on, Ana would find someone to buy it. Ana was ready to dismiss Roberto as a serious customer, but I wasn't—I was afraid to let him leave Tucson a free man.

Ordinarily, I shouldn't have been so concerned. In front of hidden cameras he and Carlos had admitted to a couple of hundred years' worth of felonies—maybe even a death sentence. But I felt uneasy. Maybe it was the way Sonia looked at me while Roberto tested the drugs; maybe it was the arsenal of weapons that stunk of CIA involvement; maybe it was the whole way Operation Hun had been run from the beginning—whatever the cause, a little voice deep inside me was warning that if Roberto was allowed to leave Tucson a free man, I would never see him again.

# 26

# When the
# Whistle Blows

1

On Saturday night, Sonia really put her hooks into Roberto, making sure he'd have a jones for her for the rest of his life. I was no longer sure why she was doing it.

After a long dinner, the whole cast sped across town to a local night-club featuring dim lights and live entertainment. Roberto asked Sonia to dance. I watched them turn slowly to the music. Roberto held her tightly, his eyes closed. Sonia's eyes found mine. She smiled and raised her hand to the back of his neck as if to say, "I'm driving this bus."

Across the table from me, Ana had finally given up trying to make conversation with Lydia; both sat staring morosely at the dance floor. Carlos wasn't talking either. His face seemed to be sagging and drooping. It was time for another trip to the john. As Carlos stood and staggered off into the darkness, I thought again of what would happen if some undercover cop busted him there. But I didn't wonder about it long. Keeping up my act had sapped me of all energy. I just wanted to lay my head down on the table.

"Miguel." Ana leaned across the table toward me. "Your sister Lydia, is she all right?"

"What do you mean?"

"She's so . . . so troubled. She never talks."

I glanced over at Lydia, and then leaned closer to Ana. "There are some things my family never talks about . . ." Ana looked shocked. "Lydia has had, well, a horrible experience."

*"Aiii, Dios!"* said Ana, covering her mouth. *"Pobrecita."*

"Yes," I said, shaking my head sadly. Ana was now looking at Lydia like she wanted to adopt her. I put my finger to my lips, signifying silence, and Ana shook her head vigorously to show she wouldn't dream of saying a word.

Carlos came back, and for the rest of the evening, while Sonia and Roberto wrestled around the dance floor, he regaled me with stories of blood and gore. I slowly tuned Carlos out until his voice was just a dull, inaudible murmur. I tried to keep an eye on Roberto and Sonia. If she had trouble, I was responsible.

Suddenly I noticed Carlos dipping his hand out of sight. I heard a metallic click. Out of the corner of my eye I saw a serrated blade as long as a small bayonet gleaming dully in the darkness. The point was inches from my rib cage, and Carlos was snarling something in my ear.

"I drove this into his heart," he hissed, his coked up eyes glazing over with the memory. "It went in easy, like butter. You know what I'm saying?" He jabbed the blade closer to me.

"I go to pull it out—to stick him again quick, before he could cry out or do something—it stuck. So I jerk it." He jerked the blade back and forth. "His blood gushes out like, like one of those geysers— *psssssh.* I'm real close, like I am to you. At that moment he knew that no power on heaven and earth could save him . . . you could see it in his eyes.

"Then he goes 'Ahhhh' and he's dead, still looking me in the eyes— it all happened this close, like I am to you." Carlos paused. Then, breathing almost sensuously, he said, "That's why I love the knife. It's personal. You know what I'm saying? You can feel it; you're part of it. You know what I mean?"

"Yes," I said forcing myself to look squarely into his dead eyes. What he really meant was that no power on heaven and earth could save me if he chose to stick me in the heart. In two seconds I would look like I was passed out drunk; he and Roberto would fake going to the john and they were in the wind.

I glanced over at the bodyguard table, only 10 feet away, where Rudy and two Chicano undercovers in dark glasses were sitting perfectly still. I couldn't tell if they were awake or asleep. They wouldn't be able to help me anyway. It would be over too quickly.

"It's like dancing," I said, wondering where the words had come from.

Carlos laughed, and the tension broke. "Dancing . . . I like that. It's like dancing—a dance of death." He laughed again and the blade was gone. It was over that quickly.

"That's beautiful," he said, downing a glass of champagne. "Spoken like a man who's been there, Miguel."

Beautiful? I thought. No—beautiful would be the sound of those steel prison gates slamming shut on you for the rest of your life.

## 2

By Monday Sonia had Roberto in such heat that he'd have to have her or explode. He was moping around Tucson like a dog, baying at the northern foothills where his beloved was ensconced in a mythical Mafia castle surrounded by squadrons of undercover agents. He called the house every couple of hours, promising Sonia that he had dispatched Carlos to Miami for money to buy "a minimum of 40 kilos"—a little over $1.6 million—and a special love gift of an Uzi and a silencer for us to use on Papo, "if Miguel decides he's got the stomach for it."

When the phone rang Monday morning, Sonia answered it with "Yes, *querido.*" She rolled her eyes in exasperation. "It's good to hear your voice too, Roberto. I can't talk too loud. Yes, Miguel is in the other room." Same as the other calls.

I hooked the earphones and recorder to the phone and sat across the kitchen table to listen.

"I just wanted to hear your voice, *mamita,*" moaned Roberto. "Carlos is already on his way. He's driving, so it may take a day or two."

"Call me as soon as he arrives, *mi amor,*" said Sonia, shaking her head and making a face.

Carlos had allegedly flown back to Miami Sunday morning to pick up the money, and had now been "on his way back" for almost 20 hours.

"Sonia, I haven't seen you since Saturday. Can't you just slip out for a little while? Don't you want to see me?"

"Yes, of course, *cariño,* I want to see you, but you know how busy we are, and we have this problem with Papo."

"Just for a couple of hours, I promise," he whined.

"Oh, no, *mi amor,* Miguel wouldn't like it. You know how he is— always business first," she said, her eyes finding mine and then looking away.

"But my *Soñita,* a woman like you should be taken care of, you should fear no man. You should have a man beside you, not a *maricon.*"

Sonia laughed mirthlessly, and pointed a finger at me.

"Is he listening to you, that . . . that *mariposa,* that *hijo de puta,* can you talk? Just say the word, *nena,* and I'll take care of him, Papo, or anyone who bothers you. Can you meet me tonight? Please *mamita.* Pretty please."

When Sonia hung up she said, "This is just a waste of time. He's not interested in that merchandise, and you know it."

"But he might come through, just to prove to you what a macho man he is."

Sonia shook her head doubtfully. "And what about Papo? He's already suspicious. If there's another delay . . ."

"It's been a month since you told him 10 days; another day or two won't matter." Sonia looked worried. "Come on, Sonia," I said, "if anyone in the world can get this guy to deliver, it's you."

"You want him badly, don't you?"

"Yes . . . badly."

"Is it just him, or do you really hate drug dealers that much?" Her eyes challenged me.

"I've had more respect for some of the drug dealers I've known than some of my bosses," I replied. I was sure she would repeat my words to someone. Fuck it, I thought, let her. I wanted them to know. "But murderers—people who get a special little kick out of killing— are in an exclusive category for me. Yeah, I want him badly."

"You don't like me, do you?"

This caught me by surprise. The house was quiet, and it was just Sonia and me, face to face, with nothing but a kitchen table and a universe of lies between us.

"Sonia, there are moments I think, 'Wow, I really like you.' And then there are moments when I think I know absolutely nothing real about you—you're a complete mystery."

"*Y ahora?*" she asked.

*"Vamos a ver que pasa,"* I said.

Ana gave up hope for Roberto as a customer and left for Miami to find us more buyers. She never said a word about our merchandise, but it was clear she was not as enthusiastic as before. She had even stopped talking to me about our trip to meet Pacho Cuervas.

The irony of the situation was ever with me. I had been assigned to a reverse undercover sting with DEA's best informant and its worst dope. There were only two possible explanations: someone was trying to kill the case or someone had stolen some of the drugs and diluted the rest to cover the theft.

Half the suits in DEA had seen the videotapes of Monica and Roberto testing the cocaine. It was obvious the stuff was tampered with. The tapes should have been more than enough to start a dozen classic Internal Security investigations. I had also complained about the dope directly to Rourke, Turghid, and South. Not only had no investigation been started, but I was being forced to continue the undercover using the same suspicious cocaine. All the while, I was under investigation, which limited my options—I couldn't protest too strongly, I couldn't refuse to work with the drugs, and I felt I couldn't drop out of the assignment.

There was no way out for me but through.

## 3

On Monday evening, while Roberto languished in his hotel room living for phone sex with Sonia, Eduardo Pineda and Mario Espinosa were leaving a steady stream of urgent messages with our answering service.

"You've got to stall them to the end of the week," I told Sonia as I attached the tape recorder to the phone in the kitchen.

Sonia's brow wrinkled with concern. "I don't know. It's too much time."

"Roberto says Carlos is on the way with the money. After all his bragging, there's still a chance he'll come through."

Sonia shook her head, exasperated. "Fine," she snapped.

I dialed the Miami phone number and handed the phone to Sonia. In moments she was speaking to Espinosa. "We'll be ready for you in a few days, Mario," she said.

"Please, *Soñita*," said Espinosa, his voice anxious. "Don't delay any longer. They've made all the arrangements—people are coming from Miami and California."

Our delays had set Mejia off like a rocket. If we didn't pay this time, Espinosa wouldn't be going home.

"The problem is we have other business we're trying to do at the same time," said Sonia. "You know how it is. But the rugs are already here. I'll be going down to check them."

"Fantastic!" said Espinosa. "Eduardo and I are leaving immediately for California. When you're ready, call us there." He left a California phone number.

"Don't worry, Mario, everything will be settled by the end of the week. Papo is going to be there, right?"

"Yes . . . yes he is."

"Good, because I'm looking forward to seeing him . . . to make amends."

"I know *querida*. I always knew you'd come through. No matter what anyone said, I knew you wouldn't betray a trust."

On Tuesday morning Rourke called me. "Levine, they want you to wrap this whole thing up," he said. "Call Mejia's people and give 'em their dope. And when the whistle blows, everybody goes. Did ya get that?"

"Who goes?"

"Whoever shows up to pick the stuff up."

"And that's it? What if Mejia doesn't show up?"

"We'll indict him," said Rourke.

"He's a fucking Colombian, Jack. There's no extradition treaty. He just sits there and we never get him." Rourke was silent. "What about the famous target? With all the bullshit about Arce-Gomez being the target, we don't even have enough to indict him yet."

"Mike, I give you my word, I'm gonna get that guy indicted. We're working on Sonia's girlfriend in Bolivia—Nati . . . Natalia—you know her?"

"I know shit about Sonia."

"Well, the two of them were like inseparable. Nati corroborates a lot of the stuff with Arce—she was right there. We're tryin' to convince her to be a witness. And we got another possible informant right in the Bolivian government, someone who was right next to Lucho, who was right there when he got the jewels. But there's problems."

"What kind of problems?"

"With the Agency."

"What does the CIA have to do with it?" I persisted.

"Mike, you don't know the half of it. Just don't ask, okay?"

"Okay. What about Roberto and Carlos; the Pacho Cuervas organization; Monica and her New York-to-Miami people; the fucking German and all the politicians, judges, and DAs he owns in Miami, maybe even DEA . . ."

"Hey, ya hump, I'm not hiding anything from anybody. Everything that happens goes to headquarters. Everything goes to the appropriate field offices."

"Jack," I said, "doesn't it seem strange to you that they go through all this trouble—Sonia, me, the undercover house, the plane, the whole fucking bit—and then they give us bullshit, yellow, garbage coke that we're supposed to convince people we're for real with?"

"What do you want from me? I don't know how many times I told you this, Levine, I'm just a grade-fucking-13. I don't call the shots."

"But you know what they're doing; we're losing these guys left and right!"

Rourke was one of the sharpest narcotics agents I'd ever known. He knew more about the drug business than any of the political appointees and suits who were his superiors, but like all of DEA's most capable agents, he had to make an important choice early in his career. He could battle incompetent and sinister bosses, lie to them, work around them, and do the best possible job in spite of them while risking their wrath—being investigated, getting shit details, being passed over for promotions and awards, being fired or jailed for some infraction of the Manual, or, as some feared, dying a mysterious death like Sante Bario. Or he could decide to accept what the system gave him, stay out of the line of fire, and not be perceived as a threat to the public images and fragile egos of the suits, or to special interests like the CIA. (Three years after Operation Hun, Kiki Camarena battled the system and paid with his life). Rourke, I was afraid, had chosen not to buck the system. I didn't think he would hurt me, but he certainly wasn't going out of his way to help me.

But I couldn't let Operation Hun die. Letting go would be like an admission that 17 years of my life had been a lie.

Around noon the phone rang. It was Roberto, the snaggle-toothed killer. "I just wanted to tell you I was leaving," he said.

"What happened?"

"Uh, I'm not sure. I've got to go to Miami to find out. If I can get it straightened out, I'll be on the way back by car myself."

"Fine," I said. He had probably used up all the government cocaine I had given him, and 72 hours of phone sex was all he could handle.

"Look, that offer still stands. If you want to use some of those things [Uzis]. Just send one of your people."

"Okay, I appreciate it. Let me think about it."

"Sonia has my number."

"Fine. Have a good flight."

"Thanks. Is Sonia there? I just want to say goodbye."

I glanced out at the pool. Sonia and Lydia were in their usual spots. "No, I'm sorry. I had to send her to meet some customers."

"Well, I've got a two o'clock flight. I'll try again. Tell her I called."

I hung up and quickly telephoned Turghid and told him about the conversation.

"You gotta alert Miami," I said. "They can take him right to his house—there's more than enough for a search warrant. He's got an arsenal there. If Miami doesn't want to do something we send Rudy and another undercover there. They pick up one of the Uzis and turn it over to ATF. An Uzi with a silencer is a 25-year federal rap."

There was a long silence. Finally, Turghid said, "What'd I tell ya 'bout gettin' offa the fuckin' target?"

"Hey," I said, remembering how vulnerable I was to this man, "I have no argument with you. I'm just trying to do my job. I'm making sure you know everything I come up with. The rest is up to you."

"I'll pass on what you said to headquarters. Believe me, Levine, they're aware of everything. Meantime, your orders are to go ahead and wrap it up. You got it?"

Minutes later the phone rang again.

"Miguel," said Ana, "how are you and my little *Soñita*?"

"Fine, Ana. You know . . . busy."

"Is Roberto still there?" Her voice sounded troubled.

"He said he's leaving, and to tell you the truth I'm glad. He's been hanging around here too long and doing nothing. I mean, no disrespect for you Ana, but I don't trust him."

"I don't blame you. This isn't like him. He's always been very honorable with me. Carlos is the one I don't trust. He visited me last night and said that he was on his way to Tucson by car and that he was bringing you the gift."

"Did he say anything about bringing money?"

"He said he wouldn't make the trip for less than 30 kilos."

"But you don't think it's true, do you?"

"I don't know. It's all very strange."

"I'm sorry Ana, I just don't trust them."

"Well, no matter, I have some other interested parties. They're not happy about traveling to where you are, but I'll try to convince them tonight."

"Wonderful," I said.

"And I gave your phone number to a friend in California; his name is Hernando Velasco—he'll be calling you soon."

"Who is he?"

"Take care of him, Miguel. He represents one of the most important cocaine dealers in California. If he likes the quality, he'll take 30 kilos."

Ana obviously wasn't taking any chances with the quality of our cocaine, and she had probably warned all her customers that it was not the best. What a waste—DEA seizes cocaine on a daily basis. There's tons of the purest cocaine in the world sitting in warehouses around the country waiting to be destroyed.

"I'll take good care of him, Ana, don't worry. How's your daughter and husband?"

"*Aiii*, Miguel, always with problems, but well enough, thank God."

"You sound tired, *mamita*. Why don't you take a rest for a couple of days? The business will always be there."

"I wish I could, Miguel. I wish I could."

At 2 P.M. the answering service reported phone calls from Pineda and Espinosa, with a California telephone number. Things were starting to heat up again. I needed to calm down and center myself so that I wouldn't screw up and miss something. I raced over to the gym for a hard workout. Sam and Morris, as usual, were standing on my pushup spot.

"Look, it's Levine," said Sam when I came out of the locker, loud enough for half the people in the gym to hear. Hello everyone, I'm Levine the deep cover agent on assignment in Tucson.

"*Nu?*" said Morris. "You found something to invest in yet?"

I shrugged. Back in February I had told them I was in Tucson looking for a nightclub to invest in.

"*Gornisht?*" asked Sam.

325

"*Gornisht,*" I said.

"So how many bars can dere be in Tucson?" asked Morris.

"What are you guys, the FBY?"

"FBY?" they both said.

"Federal Bureau of Yentas."

I managed to get in a good workout while carrying on a conversation with Sam and Morris. I left the gym feeling good; the two old guys had a great effect on me. But as I pulled up to the UC house I saw South's car in the driveway. Whatever good feelings I had vanished.

"Mr. Turghid wants to know what day the thing's going down," he said the moment I walked in the door.

"I was gonna have Sonia call them now. You wanna listen?"

I didn't wait for his answer; I went directly out to the patio to get Sonia. Turghid was not going to let me stall any longer.

South stood back and watched as I hooked the recorder to the phone, dialed, and passed the receiver to Sonia.

"*Ola,*" said an anxious Espinosa. Somewhere in the world a raging Mejia waited for news. It had been almost six weeks since Sonia had told him he'd have his drugs in eight days. To Mejia, this debt must have by now transcended anything that could be measured in either money or drugs.

"We are almost ready for you," said Sonia as I had instructed.

"*Fenomino, Soñita.* I cannot tell you how delighted I am. We're leaving for Tucson immediately."

I signaled Sonia—two days. There was still a slim chance that Roberto would come through.

"We won't be ready for two days, Mario."

A pause, then Mario said, "That's alright, dear Sonia. We're coming anyway."

After Sonia hung up, I told South, "It's all set. You can tell your boss the whistle blows on Thursday."

South nodded. "So you basically don't have much to do until then, right?"

"That depends on, basically, what you mean."

"Mr. Turghid wants you to keep working on the tapes," he said. "I have them in the car."

❊   ❊   ❊

# 4

Early Wednesday morning the answering service called. Pineda was already at the Howard Johnson in Tucson. He said it was urgent that I call.

By 10:00 I had awakened Sonia, hooked the recorder to the phone, and was dialing Pineda. Espinosa answered on the first ring. "I just wanted you to know, my *Soñita,* that we're here," he said tensely.

"We'll be ready for you tomorrow," said Sonia.

"Fabulous."

"One thing, Mario. Where's Papo? I'm supposed to speak to him."

"Guacho?"

"He said he'd be here," said Sonia, her brow suddenly furrowed. "He told me the last time I talked to him."

"Wait . . . wait a second, Sonia." I could hear muffled voices. Pineda came on the line. "That's impossible," he said, "he's not even in the country."

"But he told me he'd speak to me before we did anything," said Sonia.

"I thought all that was straightened out," said Pineda, his voice rising.

"He told me he'd be here," Sonia insisted, "that he'd speak to me."

Once again there was a long silence; then Pineda, his voice tight with suspicion, said, "I'll do what I can."

When Sonia hung up she looked drained.

"It makes no sense to arrest them and not Papo," she said. "If he's in Colombia he knows *la DEA* can't touch him."

"I'm on your side," I said. It was the first time I had felt that way since I'd met her.

The phone rang again. "My name is Hernando Velasco," said a man's voice in Colombian-accented Spanish. "Ana Tamayo gave me your number."

"Yes?" said Sonia.

"Ana said I could get hold of a sample of those items," said Velasco. "I'm not the person in charge, mind you, I'm . . ."

"What?" Sonia was confused.

I had forgotten about Ana and her California customer. Maybe I had blocked it from my mind, knowing that the call might bring Ana back to Tucson for her arrest.

327

"I'm not the owner of the boat," said Velasco. "I'm part of the crew."

"I don't understand you," said Sonia.

"Didn't Ana explain?"

"She said a customer was going to call, but I don't understand what you're talking about."

"Yes," said Velasco, "that's me, and I am interested in buying all you have."

"We have 50," said Sonia, impatiently.

"That's very little, my dear. What I'd like to do is first come where you are and buy one. If the people in L.A. are happy with the quality I'll fly back with my own plane the same day for the rest."

"Well, I don't know," said Sonia, looking at me for a signal.

I nodded my head vigorously. I had never in my career turned down a drug dealer who was asking to be arrested. Let Turghid or someone else tell me no.

"We have customers coming tomorrow. I'm not sure we'll have anything left," said Sonia eyeing me. "Why don't you call late tomorrow."

By "late tomorrow" Operation Hun would be history. She had just ensured that Velasco would not be arrested.

"Wait a second," said Velasco. "I thought your voice sounded familiar. You know me."

"How do I know you?"

"I was supposed to meet you in Cartagena. Ana set up the meeting."

Sonia's face lit with recognition and anger. "Oh, I remember you now. I needed to find Roger the Pilot's number. You never came through with it."

Sonia was talking about an American pilot named Roger Reaves, who was alleged to have flown many drug loads into the United States for both the Bolivian and Colombian drug cartels. He was listed in as many drug files as Noriega, only until this phone call no one had been able to locate him.

"I can explain," said a flustered Velasco.

"Yeah," said Sonia, "I remember. I needed it badly."

"Ana made a mistake. I had my own pilots then. I still do."

Sonia was thinking. Here was another opportunity created by DEA to hurt someone else who'd pissed her off.

"Look," persisted Velasco, "we can do a lot of business with you people. We buy a lot. You won't be sorry."

He was begging to be locked up.

328

"Where do you handle the items?" asked Sonia.

"Some right there where you are," he said. "And here in California. Is the price the same that Ana quoted?"

"Whatever Ana said is correct."

"Well, can we do business?"

"When?" asked Sonia, watching me.

"Whenever you say," said Velasco.

Sonia took his home phone number, hung up, and said, "What do we do?"

"We stall for one extra day," I said. "That'll give Velasco time to get here and maybe a better chance to get Mejia. And who knows, maybe even Roberto will surprise us."

"Will they let you?"

"I'll find that out right now," I said, picking up the phone.

I telephoned Rourke. There was no sense talking to Turghid—Velasco was way off "the target." When Rourke came on the line, I told him about the call, and said, "The guy could give us Roger Reaves."

"So what is it ya want?"

"We just need one extra day to play with him. I want to tell Pineda Friday."

"Friday! Turghid's gonna go batshit."

"And what about Mejia?" I said.

"Christ."

"I'm serious—I can't even talk to the guy; he's got me transcribing tapes now, maybe he'll have me washing cars next. Just find out, are we gonna take these guys off even if Mejia doesn't show?"

"Fuckin' Levine. You know what he's gonna say."

"If it's yes, I'm just asking for a 24-hour delay. We wasted a month in Washington when we coulda been doing half the people in Sonia's black book; what's one more day?"

Rourke was silent for a long moment. "Let me call you back."

The phone rang again. Sonia answered it. "I've got everything together," said Velasco. "I'll be on the afternoon plane to where you are." To do business with the Queen of Cocaine was a once-in-a-lifetime opportunity. Velasco said he was coming with $400,000 for 10 kilos. "If the merchandise is good, I'll take everything you have," he repeated.

After Sonia hung up, she asked, "And what do we do when he sees the quality of our cocaine?"

"That's a good question," I said.

"And when Papo's chemist tests it? I thought the object of this game was to make them talk about Lucho in front of the camera—how much talking will they do if they think they're being cheated?"

"You knew this from the time Monica tested the stuff. No! From the moment you saw it. Why did you wait until now to say something?"

She laughed an angry little bark.

"What difference would it have made if I said something to you? Your people don't listen to you. Besides, they know very well what they're doing."

"Then why ask?"

She paused to light a cigarette. She inhaled deeply, and then underwent an incredible transformation. All signs of anger vanished as quickly as a summer shower. She slowly exhaled in my direction. "I don't know how long you and I are going to be together," she said softly, seductively, "or what's going to happen. I just didn't want you to think I'm a fool."

"Sonia, a fool is the last thing in the world anyone would think you are. But neither am I."

Sonia looked at me, and then without a word turned and started toward her room.

"Where are you going?"

"To call my husband and children. I want to make sure they're all right."

A half hour later, Rourke called. "Turghid's not happy—but you can stall an extra day . . . that's it."

"Mejia or no Mejia?" I said.

"If he doesn't show we'll indict him and try to find him."

"Is anyone working on finding him?"

"Someone should be," he said, sounding doubtful.

"And what about Monica, Roberto, the others?"

Rourke drew an exasperated breath; I pictured him in his hotel room, his head in a cloud of smoke, notes and files scattered all over the room.

"Mike," he finally said, "I'm passing on everything to headquarters. From that point on its outta my hands. If you have any questions, call them yourself."

*　　*　　*

# 5

On Thursday morning the phone wouldn't stop ringing. Velasco called four times to tell us he was on his way to Tucson with the money, and to make sure we kept at least 10 kilos for him. Pineda and Espinosa were leaving angry messages again with the answering service.

Sonia laughed. "They still think they're getting paid today. If we don't call them soon, they'll blow up the hotel."

Ana called from Miami to find out about Velasco. "He said he's leaving today," I said.

"Don't worry, he'll come, or he'll send somebody," said Ana. "How many rugs did he say he wanted?"

"Ten."

She was quiet for a moment, probably calculating her $25,000 commission. She had mentioned money problems—that was probably what kept her trying to sell our bargain-basement merchandise, along with her loyalty to Sonia.

"I know a few more people here, but not many want to travel to where you are. I have a meeting later today. If it works out, I will be on the way out to you, personally." That meant with money.

After I hung up the thought of Ana's arrest crossed my mind. I pushed it away.

It was close to noon when I dialed Pineda's number. "Hello," said a voice so low and tight that I didn't recognize it.

"Is this Eduardo?" I said.

"Yes. What's happening?"

"Look, I'm calling you to tell you that we have everything ready, but there's a small problem."

"There can't be any more problems," he said flatly.

"It's just one day," I said. "We're trying to do two transactions at once." I heard myself speaking too quickly, too nervously. I had to calm down.

"Go ahead."

"The delay is the other people."

"So what are you saying?"

"How much time are you going to need to fix your jeep?" That was the jeep with the hidden drug compartments that had been collecting dust in the garage of the UC house for the last six weeks.

"About two hours," he said.

"Okay. Two hours. So then, we'll do the whole thing tomorrow."

If Velasco showed up in the morning we could arrest him and then have the Mejia people out to the house for the final roundup. Then I could get the hell out of here.

"Is everything okay?" I asked.

"Not quite," said Pineda.

"What's up?"

"Could we talk today . . . in the afternoon . . . in person?"

Something was up.

"It's nothing out of the ordinary," he persisted. "Even if it's for 10 or 15 minutes. Just two or three questions we'd like to put to you . . . personally."

The tone of his voice said it was anything but ordinary.

"I have to talk to some people first," I said. "I'm not making excuses. Like I told you, I'm trying to do too many things at once."

Pineda persisted. "Yes, I understand, but . . . this is nothing out of the ordinary. Even if it's just 10 minutes, so that we can talk."

"Yes, okay," I said. I had no excuse not to meet with him. "I'll have to call you back."

"I'll be waiting."

When I hung up, I had to take a deep breath and just sit still. Pushing people like Pineda and Mejia this way was like climbing Mt. Everest without a rope.

"What about Mejia?" said Sonia.

"Damn! I forgot."

"How could you forget that!" she screamed.

I was handling too much and getting careless. "They want to meet me, anyway," I said. "I'll ask them in person."

Before I could pick up the phone to call Turghid, it rang again.

"Miguel," said Roberto, Ana's snaggle-toothed killer. "Sorry things didn't work out."

"What happened?"

"Like I said, come to Miami, we got a deal. The people don't want to travel."

"Forget it," I said, my mind still on Pineda.

"Well, just so there are no hard feelings, why don't you send one of your employees here. I'd like to give you one of those gifts."

"I might take you up on that," I said, "Look, I have to get going."

"Is Sonia there? I just wanted to say hello."

"No, but I will tell her you called. I'm sure she'll be pleased."

I hung up and called Turghid.

"There are a couple of things going on," I said, trying to keep my voice neutral. Turghid was silent. "I was just gonna call you about something else and Roberto called from Miami."

"Yeah."

"He's sitting there with an Uzi and a silencer. All we gotta do is put Rudy or someone on a plane to pick it up and that's another 25-year rap."

Silence. I was about to ask if he was still there when he said, "That what you called about? Haven't we already discussed this a few times?"

"Yes, we did," I said, straining for control. "I'm just doing my job as an undercover. The guy called, I'm telling you what he said."

"Right now, s' far as I know," snapped Turghid, "our orders are still to focus this operation on Arce-Gomez. You got that straight?"

"I sure do," I said feeling like my heart was in a vise.

"There somethin' else?"

"Yes," I said, "the other reason I called is that Mejia's men are getting nervous. They want to meet me for a face-to-face talk."

"Why don't ya tell 'em to fuck off? You'll call 'em when you're good 'n' ready!"

"I wish I could, but I think they already smell something."

"What do you mean?"

"It's been six weeks since we told 'em we're coming back in eight days. If you were them, wouldn't you smell something wrong?"

"So what is it you wanna do now?"

"I'll tell 'em to meet me at Tequila Willy's at four—that's two hours from now. I'd like a couple of guys covering me."

"Okay. What else?"

"I'd like to give them a sample of the coke. It'll let them know we're for real, not trying to pull something funny. I know you've gotta get headquarters approval first, so when I meet 'em I won't say anything. If you get the approval just have one of the guys walk up to the table with the stuff in a sealed envelope and lay it down in front of me. I'll slide it across to him. That way it'll be in clear view until he picks it up."

I had a more important reason for doing this, although I couldn't tell Turghid without him blowing up at me. I didn't want Pineda's first sight of our yellow drugs to be when he was in front of the cameras. I wanted him to know beforehand; to have 24 hours to calm down and realize that poor coke was better than none, and that he'd be able to recoup the loss in a future deal. If I handed him garbage at the last moment, I was sure he'd go bad. And he had to have at least a couple of *pistoleros* in Tucson.

I also wanted Mejia's men talking freely about Arce-Gomez, Mejia, the German, and every other drug dealer they knew. It would be our last and only chance to get that important and dramatic testimony on videotape. It was the kind of evidence juries always convict on, and the kind of evidence someone could go to Congress with if DEA didn't act on it. I was still naive enough to think Congress might really do something.

"Anything else?" asked Turghid.

"Nothing I can think of."

# 6

Mariachi music was blasting from a powerful stereo inside Tequila Willy's as I drove up at 4:00. I walked slowly across the lot, checking around me for sudden movements, for heads in parked cars, for the sound of idling engines. If they were going to pull something, this was where it would happen.

Inside the crowded bar, I didn't see Pineda, but three Latinos wearing dark sunglasses and guayaberas and seated at a table just inside the entrance immediately drew my attention. They stopped talking as I entered and made a point of not looking at me. I hoped they were undercovers.

I moved to the bar, but before I could order a drink Pineda and a nervous-looking Latino in his mid-thirties appeared, framed in the bright sunlight of the doorway. I could feel their tension from across the room. They must have been watching the place when I came in, and I had missed them. I was reminded of how easy it was to catch any man unaware—even someone who had spent his life trying to see around corners.

"*Como estas, Eduardo?*" I said, moving toward Pineda with my hand out. All I read in his face was suspicion.

He gave me a brief, cold handshake and introduced me to Espinosa, who gripped my hand as smiling and eager as an insurance salesman.

"I'm honored to know you," he said, addressing me with the polite form in Spanish. His frightened eyes were darting all over the place. Sweat beaded on his forehead.

"Let's sit someplace," said Pineda. As he and Espinosa led the way toward a table near a wall, I watched them for telltale bulges under their shirts. I saw no sign of weapons.

For the first minute or so they said nothing. Pineda scanned the place carefully with alert eyes, while Espinosa fidgeted and smiled nervously. They asked for the meeting, so I waited for them to speak.

A waitress appeared and took our order. After she left, Espinosa broke the silence. *"Hace un calor tremendo,"* he said, pulling out a handkerchief to wipe his brow. He had kind of a pudgy round face and looked like a real cream puff. I wondered how he'd survived at all in the drug world.

"I guess you've never been here before."

"No."

More silence as they both scanned the place. Finally, I lost my patience.

"Well, I'm here, what's this about?"

Pineda looked me squarely in the eyes as if trying to discover something in them. "I want to explain how we work before we do anything," he said.

"Okay," I said, "I'm listening."

"How far are you?"

"From here, about a half-hour ride."

"When are we going to do this?"

"In the afternoon. I've got other business programmed right after you."

"That's what I wanted to explain to you. We open every bag. The chemist tests each. I witness the test. Then we repackage it in our own bags which I seal and mark with my initials. That's my personal guarantee of the purity."

The drinks came. Espinosa immediately downed a healthy shot of vodka and followed it with half a beer. Pineda suddenly looked past me. South and Rudy were moving toward the bar. South looked a nervous wreck.

"Those are your men," said Pineda.

"I thought it would be a good idea that you got a sample of our merchandise before you came out to the house. It might save some time tomorrow." Pineda stared at me blankly. I shrugged. "It's up to you."

335

Pineda seemed to nod, but he was so tense that I wasn't sure it wasn't a nervous tic. I nodded at Rudy and he started toward us with what seemed like every eye in the place following his progress. When Rudy reached our table, he leaned over and whispered "Everything okay?" in my ear, at the same time leaving a sealed envelope on the table before me.

I nodded, placing my hand over the envelope. I could feel the lump of grainy powder inside—a nice healthy sample. Pineda stared at the envelope like it was about to attack him, and Espinosa's frightened eyes were darting all over the room. He was tearing little strips off a napkin. Rudy turned and headed back toward the bar.

"He's a good man," I said.

Pineda nodded; his eyes stayed on the envelope. I pushed it across the table to him, but he didn't make a move to touch it.

"We're still going to test every bag," he said.

"I know. Just tell me how many are coming to the house so that I'll know how many cars to send."

"We have our own cars. Just tell us where the house is."

"My neighborhood's a very quiet place. It's better that no strange cars are seen—especially with out-of-state plates."

Pineda nodded, his eyes going from the envelope to me and back again. Espinosa sweated and tore more strips.

"What about Guacho?" I said. "He told Sonia he'd be here."

"We already spoke about this," said Pineda.

"Don Miguel, excuse me," said Espinosa putting a clammy hand on my forearm. "I was there from the very beginning in this . . . We were, the three of us, equal partners. Any one of us is equally authorized . . ."

Pineda silenced Espinosa with a murderous look.

"Does this mean you're not going to pay?" Pineda was furious and barely able to control himself. His hands slipped beneath the table again.

I glanced around; Rudy and South were gone. I knew that DEA wanted this case over, yet I wanted to tell Pineda, Fuck no, I'm not paying till Mejia's across a table from me. I could feel all the rage and fear that Sonia had produced focused on me through Pineda's eyes. I could also feel his desperation. His life was as much on the line as Sonia's . . . and mine. I could go no further with the bluff.

"No," I told him. "I'm going to pay as I agreed. I'm just not happy about the way it's happening."

A loud sigh escaped Espinosa, and he signaled the waitress for another double shot of vodka and a beer. Pineda said nothing, but he relaxed and ordered a beer. The waitress wiped the small mountain of napkin strips onto her tray and left Espinosa a fresh napkin. Espinosa immediately went to work on the second napkin.

"I just need to know how many of your people are coming," I said.

Pineda appeared deep in thought, staring at the envelope still untouched in front of him.

"Six to the house, no, Eduardo?" blurted Espinosa. He seemed duty-bound to fill every silence. Pineda shot him another look and said, "I want as few as possible."

He seemed as concerned about this point as he was about the drugs. There were at least four more of their gang in town—maybe Mejia was there, too. Whatever the case, Tucson was a small town, and Turghid had 24 hours to locate the others.

"I'll send two cars at two in the afternoon. If you think you'll need more, call me."

"I won't need more than two."

"Fine," I said, shoving back my chair and getting to my feet.

Espinosa got to his feet, knocking over his chair. Pineda looked skyward; I knew exactly how he felt.

"It was a pleasure to meet you, Miguel," said Espinosa, grinning. He offered me a sopping wet hand. "Please say hello to Sonia. Tell her I'm really looking forward to seeing her tomorrow."

"I will."

Pineda, a troubled look in his eyes, hadn't moved. I offered him my hand, still damp from Espinosa's. He put his hand in mine and quickly withdrew it.

"Hasta mañana," I said.

When the whistle blows everybody goes.

# 27

# The Big Bust

## 1

Sonia, Lydia, and I were about 15 minutes late to Turghid's office, and the pre-bust meeting was already in progress. The DEA office was packed with undercovers, uniformed cops, sheriff's deputies, a SWAT team, and a couple of helicopter pilots.

Turghid paused before a blackboard on which someone had drawn a diagram of the area surrounding the UC house. He glanced down at his watch and then focused his beady eyes on me.

"Glad ya'll could make it," he said. "Just in case shootin' breaks out, I wanted to be sure everybody knew what you look like."

I nodded and led Sonia and Lydia to a corner of the room near a cloud of cigarette smoke that I guessed Rourke was under. We had been delayed by a call from Velasco, who still hadn't left California. He had droned on and on until I hung up on him. I hoped he never came. Then Ana would have no reason to return.

Turghid picked up his briefing. "The organization we're gonna be takin' down today is one of the most dangerous in the business. These people are known to carry automatic weapons and they ain't afraid ta use 'em." This statement gave him the rapt attention of all the heavily armed law officers. By the time he finished describing the Mejia organization's reputation, every man in the room was ready for heavy combat.

Turghid's plans for the bust were elaborate. Half a dozen undercover agents, in addition to South and Rudy, were assigned to the inside of the house during the deal itself. South was in charge of perhaps the most crucial part of the operation—ensuring that everything was faithfully recorded. The whole alleged purpose of Operation Hun—the indictment of Luis Arce-Gomez—might very well rest on this final recording.

Another 20 or so undercover agents armed with shotguns and automatic weapons were to conceal themselves in the area immediately surrounding the house. An additional 20 were assigned to an outer perimeter, along with a half-dozen uniformed sheriff's deputies in patrol cars and a SWAT team. "Just in case they manage to break through and make a run for it, or there's a hostage situation," said Turghid.

"And from the moment the bad guys are in the house," he continued, "I want the helicopter up in the air covering the area—you men got that?"

Two men in dark uniforms, sunglasses, and baseball caps nodded.

Turghid strutted before his audience, taking a couple of quick slices at the air with a pointer—Field Marshal Montgomery facing his desert troops. "Ain't nobody gonna move up there 'less I want the son of a bitch moving," he said. He peered around fiercely at his silent audience. "Any questions?" he barked.

There were none.

"For those of you that don't know him, that's Special Agent Mike Levine, the UC." He pointed at me with his stick. "Get a good look at him."

Every eye turned toward me. This was a standard safety precaution before a large-scale operation, so that if shooting broke out everyone involved would know the good guys. But why didn't he do the same with Lydia and Sonia?

"Y'all know your assignments. Let's get going!"

Chairs scraped as officers got to their feet; equipment was checked and the mob of burly, unsmiling officers began to shuffle toward the door.

"Like a word with you," said Turghid, moving past me, his eyes angry black dots in a mass of swollen red flesh. I started to follow and noticed Sonia and Lydia moving toward one of the small offices. Sonia gave me a strange look.

Inside Turghid's office I took a seat; Rourke, South, and Rudy were there, too. Rudy was once again dressed in his green Izod shirt and penny loafers, signifying the end of Operation Hun and his return to the fold. I looked at South. He averted his eyes. It was like the day I met them.

"Headquarters's right on top of this," said Turghid. "This thing's goin' off without a hitch—y'all got that?" His eyes were on me.

"Anything new about Papo?" I said.

"Nothin' you ain't been told."

"What about the people in town with Pineda? There's supposed to be at least six. Any of them identified yet?"

Turghid looked at South. "Anybody identified?"

"No one."

"Anything else?" asked Turghid.

"Yeah, one more thing," I said, unable to stop myself. "What about sending an undercover to Miami to get the Uzi from Roberto? We get someone on a plane now, we can get to him before the news of the bust gets to Miami. This is our last chance, not only to get his whole arsenal but to maybe solve a couple a dozen homicides."

"I told you we're concentratin' on Arce-Gomez," said Turghid.

The room was quiet for a long moment. I wanted to scream that this was bullshit—they could have gotten Arce-Gomez during the Suarez case if they really wanted him. Instead I said coolly, "So lemme just get this straight. The sum total of all this, this whole operation, is just gonna be the arrests of whoever shows up at the house today?"

Turghid shook his head in disbelief. He turned to Rourke. "You wanna tell him?"

"If you get some good conversation," said Rourke, "and the deal with Nati works out, we'll put it before a grand jury."

My mind flashed on the events of the last few years in Argentina and Bolivia. Who were they kidding? The CIA had put the whole Bolivian crew—including Sonia—in power in the first place. There was no way anyone important would be indicted after today.

"Pineda told me there's six others here. Mejia could be one of them."

Rourke shrugged and looked at Turghid.

340

"The man jest told you ain't nobody else been spotted. You got any mo' questions?"

"None."

"You know what you need t' know," said Turghid. "So jest do your job. We'll take care of the rest." The room was silent. "Oh yeah," Turghid continued. "When the bad guys get there, tell 'em Sonia's doin' some business or somethin'. Headquarters don't want her out there, in case there's shooting. Lydia's gonna stay here with her."

## 2

The UC house was buzzing with activity when I got back. I watched as tense men, some already wearing bulletproof vests, rearranged the living room furniture. No one said a word to me or even acknowledged my presence.

A sectional couch, two loveseats, two easy chairs, and two end tables in which microphones were concealed were moved closer to the middle of the room to form a U around the Evil Eye so that anyone seated on any piece of furniture in the room could not avoid being on camera or near a hidden microphone. A long coffee table on which were an electric thermometer, some test tubes, and glass slides was placed directly in front of a section of the couch, center-screen on the hidden camera.

Agents and cops entered the house with bulletproof vests, flak jackets, and shotguns, and began checking for places to conceal themselves. A helicopter chugged overhead for a minute or two and then flew off. There was a surreal feeling about the whole scene.

South arrived with some fresh videotapes and cassettes. Looking as important as he could, he began going back and forth between the pool house and the living room, testing the recording equipment.

At 1:45 P.M., the two Lincolns left to pick up Pineda and his men, followed by a half-dozen cars sending up billowing clouds of desert dust. The agents assigned inside the house—all except South were Spanish-speaking Chicanos—seemed to blend into the woodwork. South disappeared inside the pool house.

I was suddenly alone.

I stepped outside and peered up and down the street. The sky was overcast, the weather cooler than usual, and the air was unnaturally still. To my right, all I could see was the mountain rising up dark and foreboding; to my left, a long dusty street lined with expensive homes.

There wasn't a car in sight, nor was there any movement or sound. The stillness was so unnatural that I wondered whether Pineda would sense something the moment he stepped out of the car.

I tried to pick out some sign of the massive ambush that was all around me. I could detect nothing except the eerie silence. I felt incredibly vulnerable.

At 2:20 the phone rang. "They're comin' your way," said a voice I didn't recognize.

"How many bad guys?" I asked.

"Four."

"There's at least two more in town," I said. Only the dial tone answered.

Minutes later the phone rang again. It was Velasco, calling again from Los Angeles.

"I just wanted to tell you that my man is on the way to where you are," he said.

"Fine," I said. "When he gets here I'll talk to him." And I hung up on him.

The phone rang again.

"Don Miguel, is Sonia there by any chance?" said Roberto, the snaggletoothed killer.

"No. She's out. Just leave a number."

"She already has it. Tell her I'm at the office. I just wanted to say that, you know, I hope there's no hard feelings."

"Forget it. Look, I'm busy."

"Like I told Sonia, that gift is waiting here for you. Just send one of your people."

"Thanks," I said, and hung up.

Minutes later the phone rang again. I snatched it up, feeling that there was a plot against my sanity.

"*Aiii*, don Miguel, it's so good to hear your voice," said Ana. "You know I miss being with you and Sonia."

"Forgive me, Ana," I said, my ear cocked for the sound of approaching cars, "Sonia's out and some people are about to arrive."

"Oh, I'm sorry to disturb you, Miguel. I just called to find out if someone from California called."

342

"Yes, he called. He says he coming, but he never seems to leave California. I'm not too sure about him, Ana."

"He'll come, Miguel. I guarantee it. Just take good care of him."

"Don't worry Ana, I will." Once again the specter of Ana's arrest appeared, and I felt a dull pain in my heart. She was just a doper—what the hell was happening to me?

As I hung up, South appeared behind me, his face flushed. "They're five minutes away," he said. "I got it over the radio."

"The equipment working all right?" I asked. I don't know why I asked the question; I had never before been very concerned with technical equipment. Technicians set it up, and I did the UC work.

South stared at me for a moment as if he had just been caught with his hand in the cash register. "Everything's working fine," he finally said.

At 2:55 I was alone in the living room. I had a terrible feeling that something bad was going to happen. I closed my eyes and took some deep breaths. On an undercover set people become emotionally supercharged and hypersensitive. The slightest sign of fear is immediately transmitted to everyone involved like a jolt of electricity. And then everything goes out of control and people die.

I had to get myself under control.

"They're here," said a voice.

Tires crunched gravel outside, car doors slammed, a muffled voice said something, and then the doorbell sounded. I got to my feet a little shaky. A tall Chicano undercover named Hector come out of nowhere and moved quickly to the front door. "Let's do it," I said, and he swung open the door.

Pineda was the first one through the door, nervous as a cat, his unblinking eyes sweeping the room. Espinosa followed him, smiling nervously. They were followed by two hard-faced young men, one tall and blond, the other hulking, dark, and bearded, lugging suitcases and a large oxygen tank. Bringing up the rear were Rudy and a Chicano undercover named Tommy carrying another oxygen bottle.

Espinosa came right at me, sweat already beading his brow. "How are you, don Miguel?" His breath reeked of alcohol. "Finally, this ordeal is over with. Where is Sonia?"

"She's out with a customer," I said. "She will try to get back as soon as she's done."

Both men froze for a moment and stared at me. Sonia's absence at this critical moment was sinister.

"Welcome," I said, shaking hands with Pineda. "My house is yours," I said, forcing as relaxed and friendly a manner as I could. "I didn't want to delay you again, so I decided we'd just begin without her." Pineda said nothing.

Pineda's men—Jose Libardo, the dark Colombian, and Mike O'Connor, the fair American—had begun unpacking and setting up their testing equipment in the space we had prepared for them. They lay their electric thermometer alongside ours on the long coffee table, along with a digital scale, a heat sealer, labels, a large box of plastic bags, and an assortment of test tubes, Clorox bottles, methyl alcohol, and laboratory flasks.

O'Connor attached a face mask to the oxygen tank, put the mask to his face, and took a deep breath. He nodded his satisfaction. "What's that for?" I asked Pineda.

"Ether bothers him," said Pineda, his eyes worriedly surveying my undercover employees. "He's been a chemist for too long. It makes him nauseous."

Suddenly South appeared in a doorway. Now there were six undercovers gawking at the proceedings, and Pineda was just standing there watching them. I felt his tension.

"You and you," I said, pointing at South and Hector. "Stop standing around and get these gentlemen whatever they want to eat or drink." Hector moved. South stared at me blankly. "You heard me," I said. "Do it!" I smiled as South turned beet red and moved toward Espinosa. Pineda smiled at me for the first time.

"How about something to eat or drink?" I said, taking Pineda by the arm and moving him a few feet closer to a hidden mike.

"No, nothing for me."

When Pineda's men finished setting up their equipment, I had Rudy put the Samsonite suitcase stuffed with the 30 one-kilo packages of cocaine next to the testing table. Now the stage was truly set and all the actors were in their places.

Libardo and O'Connor began stripping off their clothing—everything, down to their BVDs. They folded their clothing neatly and put it into plastic bags.

"What the hell are they doing that for?" I asked. I knew, but I wanted Pineda to say it for the camera so the jury wouldn't be wondering. It was always better to have the bad guy explain it for them.

"They're professionals," said Pineda. "That's to keep the smell off their clothes, in case they're checked by police sniffer dogs."

"*Conio,*" I said. For a moment, O'Connor glanced at me.

"I'm impressed," I said. "But tell me he's not a cop. He could give me a traffic ticket and he wouldn't need a uniform."

Pineda laughed, a nervous little bark. "Everybody thinks Mike's a cop. You'd laugh if I told you how we found him. He was just a kid, eight years ago, coming down to Colombia buying coke on his own. He's been with us ever since."

O'Connor and Libardo helped each other don plastic gloves, then each took a swig from beer bottles. Their movements right down to the hoisting of the bottles were made in the kind of semiconscious unison that comes only from years of working as a team. They had spent 20 minutes setting up their equipment without uttering a word, their faces devoid of expression. There was something fascinating about watching them. The room had grown silent and all eyes were on them.

O'Connor spoke for the first time. "Okay, let's get started." The hefty Libardo unzipped the suitcase and extracted the first package of coke, holding it up for a moment in a massive hand to examine it. The powder looked yellower than ever, but he remained perfectly expressionless. He weighed the package on the digital scale—an even 1,000 grams, one full kilo of cocaine.

"So far, so good," said Libardo in lightly accented English as he handed the package to O'Connor.

O'Connor held the package up to the light, and then examined it beneath a large handheld magnifying glass. After a moment he glanced over at Pineda and shook his head.

"What's that mean?" I said, feeling a tightening in my stomach.

"We'll see," said Pineda. "Let him test it."

Libardo held the package as O'Connor made a tiny incision in the plastic with a small pocketknife. He shifted the blade around inside and then slowly withdrew a small mound of fine powder. He deposited some of the powder on each of two glass slides on the table in front of him, and Libardo quickly and deftly sealed the incision with scotch tape.

Everyone in the room crowded around the couch as O'Connor placed each slide on a heating plate—one on theirs, one on the government's. Pineda and I stood right behind him. Espinosa, scarcely paying attention to the testing, stood across from us with a tumbler of whiskey in his hand, chatting with Rudy. O'Connor twisted the heat dial on each instrument. The digital reading of the government thermometer began to climb and drop erratically. "This thing is off," he said.

The idiots had given me the same broken thermometer. If they wanted to burn the case up that bad, why didn't they just put a DEA hiring poster on the fucking door?

The dopers' thermometer, however, was functioning perfectly. We all watched as the temperature gradually rose to 70°C, then 80°. Then something totally unexpected happened.

Before the temperature hit 90°, about half the powder on the slide started to turn brown; at 100° the powder was a bubbling brown liquid; at 110° it had burned to black ash. At 130° the rest of the powder began to melt. O'Connor looked at Pineda and shook his head.

"This is garbage," he said. "It's been hit. I give it no more than 50 percent."

The cocaine for the most important case in DEA had just tested out no stronger than 50 percent pure—a quality that most street users would reject.

Pineda was waiting for an explanation. The surprise and suspicion I saw in his eyes wasn't faked. Either he had not tested the sample I gave him the other day in the bar, or the powder in the envelope was different from the yellow garbage now on the table.

But what could I say? Turghid had told me the cocaine had been withdrawn from a DEA laboratory where it was tested at 89 percent pure. I was totally unprepared for street garbage. Either someone had stolen some of the coke and replaced it with mix, or it was sabotage.

"That can't be," I muttered.

"Hey," said O'Connor, "I've been doing this shit for 10 years. This stuff's cut!"

"No," I said quickly, "I'm not arguing with you. Either some of my people have been fucking with it or you just happened to choose a bag with bad stuff. Either way," I said, "I'd like to know myself. If I'm being fucking robbed, I wanna know about it."

O'Connor and Libardo sat motionless, waiting for a cue from Pineda. I was raging inside, and not bothering to hide it. Pineda and Espinosa exchanged a look that was a combination of desperation and recognition. They had an intimate understanding of my problem.

Sonia had not only ripped off Mejia, she had had serious problems with other drug dealers. Both Ana and Mejia had alluded to them. Her explanation for one of these incidents was that her uncle had stolen a customer's coke and replaced it with sugar. And now she was suddenly absent. They had to suspect that she was ripping me off as well.

Pineda nodded his head. Libardo, with a wary glance around the room, selected another bag and O'Connor repeated the test procedure. This time the cocaine tested out to about 60 percent.

"The stuff's shit," said O'Connor.

The room was still. Pineda stared at me; Libardo and O'Connor were intent on Pineda. All the undercovers had positioned themselves against the walls or in the doorways.

I knew the look in the agents' eyes well—they were a hair'sbreadth from going for their guns. All they needed was a sudden move by anyone. I had not been able to spot any guns on Pineda or Espinosa, but it didn't matter. If either man made a move that might be construed as going for a gun, they'd be cut to shreds in a crossfire before their next heartbeat—and maybe me with them. The thought that that might be exactly what someone wanted galvanized me.

"Listen, Eduardo," I said quickly, wondering whether I would look as frightened on the videotape as I felt, "you've got to know that I'm not looking for any trouble with Mr. Mejia. I'd be an idiot to invite you here to try and fool you with bad merchandise. You didn't find us, we called you. We have no reason to pull anything funny. I'm just as surprised as you are, more surprised. Either the people in Bolivia have screwed Sonia again, or it's one of my own people." I glared around suspiciously at my own men. It was not unheard of for underlings to steal merchandise.

Pineda nodded his head thoughtfully. "So what are you proposing?" he asked.

Espinosa gulped down another drink. He looked at me, his eyes as wide as saucers; he was scared to death—and with good reason. If I didn't somehow make Mejia happy, he was a dead man.

"Don Miguel," began Espinosa, "might I suggest . . ."

"Shut up!" snapped Pineda.

What was I proposing? What could I possibly propose that would get these men talking freely on camera?

The phone rang and Rudy snatched it up. He listened for a moment and looked at me. *"Es para usted."*

I took the call in the master bedroom. "Miguel," said Ana. "I just spoke to Hernando in Los Angeles. His man is on the way to where you are."

"He already called me twice to tell me that, Ana. Is he the real thing or another Roberto?" *Get pissed off, Ana—don't come back here!*

"Miguel, please take good care of these people. His word is good. He said they'll arrive at 5:40 in the evening. They're very, very important people. They'll buy at least 10 kilos. And I'll have an excuse to spend more time with you and Sonia."

"Ana, right now I'm in the middle of business, but as soon as they get here I'll take good care of them, personally, like they were family."

Ana laughed. "I know you will. My commission is the same as we said before, right?"

"You don't have to worry about us, *mamita.* Your money will be as safe with me as in a bank."

"I know, Miguel, but unfortunately I need it now. My daughter is going back to Colombia and I have to have the money before she leaves. So I'll catch a plane for you in the morning."

I felt a pressing around my heart and took a deep breath. "I look forward to seeing you, Ana." *Listen to my voice, hear what my heart is saying! Run!*

"I feel the same, Miguel. I also wanted to tell you that I spoke to Pacho again. Those items are still waiting for you in Colombia. You said after this we'd go together, no?"

"Yes."

"I can't tell you how happy that makes me." Her voice became grave. "Please don't fail me this time, Miguel. To fail Pacho twice is to lose the biggest opportunity you'll ever have, and you'll be hurting me badly."

She didn't know the half of it. "I won't fail him this time."

*"Un beso, Miguel, y saludos a Sonia."*

*"Un beso grandote, mamita,"* I said.

I returned to a silent living room full of undercover agents and drug dealers. O'Connor was waiting to show me the results of his last test. "This bag also tested out at less than 60 percent," he said holding up a glass slide coated with the blackened remnants of the heat test. "And see the way that burned, like ash?"

"Yes," I said, feeling sick inside. It was far worse than I had anticipated.

"The only thing that burns like that is Inositol. This stuff's been cut." Inositol was one of the common substances used to cut cocaine. "And look at this," he continued, putting the slide to one side and picking up the magnifying glass. He held it over another glass slide half covered with powder. "Look for yourself." I sat down beside him and looked. "You see what I mean?" he pressed.

"What am I supposed to be seeing?" I said for the videotape. This time I wasn't only thinking jury—this was one video that our elected officials ought to see.

"This stuff's been cut after it was processed," said the chemist. "Look at the rocks—some of 'em have been chopped and cut. And there's at least two kinds of powder granules there." About half the naturally formed crystals had obvious sheer sides, indicating that someone had been chopping them down to powder so that they'd mix more evenly with the diluting substance.

"You're right," I said, putting down the magnifying glass. I turned to Pineda. "I can't let you take this stuff. I have a big problem now, not only with you, but I have others on their way here expecting to get quality merchandise. I don't want our reputation to be ruined before we even get started.

"We can do one of two things. Either we call it quits right now and as soon as I'm back from Bolivia with a new load we settle, or you accept these 30 kilos as partial payment, calculate how much is missing, and when I return from this trip I'll make up the difference."

I was counting on their fear of returning home to Mejia empty-handed to convince them of the latter choice. If Pineda called it quits now, I would never be able to get him talking freely in front of the camera.

"I don't understand," said Pineda.

"Let's say," I said, "that if I had given you 30 kilos at 90 percent pure, it would have satisfied the debt, right?"

"Okay."

"Then let's say the stuff we have here tests out to an average of 60 percent pure. You follow me?"

"So far."

"Then we still owe you a third of the original debt. And when we come back from down there, I have to pay you another 10 kilos."

Pineda looked at O'Connor and Libardo as if the three were in telepathic communication. Drops of sweat flew from Espinosa, who had been Hoovering cocaine off the testing table. He had no say in the decision, but he would have to live or die by it.

Some of the undercovers were now nervously eyeing the three men around the testing table and a leather bag that was now lying half open at their feet. No one had checked the bag for guns, nor could we tell if Pineda's guayabera concealed a gun. Hands edged back toward concealed holsters. A feeling of nervous energy crackled in the air. If Pineda refused my offer, Operation Hun would come to an abrupt and possibly violent ending.

Pineda gave a barely perceptible nod; the three had come to some silent agreement. Libardo selected another bag from the suitcase for testing.

"Let's see what it is," said Pineda.

"You have nothing to lose," I said taking a deep breath. "If you lose a little on selling this stuff, you'll more than make up for it when we come back."

"You know," said Pineda, "if we do this, we're going to take into consideration the inconvenience you put us through, plus additional interest on the original amount."

"Of course," I said, too quickly. "I'm embarrassed. The last thing I want is more problems with Mr. Mejia." Before he could answer I turned to O'Connor and said in English, "You're good, man . . . really good. How about going down south with me in a couple of days? I'll cut you in for a piece of the action."

"You better ask him," said O'Connor. If he was pleased with my praise he wasn't showing it. "I don't do anything without their OK."

"What about it?" I said to Pineda. "We're going to be doing business together. You'll be protecting your own investment and I'll be paying for it. What could be wrong with that?"

I was now "throwing shit into the game." I was overloading Pineda, and hopefully distracting him from the many obvious flaws in our act.

"Something can be arranged," he said, "after I talk with Guacho. When you get down there, I'll give you a one-time number. You call me, then throw it away and never use it again. If we don't send you Mike, we'll send you Jackie. Jackie is even better than Mike." I glanced over at O'Connor. "He doesn't understand Spanish, but I would tell him to his face. He knows that Jackie is better."

"Whichever one is fine with me," I said. "I really appreciate it."

"Sure," said Pineda, smiling a predatory smile. He had gone for the bait. He thought that since he knew where Sonia and I lived, there was no longer any need to rush things. He could take whatever we had and then hand Sonia and me to Mejia gift-wrapped.

South suddenly reappeared, sidling into the room and just standing there, the fearbiter look more pronounced than ever. O'Connor and Libardo relaxed from their chores and drank some beer. After a moment they nodded to each other and got back to work. And I set to work loosening Pineda's tongue in front of the camera.

By 4:00, another 10 kilos of coke had been tested, and I had wheedled out of Pineda as much as he would ever say out loud to an undercover agent for the rest of his life. He repeated everything he had told me before about the German, emphasizing his government connections; he reaffirmed everything Sonia had said about the jewelry-for-cocaine trade with Mejia; and he repeated all his earlier statements about the size and importance of Mejia's organization.

This wouldn't be like the Suarez case, I thought. No matter how they try to hide Operation Hun, the video will be there as proof.

While it was tricky getting Pineda to talk freely and clearly, and to keep him near the Evil Eye or one of the hidden microphones, Espinosa took no prompting at all. The moment Pineda moved away from me to observe O'Connor and Libardo, Espinosa was at my side snorting coke, guzzling vodka, and talking my ear off. I had only to mention how unfair Sonia's treatment had been at the hands of Arce-Gomez, and the floodgates opened.

Espinosa, astonishingly sober for the amount of coke and alcohol he'd put away, recounted his role in the jewelry-for-cocaine deal. He bragged of other drug deals he'd taken part in, involving top figures in the Bolivian government.

I thought of Mario's words when I was trying to get him to let Hugo Hurtado live—"What he is saying will embarrass your government and mine." Now, listening to Espinosa talking about the same people, I wondered how many of those he had named were CIA assets. The spooks would go batshit if this videotape ever got leaked to the press.

By 6:00, only about half the cocaine had been tested and Ana's L.A. customers were due to arrive at any moment. It was time to blow the whistle.

Pineda was helping Libardo repackage the tested cocaine; O'Connor was working on his second tank of oxygen; Espinosa, slumped in a chair, looked like he needed oxygen.

"Eduardo " I said, looking at my watch, "let me make a suggestion

351

to save time." He paused and waited for me to continue. "Why don't you just take the rest of the stuff with you now and test it when you reach wherever you are going? I've got other customers in town and I'm way behind schedule."

The undercovers seemed to come alive with a barely perceptible but definite movement. Their eyes were suddenly wide open and watchful. Showtime!

"What if there's a serious problem with one of the bags?" asked Pineda, sensing the change in ambience.

"Look," I said, putting my hand on his shoulder, "I trust you." A great salesman had once told me that touching the customer somewhere is a great technique when making a sale. He stared at my hand as if to say, "What the hell is that doing there?" I quickly removed it.

"We've already tested about half the stuff," I persisted. "I'd say the average is about 50 to 60 percent pure, right? How far off can the rest be?"

Pineda was silent, his brain still absorbing the subtle change in attitude of the men in the room.

"I'll take the responsibility," I said. "I think I know enough about you by now to know that you're a man of your word."

"Do you?" he said, his wry smile telling me he wasn't buying it. There was something going on. He glanced around the room. Each of the eight undercovers had taken positions behind his men and covering the doors. There were no guns in sight, but the stony faces conveyed a threat just as deadly. I watched his face as he realized that he'd been finessed into a corner.

"Okay, then that's the way it'll be. Let's load the jeep," said Pineda with a strange air of resignation that amazed and depressed me. It was as though he knew what was about to happen and was telling me, "Okay, I'm dead, but was all this worth it?"

If O'Connor and Libardo had any idea that something was amiss they didn't show it. They went automatically and mechanically about the business of packing the drugs into the jeep, which was made difficult because they had to stuff 30 kilos into a secret compartment made to carry only 25. With the help of two or three undercovers, the packing took about an hour.

The job had just been completed when the phone rang. I took the call in the bedroom.

"My name is Victor Marini," said the caller. "You are expecting me."

"I'm expecting you?"

"Of course. I am here in Tucson representing Mr. Velasco. I am here to look at the contracts."

"Contracts?"

"Yes, the contracts," he repeated. "The items that I have the paper documents for."

"Look, I'm right in the middle of something. Can you call back, like in about 15 minutes?"

"You do have some contracts remaining, I expect?"

"Yes," I said, "I have more contracts than you can handle."

"Well I just wanted to make sure I could read the contracts first."

"When you get here you can read them, eat them, wipe your ass with them, anything you like. I'm busy."

When I returned to the living room, Libardo was fully dressed and ready to leave in the jeep.

"We'll give him about a half an hour head start," said Pineda, "time enough to get well out on the highway. Then your people can drive us back to the hotel."

"Of course," I said. "Why not relax for a few minutes and have a drink?"

The tough little Colombian was only minutes away from being arrested, and I felt oddly uncomfortable with the knowledge. I used to love the closing minutes of a case; seeing the shock on the face of the doper as instead of a suitcase full of dollars or dope he found himself at the wrong end of a dozen guns and glittering gold badges. Every third or fourth arrest ended with the doper losing control of his bowels. Some fainted, some had convulsive fits; during my career I had seen three die of heart attacks on the spot. I used to think they were just miserable fucking dope dealers who deserved whatever they got. I used to love what I did. But this day, all the joy was gone.

I stood in the doorway watching Libardo drive off in the jeep, following a car with two undercovers in it. They were to guide him directly to the highway. The two vehicles moved slowly down the deserted street, and then they were gone out of sight. Distantly I could hear a helicopter beating the air, then all was silent. I turned and went back into the house.

In the living room Espinosa, Pineda, and O'Connor sat quietly, drinks in hand. I entered the room and sat next to Pineda. All the undercovers were out of sight—an ominous fact that had not gone unnoticed by Pineda, who kept looking from one empty doorway to the other.

No one spoke for a long time. I could feel my heartbeat pulsing in my chest. Espinosa, his eyes wide, gulped down the remainder of a drink; his shirt was blotched with fresh patches of perspiration. O'Connor sat almost rigidly, his eyes fixed on Pineda as if looking for a cue.

Suddenly, several sets of wheels crunched in the driveway. Pineda looked at me, his face twisting into a purple grimace. He knew.

The front door crashed open. Gun-toting agents and cops charged into the room from every direction, shouting "Police!" "*Policia! Policia!*" "DEA! Don't move motherfucker!" "*No te mueves, hijo de puta!*" They piled on the three drug dealers like football players after a fumble. "Down! Get down on the floor, motherfucker!" "Spread 'em wide!"

One agent, who had spent the afternoon keeping Espinosa's glass full, kicked his legs out from under him. I quickly backed into the hall-way.

"You don't have to say nothin', motherfucker!" shrieked a voice. "*Vds Tienen el derecho a permanecer callado. Cualquier cosa que ustedes digan puede ser usada les encontra.*" "Whatever you say may be used against you!" "Where the fuck did you come from, blondie?"

The agents need not have said a word; the three men didn't utter a peep. They submitted quietly and followed all orders. As he was being handcuffed, Pineda looked around the room until he found me in the hallway. The look on his face was a promise that his hatred for me would never die, and would outlive any sentence a court might give him.

Minutes later I cracked the blinds open to watch the three being led to the cars. A crowd had materialized outside as if transformed from desert dust. They watched in silence as agents piled into cars, engines revved, and a caravan of a dozen cars roared away from the house.

Once again everything was strangely still. And I was utterly alone.

# 28

# Ana's Day
# of Reckoning

1

I stood in the hallway listening to the silence of the house trying to fathom what had just happened. I began pacing like a wild man. I had to stop the raging images of the past three years from overwhelming me.

I hit the floor doing a pushup-situp routine I had learned in martial arts training, driving my body as hard as it would go. I was right in front of the Evil Eye, but for the first time I didn't care. I had to burn the screaming hatred out of me. When the inspectors saw me on the video, they'd probably start wearing their guns to bed with them.

The phone rang, and I was immediately on full automatic. I sprang to my feet, raced to the bedroom, and had the recorder hooked to the phone before the third ring.

"I'm here," said Victor Marini, Velasco's man.

"Where's here?" I asked.

"The Granada Royale Hotel."

"Where is that?" I'd never heard of it.

He gave me the phone number and I wrote it down.

"Are you ready to do business or aren't you?" I no longer had any patience for the game.

"Yes, but I want to read the contracts before I sign them, if you know what I mean."

"But if you don't have any fucking documents, you can't read any fucking contracts."

"Look," persisted Marini, "no one signs a contract before reading it."

"I don't know you," I said. "You sound dumb enough to be a cop. For all I know you could be the head of the DEA."

"Hasn't Ana told you who we are?"

"Yes," I said.

"When is she coming to Tucson?"

"Why don't you ask her yourself?" *Please hang up on me. I've had enough. I just want to get on a plane and get out of here.*

"Are you sure you know who we are?"

"All I hear is blah, blah, blah, and I'm busy. I'll call you back when I'm ready."

For a few minutes I toyed with not saying a word about the phone call. Ana would get a get-out-of-jail-free card. If we were letting stone killers like Mejia, Roberto, and Carlos walk, why not Ana?

Then, as if there were a court battle raging in my head, I thought of one of my early supervisors—Al Seeley, chief of U.S. Customs Hard Narcotics Smuggling Squad. Al believed in the sanctity of an oath. I remembered him verbally savaging an agent for releasing a suspected cocaine smuggler because he "didn't think we had enough on him."

"You took an oath to put criminals in jail, not release them," Al said, sticking his forefinger in the man's chest. "Judges, juries, and district attorneys, they release people. You took the easy way out," he accused with another jab of his finger. "You were afraid of problems. You didn't want to take a chance. But taking chances is what you get paid for; that's why they gave you a gun and badge; that's what you swore you would do."

I never forgot that moment. Those words meant a lot to me; they made things really simple. Letting Marini go was the easy way out.

I was back to pacing when I heard a car pull up in the driveway. I raced toward the bedroom for my gun. I was still skidding down the hall when Sonia and Lydia rushed into the house.

"What happened?" asked Sonia, her eyes lit with excitement.

Lydia interrupted. "I'm gonna try and make some flight reservations. This thing's over, isn't it?"

"Ana's L.A. customer is in town," I said.

"But it won't go past tomorrow, will it?"

"I don't want it to. But I've gotta call Turghid."

"Well, I'll make reservations for tomorrow," she said, leaving Sonia and me standing in the vestibule. "If I have to cancel, I'll cancel."

"How did they take it?" Sonia asked impatiently. "Were they surprised? How did Mario react?"

"They were surprised, but they said nothing."

"Nothing?"

"Not a word. I'm sure you and I are never going to be far from their thoughts, but they said nothing. They were very calm."

She looked disappointed and afraid.

"Ana called," I said. "She sends you a big kiss."

"Oh?" Sonia was suddenly wary. "What happens with her now?"

"She's coming in the morning. Her customer is here from Los Angeles and she wants her commission."

"Will she be arrested?"

"It looks that way. You're not surprised, are you?"

Sonia hesitated a moment, trying hard to convey with her pretty face an empathy for another human being that perhaps she had never really experienced. She and Ana had lived through incredible adventures together. She shrugged. "And when will they get Papo?" Ana was now history.

"I don't think they have the slightest idea where he is."

"*La DEA*," she said, bitterly. "What fools."

I heard the sound of tires crunching gravel and moved quickly to the window. A car drove slowly by the house. I could see only its headlights in the dark. "What do you think Papo will do?" I said as I watched the taillights disappear down the block. "Run, or come after us?"

I turned, but Sonia was on the way down the hall to her bedroom, both hands clenched tightly.

"I don't know," she said over her shoulder. "You tell me."

Ten minutes later, I was speeding through the desert night to Turghid's office. I had called him to tell him about Marini's phone call and he had asked me to come in. He had actually sounded friendly, and that had me completely unnerved. But something else had me even more disturbed.

Just before leaving the house, I had picked up the kitchen phone to make a call and heard Sonia say, ". . . because he's a fool." Then a man's voice asked, "They said nothing? My name never came up? How can you be sure?" Then Sonia said, "*Callate!* Someone is on the line!"

I had hung up and moved quickly out the door. The man's voice sounded like Pachi's, but I had only heard his voice once; I just couldn't be sure. And to call him from the UC house? And who was "the fool?"

"Headquarters 's tickled pink," said Turghid when I walked into his office. "They're gonna hold off on a press release till the Arce-Gomez indictment."

"That's great," I said, wondering if Turghid really believed Arce-Gomez would be indicted. "And what about Papo? Anybody have any idea where he is?"

"He sure ain't in Tucson," said Turghid.

"Well, what about this guy Marini?"

"Somethin' fucked up about that guy. The Granada Royal ain't even in Tucson—it's in Phoenix."

"Phoenix?"

"He's there, which means he sure ain't here," said Turghid, really enjoying himself.

"Whatever," I said, finding the cheerful Turghid a lot harder to swallow than the one I was used to. "I'd like to get outta here as soon as I can, so just tell me what you want me to do."

Turghid's smile disappeared, and he drummed his thick fingers on the desk. "You jest tell that son of a bitch if he wants ta do a dope deal he better get his ass to Tucson."

I got to my feet. "If it's all the same to you," I said, "I'd like to finish my part in this thing and get out of here as soon as I can. I have some family problems."

"That's fine with me," said Turghid, his eyes unblinking black dots. "You can get outta here 's fast as you like."

As I started for the door, he added, "Real sorry to hear 'bout your family problems. By the way, how's that other li'l problem you got with Internal Security goin'?"

He wasn't even trying to be cute anymore—there was pure malice in his eyes.

"I guess it can't be too bad," I said, "they're letting me work for you."

At 10:30 P.M., alone in the kitchen, I hooked up the recorder and telephoned Marini in Phoenix.

"What the hell are you trying to pull?" I accused the instant he came on the line. "You're in Phoenix, not Tucson."

"I'm where?"

"You're in Phoenix, Arizona, and I'm in Tucson."

"How is this possible if I am in the same code of dialing with you?"

"Are you really that dumb?" I asked. *Come on, asshole, hang up so I can get out of here on the next plane.*

When Marini finally understood that he was 70 miles away from me, he said he would rent a car and be in Tucson in the morning. Even after I called him the Spanish equivalent of a jerk, idiot, and buffoon, he was still coming.

I hung up and called Turghid.

"Marini says he'll be here tomorrow."

"How 'bout when he gets here, you introduce another UC to replace you? And why don't you call Ana and make sure she gets here for her commission."

"She's already called. She's leaving Miami for here in the morning. Anything else?"

"Yes," said Turghid. "If you're not doing anything else, why don't you get back to work on those tapes."

## 2

The next morning, I awoke to bright sunlight. Dimly I could hear a phone ringing. A few moments later Sonia called through the door, "It's for you."

The house was quiet. Sonia was waiting for me by the kitchen phone. "I think it's the one from Ana," she said. "He's very polite."

"Yeah," I said, "that's him."

"I didn't want to say anything. I didn't know what you told him."

"Where's Lydia?"

"Where she always is, sleeping."

"Is anyone else here?"

"No one."

I picked up the phone. *"Hable."*

"It is I," said Marini.

"Don't tell me. Are you the same Victor Marini who couldn't find Tucson?"

"I have a reservation on the 10:40 flight to *Took-sone*," he said, still determined to ignore me.

"Marini, you're dazzling me with your footwork. One minute you're coming, the next you're not. Yesterday you were renting a car, today you're flying. Stop calling me. Just call me when you get here. In fact, I'm so fucking tired of talking to you, maybe it's better we call the thing off."

"No, no," said Marini quickly. "There are many others involved, and they are waiting . . . People of great importance."

"Yeah, I know all about it," I said. I hung up.

Sonia was watching me intently. "When will Ana be arrested?"

"It looks like very soon."

"It doesn't seem right," she said, for the first time looking genuinely concerned. But the hunted animal look in her eyes gave her away. Her concern wasn't for Ana. She was personally threatened by Ana's arrest—somewhere along the line her carefully protected world could collapse on her.

You know the truth better than anyone, Sonia. While you were queen, you kept these people in business. Whatever dope they got, they got from you; and to you they were nothing. You had hundreds of them living off you. You were the source of sources . . . the Queen of Cocaine. And now you're sending them to jail and you're not going. It doesn't seem right, does it Sonia? Not even to you.

"I already told you how it works," I said. "I don't make those decisions."

Sonia stared out at the pool, her jaw twitching slightly, the pupils of her eyes flicking back and forth.

The phone rang. "My people are now experiencing a great reluctance to come to *Took-sone,*" said Marini.

"Marini, you and your people can go fuck yourselves."

"No, no, no, listen. I beseech you . . ."

"The only reason I ever listened is that I respect Ana."

"Please, I wanted to communicate something to you . . ."

"Enough communicating!" I shouted. "Ana is on her way here because of you idiots. I only hope I can stop her." I slammed the phone down.

I thought about calling Ana. Perhaps there was time to stop her from coming. It would save her an arrest. What could they do to me? I was following orders, staying "on target." If whoever was running this madness wanted her badly enough they could indict her the way they were allegedly going to indict Arce-Gomez.

I thought of Al Seeley's words. I had taken an oath to put criminals in cages. But it didn't make sense to put someone like Ana in jail while we gave huge drug dealers like Sonia immunity and allowed murderers to go free. In a flash I understood the mind-boggling truth I might be forced to accept if I applied this newly discovered principle to the thousands I'd already arrested. Startled, I smashed the thought from my consciousness.

The phone rang again.

"This has all been a confusing mistake," said Hernando Velasco.

"Mistake, shit!" I said, "If you want to do business, say when and how, or stop wasting my fucking time." I slammed the phone down again.

It was now 10:30. Maybe there was time to catch Ana. Without a deal with Velasco, the case against her was no stronger than the case against Monica Garcia, and no one was even investigating her.

The phone rang.

"Miguel, this is Candy, Ana's daughter."

"Great! I was just about to call you."

"My mother just called me from the airport. Her flight just left, and she's on the way to you. She wanted me to call you to make sure someone met her."

By 2:30 Rudy, Sonia, and Lydia were on their way to the airport to meet Ana's flight. South had arrived at the house and immediately headed out to the pool house, supposedly to check on the recording equipment. No one had said a word about arresting Ana. Maybe after I told her that her California customers weren't going to show up, she'd be permitted to leave, just like all the others.

A little past 3:30 Ana walked through the front door followed by a good-looking young Latino in jeans. Ana, in sequined glasses, tight Capri pants—as usual a little baggy in the butt—and high-heeled clogs that she had difficulty walking on, clip-clopped straight for me with a big hug and a kiss.

"*Aiii*, Miguel, it is so good to see you again," she said.

"Me too, Ana," I said, feeling her warmth against me and a kind of numbness in my chest.

"This is Antonio," she said putting her arm around the young man's shoulders while holding her grip on me. "He's Candy's boyfriend. Isn't he adorable?"

"Nice to meet you," Antonio said in perfect English. He was a clean-cut kid no older than 20, with long, sun-streaked, dirty blond hair and an easygoing Miami smile. "Nice looking place."

"You ever been to Tucson before?" I asked in Spanish.

He answered me in English. "No, it's my first time." He looked at Lydia and lit up with a smile. He had a thing for her. Lydia looked away uncomfortably.

"What do you do?"

"I'm in my second year of college," he said. "Miami U."

Your college career might be coming to an end, my new young friend, I thought. It all depends on what you say.

"Those pants look so sexy on you," Sonia said to Ana, holding her hand and turning her with a touch and smile so loving and genuine that it chilled me.

"Do you mean that," said Ana, twisting and trying to see her own behind, "or are you just trying to make me feel good? You always do that. I can't tell whether you mean it." She kissed Sonia. "Miguel, do you know how wonderful she is?" She kissed Sonia again.

Sonia laughed. Her eyes twinkled brightly. They were a child's eyes, happy, innocent, and devoid of guilt. How did she do that?

"Is something wrong, Miguel?" said Ana. "You seem so . . . troubled. Something with your little girl?"

"It's your friends from California, Ana. They're acting strange." I summarized my conversations with Velasco and Marini.

"I'll call him right now," said Ana, and she dialed Velasco in Los Angeles while the rest of us took seats around the living room. Rudy opened the drapes to the pool area and let in the afternoon sunlight. "Does anyone want something to drink?" he said in Spanish.

"I'll have a coke," said Antonio, staring eagerly at Lydia, who was thumbing through a magazine as if she were in a doctor's waiting room.

South slithered into the room and stood near a wall watching us, an odd flushed expression on his face.

Ana's voice invaded from the kitchen, "You should have called me before I left Miami," she said. "No, of course not. You can't tell me one thing and then later change to another. No, this isn't just business; these people are my friends."

Antonio tried to get Lydia's attention. "Are you from here, Erica? Erica?"

Startled, I remembered that Erica was Lydia's undercover name. We had used it so little during the operation that I had almost forgotten it. I hoped that Lydia hadn't.

"Excuse me?" said Lydia, lowering the magazine.

"You from Tucson?" said Antonio.

"No. New York City."

"That's cool. I love the Apple—I go there a lot."

"Very nice," said Lydia, raising the magazine again.

I got to my feet and started toward the kitchen. Sonia followed me. Ana was still on the phone. She looked upset.

"So that's the way it is," she said. "Wait, I'll tell him." She turned to me and said, "The people with the money don't want to come to Tucson. Hernando says that he wants to come here with his own plane and pilot to pick up the 10 kilos, return to Los Angeles, and then return tomorrow with the money."

"Just tell him no, Ana," I said. "Tell him to forget about ever doing business with us."

"No," Ana repeated into the phone. "He said no."

Ana hung up. She was completely deflated. For a major *comisionista*, the loss of a $25,000 commission seemed to be hurting a lot more than it should have.

"I am truly sorry," she said, looking from Sonia to me. "You're my friends. I feel ashamed."

"Don't worry about it," said Sonia, taking her hand and rubbing it. She kissed Ana's cheek.

"If you don't mind, Miguel," said Ana, "I'd like to catch the next flight back to Miami."

I was relieved. I ordered Rudy to make reservations for Ana on the next flight out. "Sure thing," he said, giving me a little smile and wink. He looked as relieved as I felt. Operation Hun was almost over.

South had vanished again, so while Rudy was on the phone I fixed drinks for everyone. Ana suddenly beamed at me and raised her glass. I raised mine and said, *"Amor, salud, y dinero, Ana, y el tiempo pa' gozarlos."* Love, health, and money, and the time to enjoy them. And I really wished those things for Ana.

Rudy came to me and whispered that the next flight to Miami was at 6:30; it was already after four. Before I could say anything, South appeared in the doorway looking more animated than I had ever seen him. He motioned with a nod of his head that he wanted to talk to me. I followed South into the kitchen.

"Turghid wants you to lock the old bitch up," he said, grinning a mean grin.

I fought to stay calm. This was inevitable—she was just another doper.

"You and Rudy drive her to the airport and arrest her on the way." I said. "Your office is right there. Or if you think that's too dangerous, call Turghid and arrange for a couple of cars to meet you on the road."

"Mr. Turghid wants you to do it," he said slowly, savoring the moment.

"He said me personally?"

"You personally—he made a special point of it. You wanna call him?" South took a half-step back and made a flourish toward the phone. "Be my guest."

"No. I believe you."

"He wants me to drive and you to make the arrest. And he wants Lydia there 'cause she's female."

"Good thinking," I said, and headed for the living room.

"You gonna do it?" he said at my retreating back.

I didn't answer.

". . . and my husband is worse than ever," Ana was saying as I entered, "he's completely helpless. I don't know what to do, my darlings. I was counting on this money." Sonia's swift glance at me acknowledged that she knew it was all over for Ana.

"Ana," I interrupted, "we have reservations for you on a flight that leaves at 6:30. Why don't we leave now so that we're there in plenty of time. Maybe we'll have a little time at the airport for coffee and talk about our trip to Colombia."

"Wonderful idea, Miguel," said Ana, getting to her feet. Antonio looked dazed; he'd just completed a five-hour flight and was about to take another. The drug business was not as much fun as he had imagined. "You are coming with us, no?" Ana asked Sonia, who had not moved from her seat.

"No," I said quickly, "one of us has to stay here for some important phone calls, *mamita,* and I wanted the opportunity to talk with you for a while."

"Then I'll say goodbye now," said Ana, taking Sonia in her arms. There were tears in Ana's eyes.

"Why are you acting like it's the end of the world?" said Sonia, glancing at me.

"I don't know," said Ana, pulling out a handkerchief and wiping her tears. "Maybe . . . I don't know. I'm going to miss you."

"If you miss me, just call me when you get home," said Sonia.

Ana moved to hug Lydia.

"No, Lydia is coming with us," I said.

As we left Sonia said, "Don't forget. Call me when you get home."

Minutes later, with South at the wheel, Lydia sitting in front, and myself seated in the rear between Ana and Antonio, we were on our way. For the first 20 minutes Ana held my hand and chatted idly about everything from the failed cocaine deals and her money problems to the trip to Colombia. South kept watching me expectantly in the rearview. Lydia was inscrutable behind dark glasses.

As we neared the airport, I could see the flag flying over DEA's fortress. Ana suddenly leaned over and kissed me on the cheek.

"Thank you, Miguel," she said.

I never asked her what she was thanking me for, because at that moment I was reaching for my leather bifold that held my DEA badge and credentials. I raised it in front of her eyes, and the gold badge gleamed brightly in the late afternoon sun. I flipped it open so that she could see my photo ID. Ana stared at it for a long moment, and then sagged against me. Antonio gawked and then paled.

"Don't you move, fucko!" shouted South, slowing the car and twisting in his seat. "You're under arrest!" He was fumbling with his gun.

"That's cool, man. I'm not goin' anywhere," said Antonio, his eyes on the gun Lydia was pointing at him.

"What is this, Miguel?" said Ana, her voice a hoarse whisper, her body trembling against mine.

"It's who I am, Ana," I said. "I'm sorry. You are under arrest."

"Miguel," she sobbed, and she laid her head on my shoulder. Lydia reached over and patted her arm. "Why me, Miguel? I don't understand. The great DEA . . . why me? I am nothing. You could have had Pacho Cuervas, the biggest in Colombia. Why me?"

I held her for as long as I could. South pulled the car to the side of the road. Grinning, he held up a pair of handcuffs. "Buck wants her in cuffs," he said.

I have always believed that one of the reasons street agents live an average of only five years past their retirement is that, whether we like it or not, we get emotionally involved with our targets, our cases, and our informers—we're just too close, and it's a losing proposition. Maybe we all die of broken hearts.

# 29

# Escape from Tucson

## 1

In a bare, windowless room at the Tucson office, Ana was quickly dehumanized—stripped nude, all her body orifices searched by Lydia, fingerprinted, given a number, and photographed.

The next time I saw her she was seated at a desk in a corner of the big room, her skin a sickly gray, answering questions that a bored Chicano agent was reading off an Arrest/Personal History form. Lydia sat at a nearby desk making her final airline reservations. Antonio, who was going to be released and sent back to Miami on the next plane, was seated across the room from Ana. Rourke, a cigarette smoldering in the corner of his mouth, was busy pecking away at a typewriter while a half dozen agents and sheriff's deputies hung around murmuring among themselves. Ana had become "Hispanic female, age 50," and Operation Hun was already slipping into memory banks that were overflowing with operations and Hispanic females.

I sat at one of the desks just outside Turghid's office and dialed my answering machine in Virginia. The only messages I had were from a collection agency and from an insurance salesman. I kept listening to

366

them over and over. I wanted to get the hell out of Tucson as fast as I could, but to do that I had to first speak with Turghid, and I wasn't ready.

I could hear Turghid in his office congratulating South on his "outstanding job." Ana looked up for a moment and our eyes met. She lowered her head and looked away. South was suddenly standing over me.

"Mr. Turghid wants you to take a statement from her."

"What?"

"Mr. Turghid wants you to take a statement from Tamayo."

I stood and crossed the room. I motioned for Lydia to join me—I needed a witness and she spoke Spanish. I took a seat across the desk from Ana, and Lydia pulled a chair up alongside me. I inserted a fresh cassette into the recorder on the desk, pushed the record button, and read Ana her Miranda warnings in Spanish. Ana listened, her head bowed.

"Do you understand your rights, Ana?" I asked, concentrating only on what I had been ordered to do.

"Yes," she said, her voice barely audible.

"Ana, I've got to ask you everything you know about drug dealers. But you don't have to talk to me. It's your right to remain silent. In this country no one can hold it against you."

She looked at me for the first time.

"You already know everything," she said. "The biggest drug dealer I've ever known is Sonia Atala."

For the next hour or so I led Ana through a narrative of her years in the drug business. She had never handled drugs herself; she only introduced major sources of drugs to middlemen and earned a commission on the amount of drugs sold. And Sonia was her main source.

"Sonia was so big," she said, "that I used to get paid as much as $50,000 just for the introduction."

"Just for the introduction?"

"Yes, nothing more . . . she was the biggest."

I looked at Lydia, but the irony of arresting Ana and protecting Sonia seemed to be lost on her. She was simply anxious to finish and get home.

"Levine!" someone called. "Telephone."

I moved over to another desk and picked up the phone.

"Is she arrested?" said an excited Sonia. "How is she taking it? Is she cooperating?"

"Is that why you called?"

"No. Marini called. He said he is in Tucson."

"Where?"

"The Marriott. What about Ana? What did she say?"

"Did he leave a room number?"

"One thirty-eight."

I hung up on Sonia and almost blasted out of my chair. I transferred all my anger and frustration onto the faceless image of the man who couldn't find Tucson. If it wasn't for that motherfucker, Ana wouldn't be here.

"Don't go anywhere!" I said to Tommy, the agent who looked like me, and the few other agents who were still hanging around the office. They gawked as I jerked Turghid's door open and stuck my face inside.

Rourke and South looked up, startled. South flushed as if he'd been caught jerking off in the john. Turghid opened his mouth, but nothing came out.

"Ana's customer—the guy from L.A.—just called the UC house. He's at the Marriott waiting for me. I wanna go over there with a bunch of guys and see what he's got. If there's anything in his room, we'll lock his ass up right now."

Turghid stared at me. I was supercharged with adrenaline and ready to explode. I had to get off, and he was right in front of me representing everything I despised. Turghid must have sensed that.

"Okay," he said. "Take South with you."

After a wild ride across Tucson, myself, Tommy, South, and one of the Chicanos were in the hallway outside Marini's room. I tapped lightly on the door. It opened slightly. Tommy and I blasted inside, almost making a skinny little guy in a T-shirt and slacks part of the wall.

Victor Marini, alleged megaton drug dealer, was a skinny, violently trembling Colombian who at the moment was unable to control his bowels and bladder. As the stench spread through the room, no one said a word; Marini just gawked and trembled as we searched through dressers and luggage. When it looked like we weren't going to find anything, I said, "Okay, you wanted to meet me. I'm Miguel."

"Oh, don Miguel," said Marini, his eyes bugged out to the size of golf balls. He reached frantically for a towel on the bed and wrapped it around his middle. "I am so pleased and honored to finally meet you in person." He shoved his hand toward me, but I let it dangle.

"You here for business," I said, "or are you still talking shit?" The Chicano agent laughed. The stench was unbearable.

Marini rattled off something in a choked, quavering Spanish about trading a load of hashish that Velasco had hidden near Hollywood for cocaine, as he watched the agents poke through his belongings a second time.

"I just want to be sure you're not an agent or a cop," I said.

Tommy finally shook his head; the room was clean. Marini looked like he was about to cry. I didn't want to lose him. If Ana was in jail I wanted to see Marini and his Hollywood drug baron boss Velasco there also.

"I'm sorry," I said. "I can't take chances. You should have been straight with me."

"Please let me call Mr. Velasco," said Marini. "Please talk to him, don Miguel. Let him explain the situation to you, or he'll believe that I failed in my mission." With one hand clutching the towel, Marini reached for the phone. Moments later I was speaking with Velasco.

"We couldn't say it on the telephone," explained Velasco. "We wanted to offer the kind of deal that was hard to explain."

"Well, I'm sorry for the misunderstanding. But I'm leaving town tonight, anyway."

"Look, we really want to do business with you people. I have my own planes and pilots. I know all about Sonia. We ought to work something together. How much are you bringing back with you?"

"Maybe 300 to 500 rugs."

"I can handle the whole thing, easily," he said.

"I'm leaving town tonight," I said. "If you want to do business, you talk to my brother Tommy."

I passed the phone to Marini; after a half-dozen "yes sirs," he hung up. Tommy gave Marini an undercover phone number and we left.

Outside on the street, Tommy and the Chicano agent were laughing. Even the humorless South was smiling. None of them believed Marini would ever call. "How can he not know we're cops?" they said.

Actually, I thought, we had acted more like drug dealers than cops, recalling the kidnaping of Martinez and McCullough. I was sure that Marini would call, but I no longer cared. Operation Hun was over and my instinct was to run away from Tucson as fast as I could.

## 2

An hour later I was in the darkened DEA parking lot looking for the Lincoln—my brain was so scrambled I couldn't remember where we had parked it after Ana's arrest. Suddenly there were footsteps behind me, and I turned to see the glow of Rourke's cigarette coming my way through the darkness. Jack looked tired and disheveled.

"Where you heading?" he asked me.

"Out of here just as fast as I can."

He put his briefcase down. "If no one else tells you, you did a hell of a job."

"Thanks," I said. "If we at least get Arce-Gomez and Mejia it'll be something."

Rourke took a deep drag. "Ain't that the truth."

"What's the game plan?" I said, not liking the surrender I felt in his attitude. "When do you think Arce will be named?"

Rourke shrugged. "Your guess is as good as mine. I told you, there's some problems gotta be ironed out first."

"What kind of problems?"

"Mike, there's people in Bolivia right now—witnesses. They corroborate everything Sonia says; they put Arce-Gomez in the middle of a hundred dope deals."

"So what's the problem?"

Rourke took another deep drag and peered around nervously at the shadows. "What else? They're fucking CIA assets," he said bitterly.

This was the second time he'd mentioned this to me, but this time there was no hesitation. It had to be difficult for him to speak openly to me, to a "rogue" agent. It was a sign of the frustration he had to be feeling. Rourke was too good a narcotics agent not to be hurt deeply by what had been done to Operation Hun, but he wasn't about to take on the suits.

"So after all this shit about 'we gotta stay on target,'" I said, "the target's not even getting indicted?"

"They're discussing it. They're looking for a way we can do it without burning any of their assets."

"Who are probably bigger dopers than Arce-Gomez, right?"

Rourke said nothing. He looked very unhappy. At least I wasn't the only one feeling that way.

"Anytime there's a dope bust and the suits aren't fighting each other for TV cameras, you know something's wrong," I said. The arrests of Pineda and the others had not appeared in the press, and never would.

"Ain't that the truth."

"What about Mejia?" I said. "Anybody even looking for him, or do we gotta get the CIA's permission for him, too?"

"It's like I said, your guess is as good as mine."

"Jack, are you kidding me? Mejia too? I mean we might not be looking for him, but he sure the fuck is looking for me. To him, I'm no different than Sonia."

"It's not up to me," said Rourke wearily. "It's up to the U.S. Attorney."

"But is there even a possibility that he won't be indicted?"

"Before you cut out of here," said Rourke, bending to retrieve his briefcase, "make sure you get Turghid's okay."

"I'm serious Jack, is there a doubt that Mejia's gonna be indicted?"

"I'm doing my best, Mike, believe me. I gotta get going." He offered me his hand. "Just watch yer ass, ya hump, okay?"

"That's all I can do," I said, shaking hands.

Rourke's moment of weakness was over. I had wanted to ask him about Sonia, but I had the feeling that it didn't matter anyway; that not even Rourke knew the truth about her.

I drove the Lincoln out into the desert, feeling like a kid who got beat up by a bully every day on his way to school. I had to do something. I had to get my breakfast while I still could.

I went to a pay phone and telephoned one of the lawyers I had spoken to in the wake of the Suarez case. He had made the mistake of giving me his home phone number and telling me to call at any time. It was Saturday night, and in New York it was close to one o'clock in the morning.

"Who?" asked the attorney groggily.

"Mike Levine," I said. "The DEA agent who did the Roberto Suarez case; you and I had dinner together about a year ago."

"Okay, I remember. Christ, do you know what time it is?"

"Counselor, please, just bill me for it. I'm in the middle of something that . . . I just thought I ought to make damn sure there was someone other than me who knew the whole story and you already know the first part of it." I launched into the story of Operation Hun.

A few minutes later, I concluded, "And now, they're not only covering up for this German, Pacho Cuervas, and the others, my bet is that they're not even gonna indict Arce-Gomez and maybe not even Mejia either. And me they're still investigating—the same fucking investigation they were running on me when I first met you."

"Can you prove anything other than incompetence?" the lawyer said.

"Proof? Remember the Suarez case, how this whole thing got started?"

"Wasn't that something to do with a federal judge, or the U.S. Attorney in Miami dropping charges?"

"The U.S. Attorney drops all charges against one of the biggest dopers in our history, and then the CIA helps the son of a bitch overthrow Bolivia," I said, dimly realizing that I probably sounded like every nut case I ever interviewed.

"Yeah?"

"And then, with every informant we had predicting it was going to happen, a federal judge lowers the bail for Alfredo Gutierrez, and the guy is allowed to walk out of jail and get on a plane back to Bolivia. And DEA refuses to send one man out to follow him."

"What's your point? We went over all this before," he said, sounding annoyed. I was beginning to feel sorry that I'd made the call.

"What's my point? This isn't just any old drug case; this is the biggest case in our history. The Argentine secret police told me they're working for our CIA to help the same people I arrested take over Bolivia—they got the biggest drug dealers in the world released from jail and then helped them take over their fucking country. I'm now, right this minute, working undercover on the same people, and it's happening all over again. They're protected; the biggest dopers in the world are untouchable."

"What's this got to do with you personally?"

"Me personally? I'm a federal narcotics agent. I've spent my life trying to bring these guys down. I write a letter to *Newsweek* magazine and I'm put under investigation. They turn around and falsely accuse me of everything from going to bed with a married agent to playing my radio too loud. Christ—now they even have my fucking motorcycle under investigation. These are all events I can prove. These bastards are attacking me as personally as they can get. And now they're doing the same thing with Operation Hun and I'm into the same people again, the same dirty Bolivian government. Doesn't that sound like more than incompetence to you?"

"Levine, last time we spoke, you said DEA was harassing you, jeopardizing your life, damaging your reputation, and so on, right?"

"Yes."

"I think I told you then that on the basis of DEA violating its own procedures in handling your investigation, we might have a case, but you decided against litigation."

"That was then. Now they're doing it again. They've got me working undercover while they're trying to put me in jail. From where I am now it looks like the whole drug war's a fraud and anyone who threatens to expose it gets trampled. And they're doing it to me."

"Wait a minute. Now you sound like you want to take on the whole government. Most of what you're talking about has nothing to do with you."

"But it does—it's got to do with everybody. Our own government is behind the cocaine explosion in this country!"

"That may well be. But as a lawyer I can only litigate on the basis of what they do to you personally, not what they do to your cases."

"But that's the reason they're coming after me."

"Let me do you a favor and save you some money. It seems to me you need a politician more than a lawyer."

"You know one I could trust?" I said.

He was quiet for a moment. "Where are you calling from?"

"A pay phone just outside Tucson."

"You think that's smart?"

"I don't know. What do you suggest?"

"I don't think this is the type of conversation we should be having on a telephone."

He was right; one of the first rules of law enforcement was say on the telephone only what you would not mind seeing on the front page of the *New York Times*. Besides, why was I trusting this attorney—because he gave me his home phone number? He knew a lot of the suits personally. The agent who had introduced me to him had said he was a man who could "work things out with the suits without going to court." For all I knew, tomorrow he'd be telling my story on some radio talk show.

"I'll be coming to New York soon," I said. "Can I count on you to keep this confidential?"

"I've been practicing law for 20 years." He was angry.

"Okay, I'm sorry. I'm sorry to bother you at home." He was silent. "I'll see you in a couple of weeks."

"Fine," he said, and hung up.

We both knew I would never call.

I stood in the darkened phone booth for a long time listening to the dead line, waiting to hear some telltale click or noise. I had the same bad feeling as when I mailed the letter to *Newsweek*. I thought I might have just made a costly mistake.

## 3

It was just past midnight when I returned to the undercover house. I had carefully checked the neighborhood for anything unusual before I approached the house. As long as Papo Mejia was a free man, I would have to be wary of every pair of strange headlights that persisted in my rearview, of every lingering pair of eyes, and of every strange sound.

Sonia was standing in the hallway as I came through the door. "There was a call for you." She handed me a note. It said, "Call Mr. Arlington in Virginia whenever you get this."

For a moment I thought it was some kind of joke. Then I remembered—Arlington was a name the Rabbi said he would use if he had to get hold of me in an urgent situation. This was strange; the Rabbi hadn't spoken to me since I had returned from Argentina, and he hadn't even acknowledged me when we met in the elevator at headquarters. Why was he calling now?

"How is Ana?" asked Sonia, looking at me anxiously.

"Ana's destroyed," I said. "You wouldn't even recognize her."

"Is she cooperating?" asked Sonia, more nervous than I could ever remember her. "Did she say anything about me?"

"I don't know. I had to leave the office."

The phone rang. "Hello," I said.

"MIGUEL YOU MOTHERFUCKER!" shrieked Candy at the other end. "WHAT DID YOU DO TO MY MOTHER?" I held the phone away from me. "WHAT DID YOU DO TO MY MOTHER, YOU FUCKING LIAR?" she wailed. "YOU *HIJO DE PUTA*, I'LL KILL YOU IF YOU HURT MY MOTHER. HOW COULD YOU DO THIS TO HER?" I pushed the disconnect button.

"She's been calling all evening," said Sonia, looking cool and detached. "How could she know so soon?"

"Maybe they let her boyfriend make a phone call."

"All the world will know," she said.

"All the world knew the moment Mejia's people called an attorney."

Sonia shrugged. She was trying like hell to look indifferent, but her telltale eyes gave her away. She was afraid.

The phone rang. I picked up the receiver and heard Candy's shriek again. I pressed the disconnect button again, and when I heard the dial tone, I left the phone off the hook.

"It's tough," I said, "it's her mother. I have to leave for a little while. If it bothers you, leave it off the hook till I get back." I had to call the Rabbi from a pay phone.

Sonia was suddenly alert. "Where are you going?"

"Just out for a ride," I said, and I started toward the door.

"What happens with someone like Ana?" she asked.

I wasn't sure what bothered her more—what Mejia might do, or what Ana might say about her. "With a woman her age, no arrest record, sometimes the judges are lenient. Maybe they'll make a deal with her. She pleads guilty, maybe testifies against someone else. Besides, this is one case they aren't going to want any publicity on."

"I don't understand," she said.

"There's nothing to understand," I said, angry with myself for opening my big mouth. "It is what it is."

"That's not what you wanted to say!" she accused.

I paused in the doorway feeling the cool desert night at my back. Sonia studied me with the hungry eyes of an interrogator. "You just lived through everything I did. Figure it out yourself."

Suddenly she put her hand on my arm. "Can I come with you, Miguel? It's such a beautiful night, and I feel nervous." Her fingertips, then her palm pressed my skin. She was smiling, looking up into my eyes.

"You've got Lydia here if anything happens."

"Sure," said Sonia, her smile vanishing, her hand slipping from my arm. "What do you do all the times you go off by yourself?"

"I pray."

I found a pay phone in the parking lot of an all-night convenience store out in the desert. I dialed the Rabbi's number, deposited a handful of quarters, and waited for the connection to be made. I looked at my rented Rolex. It was almost 2:00 A.M.

The Rabbi picked up the phone on the first ring. "I hope it's you, you hardheaded Polack," he said, as if we spoke daily. "Where are you calling from?"

I looked around. "A phone booth out in the desert someplace."

"You check yourself for a tail?"

"Of course. Hey, what's going on? You got me scared shitless."

"You should be. Don't you remember I once told you that if you wanted to survive you'd have to learn to keep a low profile?"

"That's what I'm trying to do," I said. I felt dizzy, and I leaned my face against the cool glass of the booth.

"Not from what I hear. A lot of people are very upset with you."

"Upset with me? They ought to be upset with disappearing drugs, prosecutors and judges who let dopers out of jail, and drug cases too phony even for their press releases."

"I'm not arguing the merits of the drug war. I'm trying to give you some advice that may already be too late for you to follow."

His words hit me like a tub of ice water. "I'm sorry," I said.

"Now I'm going to ask you some questions, and I want truthful answers. Have you touched that woman?"

"Touched what woman?"

"The CI you're with."

"Did someone say that?" I punched the phone. "Am I being accused of that too? Did she accuse me . . ."

"Just calm down!" the Rabbi snapped. "You didn't answer me."

"An emphatic fucking no."

"If you're telling me the truth you have nothing to worry about."

"Then I have nothing to worry about."

"One more question. Have you contacted anyone outside the agency about the case you're working on?"

"Why, has anyone said I did?"

"That's not a negative answer."

"Why, is someone afraid of something?"

"Mike, I called to try to help you, not to joust with you."

"You know, I'd like to see the faces in headquarters when a judge sees a videotape of the defendants in this case testing drugs—that supposedly came out of the DEA lab at almost 90 percent pure—at 50 and 60 percent and hear the dopers calling it 'garbage.'"

"It might not work out quite the way you think," he said flatly.

I went cold inside. "What do you mean?"

Way out in the desert, a car hit its brakes and started to turn around. I had not seen it pass.

"I mean," he said, "don't count on that little scenario you just painted ever happening."

"I don't understand," I said, my heart starting to pound. Now the car was approaching rapidly.

"If I say anything further, I might be putting you in a position that you'd have to either perjure yourself on a witness stand or testify about this conversation. And if for some reason there is no trial—if they all, for instance, plead guilty—you'll never know the difference anyway. There's no way you can officially know what I know, so I'm not going to say anything."

"I can't believe this," I said.

The car pulled into the parking lot. There were two men inside, and both eyed me closely as they parked beside my car.

"Believe it," said the Rabbi. "Have you heard anything about your own investigation yet?"

"All I know is they're still working on me."

"Your file's been sent to the U.S. Attorney's office for a decision on whether or not to prosecute you."

"Prosecute me! For what—playing my radio too loud?"

"I don't know. But they're going to be looking for anything they can find. If I were you I'd take it seriously."

"To me these bastards are as serious as cancer. You know what they pulled on me in Miami?"

"I saw your memo," he said, "and so did a lot of other people. You know an assistant U.S. attorney named Pat Sullivan?"

"Miami."

"He has your case file."

"Oh Jesus. He's the same guy who released Gasser; now he's gonna decide whether or not to prosecute me? I don't even know what they're prosecuting me for. What am I supposed to do?"

"First of all, calm down. No decision has been made yet. So if I were you I'd try to make all the friends I could and get my butt out of Tucson fast."

The two men were out of their car, and walking slowly toward me around opposite ends of the car. I slipped my 9mm out of the leather bag.

"Are you still there?" said the Rabbi.

"Hold on just a sec," I said, straightening and holding the gun behind my hip. I flicked the safety off and pushed the accordion door open a crack.

"Can I help you?" I snapped at the closest of the two, his features obscured by the shadow of his cowboy hat. The other had halted in the shadows behind me.

"Jest waitin' to use the phone, partner; you gonna be long?"

"Yeah, sorry," I said.

"This here Lincoln yours?"

"Yeah."

"Nice lookin' machine. Ain't it, Will?"

"Sure is," said the other guy.

"I don't know what you two motherfuckers got on your minds," I

377

said, gripping my gun tighter. "But you're in the wrong place. The phone's busy and the car ain't for sale."

The guy in front of me chuckled softly. "No problem," he said. He and the other retreated to their car.

"I'm sorry," I said, "a couple of wiseguys wanted to use the phone." I slipped my gun back into the bag.

"I heard," said the Rabbi. "This time of night, your particular phone in all Tucson? You must be getting slow in your old age."

The car rolled slowly out of the parking lot, its lights off. Once it hit the highway, its engine roared, its lights came on, and within seconds it disappeared in the distance.

"I once told you to watch out for a peanut butter sandwich, didn't I?" said the Rabbi.

"Yeah, and I guess I didn't believe you. I still don't want to believe you."

"That's unfortunate." His voice was suddenly tired. "It's late."

"I don't know how to thank you."

"Forget it. There are a few of us besides yourself who don't agree with some of the things we see going on. But unlike you, we don't feel we have all the answers."

"Answers?" I laughed. "Did I ever say I had any answers?"

"I'm afraid I've been on the phone too long," he said. "Watch your back. I wouldn't want to see anything happen to you." He hung up.

After I replaced the receiver I waited for the phone to ring. There must have been 10 or 15 minutes of overtime on the call, and I didn't want the phone company billing the Rabbi for it; that would provide a permanent record of the phone call. We hadn't committed any crime, but why take a chance? I waited about five minutes, and the phone never rang. It was strange.

On the drive back to the house I thought about the Rabbi. It was hard for me to believe his motivation in warning me was simply his professed admiration for my career or his disagreement with some DEA policy or whatever it was that his veiled reference referred to. He was, after all, a suit. But I knew there were some who hadn't sold out to the politicians, the CIA, and everyone else who had their hands in the drug war grab-bag; Ralph Saucedo had said that some people in headquarters supported what I was trying to do. I had to believe the Rabbi was one of them. I had to believe in someone.

✽  ✽  ✽

# 4

I returned to the house a little after 3:00 A.M., and didn't fall asleep until well after dawn. I awoke in the afternoon, and I felt better. At least I knew the score. Knowing the worst is better than knowing nothing; you do what you can to remedy the situation, then sit back and relax. It was in God's hands.

I telephoned Turghid to ask permission to leave Tucson. He sounded jovial. "We jest busted yer good friend Marini, along with some asshole pilot from San Francisco named Don Wilson Camp. You know the name?"

"No. He must be Velasco's pilot."

"Yeah, well he can kiss his fucking plane goodbye; the asshole brought a sample a hash in it. Had a real good-looking babe with him, but we're prob'ly gonna let her go."

"Too bad," I said.

"Yeah. Tommy did a hell of a job." He laughed.

"Well, you're not going to need me any longer, are you?"

"I want you around till the AUSA's in tomorrow; just in case he needs you for anything. And don't forget. While you're here, keep workin' on those tapes."

I told Lydia she would have to cancel her reservations one more time—no way was I going to spend the night alone in the house with Sonia—and I hopped into the car and headed to the gym. Besides wanting a tough workout, I wanted to say goodbye to Sam and Morris. I found Sam alone in the sauna. He didn't look so good.

"So, Mr. Big Shot," he said. "I don' see you in a vile. I thought you vent back already."

"No," I said, gingerly taking a seat on the hot bench beside him. "I'm leaving though. I wanted to say goodbye to you guys. Where's Morris?"

"Morris," he said nodding his head up and down, and then shaking it sadly. "Morris is not so good."

"What happened?"

"A stroke . . . three days ago in the middle of the night."

"Damn! I can't believe it. He was like an ox. How is he?"

"Like an ox," he repeated, still shaking his head. "It's not good. God should only forgive me, but vat's left of him . . . *Gornisht halfin.*"

"Sam, I'm so sorry," I said, putting my hand on his shoulder. He covered it with his gnarled old hand, and looked into my eyes. There was a sadness in those faded blue eyes that jabbed something deep and tender inside me.

"You're a good *boychick,* Levine. I told Morris—Morris thought maybe you vas in a little hanky-panky—but I said 'Morris, dis is a good *boychick.* I can tell.'"

"Thanks Sam. I hope I deserve that."

"You should listen to an old man, Levine. You got children?"

"Yes."

"You should enjoy dem vile you can. Hug dem, squeeze dem. Soon they're big and you're old and it happens so fast you can't believe it. It's like a dream."

He used my grandma's words. Michaela, life is like a dream . . . like a dream.

On Monday morning I awoke to the sound of the telephone ringing. It was 7 A.M., an odd time for drug dealers or government agents to be calling unless there was an emergency. It kept ringing. I groped around for the recorder. By the time I got out to the kitchen Sonia was coming down the hall. I picked up the phone. It was our answering service.

"There is an urgent message for Mr. Miguel and Sonia," said a woman I didn't recognize as one of the regular operators.

"Go ahead," I said.

"Someone named Guacho called and said you should call him right away." The woman gave me a local phone number.

I thanked her and hung up. Sonia was staring at me. I must have turned pale.

"It's Papo," I said, dialing the number. "He left a phone number here in Tucson."

I let the phone ring for a very long time before I hung up. It was probably a phone booth.

"He's not there," said Sonia coolly. "He'll never be there. He's just letting us know that he won't forget; that he doesn't care where we are; that we can be reached. You think he fears *la DEA*?" She laughed a short, nasty bark. "He'll have patience. When you think he's no longer a danger is when he'll strike."

"You know that man ain't here," snapped Turghid, annoyed that I had called him at home.

"I just thought I'd pass it on to you," I said. "It's my job."

*   *   *

I made flight reservations for New York, leaving at midnight Monday. Operation Hun—and maybe the whole bogus drug war—was over for me. But without the drug war, what kind of life did I have? For 17 years my career had replaced all that makes a life worth living—family, friends, just watching a sunset with someone you love. Besides being my only source of income, my job had become my identity. Now both my identity and my freedom were in jeopardy.

Later in the afternoon, Rourke came by to take Sonia and Lydia to the airport. I helped them load their bags into the car.

"Goodbye," said Lydia, shaking my hand, looking like she was about to cross the finish line of a marathon.

"I guess we'll see each other at the trial," I said, opening the door for her. She nodded and got in the car. There really wasn't much else to say.

"See you in headquarters, ya hump," said Rourke, already seated behind the wheel. We shook hands.

Sonia was already in the back seat, and I looked at her feeling awkward, not knowing what to say. Rourke pulled the car out of the driveway, and Sonia turned and waved out the back window. She was smiling.

I was alone. Suddenly, a terrible chill hit me. The last place I wanted to be alone was that undercover house. I had to get out of there as fast as I could.

I rushed through the house gathering my belongings. Every little noise suddenly became a threat. The air conditioner clicked on and my heart almost stopped. I kept checking the windows, expecting to see strange cars stopping in the driveway.

It was a natural setup. I had been forced to stay an extra day; everyone knew I was alone. Papo's call had come that morning, and a lot of people thought I knew too much. If I were killed, the blame would automatically be placed on Mejia.

By 4:00 I was packed and on the road. I had eight hours to kill before my flight, but I didn't mind in the least. I tore out of that driveway and never looked back. I was supposed to wait for the AUSA's approval to leave, but I no longer cared.

# PART THREE

# SONIA'S SECRET

The presidents and prime ministers are the ones who make the underground deals and speak the true underground idiom. The corporations. The military. The banks. This is the underground network. This is where it happens. Power flows under the surface, far beneath the level you and I live on. This is where the laws are broken, way down under, far beneath the speed freaks and cutters of smack.

—Don Delillo, *Great Jones Street*

# 30

# Protecting the Oasis

*I personally am convinced that the Justice Department is against the best interests of the United States in terms of stopping drugs. . . . What has a DEA agent who puts his life on the line got to look forward to? The United States government is not going to back him up. I find that intolerable.*
—Representative Larry Smith, chairman of the House Task Force on International Narcotics Control, investigating our government's actions pursuant to the torture death of DEA agent Enrique "Kiki" Camarena.

On Monday, May 17, three weeks after my escape from Tucson, one of the most bizarre bureaucratic reorganizations in law enforcement history threw our federal drug enforcement effort into hopeless disarray, and probably saved me from being fired.

It happened just like Tony Buono said it would. All of DEA headquarters was shifted to the desk concept, and Monday was moving day. I was transferred from the abolished South American Unit on the fourth floor to the Heroin Desk on the sixth floor. The move rescued me from Terry Burke, the Marijuana Desk, and the relentless scrutiny of Tommy Dolittle, and placed me under the command of Kevin Gallegher.

Gallegher, a dapper, gray-haired veteran of decades of drug wars in Europe and Asia, was too much his own man to do a hatchet job for the suits. He had only one question for any subordinate: Can you lock up drug dealers? If you could do that, you could do no wrong. He was neither politician nor suit—he was a professional narcotics agent. I thought perhaps he was one of those quiet dissenters in the upper ranks whom the Rabbi had mentioned.

On that insane Monday, every DEA employee in headquarters was ordered to move to his or her new assignment at the same time. Elevators and stairways were jammed with people carrying files, office supplies, and personal belongings. The havoc the absurd restructuring of DEA caused in those halls was soon mirrored in all the agency's enforcement efforts. It continues to this day.

I ran into Tony as he struggled to free himself from a jammed elevator. "Hey, Mikey!" he called, laughing. "What'd I tell ya?"

"You sure did," I agreed.

He took a furtive look around. "Hey, whatsa difference between DEA and the *Titanic*?"

"What?"

"The *Titanic* had a fucking band." He guffawed and continued on his way.

On May 18, Rourke came into my office. I hadn't seen him or heard his voice in three weeks.

"You ready to go back to Tucson?" he asked.

"Do I have a choice?"

"Nope! They want you to get your undercover reports up to date. We're going to trial." He pulled up a chair across the desk from me.

"How's Ana doing in jail?"

"You mean you didn't hear?"

"I haven't heard a thing about anything," I said. "How would I hear unless you tell me?"

"Ana made bail—they lowered it from $1 million to $20,000. She's skipped back to Colombia. We're declaring her a fugitive now."

The news caused an odd mix of emotions in me. I was glad that Ana was out of harm's way—under Colombian law, their citizens could not be extradited to other countries for drug charges. Ana would never be able to return to the United States, which seemed enough of a penalty for her. But the radical dropping of her bail smacked of cover-up, CIA style.

I wondered how long it had taken the suits and the CIA to realize that if Ana went to trial, her attorneys and the press would have a heyday with all the unanswered questions left by Operation Hun, not the least of which was how much she really knew about Sonia Atala, their star informant and asset. Just like in the Suarez case, when CIA operations and programs were threatened, defendants were mysteriously released from jail and the case was destroyed.

"What about Mejia? He's been declared a fugitive, hasn't he?"

Rourke looked embarrassed. "He hasn't been indicted."

"That sucks!" I snapped. "The son of a bitch is out there hunting me, and my own agency hasn't even gotten an arrest warrant for him?"

Rourke frowned and nodded his head, "You're right. I wish there was something I could tell you, Mike."

"Is he gonna be indicted?"

He shrugged. "I wish I knew."

"You mean he might never be?" I had a feeling that Rourke wanted-ed to tell me something, so I had to control myself; one wrong word and I'd turn him off. My life could depend on what Rourke did or did not tell me.

"I'm saying I just don't know, Mike."

"Well, who is indicted?"

Rourke looked around unhappily. "Right now," he said, "the only ones indicted are the four guys who came to the house and Ana. And we've got Ana on a separate indictment with your friend Marini and that pilot."

"You mean, after all this shit, Mejia and Arce-Gomez are off the hook and we indict Ana Tamayo twice?"

The ludicrous words seemed to hang between us. Rourke looked as upset as I felt. Neither of us had become DEA agents to take part in anything like this.

Rourke shook his head sadly. "It's the Agency," he said so low that I could hardly hear him. It was as if he were afraid of hearing his own voice.

"What?"

"It's the Agency," he repeated. "They're claiming that if we go ahead with the Arce-Gomez indictment we'll be jeopardizing important programs in Bolivia."

"Yeah," I said, forcing a laugh, "important programs. They're afraid the world'll find out there wouldn't be a cocaine government in Bolivia if it wasn't for the CIA. What about Mejia? Is he also under their wing?"

He was thoughtful for a moment. "I doubt it. The AUSA doesn't think there's enough evidence to indict him."

I felt the blood rush to my face. "Even with that tape recording of him and Sonia?" I said, my voice rising in spite of my best efforts.

"That's enough to convict Mother Theresa. The guy's a stone killer. If DEA doesn't care about me, what about Sonia? Mejia's not gonna forget her. How do these people do it? How do they let murderers off the hook and live with themselves? And who do we indict? Ana Tamayo—twice. Wow!" I threw my hands up. "Another major victory in the drug war."

"Do you think it's me making these decisions, ya hump? I'm working on the fuckin' Marijuana Desk, and my boss is already breaking my balls wanting to know when I'll be finished with this thing. Meanwhile, I'm still pissing people off pushing for the Arce-Gomez indictment. In the meantime, what are you doing?"

"What am I doing? Whatever I can to survive, Jack. Whatever it takes."

I had still gotten no word on my Internal Security investigation, and I was frankly a frightened man—frightened of every strange face I saw more than once, of every strange click on my telephone, of every official envelope addressed to me that might announce my firing or my indictment, of every knock on my office door and every phone call. The inspectors were still rummaging through my life, and I had to wait for them to finish before I could even start rebuilding it. Right then, I was hardly the man to blow the whistle.

But I was also having a hard time living with myself doing nothing. After Rourke left, I dialed the Rabbi's extension. We hadn't spoken since my phone call from Tucson. I'd been hoping that he'd call me or give me some signal that there was no problem between us.

"How about meeting me for coffee?" I asked him. "Something just came up, and I need to talk to someone."

He was quiet. "Okay," he said finally. "Why don't you take a walk in the park across Fourteenth Street. I'll join you in a little while." He almost sounded as if he'd been expecting my call.

I crossed Fourteenth Street to a small park on Franklin Square directly across the street from headquarters. The park, easily visible from the DEA building, was a depressing montage of dead trees, rotting benches, graffiti, and dog shit. It was populated by vagrants, winos, druggies, and legions of aimless, vacant-eyed madmen. I thought it an odd choice for our meeting.

I sat on a bench that seemed almost shielded from the DEA windows by the heavy branches and sparse greenery of an old oak tree. About 40 feet away I watched a kid of about 15 in a baseball cap make a drug sale to another kid his age. Baseball Cap glanced in my direction and for a moment our eyes met. He tapped the bill of his cap and nodded his head. He wanted to know if I was buying. I looked away and saw the Rabbi approaching. He was eating an ice cream pop. The kid saw him too, and took off. The Rabbi looked like "official business."

The Rabbi carefully cleaned a spot on the bench beside me with his handkerchief and sat down.

"Beautiful day," he said.

"Aren't you a little nervous?" I asked, looking up toward the DEA building.

"Why should I be? You and I know each other; we work for the same agency, don't we? If people saw us meeting in an alley or looking like we're trying to hide I'd be nervous. I don't have anything to hide. Do you?"

"I don't, but evidently a lotta other people do," I said, and quickly summarized my earlier conversation with Rourke. "Look," I concluded, "I know there's nothing I can do about anything, but doesn't anyone on the twelfth floor lose sleep when we intentionally destroy drug cases? Especially one that had the potential this one had."

The Rabbi ate the remaining morsel of ice cream, and sucked the stick clean. "The best part," he said. He peered around the garbage-cluttered park for a wastebasket. The nearest one was about 50 feet away and was overflowing. He folded the stick and paper into a small wad and held it tightly in his fist. For a moment I thought he was going to shove it into his pocket, but he didn't; he just held it.

"You know, Levine, this is far from a perfect world. As much as we hate to admit it—as important as we think we are, and what we're doing is—sometimes there are other interests that take precedence to ours. Now that's a hard thing for some of us to admit—especially when we lay our lives on the line for what we believe in. But sometimes we have to just have faith that there are people running things who may know a little more than we do."

"You mean like the people who decide which dopers get get-out-of-jail-free cards?" I said.

He stared at me. "Yes."

"But how do we justify it? How do we send guys out to die trying to take a couple of ounces of powder off the street, while people cashing the same green paychecks are protecting the guys who put tons of powder out there? And what about the kids the politicians keep bleating about—is it all hype?"

"You're no fool, Michael," he said. "The world is a lot more complicated place than that."

"Boy, am I learning that the hard way."

"DEA doesn't function in a vacuum. America is like a sweet-smelling oasis in the middle of a shithouse; everyone wants in. If you're lucky enough to live here you lead a blessed existence. But with our blessings come lots of enemies who want to take it all away from us. In the 1940s it was the Nazis and the fascists; now it's the commies. God only knows who's next. The point is, maintaining our strength and defending our way of life are priorities that come before everything."

"Including the drug war," I said.

"Especially the drug war," said the Rabbi.

"Especially?"

"Especially," he repeated. "Who do you think the strongest, most violently anti-communist faction in the Third World is?"

"American bankers."

The Rabbi laughed. "Them too. Hey, you ever think of joining the spooks?"

"I doubt if they'd hire me."

"You never know." The Rabbi looked at me. "You know what the domino theory is?"

"Whoa! DEA didn't kill all my brain cells yet. I was reading newspapers during Vietnam."

"You weren't there were you?"

"Nope. I got discharged from the service in '61."

"But you served."

"Sure. It was the law."

"Well, what would you have done if they'd ordered you to Nam?"

"Back then . . ." The image of a 19-year-old, gung-ho sentry dog handler in spit-shined boots and Ridgeway fatigue hat flashed in my mind, ". . . I'd have gone and probably died," I said.

"Sure, you'd have gone," said the Rabbi.

"But I was 19 and didn't know my ass from my elbow. Don't ask me what I'd have done if I knew what I know now. The trouble is, the same thing is happening to me with the drug war."

"I understand," said the Rabbi, "but try to visualize a Vietnam-type situation in this hemisphere; right next door maybe, in Mexico."

"Okay," I said, "I see your point." I didn't, but if I got into an argument with him, I didn't want it to be over Vietnam.

"You know a lot about Bolivia. Why do you think that black-heart-ed son of a bitch Castro chose Bolivia as a primary target for communism and sent in Che Guevara, his top man?"

"I suppose because it's the poorest country in South America."

"Give the man a lollipop," said the Rabbi. "Hungry people do have a tendency to change governments. And do you think just because old Che ended up where all good commies belong, they're going to give up trying to turn Bolivia?"

"I don't suppose so," I said.

"And if the domino theory is correct and they get Bolivia, what's next?"

I shrugged. "The South Bronx, I hope."

The Rabbi laughed again. "The point is, Michael, we cannot let them take Bolivia, no matter what."

"Even if we have to support drug dealers?"

"When I said 'especially the drug war,' I was thinking of countries like Bolivia where drug crops feed a lot of people. These people have to keep eating, Michael, or they become vulnerable to change. And 'change' in our hemisphere is something America must keep a tight control over."

"You left something out," I said.

"What's that?"

"The only export Bolivia's got that's making any money is cocaine, and they supply Colombia with most of their coca base; and for two flat-on-their-ass broke countries, they sure owe our bankers a lot of bucks. We wouldn't want to see our bankers lose any money now, would we?"

"Let's not get cynical."

"Cynical? It's a fact, isn't it?"

"It may be a fact, but protecting banking interests is not a DEA consideration."

"What about mass murderers?" I said, unable to contain myself any longer. "Anybody upstairs lose sleep when we let 'em go? Mejia killed a man because he owed the guy money. Then he wipes out the guy's whole family—women, kids, old men, the works. He once shot a guy for not saying hello to his father. What reason could anyone possibly have for protecting a beast like that? If you call yourself a lawman and have the chance to put that animal in a cage and don't—for any reason—how can you continue calling yourself a lawman?"

The Rabbi's eyes looked troubled. "Mistakes happen, Levine; the wisest of us make them."

"Yes," I said, "and then somebody in charge jumps in our face and says, 'Hey, you screwed up!' Or you get arrested. But what happens when the people in charge are screwing up and they are the law? Or worse, they're above the law? And who does a DEA agent turn to when he lays his butt on the line against a murderer, gets enough evidence to arrest and convict him, and ends up with the killer hunting him and his own agency not lifting a finger to protect him?"

The Rabbi once more stared at me thoughtfully. I noticed the bent pop stick and paper fall from his hand. He suddenly looked at his watch. "I've got to be heading back," he said, getting to his feet. "I can't promise you anything, but I am going to make a couple of inquiries."

"I'll come with you," I said.

"No," he said quickly. "Why don't you just relax for a few minutes."

"Look, if I got a little out of line . . ."

"You think you were out of line?"

"Not really. For all I know Mejia's somewhere in this park."

He smiled. "Let's hope not."

I watched him walk quickly out of the park and back to headquarters.

As it turned out, whatever "inquiries" the Rabbi made must have worked a minor miracle. On Wednesday, May 20, I got a call from Ollie South.

"Mr. Turghid asked me to call," he said curtly.

"What can I do for you?"

"Well, you know the phone call that Sonia and you taped with Mejia?"

"Yeah, what about it?"

"Mr. Turghid wants to know if it incriminates Mejia."

The question was either incredibly dumb or incredibly sinister. It took me a moment to gather my wits and decide on the latter. "I already translated that tape; I left it with you."

"Yeah, I know. But it's in Evidence [DEA evidence vault] and I'm supposed to get the information for the AUSA."

"You're indicting Mejia?"

"I suppose so," said South.

I allowed myself the quiet joy of one of the few moments of triumph I would experience during the 1980s.

"I don't understand your question. I wrote out the translation of that tape and gave it to you, along with the others. Couldn't you see that it was incriminating?"

"Uh, I, uh, don't have it."

"You don't have my translation?"

"Uh, it was probably put in the evidence envelope with the tape."

"So I guess you didn't read it and you don't have it."

"Uh, it must've been one of those things that fell through the cracks. You know how many tapes I had to handle?"

"If that's the case," I said, "let me tell you that the Mejia phone call is the single most damaging, most incriminating piece of evidence I've ever seen or heard against any doper I have ever gone to trial against in my 17 years as an agent."

"Um-hmm," said South.

"In fact, it's probably the most important piece of evidence in that whole case."

"Um-hmm."

I felt a pang of fear. "You haven't lost that tape, have you?"

"I haven't lost anything," said South.

"If it's lost, you just blew the whole case against him."

"As far as I know, it should be in Evidence."

"What do you mean, 'As far as you know?'"

"As far as I know, I put it into Evidence," he said defensively.

"Then it should still be there, right?" I said.

"Yes . . . as far as I know."

"As far as you know," I repeated, wishing I could reach through the telephone and grab him by the neck. But his day was coming, I thought. Sooner or later he and Turghid—or somebody—would have to explain the cut cocaine we had in Tucson. If South wasn't dreading that day, somebody was. I couldn't resist a little probe.

"Is anyone transcribing the videotape of the drug testing?"

"As far as I know," said South.

Alarm bells went off in my head. When I had talked about the videotape with the Rabbi, he had said, "don't count on that little scenario you just painted ever happening."

"There's no problem is there?" I asked.

"Not that I know of," he said.

"They're gonna need my help transcribing that tape," I said. "Tell whoever's doing it to call me."

"Why would they need you?"

"It's a four-and-a-half-hour tape," I said. "There was a lot going on, a lot of talking at the same time, that kind of stuff. I was right there, so I can clear up any confusion. I also want to make sure the translation is accurate, and it'll give me a chance to go over the whole thing before I testify. You know, refresh my recollection."

"I'll pass it on."

"You do that."

I was never called to help transcribe the tapes. When I arrived in Tucson to testify in the trial of Mejia's drones, I learned that the sound was missing from all the drug testing videotapes. I was told that South had made some kind of error—no one knew what kind—with the recording equipment. South swore that to his best recollection he had checked the equipment and it was operating properly. No one questioned him nor was the matter investigated any further.

On June 29, Papo Mejia was finally indicted and an arrest warrant issued. On August 2, Mejia and Ana were finally listed as DEA fugitives, but with no extradition treaty with Colombia, there was little hope that they would stand trial in the United States. Arce-Gomez, the "target" of Operation Hun, would not be indicted in an American court. The CIA's wishes prevailed, and their secret programs were safeguarded.

# 31

# Pandora's Box

On August 11, 1982, the U.S. government went to trial against the four Mejia drones. The case received very little local and no national press coverage, totally out of character for the DEA suits, who usually scramble after the media like monkeys after a banana. However, the real Underground Empire could not have given the court case more attention.

A special attorney, allegedly out of the Department of Justice in Washington, was assigned to Tucson to assist the local AUSA, Negatu Molla, prosecute this relatively easy reverse undercover case. In all my years of federal service, I never saw "Main Justice" show that level of concern for any drug prosecution.

"How come an attorney all the way from Washington?" I asked Molla, an easygoing African emigre officially charged with the prosecution.

"They said that she's new, and they wanted her to get some trial experience," said Molla.

"In Tucson? All the way from Washington to Tucson for experience? You think they could have found some big drug trials in Miami or New York, or right there in D.C.?"

Molla laughed. "Who knows? That's what they told me."

Jane (name changed) had curly hair and the wide-eyed look of a perpetually amazed high school senior. She looked more like an understudy for the lead in the musical *Annie* than a special attorney. But after talking to her for two minutes I knew she was neither an innocent nor a young attorney needing experience. She was full of questions, curious about everything but divulging nothing. If she had been sent to Tucson for experience, it certainly wasn't as a prosecutor. Rourke later confided that she reported to the CIA. It was no surprise. I named her "CIA Girl" and tried to steer clear of her.

However, it became impossible to do this, as CIA Girl turned out to be ever-present. She stayed in our hotel, ate with us, and socialized with us, yet we knew almost nothing about her except that she spent much of her time on the phone to someone in Washington reporting on the "progress" of this less-than-spectacular drug trial.

And wherever Sonia went, CIA Girl would go. Although CIA Girl claimed to speak very little Spanish and Sonia supposedly spoke no English, the two never needed a translator. CIA Girl went on to become an intimate part of Sonia's life over the next several years, not only taking part in her supervision and preparation as a government witness and acting as a co-prosecutor in a subsequent drug trial in Miami, but also attending meetings with the CIA during which decisions were made not to indict Arce-Gomez.

So the videotape of the drug testing had no sound, and we had what appeared to be a CIA plant in the prosecution; but I wasn't going to start asking questions. My Internal Security case was still pending, my daughter's drug problem had taken a turn for the worse, Suarez's contract on me was still active, and I was praying that someone would find Papo Mejia before he found me. It was all I could do to keep my little world from crumbling—I wasn't about to take on the Underground Empire again. But I had one ace up my sleeve—or so I thought.

I would be testifying as to what the conversation was in the mute videotape. I was to sit in front of a television set in court and narrate the action. If the defense attorneys and the media were astute enough, my testimony might help blow the lid off the whole phony drug war.

I figured that Mejia's men had said and done more than enough to convict themselves several times over, so I didn't think the truth about the cut drugs would hurt the prosecution's case. But it might be enough to get some hungry investigative reporter interested in a cover-up story, as happened after that little burglary at the Watergate Hotel in 1972.

Once the press started the ball rolling, I thought, nothing would stop it. Congress would be forced to stop looking the other way. I was sure that a congressional inquiry would find that the Minister and Queen of Cocaine would never have existed were it not for the CIA's covert support of the Bolivian cocaine cartel.

On a brutally hot August day in Tucson, my chance to testify about the drug testing arrived. The suits had not done their customary "victory dance" for the press about this case, so there were no national media members present. But there were enough local reporters there to pick up the story.

The key to Pandora's box was how the defense attorneys reacted to my testimony. Each of the four defendants had his own counsel. I figured that after they heard my testimony, at least one of the lawyers would demand that the government explain how we ended up with 50 percent street garbage. The difference in purity indicated that a minimum of 12 kilos of cocaine, having a street value of $2.4 million, had been removed or stolen in the midst of what DEA had described as its highest-priority investigation—more than enough scandal to cause an independent inquiry.

And that would just be the beginning. I would then do everything I could to make sure the inquiry was enlarged to include the suits' lack of interest in investigating, arresting, or indicting all the other defendants in the case, from the German and Roberto to Papo Mejia and Arce-Gomez himself. Then I would do my damnedest to see that it included the disappearing defendants in the Suarez case and the CIA's role in the Cocaine Coup. The CIA had shot a bullet into the heart of America, and I wanted the world to know it.

It was time to show the jury the climactic silent video, and court was adjourned to a special room rigged with television screens so the jury could get a close look at the action. As I took my seat in the witness box, I was dizzy with anticipation. I took a deep breath and hoped I looked composed.

Early on, Alfred Donau, Pineda's attorney, rose to ask me some questions. The judge had given all the defense attorneys the right to interrupt the proceedings to cross-examine me.

"Agent Levine, you had, did you not, a recording instrument along with this video?"

This is it, I thought. Donau is sharp—he smells the government is hiding something.

"Yes, sir," I said, my voice echoing in the courtroom.

"And it was your intention to have sound, was it not?"

"It certainly was." My insides were crying out in joy.

"But you do not have it?" Donau looked incredulous.

Prosecutor Molla interceded, and asked if I knew what had happened.

"What the foul-up is, I really don't know, but it had to be something to do with something that happened by someone. Who? I don't know." I hoped that my own confusion would attract the defense like sharks to blood. "At that particular time there were seven or eight people setting up the house for [the final drug testing]." That was enough for Donau to demand that everyone in the house be questioned.

But none of the defense attorneys continued the line of questioning. CIA Girl, who was staring at me hard from the prosecutor's table, seemed to be the only one in court who knew what I was trying to do.

I narrated the on-screen action for several more hours, emphasizing and reemphasizing that Pineda and his men were unhappy with the quality of the cocaine, that they had accused me of cutting it, and that they had called it "garbage."

At one point, the video showed Pineda, O'Connor, and Libardo visibly upset. I explained that they were upset because the drugs were diluted. I stared at each of the defense attorneys as I tried to hammer the point home.

"O'Connor and Libardo are complaining that the [cocaine] is not [pure]," I said, "that it's cut with something. Pineda is also telling me that [the cocaine] is not pure."

I kept expecting the defense attorneys to jump on me. Each had a copy of the DEA laboratory report sitting right in front of him indicating that Turghid had received cocaine that was tested at 89 percent pure. What explanation could the government have for the discrepancy? Who had diluted the drugs and why? The defense could have demanded the cocaine be retested and compared with the original reports. DEA would have been, at the very least, forced to investigate itself. But they said nothing. So I kept hammering away.

Later there was about a four-minute segment during which Pineda and O'Connor were talking to me heatedly as we examined some of the cocaine under a magnifying glass. Dan Pykett, Espinosa's attorney, seemed to sense something.

"Do you recall what you were saying?" he asked.

"Yes. I believe at this point they are saying that [the particular sample was cut]."

"Who said that, Agent, if you remember?"

"O'Connor said, 'This has been cut.'" *Come on, counselor—please. You've got a government report right in front of you that says the stuff had never been cut. O'Connor's an expert! Jump on it, damn it, jump on it!*

Once again the line of questioning was dropped.

But I was not going to let it die. I described most of the conversation as having to do with the cocaine's quality. "It was so bad," I said, "that at one point I thought Pineda wasn't even going to accept it." But as the hours slipped by I realized that the defense would never pick it up. The last opportunity came moments after the videotape had been completed, when Molla asked, "Now, as to the sound on the video, when was the first time that you knew there was no sound going along with the video, or that the microphone didn't work?"

"Sometime last week just after I arrived here in Tucson for the pretrial," I said.

"That's the first time you knew about it?"

"That's the first time I knew about it," I repeated, wishing that the defense lawyers could read my thoughts.

"And is it true that to this day you don't really know what was wrong with it?"

"Yes."

In my mind's eye, I envisioned Dan Pykett questioning me.

*"Agent Levine, you've been an undercover agent for many years, haven't you?"*

*"Seventeen long years, sir."*

*"And during those years how many undercover cases would you say you took part in?"*

*"Several thousand, sir."*

*"And many of them involved the use of electronic recording devices, isn't that correct?"*

*"Yes sir, most of them."*

*"And there were many of those cases that involved an undercover house or some other location that was wired to record conversation, isn't that correct?"*

*"Yes, that's exactly right, sir."*

*"Now on how many of those occasions did the recording devices pick up absolutely no sound?"*

*"Never, sir. This is the first time in my career that anything like this has happened."*

*"Isn't it highly unusual for the undercover agent to be told of a defective four-and-a-half-hour videotape only two days before he is to testify?"*

*"It's very unusual! If it were truly an error, I would have been told immediately so that I could better prepare myself to testify."*

*"Now, Agent Levine, does DEA consider you an expert on cocaine testing?"*

*"They sure do."*

*"Would you say the defendants were correct when they described the cocaine they were testing as 'garbage?'"*

*"It was so bad, sir, that I almost had to beg them to accept the stuff."*

*"So your testimony, Agent Levine, is that you think there is evidence that a substantial amount of cocaine is missing?"*

*"Absolutely and unequivocally yes."*

*"And doesn't DEA have hundreds if not thousands of pounds of almost pure cocaine in its warehouses?"*

*"Absolutely, sir."*

*"Isn't it highly unusual for a case as important as this—or any reverse undercover case—to be supplied with yellow cocaine that is less than 90 percent pure?"*

*"Absolutely, sir. Unusual enough to call for a congressional inquiry."*

*"Why would they give you substandard cocaine?"*

*"So that top drug dealers would not want to deal with us."*

*"And what would that accomplish?"*

*"It would kill a case that should have netted us hundreds of millions, maybe billions, in drug money, and enabled us to cripple a vast South American drug network."*

"I object to that line of questioning," said one of the defense attorneys. I was back in reality.

"Objection sustained," said the judge.

"I have no further questions," said Molla.

The drug testing tape was over, and no one had asked the essential questions. Perhaps I should have been more direct in my testimony;

perhaps I should have just stood up in court and called for an inquiry myself. But I had tried to blow the whistle 18 months ago with my letter to *Newsweek,* and ended up under investigation by Internal Security. A DEA agent—like any professional law enforcement officer—is trained to volunteer nothing in court. You answer only what you are asked. And I was afraid to do otherwise.

Days later I realized that I had been so focused on the cocaine that I had not really thought through why someone would want to kill the sound on that video. The answer came to me one afternoon during a recess in the trial. Sonia, Rourke, CIA Girl, and I were gathered in Molla's office when CIA Girl left the room to make her afternoon report to Washington.

What the hell could she be reporting, I wondered. There was no progress to report—the trial was about as routine as any low-level drug case. Even the press had lost interest. Yet she was calling her office three or four times a day. Then it dawned on me. It wasn't progress she was reporting, it was damage control.

If Operation Hun was a threat to CIA programs, as Rourke had indicated, then information revealed during the trial was the Agency's biggest fear. That was why the video had no sound—it was four-and-a-half hours of conversation naming dozens of people in the drug business—from Bolivian cabinet officials to the mysterious German in Miami. These were names that were being protected, that someone wanted kept off a videotape that might attract media attention. At least one of those names, as Rourke would later confirm, was a drug-dealing CIA asset placed high in the Bolivian government.

When Sonia took the stand, she was the perfect witness. She was soft-spoken and demure; she looked the defense attorneys right in their eyes; she met the baleful glare of Pineda calmly and evenly; she listened carefully to every word of every question, giving the prosecution plenty of time to object to defense questions. It was as if she'd been doing it all her life.

Her testimony was handled exclusively by none other than CIA Girl, who had been sent to Tucson for "trial experience." While Sonia was on the witness stand, Molla said not a single word.

Not one of the four top-notch defense attorneys came near breaking her down during cross-examination. During her testimony, one of them, Herbert Abramson, made a remarkable observation. He noticed that Sonia was reacting to questions that were put to her in English before the interpreter had a chance to translate them in Spanish.

"Do you speak and understand English, Mrs. Atala?" asked Abramson.

"No, I understand very few words."

"Do you remember yesterday when the interpreter was asking the judge in English about the words *arrangement* and *agreement,* and you said to the interpreter that these words both meant the same thing; do you remember that?"

"No, I don't remember."

The questioning went no further. Too bad.

On August 25, with the CIA, the State Department, and Justice monitoring every word of the trial and the American media ignoring it, Papo Mejia's drones were found guilty of all charges.

Not long after the trial, the suits began the cover-up. In violation of all DEA and Department of Justice regulations, administrative procedures were begun with the intention of destroying all evidence and closing Operation Hun.

That was how all the special interests in our government wanted the operation to end, for as long as that evidence existed and the spotlight was on Sonia, their secret was in danger. This was a case like the Suarez case, that the special interests never wanted to happen; it had been a monster put together by maverick DEA agents whom the CIA couldn't control. Damage control was necessary. Under the law, evidence could not be destroyed in any case where there were living fugitives. But the law didn't consider cases that the government wanted to kill. If it was up to the suits, no one else would have been arrested in Operation Hun.

# 32

# Papo

On Wednesday, September 15 at approximately 2:45 P.M., the "No Smoking" and "Fasten Seat Belts" signs illuminated on Avianca flight 142, originating from Bogota, Colombia. A stewardess announced the flight's imminent arrival at Miami International Airport in Spanish, English, and Portuguese. "All passengers are advised to have their passports available for Immigration and Customs checks and to review all arrival forms."

The passenger in seat 24A, a squat, powerfully built man with bushy dark hair, a bulldog jaw, and the coldest eyes any of the flight crew could remember, slipped a gray, custom-tailored jacket over his pale pink silk shirt. His diamond-and-gold Rolex caught the sunlight as he withdrew an alligator-hide wallet from his inside pocket and gave his entry documents a final examination—a Colombian passport in the name Luis Fernando Arcila-Mejia, a U.S. Immigration entry form, and a U.S. Customs Declaration form. Do you have anything to declare? the Customs form asked. He checked no, signed the form, and laughed to himself.

The plane began to bank for its final approach. The Miami skyline gleamed golden in the afternoon light. The man smiled. He loved this country—this golden place where all things were possible; where everything had a price and what wasn't for sale you just took. It was a

place where a man with *cojones,* who was unafraid of slicing and dic-
ing to get what he wanted, could live the life of a god.

Life was good for Papo Mejia. At 27, he had a beautiful wife, a new
baby son, and the kind of money and power few men even hope to
attain. And none of the *comemierdas* who had tried to challenge him,
who wanted to hurt him, amounted to enough of a threat to lose a
minute of sleep over. He had become too powerful for all of them.
Even the great gringo government itself could be bought and controlled if you were smart and knew the right people.

The Tucson thing hadn't amounted to much. That idiot Pineda had
walked into a trap. He should have known better. And that *maricon*
Espinosa should have been killed when the deal first went bad.

Papo had sensed something wrong the moment he heard Sonia's
voice on the phone. He should have followed his instinct and just
hung up. But he had allowed Pineda to convince him. "Just talk to
her," he had pleaded. "Just until we can find out where they live and
what they've got."

Papo had been right all along. He had warned Pineda to be wary
of a trap; that fucking *lesbiana* was as treacherous as a pit viper. Just
three years ago she had been trying to hire *pistolocos* in Colombia to
kill Bolivian politicians. A woman like that was not to be trusted for a
second.

Papo cursed himself for not killing her the first time, when she
came begging to him in Colombia, pleading with him for time, blaming the whole thing on Arce-Gomez and the Bolivians, claiming they
had his money. He should have seen through her act then. Arce-
Gomez was squeezing her out of the business, so she tried to get Papo
to kill him. That didn't work, so the *puta traicionera* ran to DEA and
got them to do her dirty work.

That first night, when Eduardo was sitting across a table from her
and the Jew DEA agent, he should have shot them both; he should
have started pulling the trigger the moment they gave their first
excuse. If he didn't escape, at least he would have died like a man
instead of rotting in a cage.

Well, what did it matter, what was done was done; they would do
their time and keep their mouths shut. Papo had been assured that
no efforts were being made to search for him and that, as long as he
was not arrested for some other charge the only evidence against him,
the one tape-recording, would be destroyed and the whole case quickly forgotten.

But Papo Mejia would not forget. While the great paper tiger DEA might forget Tucson, he would never forget it until it was avenged by the blood of Sonia Atala and *El Judío Triqueño*. For the time being patience was required, but discreet inquiries were already being made; information was being gathered; the hunt had already begun. And when the Bolivian whore and the Dark Jew least expected it, when the name Mejia had begun to fade from their memories, he would suddenly be there. He smiled at the thought.

Fifteen thousand feet below, a strange scene was developing in the International Arrivals terminal. A massive 6'3", 260-pound black man with wild staring eyes moved slowly through the sweating, multihued mob of people. Flimsy ropes attached to metal stanchions separated the crowd from an opaque glass door that led to the U.S. Customs area. Every few seconds the door would swing open and new arrivals would feel their first blast of Miami heat and take their first rubber-carpeted steps into a bedlam of screaming children, caterwauling babies, and people shouting in a dozen languages—the Promised Land.

The atmosphere in the terminal that day, as many would remember, was unusually tense. "You just knew something was going to happen," said a witness later. The crowd, comprised mostly of boisterous families of Latinos who had come to the airport to greet loved ones arriving from Colombia, seemed bigger and noisier than usual.

The waiting man was clutching a large paper bag. He positioned himself toward the rear of the crowd, not even glancing down as a little boy at play crashed into his hip and fell to the ground yowling and holding his head. The man was watching the glass door, his eyes wide and unblinking.

On the other side of the glass door, Papo Mejia handed his passport to an Immigration officer, who fed the name and date of birth on the phony passport into a computer terminal. The screen flashed "No Record." The officer handed Papo back his passport and said, *"Bienvenido a los Estados Unidos, Señor Arcilo."*

To pass through Customs, Papo next had to walk about 40 feet to the baggage carousel, retrieve his suitcase, and get on line at the Customs desk. Passing through Customs was easier than Immigration. The Customs inspector studied him, trying to decide whether the burly Colombian, whose passport described him as a *comerciante*—a businessman—merited a full search. Papo met his gaze evenly—he had nothing to hide. He wouldn't be on the same plane with drugs, let alone carry them.

This guy ain't carrying, thought the inspector. He's too cocky; too much jewelry on him for a mule. No sign of nerves.

The inspector waved Papo through. Papo picked up his suitcase and started toward the glass door and the streets of Miami. No muss, no fuss. Once again he had been admitted to the United States, as he had been innumerable times in the past. It was so easy.

On the other side of the door, passengers emerged and stood stunned and bewildered by the sudden cacophony and the writhing, pushing mob. Groups of people charged through the hopeless tangle to meet their loved ones as if a moment's delay might cause them to evaporate. Two undercover cops shook their heads at one another. This was a brutal day at the office for them. Their attention was concentrated on the new arrivals, looking for fugitives, drug smugglers, and suspected terrorists. No sense watching the crowd.

No one could have expected what was about to happen. The door swung open and a half-dozen more arrivals froze in shock after their first steps into the Promised Land. Papo moved quickly past them, his mongoose eyes scanning the faces ahead for his wife and maid. His street instincts, honed in the slums of Bogota and in a thousand back alley Miami drug deals, urged him to move faster. He was too vulnerable.

Papo hustled forward into the shuffling herd heading for the exit. He usually felt safer moving in a large crowd, but not this time. He was caught in the tide of humanity, weighted down by his own baggage. He failed to see the huge man surging through the crowd like a mighty whale, bodies bouncing off him like ocean spray, clutching the soiled paper bag out in front of him, angling ever closer. Suddenly the bag dropped and a chorus of shrieks exploded. A 12-inch bayonet was raised high above the crowd.

Papo didn't hear the pounding footsteps behind him until the last moment. He turned just as a gargantuan hand tightened around his throat. He saw the long, rusty blade poise high above his head and then plunge toward him. Oddly, he felt no pain as it drove into his body near the base of his neck. Blood exploded outward from him, blinding him, turning his world into a red, shrieking frenzy. The blade rose high in the air again, and then buried itself to the hilt at the top of Papo's stomach. The huge man screamed something unintelligible and drove the blade into Papo a third time.

Papo, no stranger to deadly violence, did not succumb to shock. His legs scrambled in mindless, hysterical flight. But he didn't get far. The massive hand encircled his throat once again, choking off a frightened cry of *"Mami."* The huge man raised the long blade seven more times, plunging it deeply into Papo's neck, chest, and stomach.

Finally, amidst a hellish din of screams, pounding feet, blaring loudspeakers, and roaring jet engines, the huge man let Papo's body drop to the ground like the half-butchered carcass of a fattened piglet, its limbs thrashing wildly and its voice squealing hysterically against the encroaching darkness—the same darkness into which Papo had gleefully sent so many.

The man loped away from the scene, followed by a plainclothes police officer. He was arrested outside the airport without a struggle. He made no statement. Police would learn that his name was Miguel Arcangel Perez and that he was a Marielito—one of the 125,000 Cubans who had emigrated to the United States in 1980 when Castro had emptied his jails and mental institutions into boats at the port of Mariel and shoved them off toward Miami. Little else would ever be known about the man. Later, police would say that Perez had probably been hunting Mejia for as long as three years, and had probably figured that the best place to trap the wily killer would be after he had cleared Customs on the return leg of one of his many trips to Colombia. He would undoubtedly be unarmed.

There are two theories of why Perez stalked and attacked Mejia. The most commonly believed one is that he was hired by Griselda Blanco, the notorious Colombian "Godmother." A government informant later claimed to have been present when Griselda, who had learned of Papo's travel plans, gave Perez the rusty bayonet. The Godmother's hatred of Papo was legend. She had long been at war with him—one of the longest and bloodiest of the now infamous Cocaine Cowboy wars.

The police investigation indicated that Mejia had been using the home of Perez's brother, whose daughter was a wheelchair-bound paraplegic, as a stash pad; that drugs were missing and a short while thereafter so too were Perez's brother and niece. It had not taken Perez long to realize that Mejia was the cause of his family's disappearance.

Which of the stories is true will probably never be known and really didn't matter in the long run. What did matter was that Papo Mejia survived.

# 33

# Papo's Trial

On February 3, 1983, I returned to Tucson to testify against Papo Mejia in a trial the U.S. government had never expected or intended to happen.

I had been transferred temporarily to Vice President Bush's South Florida Task Force and was shuttling back and forth between Miami and New York. I was fully engaged in my daughter's war on drugs and at the same time doing undercover work in Miami and the Carolinas. Internal Security was still investigating me, and the rumor mill still maintained that I would be indicted for something, although nobody knew what.

My first night in Tucson I had dinner with Sonia and CIA Girl, Rourke, Maria Montez, and Lydia. Sonia was in a buoyant mood, laughing and teasing about Rourke's cigarette smoking. She had every reason to be happy. She had stolen a bag of jewels, $500,000 cash, and a Mercedes from Papo Mejia, one of the most prolific murderers in the world, and had not only gotten away with it, but was now about to see to it that he spent the rest of his life behind bars.

On February 9, I saw Papo in the flesh for the first time. He looked remarkably fit for a man who had been stabbed 10 times with a bayonet only five months earlier. In fact, I could see no outward signs of any damage. He was well dressed in a pale-colored business suit, looking robust and full of venom. From the moment I took the witness stand, Mejia's jaw set in a tetanus grin while his eyes sent an unwavering message. During my two days of testimony, he took his eyes off me only once. As I detailed how Sonia and I had manipulated him into the recorded phone call that would convict him, he took a sudden deep breath, turned his body, and seemed to stare at the wall. His jaw twitched as though there were a small rodent trapped between his teeth.

"I wanted to make sure I had Mr. Mejia's voice on tape," I testified as I studied his profile, wondering how many lives he had snuffed and whether their spirits were conscious of what was happening. "I wanted to prove his role in the conspiracy; that he knew he was getting drugs he had bought and paid for." I imagined I felt those spirits patting me on the back and saying, "You did a good thing Levine; you balanced the books." For a moment I felt fulfilled. I had made a difference.

When Papo turned toward me again, his face seemed to bloat with hatred. The fact that Sonia and I were living would provide him with the rage to survive any jail sentence he might receive. He would need that inspiration, for on March 18, Judge Marquez sentenced Mejia to 30 years in prison and special parole for life.

At a recess during my testimony, Lydia approached me. "Mike, I'm leaving for L.A. tonight," she said. "Would you mind driving me to the airport after court?"

I was speechless. Lydia hadn't addressed me this directly since that day in Miami, almost a year earlier, when the inspectors called our undercover room to demand that she appear for interrogation.

"Sure thing. I'd love to."

"Are you sure it won't put you out?" she asked, looking as if she were already changing her mind.

"Not at all," I said.

Right after court ended for the night, Lydia and I headed out to the airport. During the half-hour ride, she just stared out the window at row after row of sun-bleached buildings. I tried to make conversation.

"How's your husband doing?"

"Fine."

"How're things in the L.A. office?"

"Not bad."

I finally gave up. But just as we were entering the airport, Lydia looked at me. "Mike," she said, her voice so low that I barely heard it.

"Yeah?"

"We might not be seeing each other again."

"You never know."

"I, uh, I just wanted to tell you that it's been a pleasure working with you again."

"For me too, Lydia."

She said nothing else. I was more upset with her now than I had been before the ride.

As I parked in front of the main terminal, Dave Gorman and Dave Kunz pulled their jeep to the curb just ahead of us. It was as if fate had sent them.

"Hey! Funny meeting you all here," said Gorman. "You following us?"

"Wow!" said Kunz, "Four members of the original Suarez under-cover team in one place. There's gotta be an inspector around here someplace, especially with Levine here." He put his hands to his eyes like binoculars and peered out at the parking lot.

"Don't remind me," I said, noticing that Lydia's olive complexion had turned a dull crimson.

"Man, they were flat trying to do you," said Gorman. "They must have tried to get me and Dave to change our testimony a half-dozen times. And I mean they were pressing hard."

"I heard that's what they were doing," I said, the torture of the past three years flashing through my mind. Something was happening to Lydia—she now looked as angry as I felt.

"Yeah, man," said Kunz, "they wanted your ass bad."

"What do you mean 'wanted'?" I said.

"That thing still going on?" asked Kunz.

"As far as I know."

"They did the same thing to me," Lydia suddenly blurted. There was a look on her face that told me she wanted to say more.

"You know," I said, "I never asked you what happened after that day they called our hotel room in Miami."

"They forced me to come back to Miami to be interrogated," she said, looking directly at me.

"What was it all about?"

"They wanted to know if I had been to bed with you," she said disgustedly.

"You're kidding," said Kunz.

"I wish I was," said Lydia.

I remembered Tommy Dolittle telling me it was over a matter unrelated to me. "What else did they want to know?" I asked, happy that there were two witnesses to hear her, but raging against the bastards that made me need witnesses.

"You were right," said Lydia, "when you said they would try to blame you if I refused to go. They kept asking me, 'Did Levine tell you not to talk to us?'"

"In other words, they were trying to get me?"

"Yes," said Lydia, looking as though a load had been lifted from her shoulders.

"Wow," said Kunz. "They're still after you."

"I guess so," I said. Both Daves were now peering around in earnest.

"One of the inspectors," continued Lydia, "the fat one with the bad teeth . . ."

"Quasimoto," I said.

"Yeah," said Lydia fuming, "that guy. He flung a memo across the desk at me; the one about agents recording agents. He wanted to know if you had recorded the phone call."

"What did you tell him?"

"I said, 'Hey, we were working undercover; we were recording all incoming calls. We didn't expect a call from you guys.'"

"How did they get you to come back to Miami?"

"Quasimoto called my boss and said, 'Send that whore back out here!' My boss said that if I wanted him to, he would testify to the exact words."

"Why don't you sue?" asked Gorman, watching a passing car.

"We might," said Lydia. My lively undercover partner from the Suarez case had suddenly returned. "My husband wanted to jump on a plane to Miami. The guys in his group had to sit on him. He wanted to go right into Quasimoto's office and say, 'I'm that whore's husband.' Mike, I thought Johnny would kill him. We're talking to a lawyer now."

"If you need me for anything, to testify or whatever," I said, "you can count on me."

Lydia nodded. Her lawyer had probably warned her against telling me anything, because I might use it to attack the inspectors, putting her and her husband in the middle of my case whether they liked it or not. All this time she had been afraid to say anything, and I had been afraid to ask.

411

"I mean it," I said. "Somebody's got to stand up to these bastards. Tell your husband. Together we have a hell of a case."

"Okay," said Lydia, looking apprehensive. "I'm not sure what we're going to do. Johnny and I have to talk about it and decide."

The momentum was slipping away. I wanted to keep talking, but the two Daves kept looking around uncomfortably and Lydia said she wanted to make some phone calls. Before she left I made sure she had every phone number and address I had.

"Don't forget," I said, "talk to your husband. I will back you 100 percent. Call me and let me know."

"I will," she called over her shoulder, and she disappeared inside the terminal.

"Somethin' else," said Kunz, shaking his head.

"Who'd believe this shit?" said Gorman.

"Maybe someday I'll put this all in a book," I said. The two Daves were silent.

I never saw Lydia again. Within months, she and her husband were both promoted and transferred overseas.

As for Sonia, throughout that final week of the trial I saw enough of her to know that she had become the perfect tool for the suits' smoke-and-mirrors show. She had honed her witness stand performance to perfection. She knew how to use her good looks and schoolgirl smile to make a jury forget that she herself was one of the biggest drug dealers who ever lived; that she herself was a willing and active partner of a government that had tortured, raped, and murdered thousands of her countrypeople, many of whom were tortured to death in her house across the street from Los Tajibos Hotel in Santa Cruz. She was an extremely valuable, well-protected player in the drug war game—a game that was destroying America.

After the trial, I slipped out of Tucson without saying goodbye. I doubted that I would ever see or hear of Sonia and Operation Hun again. DEA, Justice, the State Department, and the CIA once more tried to close the books on Operation Hun. Finally, the DEA suits, in violation of their own regulations, officially closed the Tucson case file and destroyed all the evidence—including the tape recordings, videotapes, and tainted cocaine. For them the case was closed. For me it would never be.

# 34

# The Last Dance

On a rainy night in mid-May, unable to sleep, I was driving around suburban Virginia. I stopped at a blue-collar club just off Route 50 in Alexandria for a nightcap and perhaps a little anonymous conversation. A country music combo was playing and most of the tables were occupied. I had just ordered a Diet Coke when I noticed her.

Sonia sat at a table with two couples who appeared to be in their mid-thirties. The women wore cocktail dresses and the men were dressed in tailored suits, and they were all deeply tanned as if they'd just returned from a vacation. Gold and diamond jewelry flashed as the five engaged in animated conversation. It was as if a table in a Bogota nightclub had suddenly been zapped through a cosmic teleporter and deposited in the Virginia countryside by some alien with a bizarre sense of humor. My instincts screamed drug deal, drug deal, drug deal.

If I had learned anything from my 18 years in the drug war business, it was how to spot a deal in progress. I could do it the way a composer can hear a single wrong note in a symphony played by 100 musi-

413

cians. But how could she be doing a drug deal if she was in the Witness Protection Program?

Months earlier I had learned that CIA Girl herself had initiated the action to place Sonia into the Witness Protection Program. This meant that Sonia and her family had new identities and either resident alien status or U.S. citizenship; that they were being paid tens of thousands—possibly hundreds of thousands—of dollars of government subsistence and DEA "reward" monies; that they had been furnished a home and jobs; and that their lives were protected and (supposedly) closely monitored by Justice. It also indicated that the informant Sonia was no longer even superficially in the hands of DEA. If she were, it would have been DEA that put her into the protection program, not CIA Girl.

I had also learned other news that was even more chilling to me personally. All prosecutions resulting from Sonia's testimony were now under the control of CIA Girl and Pat Sullivan, who was still deciding whether or not to prosecute me. What a nice, neat package.

Sonia, as if receiving some telepathic alarm, suddenly turned and looked directly at me. For a moment she turned as pale as death. In the next instant she was smiling.

I smiled back.

She motioned with her head toward the dance floor where a half-dozen couples were dancing to a slow country tune. I nodded and started toward her. Sonia said something quickly to her companions and laughed that nervous little bark I knew so well. Her companions, now grim and apprehensive, turned to study me.

As Sonia came toward me, her smile vanished and her eyes darted all over the place looking for some sign that this was not a chance meeting. Perhaps the stunned look on my face reassured her that I had merely stumbled upon her innocently, because suddenly she was smiling radiantly again. Her tablemates watched us with dark concern.

"I promise you I am not following you," she said with a laugh as she came into my arms.

"Why would I think that?" I said. "You were here first." She laughed her nervous laugh.

We said nothing for a few minutes, just moving to the music. I remembered our first dance in Miami more than a year before. I had the feeling then that we were being watched; now I was certain of it. I turned Sonia in a circle, my eyes scouring the faces around us. I felt

Sonia's hand move up along my back and come to rest on the back of my neck.

"So how is the great gringo drug war doing?" she said, suddenly confident. "Are you still all business, no pleasure?"

"That depends on what the pleasure is," I said, feeling my stomach tighten and a pressure in my head that I hadn't felt in months. I had begun to pick out eyes that seemed to be watching us intently.

"You'll never change," she said, pressing closer. "Too bad."

"How is your English coming?"

She shrugged. "I prefer Spanish."

"And how is your family doing—Walter and the kids?"

She smiled. "Everyone is fine. We are getting used to things here. But it will be nice to go home again, permanently."

She had said *permanently* as if she had recently been there on a trip. And such a trip could only mean drugs. But how could that be if she was in the Witness Protection Program?

"You're going home to Bolivia?" I said.

"Of course. Eventually I will."

"But you've been back there recently?"

Once again she paled. Her hand dropped from my neck. "How could I?"

"That's what I was wondering. You said, 'go home permanently.'"

"And that's what I meant."

"Aren't you afraid?"

She shrugged. "What should I fear? Governments change. I have friends."

We danced quietly for a few moments. In the three months since the Mejia trial I had blocked Sonia and Operation Hun from my mind. I had other problems to worry about. The Internal Security investigation was still hanging over my head, and my daughter's drug problem had deteriorated to the point that I had requested a hardship transfer to New York.

The down-and-dirty street narc deep inside me was screaming for me to walk Sonia back to her table and ask her companions to identify themselves, to call out a squad of DEA agents to interrogate them, to get search warrants for wherever they were staying and wherever Sonia was living. I was sure we'd learn that she was back in business.

But my last five years' experience were also calling to me, telling me that whatever Sonia was doing was no secret to the CIA or the DEA suits, and that if I made any move that jeopardized her, the charges hanging over my head would become a criminal indictment.

"Your friends seem a little upset," I said.

"Why do you say that?" she said, tensing.

"Where are they from?"

Sonia stopped dancing. "You're right, I'm probably being rude." She started back to her table.

I followed her, unsure of my next move.

She turned and gave me a soft kiss on the cheek. "It was really nice to see you again, Miguel. I hope all your troubles work out in your favor." Her eyes lingered on mine for a moment. It was a warning.

I stood there for a moment, unable to move. As Sonia rejoined her companions, they all stared at me. *Haven't you had enough? Just get your ass out of here before you're in over your head again.* I left a $10 bill on the bar and hustled out into the night.

I never saw Sonia again. But it would not be the last I heard of her.

# 35

# A Deal with the Devil

*Sometimes the philosophy of this agency is, a pact with the devil is better than no pact at all.*
— DEA spokesman Robert Feldkamp

## 1

Jack Rourke was causing a crisis. Despite being assigned to the Marijuana Desk, despite covert opposition from the suits and overt opposition from the CIA, he continued to push for the indictment of Arce-Gomez and other Bolivian government officials. Some were CIA assets who were paid U.S. tax dollars and protected from prosecution while they flooded our streets with cocaine. The CIA claimed that indicting these people would irreparably damage "important programs."

In November 1982—as a result of Rourke's persistence—secret meetings had been called between DEA, the Department of Justice, and the CIA to discuss whether or not such an indictment could be reached without jeopardizing CIA programs. CIA Girl took part in all these meetings, as did Pat Sullivan and Rourke.

If any of the CIA assets were indicted, the Agency's role in the takeover of Bolivia by drug dealers, rapists, and murderers—and perhaps their role in drug dealing, too—might be revealed to the

417

American people. Thus, the result of the secret meetings—which were probably held more for the purpose of placating Rourke and the quiet dissenters in DEA management than any law enforcement reason—was that there would be no indictment. The CIA's drug-dealing assets would be permitted to continue their criminal ways unhindered by the war on drugs.

In the meantime, Sonia had remained a numbered DEA informant, although under the watchful eye of the CIA. DEA had been permitted to use Sonia far too extensively in Operation Hun for the Agency to just snatch her away without risking real problems with street agents like Rourke who still believed a drug war could be fought in spite of CIA programs. It was easier and less risky to hinder DEA investigations covertly by refusing to cooperate and by setting up obstacles through DEA suits who were willing tools. But, once again, they didn't count on Rourke's dogged determination.

Rourke—still working at a nonsupervisory grade—continued to push for the Arce-Gomez indictment. The DEA suits shuffled responsibility for the remnants of Operation Hun from one supervisor to another. Little by little the case became unwinnable due to evidence that had "disappeared" and investigative leads that were strangely never followed. Rourke, however, never let up. He continued pushing for cooperation of other informants not controlled by the Agency who could incriminate the Arce-Gomez gang.

By early 1983, Rourke had obtained the cooperation of Natalia "Nati" Justiniano, Sonia's friend and constant companion. She had accompanied Sonia on many of her drug-dealing trips and had also claimed to be an old friend of Arce-Gomez. On February 1, she testified before a Miami grand jury, corroborating much of Sonia's story. Her testimony also incriminated some of the CIA assets who were Arce-Gomez's accomplices.

By mid-February, Rourke was able to get a second trafficker—a customer of Sonia's whom DEA had arrested in a separate case—to testify before the same Miami grand jury. He also incriminated Arce-Gomez and his cohorts. It began to look like Rourke was going to get his indictment whether the CIA cooperated or not.

On February 17, CIA Girl and Pat Sullivan had a secret meeting with one of the CIA assets whom Sonia had implicated as a drug trafficker. Operation Hun had once again delved uncomfortably into the CIA's drug world activities, and it had to be stopped. The CIA now claimed that Sonia had lied. A week later, on February 25, the CIA asset was given a polygraph examination by a Justice examiner. The CIA asset failed.

Immediately after this mysterious event the DEA suits suddenly realized that one of the most damaging witnesses against the Bolivian government—in many ways more damaging than Sonia herself—had been right under DEA's nose all along: Sonia's husband Pachi.

Pachi, Undersecretary of Labor in the Bolivian government headed by General Hugo Banzer (1971–1978)—a CIA-supported government under which the Bolivian cocaine business first flourished—had not been as innocent and oblivious to Sonia's drug dealing as she had claimed. He turned out to be an old friend of Arce-Gomez and his henchmen, some of whom he'd known since childhood. Walter admitted to having taken an active part in Sonia's drug dealing; he not only corroborated his wife's testimony, in many instances he was more willing to talk than she was about what went on behind the bloody doors of his country's drug-fueled government.

How Rourke was finally able to learn about Pachi's role after having Pachi in his custody for almost two years may only be answered when our elected officials seriously investigate the CIA's true role in international drug trafficking.[1]

On March 21, 1983, after a month of debriefing Pachi, Rourke had him testify before the Miami grand jury. Then, on April 25, Rourke once again dragged the U.S. government kicking and screaming into a grand jury room. In spite of the suits, the Department of Justice, and the CIA, Arce-Gomez was finally indicted along with 16 others. Among the Bolivian government officials indicted, at least two were CIA assets. The nongovernment indictees were midlevel drug dealers and customers of Sonia.

The indictees:

Luis Arce-Gomez, a/k/a "Lucho," Bolivian Minister of Interior

Alberto Alvarez, a/k/a "El Gato," representative of Arce-Gomez and quasi-official Bolivian government functionary

---

[1] Despite statements like "our covert agencies have converted themselves to channels for drugs" by Senator John Kerrey, not a single U.S. government official has been charged with a drug-related crime. In her book *Out of Control* (New York: Atlantic Monthly Press, 1987), investigative journalist Leslie Cockburn shows quite conclusively that the only official inquiry into the U.S. government's involvement in the trafficking of drugs to its own people was a sham, the purpose of which was to cover up the very crimes it was supposed to be investigating.

> Juan Carlos Camacho, Bolivian Attorney General and drug-dealing representative of Arce-Gomez (suspected CIA asset)
>
> Jose Tito Camacho, head of Bolivian Narcotics Police and drug-dealing representative of Arce-Gomez (suspected CIA asset)
>
> Herlan Echeverria, Bolivian government official and drug-dealing representative of Arce-Gomez (suspected CIA asset)
>
> Jose Nelo Callau, Bolivian government official and drug-dealing representative of Arce-Gomez (suspected CIA asset)
>
> Jon Doe, a/k/a "Mendieta," Bolivian government cocaine chemist
>
> Ana Rodriguez de Tamayo, *comisionista* friend of Sonia's (the only target of Operation Hun to be indicted three times)
>
> René Benitez, customer of Sonia's (already in custody for the shooting of DEA agents McCullough and Martinez)
>
> Jorge Baron, customer of Sonia's
>
> Carlos Gallo, customer of Sonia's
>
> Humberto Montero, customer of Sonia's
>
> Roberto Bernabe-Suarez, customer of Sonia's
>
> Rolando Rafael Franco, customer of Sonia's
>
> Alejandro Vasquez-Caicedo, customer of Sonia's
>
> Rafael Sanchez-Jerez, customer of Sonia's
>
> Nestor Villalta-Ramirez, customer of Sonia's

It was a great personal victory for Rourke. He had overcome forces in his own government a lot more powerful and sinister than any drug dealer. As a DEA agent who had lived, breathed, and believed in the Big Lie, I knew the exhilaration he felt. But as far as any value to the alleged drug war, the indictment of Arce-Gomez was meaningless. Since there was no extradition treaty with Bolivia for drug violators, no one ever expected to see Arce-Gomez or any of the CIA assets stand trial. The joke was once again on the American people.

When Arce-Gomez learned of his indictment, he was so disdainful of the phony gringo drug war that he almost made a fatal mistake. To give Congress the impression that Bolivia was cooperating in the war on drugs so that it would continue paying the Bolivian government massive amounts of foreign aid, Arce-Gomez resigned as Minister of Interior to prove his "innocence." He became Bolivia's Military Attache to Argentina, where he planned to lay low until the heat blew over. When Arce's formal indictment was made public, he stayed put despite his vulnerability to arrest and extradition in Argentina. He couldn't conceive of the Argentines who had helped put him into power turning him over to DEA. Neither could I; nor, I'm sure, could the CIA.

Rourke, undaunted by all the intrigue, pushed for an international arrest warrant and requested that the Argentine authorities honor their extradition treaty by arresting Arce-Gomez. To the surprise of many in our government, the Argentine authorities complied. On May 16, 1983, Arce-Gomez was arrested for the first time in his life.

Soon after that, Rourke, beaming with delight, appeared in my office. "They got him!" he said.

"Congratulations—you really earned it."

"Thanks," he said, closing the door and taking a seat.

I debated telling Rourke about my last dance with Sonia, and decided not to. Sonia was in the Witness Protection Program and under the supervision of the Department of Justice, DEA, the U.S. Marshals, and the CIA. The President didn't have that many badges watching him. How the hell could I dare say that I had stumbled onto this star asset right in the middle of a drug deal?

"You think the Argentines will actually give him to us?" I said.

"Why wouldn't they?" Rourke said.

"They put the guy in power in the first place," I said, "and the Agency used them to do it. They're as responsible for the Cocaine Coup as Arce-Gomez himself. What're you gonna do, indict them, too?"

Rourke glanced quickly at my closed office door. In a building full of CIA agents and suspected CIA informants, speaking this way was close to treason. But every time I saw Rourke, I'd flash back through the whole miserable experience; then I wasn't responsible for anything I said.

Rourke took a deep drag on his cigarette and said nothing. I noticed dark rings around his eyes. His shirt looked slept in. I knew he regretted having mentioned the Agency to me; the fact that he had was a testimonial to his frustration.

"Let me ask you something," I said. "You've been battling them right from the start. They flat didn't want this indictment to happen. You think they're all of a sudden going to roll over and play dead and let us have this guy? Right now there's contacts being made and buttons being pushed that you, me, and nobody else will ever hear about, and you know it."

He sighed deeply. "We'll see, ya hump. We'll see."

Two weeks later an Argentine judge ruled the case against Arce-Gomez was lacking in evidence; the ex-Minister of Cocaine was released from jail and he immediately returned to Bolivia.

# 2

Humberto Montero and Jorge Baron, who had been charged in the same indictment with Arce-Gomez, were arrested. In May 1984, the two men stood trial on charges of possession of cocaine with intent to sell. Their chief accusers would be their sources—Sonia and Pachi, who were accused of no crime. The prosecutor was Pat Sullivan, assisted by wherever-Sonia-goes-I-go CIA Girl.

Throughout the trial, the defense attorneys hammered away at the nature of a drug war that rewarded Sonia Atala—one of the biggest drug sources in history—with large sums of money, U.S. government protection, and resident status in the United States while using her to penalize alleged drug dealers who were, in effect, nothing more than her customers. Their arguments did not sway the jury. Both men were convicted and sentenced to lengthy jail terms.

But the defense was successful in getting Sonia and Walter to reveal a sordid picture of the U.S. war on drugs in general and the Atalas in particular. The testimony revealed the important role Sonia played in the "cocaine invasion" of the United States and how well she was protected by the very people she was invading, and it shed light on Pachi's part in Sonia's drug trafficking. Most significant was that it foreshadowed some of the incredible events that followed.

Jose Quinon, Montero's quick-witted defense attorney, cross-examined Sonia, the cool veteran of the witness stand. She had mastered the role of the innocent victim of circumstance who'd been taken advantage of by all the big, mean men around her, while firing verbal torpedoes with unerring accuracy at every opening the defense gave her.

Quinon, a Cuban American, was no slouch. The one-time defense attorney for the infamous Carlos Lehder quickly established that

Sonia had been a high-level trafficker long before the Cocaine Coup; that in Bolivia, Sonia and Walter had owned three homes, a huge ranch where 10 or more peasant families lived as virtual slave labor, airplanes, a cotton plantation, and a cattle ranch; that in Rio de Janeiro they owned apartments and offices; that during Sonia's stay in the United States, the U.S. government had already paid her $75,000 and had promised her substantial additional payments when she testified; and that none of the money had been reported as income to the IRS.

Through his cross-examination of Sonia, Quinon also revealed that when DEA had asked the Garcia-Mesa/Arce-Gomez government to prepare a list of Bolivia's top cocaine traffickers, Sonia was at the top of the list; and that Sonia had motives for going after Arce-Gomez that were quite different from what she had told DEA.

QUINON: And what was it that prompted you to go to [DEA] to complain about Luis Arce-Gomez and the others in the Bolivian government?

SONIA: In order to get [their] help.

QUINON: You wanted [DEA] to protect you from the Bolivian government officials who were squeezing you out of the cocaine trade; is that correct?

SONIA: Not getting me out of the cocaine trade.

QUINON: Well isn't it a fact, that by March of 1981, the beginning of March of 1981, much of your capital had been depleted because you gave it to Juan Carlos Camacho and Alberto Alvarez; is that correct?

SONIA: Yes.

QUINON: In addition to that, all your [Colombian cocaine customers] were known to them because you took Nelo Callau with you to Colombia to meet your clients; isn't that right?

SONIA: That I took him to Colombia, yes.

QUINON: And the other two, Juan Carlos Camacho and Alberto Alvarez had [access to the Bolivian government] cocaine; is that right?

SONIA: Yes.

QUINON: So they didn't need you anymore, did they?

SONIA: Exactly.

QUINON: And you weren't too happy about the fact that [Arce-Gomez and his people] were cutting you out of millions of dollars; correct?

SONIA: Correct.

Quinon also established that immediately after the Cocaine Coup, Sonia was assigned her own personal squad of Klaus Barbie-trained neo-Nazi mercenaries whom she fed, housed, and was instrumental in buying weapons for. Sonia claimed that while she supported the group, she did not have the authority to command them.

QUINON:  Are you saying that you did not have any say so concerning what those [mercenaries] did?

SONIA:  No, because they had their own boss.

QUINON:  Did they not in fact protect you and your drug trade?

SONIA:  No.

QUINON:  You're sure of that?

SONIA:  Yes.

QUINON:  And your husband Pachi, did he have any disposal over that [mercenary] group?

SONIA:  No.

QUINON:  And he would not use that group for protection, your husband, to your knowledge?

SONIA:  No, we never used it for protection.

QUINON:  And that is the very [same mercenary] group that used to take drugs from other [drug dealers who were not paying protection money to Arce-Gomez] and bring it very early in the morning to your house; correct?

SONIA:  Yes, but because they were sent. They were sent.

David Finger, the hard-driving defense attorney for Jorge Baron, took over the questioning and continued to explore Sonia's relationship to the mercenaries.

FINGER:  Ma'am, were you in fact bothered by the fact that these [mercenary] groups, that you were housing and feeding, tortured people?

SONIA:  Yes, but there was nothing I could do.

FINGER:  You had to give them your house and you had to feed them; you had to do it?

SONIA:  To part of the group, because there are many.

FINGER:  Ma'am, I believe you told Mr. Quinon on cross examination that the [mercenary] group was not at your disposal, but only stayed at the residence you provided them and where you fed them?

SONIA:  Yes.

FINGER:  Isn't it a fact, ma'am, that you were at a meeting attended by Mr. Juan Carlos Camacho, Alberto Alvarez, and your husband Pachi, and that you were told by Camacho and Alvarez that you could use the group to spread the word to your friends that you had a security group that was furnished to you by the government to avoid tax on the house; do you remember that conversation . . . ?

SONIA: Yes, sir, but it's different from my having been able to use them, from that to them having been under my command. The two things are different.

FINGER: What did you understand Camacho and Alvarez to mean when they said, spread the word that the government is giving you a [mercenary] group; what did you take that to mean, ma'am?

SONIA: Spread the word for me, I understand that to mean, that other people will think that I have my orders or that I am giving orders to a group of [mercenaries]. . . . But in reality, I didn't have it. Spreading the word is like propaganda only.

FINGER: So Camacho and Alvarez didn't mean it, as far as you know, when they told you that? They didn't mean it? You didn't really have them to use, as far as you know; even though they were living at your house under your roof and being fed by you?

SONIA: In many opportunities, they told me when—in many opportunities, Camacho, as much as Alvarez, told me that I could use—or that if I needed anything, that I could count with the help of the [mercenaries]. But I never did receive their help.

FINGER: The point is, ma'am, it was there for you to utilize if you wanted to; is that right?

SONIA: Yes.

Sonia's testimony revealed that she was as capable of murder and mayhem as any of the people she was accusing. When Rolando Franco, a midlevel drug dealer, refused to pay Sonia for some cocaine that he'd bought, accusing her of replacing some of the cocaine with sugar, Sonia held Roberto Bernabe-Suarez, one of Franco's partners, captive and threatened to kill him unless Franco paid. Incredibly, under direct examination by CIA Girl, Sonia freely admitted to holding Bernabe-Suarez hostage and making the threat. (Ironically, Sonia had testified against both Franco and Bernabe-Suarez; both were indicted along with Arce-Gomez.) When Finger cross-examined Sonia, he highlighted the incident.

FINGER: And that's why you held Bobi [Bernabe-Suarez] hostage and threatened to kill him?

SONIA: I threatened that he would not leave until they had paid, but I let him go without them having paid me.

FINGER: Ma'am, didn't you come to an agreement with Mr. Franco, a compromise, whereby he agreed to pay you a portion and you would let [Bernabe-Suarez] go?

SONIA: I got two agreements with him, but he did not comply with any of them.

FINGER: But when you let [Bernabe-Suarez] go, it was with the understanding that there was going to be a payment? You didn't let him go because you thought it was a nice thing to do, did you?

SONIA: I let him go, because they told me that they were going to pay me. That's the motive.

To admit to kidnaping, Sonia had to be supremely confident in her U.S. protectors. An indication of what else she was involved in came when Finger returned to the theme of torture after the Cocaine Coup.

FINGER: Before [the mercenaries] took and used [your] house, you had occasion to go and look at that house with [your husband Walter] and Juan Carlos Camacho and Alberto Alvarez; correct?

SONIA: Yes.

FINGER: And Camacho told you that he liked the house, because it was so isolated that the screams could not be heard; didn't he tell you that?

SONIA: Yes.

FINGER: Now, I believe you testified yesterday, that you let them use the house because Camacho asked you [for permission to use it]; is that right?

SONIA: Yes.

Finger explored Sonia's participation in Arce-Gomez's alleged plot to flood the United States with cocaine. His questioning brought out a Sonia who was far from intimidated by the Minister.

FINGER: [After the coup] you returned from Colombia to Santa Cruz on September 14, 1980; is that correct, ma'am?

SONIA: Yes.

FINGER: And you were contacted by [Herlan] Echeverria to contact Mr. Arce-Gomez?

SONIA: Yes.

FINGER: And he was a very powerful man in the government?

SONIA: Yes.

FINGER: And you had never met him before?

SONIA: No.

FINGER: And you told Mr. Echeverria that you couldn't meet him that night, but you would meet him at your house at seven o'clock the next morning?

SONIA: Yes.

FINGER:    And the next morning you were an hour late for the meeting with Mr. Arce-Gomez?

SONIA:    Yes.

FINGER:    So you agreed to meet him the next day?

SONIA:    I don't know whether it was the same day or the next day.

FINGER:    But you agreed to meet him later on?

SONIA:    Yes, I agreed to meet him later on.

FINGER:    And you finally met him on September 23; is that right?

SONIA:    Yes.

FINGER:    And that's when you had the discussions about the protection money?

SONIA:    Yes.

FINGER:    Since the United States had cut off economic aid to Bolivia . . .

SONIA:    Yes.

FINGER:    . . . and since the United States had cut off aid, [Arce-Gomez] told you that he was going to invade the gringos with cocaine; [isn't that correct]?

SONIA:    Yes.

FINGER:    Now, when I use the word *gringo,* we're talking about the same gringos who have paid you $75,000, are we not; we're the gringos . . . well, who are the gringos?

SONIA:    [The people] in the United States.

FINGER:    The people of the United States are the gringos you were going to help Arce-Gomez invade with cocaine?

SONIA:    Uh-huh.

Walter "Pachi" Atala was not a very good witness for the government. Despite the prosecution's attempt to portray him as being coerced into trafficking to save his wife and children, despite admitting on the witness stand to numerous specific acts of trafficking, and despite having received full immunity from prosecution, Walter refused to acknowledge either his direct involvement in the trafficking or that he had been coerced into anything. Perhaps because of his ego, perhaps because of his aristocratic background, Walter could not bear to portray himself in any way that might be inconsistent with his own strange, super-macho image of himself. Quinon was first to question Walter about his involvement in the cocaine business.

QUINON:    Are you still saying that you were indirectly involved in the trafficking of cocaine?

WALTER:    Counsel, after the government of Gen. Garcia Mesa went to power, the cocaine trafficking was a legal thing in my country. All of those who paid to the Minister of the Interior could [traffic in cocaine] freely with their protection.

QUINON: Mr. Atala, you are not answering my question. I'm not asking you about the President . . . and whether trafficking was legal. It's a simple question. Please listen to it. Are you saying that you were indirectly involved in the trafficking of cocaine?

WALTER: I was connected directly, because it was already a legal thing in my country. In the beginning, to clarify, so the members of the jury know about it, in the beginning before [the Cocaine Coup] I tried to camouflage the situation. But not after that, because it was something that was going to be made legal.

QUINON: So . . . when you told Tito Camacho that "you force us to be traffickers," surely you're not suggesting to this jury that Tito Camacho was twisting your arm and saying, "Okay, Pachi, you have to go out and traffic in cocaine"; he wasn't doing that was he?

WALTER: No, he did not force, but rather moral pressure. There are different types of pressure. There is moral pressure and physical, inside any proceeding, and the psychological pressure.

QUINON: So you were being morally and psychologically pressured to traffic in cocaine, painfully so?

WALTER: No, so, because I tell you in honor to the truth, I was always involved in dangerous matters. I always liked danger. And then I couldn't feel ashamed, because of the words of Mr. Tito Camacho. And when I tell you that I'm not afraid, [it's] because I have been a race car driver. . . .

Later, Quinon tried again.

QUINON: Mr. Atala, before you mentioned that you came from a very good family; correct?

WALTER: Yes, sir.

QUINON: And somewhere down the line, you got involved with cocaine?

WALTER: Yes, sir.

QUINON: All right, how did that come about?

For the next three or four minutes, Walter, like the politician he is, spoke about the suffering Bolivian people, the price of coca leaves, and the failing Bolivian economy. When it appeared that he had only just begun his filibuster, Quinon interrupted.

QUINON: Mr. Atala, I don't mean to interrupt you. I believe the question directed to you was more personally, rather than about

428

<blockquote>

<table>
<tr><td></td><td>your country. The question is: why did you get involved in cocaine, if you were from a good, honest, wealthy family?</td></tr>
<tr><td>WALTER:</td><td>In the face of this situation, which already generated, and I reiterate to you again, they went to my house to invite me, so I would participate too. Because I was a personal friend of the Minister of the Interior. And supposedly, the persons that [joined forces with the new government] were also people that had been with me in school.</td></tr>
</table>

</blockquote>

Sonia claimed to have been "forced" into dealing for the Minister of Interior, but Walter said he was "invited" to participate by Arce-Gomez, his personal friend. Sonia said she never met Arce-Gomez before the Cocaine Coup, but Walter said he went to school with him. Incredibly, the Atalas hadn't even tried to coordinate their stories.

Perhaps the most revealing answer Walter gave—one of the few that directly corresponded with Sonia's—was when Quinon asked about his reasons for suddenly cooperating with the DEA investigation.

<blockquote>

<table>
<tr><td>QUINON:</td><td>Okay. Now, let me ask you this: why did you decide to cooperate with the DEA?</td></tr>
<tr><td>WALTER:</td><td>That is a very interesting question.</td></tr>
<tr><td>QUINON:</td><td>I agree. That's why I asked you that.</td></tr>
<tr><td>WALTER:</td><td>Look, in my country . . . generally, the general population is blamed of being . . . of being the ones that push the drug trafficking. However, this trafficking comes down from the government. That is why when I was detained, very many people were detained. [Walter had been detained by Arce-Gomez's mercenaries when DEA spirited Sonia away from Bolivia.] However, the ones that were guilty of the situation existing in my country, were enjoying very nice vacations outside [the country] and enjoying the money and were working already directly together with the [cocaine customers] that my wife had already introduced to them from the United States as well as Colombia.</td></tr>
</table>

</blockquote>

Quinon, perhaps expecting the usual drug-dealer-turned-government-witness-I-have-seen-the-error-of-my-ways bullshit, was taken aback by Walter's candid admission that he was using the U.S. government to take revenge on the people who had cut him and Sonia out of the business, and continued the line of questioning.

<blockquote>

<table>
<tr><td>QUINON:</td><td>All right. Now, my question was . . . and maybe you misunderstood . . . why did you cooperate with the DEA? You're telling me about the [Bolivian] government officials and I</td></tr>
</table>

</blockquote>

understand that, but I want to know why you cooperated with the DEA. . . .

WALTER: Being before in the situation, I had the great opportunity that was offered to me by this government. [A little sarcasm from Pachi.]

QUINON: This government; you mean, the United States?

WALTER: Of the United States, through the department of the DEA, of cooperating and of telling the truth about the existent situation in my country. And I offer myself to do that.

QUINON: So you decided to cooperate, because all of a sudden you decided that cocaine is bad for society; correct? [Quinon had a sarcastic streak himself.]

WALTER: I do not want to go into details, counsel, but I will tell you that, yes.

QUINON: It was a situation where your conscience was bothering you and you decided this is as good a time as any to do something about the problem; correct?

WALTER: Yes, sir.

Another series of questions by Quinon resulted in an interesting insight into Pachi's mobile morality.

QUINON: Were you present when Arce-Gomez offered to your wife as many coca leaves as she could handle?

WALTER: No, sir. Let me add something to what you say about the coca leaf. When Mr. Mendieta [the Bolivian government chemist working for Arce-Gomez] offered to us on behalf of the Ministry to establish a factory of cocaine, my opposition was negative. I expressed to him that we may have been traffickers, but that we were not producers or owners of factories. So it's rather too much that you ask me if the Minister offered coca leaves.

QUINON: All right. Why were you somewhat offended that you responded to Mendieta, "I may be a trafficker, but, my God, not a manufacturer?" Why were you so offended? What offended you about the manufacture [of cocaine]?

WALTER: It's not a question of having been offended, counselor, but rather that it's not so much if a weapon situation . . . if a weapon situation and I use that arm to fire at someone there is someone behind me that fabricated that weapon or manufactured that weapon for me to commit a crime . . . It never crossed my mind to be a manufacturer.

I had already been used [by the Bolivian government] so that we could sell their [cocaine] for them, counselor. I want you to understand my ethical position.

QUINON: In other words, you were not a manufacturer, because ethics prohibited you from doing it?

WALTER:  Ethics and my morality did not permit that and never did.

QUINON:  All right. The ethics and morality did not affect [you selling cocaine]?

WALTER:  The distribution [of cocaine], because there was something already premanufactured already. My wife and I didn't go to the bank [where the Bolivian government stored cocaine in bank vaults] and say, "give us these bags," that we are going to manufacture them. They were taken to us to our home. When I expressed to Mr. Mendieta that [the Bolivian government's] cocaine was lousy, it was no good, he expressed to me, "but you [and Sonia] have a good chemist that can reprocess it."

Finally, Quinon brought out how incredibly selective the U.S. government had been in choosing who would be indicted. When Walter answered, it was with barely concealed disdain for the American drug war.

QUINON:  With the exception of Ana Tamayo, none of the people that used to work for you and your wife have been indicted in this case; correct?

WALTER:  That's not my problem, counselor.

QUINON:  I'm simply asking the question, sir. Isn't that a fact?

WALTER:  That's the problem of the DEA, not mine.

When Finger took over the cross-examination, he explored the mystery of Rourke's belated discovery of Pachi as a witness.

FINGER:  Why did it take you a year and a half before you started talking to the DEA after getting to the United States of America?

WALTER:  Because they never spoke to me before.

FINGER:  Well, you had seen the DEA agents at your home to talk to Sonia, hadn't you?

WALTER:  When Sonia came [to the United States], I believe she gave all her information by herself. Subsequently, when the DEA agents were going to my home, I was leaving it, because I don't like to listen sometimes to what is not convenient for oneself.

FINGER:  Did you know they were DEA agents?

WALTER:  Yes, sir.

FINGER:  And you knew they were there to talk to Sonia about narcotics smuggling?

WALTER:  Yes, sir.

FINGER:  And you told Mr. Quinon yesterday that the reason you are cooperating, is because you have a moral conviction against cocaine?

WALTER: I gave that answer to [Quinon] because my wife had certain agreements with the DEA. However, I didn't. When they asked me if I could cooperate, I said I could. I never said, "But what is going to happen to me, are you going to pay me money or what are you going to give me?"

FINGER: I'm not suggesting that you did that, Mr. Atala, All I want to know is when the DEA was visiting your wife for more than a year, why didn't you go up to them and say, "Hey, I've got some information, I can help you out and help you fight this war on drugs"; why didn't you do it?

WALTER: When I arrived from my country, I brought certain information for them, written information. And I also had a problem, I neither sell myself nor do I excuse myself. Then, since they didn't invite me, I didn't tell them, either. I don't want that, I don't like that.

FINGER: So you weren't going to volunteer your services to the DEA until they asked you?

WALTER: Yes, sir.

FINGER: When the DEA finally did approach you, did you ever ask them, "What took you so long?"

WALTER: No, sir.

FINGER: Did they ever tell you why they're talking to you in February of 1983, since you have been around since October of 1981?

WALTER: They are investigators and they must have known the reason why.

Finger also delved into Pachi's relationship with Arce-Gomez. Walter's answer seemed to emphasize the possibility that one of the CIA's reasons for supporting, if not instigating, the Cocaine Coup, might have been to defeat President Carter in the 1980 elections, something that the Doctor had told me back in Argentina.

FINGER: How was it that you knew [Arce-Gomez]?

WALTER: If I'm not mistaken, he comes from the city of Sucrez [phonetic]. And when I started racing, well he . . . was stationed in Sucrez and that's when I met him. So every year at the parties, which are on May 25, I used to see him there in Sucrez. We used to talk, play, like good friends. He was like they say, my pal. He was . . . He liked racing. He was a fan of racing.

FINGER: He was a personal friend of yours or just a racing fan?

WALTER: Well, he was my friend, because when I arrived, he would do everything he could for me. He was simply a captain [in the army] at that time.

FINGER: Now you had a meeting with Arce after he assumed power where he discussed with you the difficult economic situation in Bolivia; do you recall that?

WALTER: Yes, sir.

FINGER: And at that time he was waiting for President Reagan's election?

WALTER: Yes, sir.

FINGER: And he told you that he had reports that 80 percent of adult Americans used or were addicted to cocaine?

WALTER: Yes, sir.

FINGER: And then he said that they better take care of their borders, because he's going to cover them with cocaine?

WALTER: If the United States denied all their help to the country, yes, it would be that way.

The Cocaine Coup occurred in July 1980, four months before Reagan's election. Whether the Cocaine Coup and the alleged "October surprise"—the effort to delay the release of the American hostages in Iran—was part of a global plot to defeat President Carter is another of the many questions that can be answered only by an in-depth investigation into the criminal behavior of U.S. government officials that is hidden behind the veil of "national security."

Near the end of Finger's cross-examination, Pachi succinctly captured Sonia's role in America's cocaine explosion.

WALTER: Look, counselor, I'm going to tell you something, if you read the entire procedure, of how things happened . . . The Minister and the gentlemen that accompanied him, what they needed were international contact, and what my wife was doing was opening a path for that so-called cocaine invasion into the Untied States.

FINGER: She was like a trailblazer?

WALTER: [She was the one] that introduced the people.

And if there was any doubt as to the Atalas' real reasons for turning to the U.S. government, Walter cleared them up.

WALTER: Because after [Sonia had introduced Arce-Gomez and his men to her customers] they wanted to eliminate us, and the way to eliminate us was by tricking us, giving us goods that were no good, giving them ridiculous prices as compared to what the cost of cocaine should be, sending their personal representatives to Colombia and Miami, and Mr. Arce-Gomez himself coming to the United States. So he was setting up quite a big operation.

433

FINGER:    They just took advantage of you and your wife?
WALTER:    And then afterward, we were the scapegoats for the whole
           thing, sir.
FINGER:    And you escaped to the United States of America?
WALTER:    I looked for a place that would offer me the opportunity to
           live in peace and to provide and that I have always wanted to
           provide for my children.

The trial of Sonia's customers ended with convictions, as everyone expected. Montero and Baron were sentenced to 10 and 5 years in prison, respectively. The irony of Sonia sending her customers to jail came out in Montero's description of his first meeting with Sonia:

FINGER:    Would it be safe to say that as of that meeting in April you
           knew that [Sonia] was a cocaine trafficker?
MONTERO:   Oh, definitely she was. She told me in the conversation, just
           before it ended, that people had a little joke [about] her and
           that she was . . . she was "the queen of Bolivia with a crown
           of snow."

In his summation, Finger said: "When they wrote the words, 'Give me your tired, your poor, your huddled masses yearning to breathe free' on the Statue of Liberty, I don't think they had Sonia and Pachi Atala in mind. I think if that grand old lady knew we'd made Sonia and Pachi Atala U.S. residents, she'd fall off that pedestal in New York Harbor in tears."

And he didn't know the half of it.

The trial over, their duty done, Sonia and Walter disappeared into the netherworld of secret locations and false identifications known as the Witness Protection Program. Rourke resigned himself to his new job on the Marijuana Desk. And the real Underground Empire breathed easy again, thinking that Operation Hun could finally be laid safely to rest.

# 36

# A Texas Drug Bust

At 3:00 P.M. on December 14, 1987, two dark, mustachioed Chicanos entered a Denny's restaurant on the outskirts of San Antonio, Texas. For a moment they stood silhouetted in the bright sunlight while their hard eyes scoured the place. The restaurant was almost empty. A family was eating lunch at a rear booth, and the little boy looked up to stare at the men. *"No mires!"* snapped the father, shoving the child's head back toward his food. "Mind your own business!" he told his son. These two were trouble, and trouble was not something you looked in the eye in San Antonio.

What the father didn't know was that the two men in the doorway were undercover DEA agents Bobby Hernandez and Rudy Gonzalez. They were there to meet Francisco Altamirano, who was watching them nervously from a booth near the counter. Sitting at the counter was another man, his eyes invisible behind dark glasses.

Altamirano nodded almost imperceptibly, and the two men moved quickly toward his booth.

For Hernandez and Gonzalez, this was the big day they'd been working toward since Altamirano first sold them cocaine back in April. It was the day of the big bust. And if they had done their job well and got a little lucky, maybe they'd bag a bigger prize than Altamirano—his most guarded secret—his source.

To get past a street dealer to his source, which Hernandez and Gonzalez had been setting up for seven months, was a tricky psychological game. You couldn't order too much dope because that would make dealer and source suspicious. And you couldn't order too little because upping the ante would make them even more suspicious. Once an undercover made several small buys and felt he had a dealer's confidence, he would then try to bait the source out into the open by ordering more dope than the dealer would be trusted with. The main man—not trusting the street dealer but not wanting to lose the sale—would show up on the set himself with the dope, and the agents would bag themselves a class-one dope dealer, maybe even a smuggler.

Hernandez and Gonzalez had bought a total of eight ounces of cocaine from Altamirano. A couple of weeks earlier Gonzalez visited Altamirano at the restaurant across town where he worked part time as a cook. Altamirano was frying eggs when Gonzalez slipped into the kitchen through the back door to ask about the possibility of getting a couple of kilos.

"What! You fucking kidding, man? My people would go bad on me if they heard that."

"Why should they go bad?" Rudy had said. "They got something against making money?"

"These people are heavies from down south," Altamirano had said mysteriously. "Peruvians . . . a brother and sister. I never asked for anything like that kind of weight before. They'd think I was a cop or something. Look what you made me do, *ese*. I burnt the fucking eggs."

"I said 'possibly,' man. I don't have that kinda bread now anyway. Hey, don't throw those eggs out. I got to say one thing about you, my man—burnt or not, you make the best Huevos Rancheros I ever ate."

A couple of days later Gonzalez and Hernandez showed up at Altamirano's restaurant to say they had enough money for 15 ounces of cocaine—$16,000 worth. The amount was definitely more than Altamirano could handle, but not enough to frighten him off. The trap had been baited perfectly.

"Well? You got it?" said Hernandez, sliding into the booth opposite Altamirano.

Gonzalez slid in beside his partner, checking the man at the counter, who was seated behind them and had his arm over a leather bag. To Rudy, who had worked and traveled all over South and Central America, the man had the kind of features that could have been Mexican or maybe Caribbean, but definitely not Peruvian. Besides, no class-one doper would be sitting in a fucking Denny's with his dope in a bag.

Gonzalez angled himself in his seat; the man at the counter would have to be watched. The whole deal could be a ripoff—about half the DEA undercovers killed in the line of duty had been targets of ripoffs. Sixteen thousand in cash attracted a lot of strange street creatures. If the guy had something heavy like an Uzi in that bag, the dozen agents cruising the streets outside would do them no good at all. It would all happen too fast.

"You got the money?" asked Altamirano, speaking in a loud enough Spanish for the man at the counter to hear.

"It's nearby," said Hernandez. "What about the stuff?"

"Fifteen is a lot," said Altamirano, loud. "My people won't risk all that *sota* at once. I got seven oh-zees nearby. You get the other eight when my people hear I got paid for the first seven."

"How far is nearby?" said Hernandez, his eyes lingering on the guy at the counter. There was no way the dope was in that bag. If he had anything in there, it was a gun.

"Just two blocks . . . five minutes," said Altamirano. He suddenly looked at the two agents suspiciously, his eyes nervously bouncing from one to the other. "These people don't fuck around, *ese*. They got at least one guy with a rifle watching them."

"*Cojelo suave, ese,*" said Hernandez, smiling easily. "You know us. We're here to do business."

Both agents relaxed a little. The fact that Altamirano was himself nervous about a ripoff was reassuring. It meant he had come to do righteous business; it meant his source was nearby.

"I'll be right back," said Gonzalez, making a decision about the game's next move and sliding out of the booth. The guy at the counter was turned toward him, his hand still resting protectively on the leather bag. Gonzalez walked slowly out the door and into the parking lot. Maybe the guy was the eyes and ears of the source. Gonzalez hoped so; he was about to make sure he got an eye- and earful.

"Where's he going?" said Altamirano nervously.

"Be cool, *ese*," said Hernandez. "He'll be right back."

In the parking lot, Gonzalez felt a rush of adrenaline; the action was on. He opened the trunk of his undercover car. The bag full of $100 bills looked like it was glowing. The air suddenly seemed unusually crisp; the smells from the restaurant more pungent than before. From the moment he started back to the restaurant with the money he would be as close to death as any undercover could get.

Gonzalez felt a dozen eyes watching his every movement. He couldn't see them, but he knew they were just a couple of heartbeats away. They were his group, his team, his backup; they were all street men like him; they were his brothers. If there was trouble they would read it in his body language, his slightest gesture. They would protect him with their lives. Thinking about them gave Gonzalez confidence.

"UC's got the flash roll and is returning to the Denny's," a voice whispered over car radios. "He's gonna flash it."

"Who's got an eyeball?" snapped the group supervisor.

"Unit 4407, ten-four."

"Unit 4409, ditto."

"Unit 4417, ten-four."

"If he's flashin it," said the supervisor, "the source's gotta be close. I want oh-seven and oh-nine to stay put and keep an eye on the UCs; the rest of you cruisin' the neighborhood lookin' for anything that might be connected."

A chorus of "ten-fours" crackled over the airwaves.

As Gonzalez returned to the Denny's with the bag of money under his arm, the man at the counter stared at him openly, his hand still resting on the leather bag. Gonzalez's elbow touched the gun beneath his shirt. If the *hijo de puta* makes a move, he thought, I'm gonna take him with me.

"Here it is," said Gonzalez, taking his seat in the booth. He opened the bag.

"Check it out," said Hernandez.

Gonzalez held the bag open and flipped through the two stacks of bills. "Go slow," said Altamirano, leaning across the table, his eyes gleaming.

"See enough?" said Hernandez.

"Yeah," said Altamirano, glancing at the guy at the counter, who had heard and seen everything.

"Okay, then let's do it," said Gonzalez, tucking the bag back under his arm. He got quickly to his feet and started toward the door.

Altamirano looked startled. "Where's he going?" He twisted nervously in his seat.

"Be cool, *ese*," said Hernandez, "he's just putting the bread back in the oven so it stays warm, that's all."

But Altamirano wasn't listening. He was watching the man at the counter follow Gonzalez out to the parking lot.

Gonzalez had the car trunk open when he noticed the man coming toward him with the leather bag held tightly under his arm. Rudy dropped the bag of money and closed the trunk. The man passed by close enough for Rudy to touch him. The guy kept on walking, slowly, out of the parking lot, pausing a couple of times to look back.

Gonzalez got into the front seat of his car and grabbed a hidden radio mike. Keeping it in his lap, he pressed the talk button. "I think the guy carrying the bag is counter-surveillance."

"That's ten-four," said a voice. "I got an eyeball on him; he's scoping the whole neighborhood."

"Stay on him," said the supervisor.

"He's heading toward Dos Pedros."

"This is forty-four ten, I'm gettin' out on foot to take him."

"Forty-four fifteen, ditto."

The man with the leather bag continued slowly up the street, cautiously checking his surroundings, toward the parking lot of the Casa Dos Pedros restaurant, about 200 yards east. Twice he stopped abruptly and turned, but saw nothing out of the ordinary. A dozen agents tried to keep an eye on him, ducked low in their cars, peeking through rearview mirrors or binoculars, or scrambling behind him hiding behind trees and crouching behind parked cars.

"Anybody see the guy?" the supervisor asked.

Silence.

"Does anybody know where the goddamn guy with the bag is?"

Three tense minutes passed, then a voice said, "I got Bag Man gettin' into a car with two people. The bag's gone."

"Gone?" snapped the group leader. "Anybody see where it went?"

Silence.

"What's the twenty?"

"Dos Pedros parking lot. He's in a blue Chevy Malibu with two people."

"You got a description?"

"All I can see's it's a man and a woman."

"They starting the engine?"

"No. They're just sitting and talking."

"All units get into goddamn position," said the supervisor. He was pissed.

Inside the Denny's, Hernandez and Altamirano finally agreed on how the deal would go down.

"I got seven oh-zees in my car," said Altamirano. "You pay for that, you get the rest."

"Okay," said Hernandez. "Soon as I see it's all there, I walk over to my partner's car and get the bread. Then we do the same thing with the next eight, right?"

"Right."

The two men left the Denny's and went to Altamirano's car on a nearby street. Altamirano, twitching nervously, had trouble getting the keys into the ignition. Finally he started the engine and put it into gear.

"Where we going?" said Hernandez. "I thought the stuff's in the car."

"It is," said Altamirano. "It's right under your feet."

A paper bag covered by a towel lay right at Hernandez's feet. Bobby picked up the bag. Inside was a can of hair spray. "What the fuck is this?"

"The can got a false bottom," said Altamirano.

Hernandez turned the can upside down and pulled the bottom off; the inside was stuffed with plastic bags of white powder. It was a beautiful, professional job. Hernandez was excited. A can like that would never be in the hands of a street dealer like Altamirano. They were close to something big. This was more than just a source; this was a prime source . . . a smuggler. "This is beautiful," breathed Hernandez.

"Isn't it?" said Altamirano, pleased. He had just pulled into the Denny's parking lot.

"Park across from my partner," said Hernandez. "I'll get the money."

Altamirano parked about 20 feet from Gonzalez. Hernandez got out and walked quickly across the parking lot to the car. "He's got the stuff in the car. Gimme the keys."

"Shit," said Gonzalez, "I'm gonna miss that guy."

"What are you talking about?"

"Ain't nobody cooks Huevos Rancheros like that guy."

"C'mon, *ese*. Stop fucking around. He's gonna catch wise."

Gonzalez tossed him the keys. Hernandez opened the trunk. It was the arrest signal.

The parking lot came alive. Cars screeched and skidded around Altamirano. Before he could react he was face down on the pavement and being handcuffed.

"We got half the stuff," said Gonzalez into the mike. "Take the other guy."

Texas dust billowed up behind a half dozen cars exploding into the Casa Dos Pedros parking lot. Three agents on foot sprang from behind parked cars and sprinted forward. Within seconds the blue Malibu was surrounded by men with guns leveled at the passengers. The slightest move from inside the car would set off a 20-second hail of bullets that would turn the inside of the car into a gory mass of blood and brains.

"Show your fucking hands!"

*"Policia! Policia! No se muevan! Manos en el aire!"*

"Show your motherfucking hands or you're dead!"

The woman was the first to get out, her pretty face placid, as if she were being helped from her car by the parking valet. The two men, chalk white with terror, had to be pulled from the car. The man from the counter identified himself as Luis Santiago. The man and woman were identified as a married couple: Pachi and Sonia Albrecht.

"She look like a doper to you?" remarked a pot-bellied agent in cowboy boots as Sonia Albrecht glared defiantly at her captors. Her husband Pachi, standing handcuffed beside her, looked confused and frightened.

"Shee-it, she looks like a goddamn cheerleader at A & M."

"Look at her eyes," said Gonzalez. "She ain't the least impressed."

"Look at her old man; he looks like he's about to blubber."

Nothing incriminating was found in the Albrecht's Malibu; but a waiter in Casa Dos Pedros told Hernandez that he'd seen Santiago put something in a gold Thunderbird a few minutes before the arrest. A quick check of the plates revealed that the Thunderbird was registered to Santiago, and within a couple of hours Rudy had a search warrant.

The search of Santiago's car revealed the additional eight ounces of cocaine hidden in two more cans. Sonia Albrecht's fingerprints were on one can and Pachi Albrecht's fingerprints were on the paper bag that contained the first seven ounces in Altamirano's car. In addition, among the items found and inventoried in Santiago's car were the following (as listed in court documents):

> a slip of paper [that] listed over $11,000 in expenditures owed by Sonia Albrecht with respect to certain trips from or to such locations as Miami—a United States hub for cocaine importation from South America—and Bolivia—one of the primary source countries of cocaine in South America;
>
> a slip of paper [that] listed various firearms, including certain automatic weapons frequently used by narcotics traffickers in Latin America and increasingly being used by those in the United States.

An expert was not able to determine if the handwriting on these lists was Santiago's. Mysteriously, no comparison was ever made with either of the Albrechts' handwriting.

Altamirano and Santiago were convicted of federal cocaine trafficking charges, and were sentenced to seven years in prison. All criminal charges against the Albrechts were dropped. Long after they were released, Hernandez and Gonzalez learned that the couple's true name was Atala.

After the Atalas' release, federal prosecutors charged that Santiago was the source of the cocaine, and his sentence was revised upward to 15 years. Santiago appealed his conviction. The Court of Appeals denied his petition, but in doing so made this observation: "Agent Gonzalez's testimony also supports the conclusion that the appearance and location of the Albrechts, the two individuals Santiago had joined inside the blue Chevrolet, were consistent with Altamirano's representations as to his source."

Court of Appeals and truth notwithstanding, the Atalas were long gone. The Queen of Cocaine and her husband once again disappeared into the shadows of the real Underground Empire.

# 37

# Resurrection

1

The resurrection of Operation Hun on October 14, 1989 was swift and unexpected. At the Bogota, Colombia airport that day, a prisoner transfer was carried out under heavy security. There was great concern among the few U.S. officials who knew about the momentous event that the Medellin Cartel had gotten wind of the plan and was preparing a full-scale military assault. They conveyed this fear to the handful of Colombian officials trusted enough to be involved in decision making. As a prudent security measure it was decided that the entire airport and surrounding vicinity had to be sealed off. Considering the significance of what was about to occur, the precaution seemed justified. Besides, it would make dynamite press copy.

In the predawn darkness, a strange caravan—a black Mercedes stretch limo escorted by a dozen motorcycle police, army jeeps, and troop carriers bristling with armed men—drove swiftly through the deserted streets toward the outskirts of town. Overhead three U.S.-made helicopters swooped back and forth, checking the streets ahead for an ambush.

At the request of U.S. officials, the Colombian military had moved thousands of men into position. The roads leading to the airfield for a mile in every direction were blocked off and lined with soldiers and police vehicles. The airfield's perimeter fence was lined with soldiers toting submachine guns. Armed men in civilian clothes and army and police uniforms were stationed on the roof of the terminal, in all passageways, and even in the johns. Inside the empty terminal heavily armed men were stationed at 10- or 15-foot intervals. Only a tank division would be a threat to the security of this operation.

As the Amazon dawn began to streak gold and burnt orange, two soldiers stationed on the perimeter fence took in the impressive array around them.

"What do you think this is all about?"

"Someone said the gringo president is coming for a secret visit."

"*Conio!* I wonder how it feels to be so important, like your ass is made of gold and diamonds or something."

Suddenly a huge United States Air Force C-127 thundered in low over the horizon. Within minutes the lumbering giant was on the ground and rolling toward the terminal.

The airport seemed to come alive. The helicopters chugged into view. The caravan powered through the gate onto the tarmac, where more military vehicles joined it, forming a protective V around the limo. The formation raced across the airfield toward the C-127, which had stopped several hundred yards from the main terminal. The rear hatch of the plane swung down, and armed U.S. soldiers and agents poured out of the plane onto the tarmac.

The vehicles came to a halt about a dozen yards from the tail of the plane. Colombian soldiers leaped from their vehicles and formed a circle around the area, each holding his weapon at a tense port-arms and staring off into the dawn light as if an attack were imminent. None of them knew exactly what they were there for. They had only been told that they were taking part in an historic operation.

Colombian President Virgilio Barco, forced into action by an increasingly violent Medellin Cartel, was for the first time in history extraditing Colombian citizens to the United States on drug charges. The cartel had overstepped its bounds by killing politicians, judges, and media people who opposed them. If Barco didn't do something to curtail the cartel's power, there would soon be no government left for him to lead.

A list of 20 "extraditables" had been prepared, among them

allegedly the most powerful and deadly drug dealers on the earth. According to the American press, it was a star-studded list of international criminals. The news of Barco's intent had rocked the world; it was open defiance against the most powerful criminal organization ever. There were many with long experience in South American narcotics enforcement who didn't believe Barco would carry out his threat. But today was to be the day he would prove them wrong; the day—according to many U.S. politicians and the media—that the drug barons would be dealt their severest blow. It was the day the first and presumably most important of the extraditables would be sent to the United States to face justice.

A heavily manacled figure emerged from the limo, leather bag over the head. The prisoner was quickly surrounded by soldiers and plain-clothes police, and the group hustled toward the plane. The prisoner clopped along in open-backed high heels and too-tight purple Capri pants. Some of the DEA agents noticed that her pants, though tight, were baggy in the buttocks.

The first Colombian to be extradited was Ana Tamayo.

Ana, whom the press called "a key figure in the notorious Medellin Cartel," was one of three Colombian traffickers that were brought to the United States on the C-127 that Saturday morning. The other two—Bernardo Pelaez Roldan and Roberto Peter Carlini—were also described as "key figures," "drug barons," "kingpins," and "most significant players." They were also said to be connected with the Medellin Cartel.[1]

I had never heard of them.

Attorney General Dick Thornburgh said, "I commend President Virgilio Barco and the government of Colombia for their continued diligence in the war against narco-terrorists." The Colombians, of course, asked for more financial aid and President Bush, of course, sent them $65 million in military equipment paid for by the completely credulous and convinced American taxpayers. Few in the media noticed when the Colombians protested that military equipment wasn't what they needed. They said the drug war wasn't really a military type of war, and they would have much preferred money. But they decided to keep the equipment anyway, as a token of U.S. support. American taxpayers were grateful.

When the news broke, I watched in wonder. Somebody must have

---

[1] UPI News Release 10/14/89 1700—"Colombia Deports Three Suspected Drug Dealers."

screwed up. Ana was never supposed to be arrested—if she went to trial, not only would I have to testify but the world press would be watching. What might be revealed would not exactly be the image of the war on drugs our politicians and bureaucrats wanted made public.

I had just lived through another Operation Hun—this mess was called Operation Trifecta and involved high government officials in Mexico, Panama, and Bolivia. I was also writing the exposé *Deep Cover (The Inside Story of How DEA Infighting, Incompetence and Subterfuge Lost Us the Biggest Battle of the Drug War)* about that operation. I was due to retire in December and the book would be on the stands in March, after which I doubted that any prosecutor with a case as wormy and full of dirty secrets as Operation Hun would want me on a witness stand. Besides, as the suits had learned from the Suarez case, I could not be counted on to keep my mouth shut and play their game. If I was going to take on the drug war suits, I wanted to do it as a civilian. Although I was due to retire in seven weeks, the memory of Internal Security ripping my life apart was still fresh in my mind.

In November 1983, the government's two-and-a-half-year attempt to indict me came to an end.

It was late afternoon when Kevin Gallegher called me into his office. "Close the door," he said. He was standing in front of his desk holding a thick packet of papers, a somber look on his face. Mike Powers, whose wife had been killed by drug dealers in Thailand, was sitting on a couch watching me.

"Should I sit down?"

"I think you better," said Powers.

"Read this," said Gallegher, handing me the packet.

The cover sheet told the whole story. It said I was being charged with a questionable transaction with an informant (a transaction DEA had ordered me to do with Tanya), unauthorized phone calls from the American embassy (the phone calls to my kids when Suarez put a price on my head), and failure to keep receipts and records of expenses while working undercover during the Suarez operation (an offense that can only be likened to charging a soldier on combat duty with failing to file an income tax form). The suits proposed a 20-day suspension without pay, and I was given an opportunity to reply.

"They just wanted to do you," said Kevin.

"Let us answer it for you," said Powers. "I know you; you'll get too emotional. You'll write a fucking 200-page manifesto."

Mike was right. I had 10 days to answer the charges and two-and-a-half years of rage built up inside me. I let Mike and Kevin answer the charges for me.

The answer was concise and unemotional. It clearly and unequivocally stated that I had done absolutely nothing to be penalized for. A couple of weeks after I submitted it, the suits decided to suspend me for one week.

"After all that shit, they had to hit you with something," said Kevin. "Why don't you take a week's vacation, forget about it, and head to New York and start locking up dope dealers."

That afternoon, the Rabbi called. "Consider yourself very lucky," he said.

"I do," I said, feeling about as lucky as a man wrongfully jailed being told by the warden to feel lucky that he didn't get the electric chair.

I ended up taking Kevin's advice. I wasn't big enough to take these people on by myself. Almost two years had passed since Rourke first mentioned Sonia Atala to me; almost three-and-a-half years had gone by since I first heard it from her uncle Hugo in the Buenos Aires Sheraton. I was no longer in the loop for cocaine investigations in general and Operation Hun in particular, nor did I want to be. The healthiest thing for me to do was to try to block thoughts of Operation Hun and the hype Americans were fed about the drug war from my mind. I managed to do that for five years.

## 2

By the end of the first week of November 1989, Ana Tamayo had been in jail almost a month and no one had told me that I would be needed as a witness. I no longer found things like this strange.

I was rarely in the office anymore. Six months earlier I had chased a crack dealer out a second-story window during a crack house raid and was trying to recuperate from three herniated discs, an impact fracture of my right ankle, and more damage to my surgical knee. I would go into the office once a week or so for a couple of hours to do paperwork, usually related to my injuries or my retirement. So it seemed an act of fate that on November 13 I happened to be in the office when Rourke called.

"Man, am I glad I found you, ya hump," said Rourke. "I thought you were gone already. You heard about Ana?"

"How could I avoid it?" I said. "It's been on every news show, every paper. It's incredible."

"Can you fucking believe it—Ana fucking Tamayo? And they delivered her to us with a fucking bag over her head."

"Jesus," I said. "It's like the Chiappe thing back in 1975."

"You were on that?"

"Sure I was. I got sued for it . . . for kidnaping."

For a moment I saw in my mind that dawn on the tarmac at Eseiza Airport almost 15 drug war years earlier. I remembered Chiappe's gaping, bloody maw where his teeth had been battered out with a rifle butt. I had thought then that he had gotten what he deserved. I no longer felt the same way.

"So what are they gonna do with poor Ana?" I asked Rourke.

"Mike, you got no idea what a fuckup this thing is. You have no idea."

"Nothing would surprise me."

"You know what attorney she got?" Rourke laughed. "She's got Carlos Lehder's attorney."

"I don't believe it," I said. "What's still trying to sink in now is this picture of Ana Tamayo with a bag over her head. Where's she going to trial?"

"She's going to trial in Miami. Guess what happened in Tucson?"

"I can't imagine."

"You can't imagine, huh? Can you imagine a bigger fuckup. We got a group supervisor comes in there, and he decides to clean out all the files."

"You mean he got rid of the whole file?" I said, feeling the hot anger in me rise a couple of degrees. This was the first time I heard that all the evidence gathered in Operation Hun had been destroyed.

"He closed it," said Rourke.

"He closed the case."

"He not only closed the case—guess what else he did. There's a bail-jumping charge on Ana, right?"

"Yeah."

"He got it dismissed." Rourke stopped talking, giving me a moment to think about the implications. "When in your life have you ever heard of a bail-jumping charge being dismissed?"

"I don't believe it," I said.

"If a guy dies they don't dismiss a bail-jumping charge against him," said Rourke.

"Who's the guy responsible for dismissing the case?"

"I never heard of him in my life," said Rourke. He's been a group supervisor for three years I guess. Not, I guess, the best-liked guy in town either."

I made a mental bet with myself that the supervisor was one of those who "transferred" over from the CIA.

"What about all the videotapes with Ana and us?" I asked, also remembering the tapes of Roberto, Monica Garcia, and the testing of the yellow cocaine.

"I got a phone call in to those guys to try to find out if any of the evidence is still around. You know I just got off the phone with Pat Sullivan a little while ago and he's in a panic. The defense attorney's got discovery and Ana's being held without bail, and all that kind of shit; you know, pretrial detention. So we got a speedy trial situation and we got 14-day discovery and shit like that. So Sullivan calls Miami DEA, right?"

"Yeah," I said. With Sullivan as prosecutor, I knew I'd never be a witness against Ana.

"So who do the suits assign the case to? Some kid who's brand new. The kid came in and sat down in front of Sullivan. This is the prosecutor, right? The senior prosecutor. He's not just an AUSA. You know he's like being looked at to be the U.S. Attorney. The kid walks in and sits down in front of him and says, 'I don't know anything about this case. I don't know why I'm here. I don't want to be here. But here I am.'"

"Oh my God," I said.

"Now we got newspaper people all over us."

"So what's the next step?" I asked. "When I heard that they got Ana I figured someone would notify me to testify, but I never got notified. I know I've got to testify."

"Yeah, you know I would have jumped right on that, and I thought you knew about it a long time ago."

"I saw the news releases."

"I was sitting at home eating breakfast when I was told about it," said Rourke. "As a matter of fact, you know what happened? They called me about three months ago when they had her arrested and were thinking about bringing her back. I almost fucking choked, right?"

"Yeah."

"I said, 'Shit, no problem, we got her on bail-jumping.' So I call up and found out that the fucking case was dismissed. I almost fell out of my chair. They dismissed the case," he repeated, as if he still couldn't believe it. "So I get a hold of Sullivan and I say, 'Pat, this is it—it's a no-dope conspiracy case.'

"He says, 'We don't want her back.'

"So I say, 'Well Pat, it may come down that we won't have a choice, 'cause somebody else is gonna make this decision for us.' He says, 'Naaah.'

"Then, guess what happens to Ana's daughter three weeks ago."

"I don't know. Nothing surprises me about this case anymore."

"Mike, this is what happens," said Rourke, his voice dropping to a conspiratorial whisper. "The fucking daughter is working for DEA to try to help her mother. She tried to work for somebody down in Cartagena . . . real cloak and dagger. So Ana gets arrested down in Colombia and the daughter figures she's gonna be the intermediary to DEA. Three weeks ago the daughter is driving down the street in Cartagena. The girlfriend jumps out of the car. A motorcycle pulls up and they blow her brains out."

"Ohhh," I said as if the wind was knocked out of me. Rourke was laughing. I had never thought of him as a cruel man, but he was laughing.

"The next thing that happens, Ana gets a bag over her head and gets shipped back to the U.S."

"This whole thing is unbelievable," I said remembering Candy's wounded screams over the phone the night I arrested her mother; remembering Ana consoling me the night I learned my daughter was on drugs. "This whole thing is too much for even Hollywood. I mean who's gonna believe this?"

I heard my voice crack and wondered whether Rourke noticed.

"Mike, am I gonna make the next book?"[1]

"Definitely," I said. "In the meantime, how's Sonia doing?"

There was a long silence. "Sonia," said Rourke slowly, his voice suddenly just above a whisper, "is the subject of three Title 3s."

"You mean she's selling dope again?"

"She's fucking doing anything and everything she can."

"Oh, my God," I said, once again thinking of Ana in chains with a bag over her head.

---

[1] Rourke was referring to *Undercover* by Donald Goddard—a book written about my early undercover career. When this phone call occurred, *Deep Cover* was still a closely guarded secret.

"I don't know what the fuck I'm going to do with that," said Rourke. "She's even fucking selling Immigration cards."

"Holy shit," I said, but I wasn't really surprised. We had given her a license to steal, and she was only using it to the best of her ability.

Rourke began to describe Sonia's arrest in San Antonio.

"She was in the car with Walter—you know, Walter the born-again Christian?"

"Yeah."

"The two of them are in the backseat of a car. The guy gets out of the car and sells dope to an undercover agent."

"You're talking about Pachi?"

"Yeah. Walter fucking-no-brains Pachi Atala."

"Oh, my God," I said again. This was the first time I had heard the story.

"They all get pinched," continued Rourke. "You know we get the arrest kind of sidestepped. You can't take an overt act and say 'Forget it!' But she apparently showed up on a couple of wires."

Long silence.

"So what's the next step, Jack?"

"What's the next step? I don't know. I'm happy as hell that you're still on the job. I thought you'd jumped out the back door."

"I'm seven weeks from retirement, Jack."

"Seven weeks . . . well, we'll bring you back."

For a moment my heart sank with the thought that I might be prevented from retiring until Ana's court case was over. But there was no way Sullivan would want me testifying.

"Are you serious?" I asked.

"Sure."

"You mean they're bringing you back to put the whole Operation Hun back together again?"

"That's what I think is going to have to happen. Sullivan is fucking ranting and raving because he's got the press all over the place. And they're looking at it as a very serious indication of what we're doing down in South America. You know, indicting and not being able to prosecute is not what they want to happen."

"This is incredible."

"What we want Ana to do is plead to something . . . anything. Just to fucking get her out of the way."

"Incredible," I repeated.

"And there's fucking Ana Tamayo, you know what she looks like."

451

"Yeah."

"Oh, she looks better now than she did 10 years ago. I couldn't believe it. She had her hair all done up and everything like that."

"We made her an international celebrity," I said. "Why not?"

"And she's looking around the room, all cow-eyes and shit like that."

"Oh, her poor daughter," I said. "I remember when I locked [Ana] up, her laying her head on my shoulder and saying to me . . ."

"What was the name of the song that was being played, Mike?"

I was astounded that Rourke had remembered. At the moment I arrested Ana a Spanish song was on the radio about a guy writing his mother from jail. I had forgotten I told Rourke about it.

"Oh, I think it went 'Desde la carcel te escribo, querida madre'; 'I'm writing you from jail dear mother,' or something like that."

Rourke was laughing. "Was it in Spanish?"

"Yeah, I think it was."

"I remember you telling her, 'I'm sorry, but I didn't plan it that way,'" said Rourke still laughing.

I had said that, but I wasn't referring to the song.

"You know what she said to me when I arrested her?" I said. "She said, 'You could have had Pacho Cuervas; you could have had all these big people and you arrested me, Miguel. The great DEA. Why? Why? Why?' And she was crying. The truth was, I felt like crying with her."

Rourke stopped laughing. This was not a subject he wanted to talk about.

"So what should I do," I asked, "just wait until I'm contacted again?"

"No, I guess you just . . . now I know where you are. I was thinking maybe you were on a world tour with your book, ya hump. You never even had the courtesy to mail me a copy."

"What do you mean courtesy? I didn't even know where you were."

"Yeah, yeah, yeah."

"What about Sonia? She a key witness in this thing?"

"Sure she's a key witness. But guess what—I remember her telling us that the only person in the whole conspiracy that she wouldn't testify against was Ana."

There was not much left for us to talk about. Yet Rourke didn't want to get off the phone. He rambled on a while, griping about the bullshit all DEA agents had to contend with. And then he surprised me.

"It's fucking getting worse and worse and worse. Expose this fucking fraud, Michael. Expose it."

"I'll do the best I can, Jack. It's just too much; nobody will believe it anymore. It's so much of a fucking fraud I wouldn't know where to begin."

Ana Tamayo never had a trial—her attorneys made a deal with the prosecutors. She pleaded guilty and was sentenced to five years in prison; which meant she'd probably have to serve about two-and-a-half years. When I heard this, I figured once again that Operation Hun and Sonia Atala would remain two of the best-kept secrets of the drug war. But the best—or the worst—was yet to come.

# 38

# Finale Fraudulente

Chimoré, the DEA outpost in the Chapare region of Bolivia, is to the people who live in the region like a festering ulcer on alabaster skin. The region is one of the most beautiful on earth. From the barbed-wire-encircled encampment with its scattering of barracks, pillboxes, helicopter platforms, and sandbag walls, you can see hundreds of square miles of emerald rain forest and the black peaks of the Cordillera peeking above misty white clouds. The Chapare is a lush 2.5 million hectares where huge quantities of the most potent coca leaf are grown.

Inside the compound the personnel—Bolivian antinarcotics police called Leopardos, DEA agents, U.S. Customs agents, and U.S. military personnel, ostensibly dedicated to the total eradication of coca in Bolivia—move about in full combat gear. Security is always tight because the compound is surrounded by the enemy—those who need the coca leaf to survive, or about 70–80 percent of Bolivia's population.

On a typical day, word would come to the encampment from supposedly confidential DEA sources of massive cocaine labs in the jungle. The agents and Bolivian police would scramble for their helicopters, but by the time they got to the spot in the jungle there would be nothing left but empty beer cans and fast-food wrappers. When it came to taking food out of their own people's mouths, you just couldn't count on the loyalty of most Bolivian cops. And the military—they were just plain corrupt.

From the Bolivian point of view the whole drug war was a haphazardly, at times comically, choreographed show run for the benefit of visiting U.S. politicians and media for the purpose of keeping American aid dollars flowing. There were also those disquieting rumors that at least one of the biggest cocaine labs—the one at Huanchaca—was run by the CIA to finance covert South American operations like the Contras. Some eyewitnesses claimed to have seen Oliver North, American hero, at the Huanchaca lab.

The target operation on Sunday morning, December 10, 1989, was far too important to risk a leak of any sort. The world would be watching, and a fuckup could have disastrous effects on the images of Bolivian and American politicians. Thus, no one participating in the action was told the identity and location of the target and the nature of the assignment until the helicopters were airborne.

At dawn, four United States military helicopters piloted by American servicemen, flying Bolivian flags, and carrying Bolivian troops and DEA agents, lifted slowly off the ground. A few miles down the road in a shabby little village called Sinaota, where the enemy—dirt-poor peasants needing to feed and clothe their families—continued to harvest coca, an old man peered up at the hovering craft. He raised his right hand high toward the rising sun, closed his fist, and extended his middle finger in the air. One of the men in the village had told him that this was a terrible insult to the gringos; that the finger represented an erect penis. The old man did not understand why an erect penis would be looked upon as an insult—it made no sense. But there was so much about these gringos and their insane drug war that did not make sense that he accepted the information as true.

The helicopters formed in a straight line and swooped directly over the old man and off into the distance, climbing in the direction of Santa Cruz de la Sierra. The old man kept his finger raised until they were out of sight. He had taken a vow to raise his finger every time he saw the helicopters for as long as he lived or for as long as they remained as trespassers on the sacred lands of his people.

On board one of the helicopters the target for that morning's operation was revealed. An American cheered. "Shut the fuck up," said his supervisor nervously. A heavily armed Leopardo stared at the gringo curiously. Another Leopardo closed his eyes and laid his head back.

"Everybody got their flak jackets?" said the supervisor. "Somebody speaks Spanish, ask the Bolivian's if they got 'em. I got a feeling this one's gonna be big trouble."

The target of the operation was none other than the Minister of Cocaine—Luis Arce-Gomez himself.

The behind-the-scenes maneuvering that convinced the Bolivian politicians to violate their own law in handing Arce-Gomez to the Americans is worth examining.

While Pat Sullivan was haggling with Ana Tamayo's defense attorneys over a plea bargain, the drug war in Colombia heated up. President Barco tried to put the screws to the Medellin Cartel by knocking off a couple of their cocaine labs and extraditing a few more insignificant drug dealers.

Barco left other, more businesslike drug dealers, like the nonviolent Cali Cartel, to expand and flourish. After all, as he and the behind-the-scenes U.S. policy makers knew, the Colombian economy was far too dependent on drugs to make real war against coca. Besides, drug money was the only thing repaying the huge debts owed by countries like Colombia, Bolivia, and Peru to already nervous U.S. bankers.

Duplicity and hypocrisy notwithstanding, the new offensive in Colombia was turning out to be a godsend to American and Colombian politicians. The press dutifully wrote the stories the policy makers revealed to them—the bombings, shootings, threats, kidnapings, and extraditions. The events in Colombia also provided a smokescreen for the high U.S. government officials implicated as drug traffickers during the Iran-Contra hearings. Americans were once more told they were winning the drug war, and President Bush got $9 billion from Congress for the drug war in 1989. (In 1990 he got $11 billion.) Most of that money went toward the new militarized war on drugs.

For the American politicians who had supported the militarized drug war, as long as there were action headlines they could keep winning elections. For the drug war bureaucrats, there was more funding and bigger empires. For the Colombian politicians, there were more dollars from both the American taxpayers and the American druggies, whose ever-increasing demand was being met by the quietly expanding Cali Cartel and others. Colombia was also getting the most favorable world press they had ever received. But for the drug war suits responsible for Bolivia, the new war was becoming a problem.

By December 1989, Bolivia had fallen far behind in the battle for headlines. Colombia had extradited 11 "drug barons," and Bolivia hadn't even extradited one. On top of that, Bolivia had not wiped out anywhere near the 12,000 acres of coca that they'd promised to destroy by 1987. They just couldn't do it without starving half the country. The Bush administration put the screws to the State Department suits charged with making things happen in Bolivia; they in turn laid it on the Bolivian politicians. If the Bolivians wanted their turn in the American taxpayers' pockets, they'd better get with the program.

The Bolivian government had an idea. Arce-Gomez had been a secret thorn in their side for a long time. The Minister of Cocaine had allegedly been in hiding for six years, wanted in Bolivia for his responsibility in murdering and torturing thousands. A trial date had been set, and he was charged with human rights violations. He was notified—the location of his mother's farm outside Santa Cruz, where he was living, was well known—but he simply didn't show up for his trial. The government didn't dare arrest him and risk a lengthy trial, because while he had many enemies from his days of killing and torture, he had many more friends who despised the gringo drug war and who looked upon Arce-Gomez as a symbol of one who had defied it. His trial might cause havoc in Bolivia.

So why not deliver Arce-Gomez 5,000 miles to the north to the gringos who suddenly wanted him so badly? The Americans would have their headlines and Bolivia would have its aid payments—maybe even an increase—and be rid of an old irritant at the same time.

"But we can't do that," a high-level Bolivian official must have observed at a secret meeting called to figure out ways to ensure that American aid dollars kept flowing. "He is a Bolivian citizen. We have no extradition treaties. In fact, our law specifically prohibits the removal of a Bolivian citizen to stand trial in another country."

This was not entirely true. The only extradition treaty between the United States and Bolivia was a very special one. It was signed in 1904—after heavy U.S. pressure—for the express purpose of capturing and returning the infamous American bank robbers Butch Cassidy and the Sundance Kid, who were believed to be hiding out in Bolivia. But they were never captured, and they weren't Bolivians anyway.

An ancient ceiling fan slowly creaked overhead as the men seated around the long table were lost in thought. Finally, an assistant to an assistant minister, who was about to win his place in Bolivian history, said, "I have an idea. Because he did not show up at his human rights trial, we take away his citizenship." There was a moment of silence; then, one by one, each of the men around the table began to smile.

Arce-Gomez would be the perfect sacrifice. It didn't matter to the gringos that he was an aged, penniless, broken man long out of the drug business and no longer a threat to anyone but himself—he would make great headlines. He would be the perfect symbol to show the world that Bolivia was as serious about its war on drugs as Colombia. He would be worth at least $50 million in U.S. aid.

And so it was that on that Sunday morning in December 1989, Bolivian police accompanied by DEA advisors "found" Arce-Gomez on his mother's farm, ending a six-year "search" for the man whom DEA agents in Bolivia had reported seeing openly shopping in downtown Santa Cruz for the past several years. The shell of the Minister of Cocaine—the only Bolivian ever to be extradited anywhere—was dumped onto a DEA plane and flown to Miami where none other than Pat Sullivan would prosecute him.

"We never gave up. We kept looking for him," said James Shedd, a DEA spokesman.

"Bringing [Luis Arce-Gomez] to trial is a significant strike against the danger posed to the United States by those who deal in narcotics," said Diane Cossin, executive assistant to the Miami U.S. Attorney. Similar statements would be made by every politician who ever won a vote supporting our war on drugs and every suit whose job depended on its continued existence. Soon after, Bolivia received an increase in U.S. aid dollars.

Two weeks later, the U.S. military invaded Panama to arrest a midlevel drug dealer named Manuel Noriega. Lee Atwater, Chairman of the Republican Party, described the invasion that killed 23 American servicemen and as many as 2,000 innocent Panamanian civilians as "a political jackpot." Arce-Gomez and Bolivia were pushed from the headlines.

✤  ✤  ✤

Three months later, after eight sleazy years of life, Operation Hun was quietly buried. In a trial that was virtually ignored by the press, Sonia Atala—by this time one of the highest-paid, best-protected, most-accomplished professional witnesses in the Witness Protection Program, and veteran of the U.S. judicial system (having seen it from just about every angle)—was trotted out of hiding to be Arce-Gomez's chief accuser. The Minister of Cocaine, of course, was convicted of all charges and sentenced to 30 years in prison; not a bad thing considering he was truly an evil man responsible for terrible things done to his people. But when you consider that Arce-Gomez would have had no drug customers were it not for Sonia, and that the coup that gave him power might never have occurred were it not for covert U.S. support, it's difficult to conceive of his extradition and conviction as a victory in the drug war.

And that's not all, folks.

It was in many ways fitting that the most chilling irony of my 25-year career seeking the source of all sources was revealed during the Arce-Gomez trial, one month after my retirement. Under cross-examination by defense counsel Stephen Finta, Sonia admitted that, with the full knowledge, cooperation, and aid of the U.S. government, all her vast wealth and properties in Bolivia had been returned to her—the three homes; *Perserverancia*, the ranch with its vast grazing lands, cattle herds, cotton plantation, airplanes, landing strips, and peasant families; the apartments and offices in Brazil. It was also revealed that Sonia was soon to return to Bolivia, still the number one source country in the world for cocaine, once again free to reign supreme as the Queen with the Crown of Snow.

# Epilogue

And here's the rest of the story.

Papo Mejia has about 22 years remaining in prison, from where he has made it known that I am number one on his hit parade. He now considers me more responsible than Sonia for his current address— perhaps the Agency got to him. During a recent trip to Miami to research aspects of this book, I met with two of Mejia's attorneys, who said they were hopeful of getting him out in eight years.

"So what should I do," I said, "go into hiding?"

"Oh, no," said one. "I think there are a few others who are ahead of you."

The sentences of the four Mejia drones were as follows.

> Eduardo Pineda: imprisonment for 10 years and special parole for life
> Mario Espinosa: imprisonment for 8 years and special parole for 25 years

Jose Libardo: imprisonment for 5 years and special parole
for 15 years

Michael O'Connor: imprisonment for 5 years and special
parole for 10 years

The hapless Victor Marini and Donald Wilson Camp, the minions of Hollywood drug baron Hernando Velasco, exchanged guilty pleas for a plea bargain. Marini was sentenced to 4 years in prison and 10 years special parole; Camp to 2 years in prison. Velasco, described by Ana Tamayo and others as one of the biggest drug dealers in California, was never arrested, indicted, or investigated despite the numerous incriminating tape-recorded telephone conversations with me and Sonia and the arrests and plea bargains of Marini and Camp.

Roberto Torrez never got Sonia, but he didn't make out badly. He got a get-out-of-jail-free card and a lot of U.S. government cocaine to get high on. The man freely admitted taking part in the French Connection heroin ring in the 1960s; possessed, tested, and conspired to distribute large quantities of cocaine; and admitted to multiple homicides and possession of automatic weapons. All of these admissions were on audio- and videotape, but he was never prosecuted or even investigated. His bodyguard Carlos, who also admitted on tape to multiple homicides and large-scale drug dealing, was never charged, arrested, or even identified.

Pacho Cuervas, believed to be one of the biggest Colombian drug traffickers and against whom we had evidence of drug dealing worldwide, was never indicted, investigated, or fully identified. For many years, his name remained absent from the DEA computer system. He and his extensive organization continued their business unhindered, and may still be in operation.

The German, identified as Papo Mejia's biggest cocaine customer and described as being "untouchable" due to political connections and as being the source of cocaine for politicians, judges, and celebrities, was never investigated or even identified.

Monica Garcia was never indicted for the numerous incriminating acts she committed both on- and off-camera during Operation Hun, nor was any effort made by DEA to investigate or identify her extensive organization, which in all likelihood is still functioning.

Nicole Levine: Thanks to Frank Gullich, a great old street agent and fellow hard-headed Polack (he was the swing vote on the hardship committee), I was granted a transfer to New York, where I watched my little girl win her drug war victory. That she hasn't touched drugs in six years makes me prouder than any victory I had in my career.

The key to winning Nicole's drug battle was ignoring everything our government has been telling us about the cause of our drug problem for the past two decades—that our children are victims of a drug epidemic caused by the "availability of drugs" and evil, dark foreigners; that we must depend on the government to stop drugs or else become hapless victims of evil drug dealers. The entire phony drug war is based on this lie—a lie that keeps more people enslaved to drugs than all the dealers who ever lived.

Telling anyone with an addiction problem that they are a victim gives the person license to continue in the addiction. This is called *enabling*. Our leaders have been guilty of enabling for more than 20 years, and the result has been hundreds of thousands of lost lives. The life of my brother. The life of my son. I would love to see those responsible go to jail, and will happily spend the rest of my life trying to put them there. But without the support of the American people, it can never happen.

At least my discovery of the fraud helped save my daughter. From the moment Nicole understood that she was not a victim of an inert powder, nor of drug dealers (who *never* give users "free" samples), nor of some mysterious epidemic; from the moment that she recognized it had been her choice to experiment with drugs and that her family would not tolerate her behavior, we were on our way to victory.

My motorcycle: Just before I left headquarters for the last time, Kevin Gallegher called me into his office. He looked embarrassed—unusual for him.

"I'm supposed to admonish you," he said, looking at some writing on his pad. "Something about your motorcycle."

"For what?"

"For your motorcycle."

"My motorcycle? What did it do?"

"What did it do?" Kevin smacked me on the arm with the pad. "If you don't know what it did, I sure don't! Don't ask stupid questions. Just get the fuck out of here before someone changes his mind."

The drug war under President Clinton is bigger and healthier than ever. It seems like every department in the federal government has a part in it—DEA, FBI, CIA, NSA, IRS, DIA, ATF, State Department,

Pentagon, Customs, Coast Guard, Army, Navy, Air Force, Marines—
and each one is fighting for more turf and a bigger chunk of the drug
war budget. When I started out as an agent in 1965, there were two
federal agencies enforcing the drug laws, and the budget was less than
$10 million. Today there are 54 agencies involved and the budget is
$13 billion. Orchestrating the whole mess is a Drug Czar who is gen-
erally a political appointment with no specific qualifications for the
job. The latest one is Lee Brown, ex-police commissioner of drug-
blighted New York City.

Perhaps the biggest problem facing the Drug Czar is that some of
the agencies supposedly fighting the drug war are schizophrenic about
their loyalty. For decades, the CIA, the Pentagon, and secret organi-
zations like Oliver North's Enterprise have been supporting and protecting the world's biggest drug dealers. Those brave freedom fighters
in Afghanistan, the Mujahedin, supply a major portion of the heroin
used in the United States. The Contras and some of their Central
American allies like Honduras have been documented by DEA as
supplying us with at least 50 percent of our national cocaine consumption. They were the main conduit to the United States for
Colombian cocaine during the 1980s. The rest of the drug supply for
the American habit came from other CIA-supported groups, such as
DFS (the Mexican equivalent of the CIA), the Shan United Army in
the Golden Triangle of Southeast Asia, or any of a score of other
groups and/or individuals like Manuel Noriega. Support of these people has been secretly deemed more important than getting drugs off
our streets.

The other big problem the Czar faces are the millions of people in
poor countries like Bolivia, Peru, Colombia, Afghanistan, Turkey,
Taiwan, Ghana, Nigeria, Iran, India, Pakistan, Mexico, and Southeast
Asia who depend on the money Americans spend on drugs (estimated as high as $200 billion a year) to pay for their food, clothing, and
shelter. The leaders of these countries say they're on our side in the
war on drugs, but it is difficult to go to war against what feeds your
children.

So with the help of American bureaucrats and gutless politicians,
they put on a dog-and-pony show to demonstrate to the American taxpayers how committed they are to our war on drugs. And out of grat-
itude we pay them billions in aid and hundreds of millions in "drug
war funds." Yet incredibly, after almost three decades of international cooperation and statistic-spouting politicians who tell us again and

again how we are now "turning the corner in the drug war," drugs keep pouring across our borders at an ever-increasing rate.

But hark! There is hope on the horizon, and it is coming from the American people themselves. As I travel around the country speaking to adults, teenagers, and children, I sense a great awakening. People are becoming disgusted with the billions of dollars thrown down the rathole of the militarized drug war; the sordid invasion of Panama, which has actually resulted in more rampant drug dealing in that country; the secret deals made in the name of "national security" that really make us less secure in our own homes; and the lack of concern of elected officials and their appointed staff for the welfare of the American people. As that sage comic strip hero Pogo first said, "We have met the enemy, and he is us." People are looking for the truth about the drug war, and when they find it, that will be the doom of the Underground Empire.

Fight back, America! Fight back!

# Index